T0135131

IFIP Advances in Information and Communication Technology 431

IFIP – The International Federation for Information Processing

IFIP was founded in 1960 under the auspices of UNESCO, following the First World Computer Congress held in Paris the previous year. An umbrella organization for societies working in information processing, IFIP's aim is two-fold: to support information processing within its member countries and to encourage technology transfer to developing nations. As its mission statement clearly states,

> *IFIP's mission is to be the leading, truly international, apolitical organization which encourages and assists in the development, exploitation and application of information technology for the bene t of all people.*

IFIP is a non-profitmaking organization, run almost solely by 2500 volunteers. It operates through a number of technical committees, which organize events and publications. IFIP's events range from an international congress to local seminars, but the most important are:

- The IFIP World Computer Congress, held every second year;
- Open conferences;
- Working conferences.

The flagship event is the IFIP World Computer Congress, at which both invited and contributed papers are presented. Contributed papers are rigorously refereed and the rejection rate is high.

As with the Congress, participation in the open conferences is open to all and papers may be invited or submitted. Again, submitted papers are stringently refereed.

The working conferences are structured differently. They are usually run by a working group and attendance is small and by invitation only. Their purpose is to create an atmosphere conducive to innovation and development. Refereeing is also rigorous and papers are subjected to extensive group discussion.

Publications arising from IFIP events vary. The papers presented at the IFIP World Computer Congress and at open conferences are published as conference proceedings, while the results of the working conferences are often published as collections of selected and edited papers.

Any national society whose primary activity is about information processing may apply to become a full member of IFIP, although full membership is restricted to one society per country. Full members are entitled to vote at the annual General Assembly, National societies preferring a less committed involvement may apply for associate or corresponding membership. Associate members enjoy the same benefits as full members, but without voting rights. Corresponding members are not represented in IFIP bodies. Affiliated membership is open to non-national societies, and individual and honorary membership schemes are also offered.

Kai Kimppa   Diane Whitehouse
Tiina Kuusela   Jackie Phahlamohlaka (Eds.)

ICT and Society

11th IFIP TC 9 International Conference
on Human Choice and Computers, HCC11 2014
Turku, Finland, July 30 – August 1, 2014
Proceedings

 Springer

Volume Editors

Kai Kimppa
Tiina Kuusela
University of Turku
Rehtorinpellonkatu 3, 20014 Turku, Finland
E-mail: {kai.kimppa, takuus}@utu.fi

Diane Whitehouse
The Castlegate Consultancy
27 Castlegate, Malton, YO17 7DP, UK
E-mail: diane.whitehouse@thecastlegateconsultancy.com

Jackie Phahlamohlaka
Council for Scientific and Industrial Research (CSIR)
P.O. Box 395, 0001 Pretoria, South Africa
E-mail: jphahlamohlaka@csir.co.za

ISSN 1868-4238   e-ISSN 1868-422X
ISBN 978-3-662-51582-2   e-ISBN 978-3-662-44208-1
DOI 10.1007/978-3-662-44208-1
Springer Heidelberg New York Dordrecht London

Typesetting: Camera-ready by author, data conversion by Scientific Publishing Services, Chennai, India

Printed on acid-free paper

Springer is part of Springer Science+Business Media (www.springer.com)

Preface

This book contains the proceedings of the 11th International Human Choice and Computers (HCC11) conference, held in Turku, Finland, during July 30th to August 1st, 2014. The conference was organized by the International Federation for Information Processing (IFIP) Technical Committee 9 (TC9), Information and Communication Technology (ICT) and Society.

The proceedings have been subdivided into 4 sections: society, social responsibility, ethics and ICT; the history of computing and its meaning for the future; peace, war, cyber-security and ICT; and health, care, well-being and ICT. The papers selected for this book cover a variety of topics and range across the subject fields of the working groups of TC9. They are based on both academic research and the professional experience of information technologists working in the field.

It is the continued intention of the TC9 that academics, practitioners, governments and international organizations alike will benefit from the contributions to these proceedings. We hope that readers will gain new insights into the field from the publication, and will engage with us in the debate about innovative technologies in both this current Human Choice and Computers conference and future ones.

June 2014

Kai K. Kimppa
Diane Whitehouse
Tiina Kuusela
Jackie Phahlamohlaka

HCC11 – 2014

Chairs and Program Committee

HCC11 Chairs

Kimppa Kai	University of Turku, Finland
Whitehouse Diane	The Castlegate Consultancy, UK
Phahlamohlaka Jackie	CSIR, South Africa

HCC11 Program Committee

Adamson Greg	University of Melbourne, Australia
Allhutter Doris	Austrian Academy of Sciences, Austria
Bissett Andrew	Sheffield-Hallam University, UK
Bonfanti Corrado	AICA - The Italian Computer Society, Italy
Bradley Gunilla	Royal Institute of Technology, Sweden
Brunnstein Klaus	University of Hamburg, Germany
de la Harpe Retha	Cape Peninsula University of Technology, South Africa
De laat Paul	University of Groningen, The Netherlands
Diaz Andrade Antonio	Auckland University of Technology, New Zealand
Djohy Georges	University of Parakou, Benin
Duquenoy Penny	University of Middlesex, UK
Finken Sisse	University of Oslo, Norway
Fischer-Huebner Simone	Karlstad University, Sweden
Flick Catherine	De Montfort University, UK
González Carina	University of La Laguna, Spain
Grant Tim	R-BAR, The Netherlands
Griffiths Marie	The University of Salford, UK
Hankel Albert	SURFnet, The Netherlands
Harviainen J. Tuomas	University of Tampere, Finland
Heikkilä Jukka	University of Turku, Finland
Heimo Olli	University of Turku, Finland
Hercheui Magda	Westminster Business School, UK
Herman Clem	The Open University, UK
Hilty Lorenz	University of Zurich, Switzerland
Holvikivi Jaana	Helsinki Metropolia University of Applied Sciences, Finland
Jain Anupam	IBM Research, India
Kelly Suzette	University of South Florida, USA
Klein Stefan	University of Münster, Germany
Koskinen Jani	University of Turku, Finland

Kosta Eleni	Tilberg University, The Netherlands
Kreps David	Salford University, UK
Lahtiranta Janne	University of Turku, Finland
Larsson Ingela	Sweden
Leenen Louise	CSIR, South Africa
Lohmann Wolfgang	Empa, Swiss Federal Laboratories for Materials Science and Technology, Switzerland
Martino John	Victoria University, Australia
Masiero Silvia	London School of Economics and Political Science, UK
Mörtberg Christina	Linneaus University, Sweden
Nurminen Markku	University of Turku, Finland
Obani Pedi	University of Benin, Nigeria
Oram Denise	Glyndwr University, UK
Paju Petri	University of Turku, Finland
Patrignani Norberto	Politecnico of Torino, Italy
Puigjaner Ramon	Universitat de les Illes Balears, Spain
Schräpel Norman	University of Halle, Germany
Simon Judith	University of Vienna, Austria
Suopajärvi Tiina	University of Oulu, Finland
Tarkkanen Kimmo	University of Turku, Finland
Tatnall Arthur	Victoria University, Australia
Tuikka Anne-Marie	University of Turku, Finland
Tuomisto Antti	University of Turku, Finland
Wenngren Gunnar	AB Wenngrens i Linkoping, Sweden
Westrup Chris	University of Manchester, UK
Vehviläinen Marja	University of Tampere, Finland
Vyskoc Jozef	VaF Rovinka, Slovak Republic
Xu Xiaoyu	University of Turku, Finland

Table of Contents

The History of Computing and Its Meaning for the Future

Peace, War, Cyber-Security and ICT

Health, Care, Well-Being and ICT

E-retailing Ethics in Egypt and Its Effect on Customer Repurchase Intention

Gomaa Agag and Ibrahim Elbeltagi

Plymouth Graduate School of Management,
Plymouth University, Mast House, Shepherd's Wharf,
24 Sutton Rd, Plymouth, Devon, PL4 0HJ
{gomaa.agag,i.elbeltagi}@plymouth.ac.uk

Abstract. The theoretical understanding of online shopping behaviour has received much attention. Less focus has been given to the formation of the ethical issues that result from online shopper interactions with e-retailers. The vast majority of earlier research on this area is conceptual in nature and limited in scope by focusing on consumers' privacy issues. Therefore, the purpose of this paper is to propose a theoretical model explaining what factors contribute to online retailing ethics and its effect on customer repurchase intention. The data were analysed using variance-based structural equation modelling, employing partial least squares regression. Findings indicate that the five factors of the online retailing ethics (security, privacy, non- deception, fulfilment/reliability, and corporate social responsibility) are strongly predictive of online consumers' repurchase intention. The results offer important implications for e-retailers and are likely to stimulate further research in the area of e-ethics from the consumers' perspective.

Keywords: E-retailing, online retailing ethics, repurchase intention, structural equation modelling.

1   Introduction

The internet has come as a strong alternative way of physical commerce. The internet itself is a global phenomenon, with over 2,7billion users worldwide in 2013, up from 420 million in 2000 and 1 billion in 2005 [1]. In the developing world, 31%of the population is online, compared with 77% in the developed world [1].The incredible growth of e-commerce presents ethical issues by the way Internet represents new environment for unethical behaviour [2]. Although many business are acknowledging the importance of e-commerce and online retailing activities, little attention has been given to the business community's perceptions of the ethicality of this new media [3].Given the latest technological developments in e-retailing, this paper advances our understanding of the ethical issues in the online retail context. In this respect we follow the call by [4].For internet researchers to make significant contribution to the retailing literature "by utilizing theories not frequently applied to internet issues as well as investigating antecedents variables heretofore overlooked ".

K.K. Kimppa et al. (Eds.): HCC11 2014, IFIP AICT 431, pp. 1–14, 2014.
© IFIP International Federation for Information Processing 2014

A number of studies have addressed consumers' ethical believes and practices [5, 6, 7, 8], as well as consumers' perceptions of retailers ethics [9, 10, 11, 12]. Yet, little research has been conducted on the potential ethical issues regarding online retailing from the consumers' perspective. In addition, the vast majority of earlier research is conceptual in nature, and has primarily focused on privacy issues e.g., [13, 14, 15, 16, 17] ignoring other important ethical marketing issues surrounding the Internet such as deception and dishonesty [3, 18]. The purpose of our study is to propose a theoretical model explaining what factors contribute to online retailing ethics and its effect on customer repurchase intention.

2   Literature Review

According to the Aristotelian moral philosophy tradition, the meaning of the word "ethics" is "human actions from the point of view of their rightness or wrongness" [19]. Ethics corresponds to "what is good?" [20], however there is not any universal answer to this question [21] "Marketing Ethics" could be defined as the standards of conduct and moral judgment applied to marketing practice or a code of morals for the marketing field [19]. There are many studies in the literature addressing various issues concerning marketing ethics [22, 23, 24]. However, previous researchers have tended to ignore other potential important ethical marketing issues pertaining to the internet, such as deception, dishonesty, and accuracy [25]. Though the CPEOR scale was developed in 2007, few studies e.g. [26, 27, 28, 29, 30] have examined the antecedents e.g. consumers' general internet expertise and consequences e.g. trust, perceived value, satisfaction, loyalty, and word-of-mouth of CPEOR. Further, it is particularly relevant to understand how consumers evaluate the ethics of their web sites in the face of competition between merchants and constantly rising consumer expectations [26]. Drawing on the above studies, in this research, online retailing ethics (ORE) is defined as consumers' perceptions about the integrity and responsibility of the company (behind the website) in its attempt to deal with consumers in a secure, confidential, fair and honest manner that ultimately protects consumers' interests.

3   Theoretical Model and Research Hypotheses

We expect ORE to be a higher-order construct composed of five dimensions. In particular, we conceive a second-order factor structure in which five distinct component factors (i.e., security, privacy, fulfilment, non-deception, and CSR) are the manifestation of a broader, more general and more abstract higher-order latent variable (ORE). This conceptualization is consistent with previous definitions of business ethics at highly abstract levels e.g., [31, 32, 33]. In such a second-order factorial structure, each factor can be considered a manifestation of ORE, and each item is a manifestation of its respective factor. Based on this reasoning, we propose the following hypothesis:

Hypothesis 1: ORE is a second-order construct composed of five dimensions (i.e., security, privacy, fulfilment, non-deception, and CSR).

3.1 ORE and Repurchase Intention

Repurchase intention is defined here as the intention to repurchase a particular brand of product again. A buyer who has higher levels of trust of the salesperson and the manufacturer with which he/she has had experience is more likely to repurchase that brand than is the customer with lower levels of trust. Holden, (1990) found that one of the outcomes of both trust of the salesperson and trust of the company is purchasing loyalty. It is understood that if a customer buys from the same supplier again and is well disposed toward it affectively, he or she is really loyal to the provider [34, 35, 36, 37]. In the financial services the main outcomes of the service will then influence the customer's attitude. But other aspects related to the perceived social behaviour of the provider can determine the final attitude too [38]. A review of the literature identified a number of studies on social programs that found positive effects of social and ethical business practices on customer attitudes toward the brand [39] with stronger identification with the company, greater brand purchase and greater intention to seek employment with the company [40]. In this sense, consumers are willing to actively support companies committed to cause-related marketing, environmentally friendly practices and ethics [41, 42]. Limbu, et al., (2011) pointed out that perceived ethics of an Internet retailer's website significantly affect consumers' trust and attitudes to the retailer's website that eventually have positive impacts on purchase and revisit intentions. The ORE is proposed to positively influence the customer's repurchase intentions. The following hypothesis is suggested regarding the impact of ORE on repurchase intention.

Hypothesis 2: As security increase, consumer repurchase intention will increase.

Hypothesis 3: As privacy increase, consumer repurchase intention will increase.

Hypothesis 4: As fulfilment increase, consumer repurchase intention will increase.

Hypothesis 5: As non-deception increase, consumer repurchase intention will increase.

Hypothesis 6: As CSR increase, consumer repurchase intention will increase.

4   Method

4.1   Sample Selection and Data Collection

To empirically test the hypotheses, we used a questionnaire survey. Data was collected from the American university in Egypt. Student samples have often been used in online shopping research e.g., [43, 44]. We obtained a usable sample of 280 students. Demographic details of the sample profile are provided in Table 1.

Table 1. Sample profile

Variable	Categories	Frequency	Percent
Gender	Male	155	55.0%
	Female	125	45.0%
Age	<20	-	-
	20<30	180	64.0%
	30>40	80	28.5%
	<40	20	7.5%
Monthly income	£1,000 or below	125	44.5%
	£1,001–2,000	90	32.0%
	£2,001–3,000	50	18.0%
	£3,001 or above.	15	5.5%
Education	Bachelor degree	10	3.5%
	Diploma	20	7.0%
	Master or doctorate.	250	89.5%
	Other		
		-	-
Frequency of online shopping within a year	<3 times	212	76.0%
	4–6 times	31	11.0%
	7–9 times	26	9.0%
	>10 times	11	4.0%
Experience	< 2	180	64.0%
	2<5	70	25.0%
	>5	30	11.0%

4.2   Measurement Scales

We used existing multi-item scales for the measurement of (Privacy, Security, Fulfil-ment/Reliability, and Non-deception). This scale developed by [26] and has four dimensions: security (5 items), privacy (4 items), non-deception (4 items) and fulfil-ment/reliability (4 items). All scales consisted of 5-point Likert questions, ranging from "1 = strongly disagree" to "5 = strongly agree". CSR was measured using a scale adapted from [45] scale of "corporate social irresponsibility" and followed the conceptualization of [46]. Repurchase intention was measured using five items scale adapted from [47].

5   Results

5.1   Descriptive Statistics

A total of 280 respondents were surveyed online. Of these 280 participants, 155 were men (55.0%) and 125 were women (45.0%). The majority of respondents were aged between 20 and 30 (64.0%), had post-graduate education (master and doctorate) (89.5%), and had engaged in online shopping three times within the previous year (82.0%). The most recent online shoppers experience for the majority of respondents was within the previous 2 years (64.0%) and the most online shoppers income was £1000 or below (44.5%). Table1 shows the respondent demographics.

5.2   Measurement Model

In contrast with LISREL, the partial least squares (PLS) method is an appropriate analytical tool in this case because it has minimal demands on measurement scales, sample size, and residual distributions [48]. The assessment of a measurement model should examine (1) individual item reliability, (2) internal consistency, and (3) discriminate validity (Barclay, Higgins, & Thompson, 1995). This study employs the structural equation modelling tool WarpPLS (version 4.0) for confirmatory factor analysis to estimate the measurement model using WarpPLS analysis to test construct reliability and validity. The results in Table 2 show that composite reliabilities ranged from 0.891 to 0.917, all exceeding 0.7 [52], and the AVE of each construct ranged from 0.651 to 0.701, all exceeding 0.5 [48]. Table 2 shows that all indices fit with heuristics. Discriminate validity is tested in the measurement model analysis to determine the correlations between the latent variables and other constructs. The convergent and discriminant validity were assessed by checking whether the AVE (average variance extracted) of each construct is larger than its correlation with the other constructs, and whether each item had a higher loading on its assigned construct than on the other constructs [53, 54]. The results indicate that the discriminate validity was achieved, as shown in Table 2.

Table 2. Results of composite reliability and convergent/discriminant validity testing

Construct	Reliability	AVE	Correlations and square roots of AVEs.					
			PV	SC	REL	DEC	CSR	REP
PV	0.891	0.672	(0.826)					
SC	0.904	0.701	0.815	(0.837)				
REL	0.896	0.682	0.777	0.800	(0.822)			
DEC	0.912	0.676	0.748	0.774	0.665	(0.820)		
CSR	0.917	0.651	0.770	0.779	0.728	0.803	(0.807)	
REP	0.874	0.662	0.803	0.793	0.763	0.797	0.712	(0.816)

Note: PV: privacy, SC: security, REL: reliability, DCE: non-deception, CSR: Corporate social responsibility and REP: repurchase intention.

5.3   Structural Model

The model explains 81% of variance for the repurchase intention. **H1** since we wanted to have stronger evidence of the existence of the five ethical dimensions, Following the method utilized by [55, 56], we performed CFA analyses using WarpPls 4.0 comparing several possible factor structures (see Table 3). We compared the fit of the six-factor model to that of a series of alternative models with fewer factors: five-factor model (privacy + security, non-deception, reliability, CSR, and repurchase intention) and four-factor model (privacy + security + reliability, non-deception, CSR, and repurchase intention) and three-factor (privacy + security + reliability, non-deception + CSR, and repurchase intention) and a two-factor model (privacy + security + reliability + non-deception + CSR, and repurchase intention). As shown in Table 3, the five factors model, one second-order factor fits the data much better than the other factor models. For example, the AARS difference between the proposed five-factor model and the others models is highly significant (AARS=0.758, p<0.001).

Table 3. Summary results of models fit indices

Models	APC	ARS	AARS	AVIF	GOF
five factors, one second-order factor	0.168	0.773	0.758	2.653	0.742
five factors	0.187	0.713	0.708	2.851	0.702
four factors	0.217	0.706	0.702	2.949	0.689
three factors	0.261	0.707	0.704	3.191	0.687
two factors	0.321	0.694	0.691	3.364	0.674

The overall fit measures suggest that the model is a plausible representation of the structures underlying the empirical data. The APC= (0.168, p<0.001), ARS= (0. 773, p<0.001), AARS= (0. 758, p<0.001), AVIF= (2.653), and GOF= (0.742). As long as the Average path coefficient (APC), the Average R squared (ARS), and the Average adjusted R-squared (AARS) are significant under 5% level, and the average variance inflation factor (VIF) is lower than 5. As well as the geometric mean of the average communality (GOF) suggests a large effect size, the overall fit indices indicate a good fit of the model [57]; [58]. These findings suggest that ORE can be modelled as a second-order construct. This provides strong support for the five dimensions as aspects of ORE as a second-order construct, thus confirming Hypothesis 1. Further evidence for acceptance of the second-order factor structure is found in the variance explained by the structural equations. ORE as a second-order construct explains 81% of customer satisfaction, as opposed to 72% in the alternative.

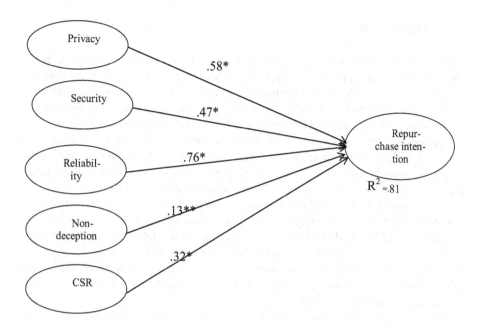

* Significant at the 0.01 level.
** Significant at the 0.05 level.

Fig. 1. PLS results of research model of main test (n = 310)

APC= (0.168, p<0.001), ARS= (0. 773, p<0.001), AARS= (0. 758, p<0.001), AVIF= (2.653), and GOF= (0.742).

H2 examines the effects of privacy on repurchase intention. Privacy is significantly related to repurchase intention (B = .58, p < .01).

H3 examines the effects of security on repurchase intention. Security is significantly related to repurchase intention (B = .47, p < .01).

H4 examines the effects of reliability on repurchase intention. Reliability is significantly related to repurchase intention (B = .76, p < .01).

H5 examines the effects of non-deception on repurchase intention. Non-deception is significantly related to repurchase intention (B = .13, p < .05).

H6 examines the effects of CSR on repurchase intention. CSR is significantly related to repurchase intention (B = .32, p < .01).

The software calculates five fit indices which are meaningful in the context of variance-based SEM [57, 58]: average path coefficient (APC), average R^2 (ARS), Average adjusted R-squared (AARS), average variance inflation factor (VIF), and geometric mean of the average communality (GOF). Their values are the following: APC= (0.168, p<0.001), ARS= (0. 773, p<0.001), AARS= (0. 758, p<0.001), AVIF= (2.653), and GOF= (0.742).

6   Discussion

The aim of this study was to examine the impact of online retailing ethics on repurchase intention with the extending research model adapted from [26]. Data were collected in Egypt. The findings of the hypotheses testing of this study were as follows.

First, we confirmed that ORE is a multidimensional construct composed of five dimensions: security, privacy, fulfilment/reliability, non-deception, and CSR.

Second, the findings of this study show the direct effect of the five dimensions (security, privacy, fulfilment/reliability, non-deception, and CSR) on consumer repurchase intention. This result confirms the findings of previous studies that online retailing ethics significantly impacts the customer repurchase intention e.g. [26, 27, 28].

A key aspect of this multidimensional conceptualization is that privacy is important. Privacy is a great concern in modern society [59]. The American Marketing Association (AMA) Code of Ethics for Marketing on the Internet states that "information collected from customers should be confidential and used only for expressed purposes." This statement recommends that e-commerce companies comply with ethical principles and protect a consumer's privacy. The results of the current study also indicate that ORE involves privacy.

Security, the second dimension, is an important issue in contemporary online transactions [60]. Prior literature argued that technological protection and security statements are significant factors that can improve consumer-perceived security [61, 62, 63]. Our study suggests that consumers desire e-commerce companies to have technological protection and security statements. Thus, ORE includes security.

Fulfilment/reliability, suggests that ORE is also related to the service quality delivered by websites on which consumers shop online. Consistent with previous research [64, 65], our results show that online consumers want to receive the right quality and right quantity of items that they ordered within the time frame promised by the online retailers, and they expect to be billed accurately by them.

The existence of the fourth dimension, non-deception, indicates that consumers' concerns arising in traditional markets due to deceptive or manipulative advertising and sales practices are somewhat exacerbated in Internet commerce by the relatively unfamiliar and impersonal nature of the Web, where the lack of opportunities for face-to-face interactions reduces people's ability to detect deception [66]. For instance, in traditional retail settings, the detection of deception relies, amongst other things, on recognizing subtle changes in a person's non-verbal behaviours, such as eye contact and body movements [67].

Finally, CSR, Several studies have investigated how consumers perceive the social responsibility of retailers [68, 41]. An international survey has been conducted on 211 scholars with expertise in business ethics. Each respondent was asked to identify the three most important issues that business ethics academia will face in the coming decade. The results suggest that the most important issues facing business ethics academia in the future will be the corporate social responsibility [69].

Fulfilment was the strongest predictor of repurchase intention. This adds further empirical evidence to previous results [65, 26]. When shopping online, consumers are vulnerable. They worry that they will not receive the products or services exactly as they purchased. Consequently, consumer concerns about fulfilment are still a critical issue for online retailers [70]. Furthermore, privacy, followed by security, CSR and non-deception, had a strong influence on repurchase ignition Overall; these results are in line with several articles and reports e.g., [71, 72].

7 Theoretical Contribution

This study contributes to the literature in the following ways. **First,** the study provides empirical support for a comprehensive model of ORE composed of five multidimensional constructs that include security, privacy, fulfilment/reliability non-deception, and CSR. Several scales developed to measure online service quality tend to collapse privacy and security concepts into one dimension [64, 65]. Prior research in the traditional marketplace addressing consumers' ethical perceptions has considered a limited number of dimensions. For example, in [73] study, the security/privacy dimension refers to: "security of credit card payments and privacy of shared information".

Second key contribution of the present study stems from the analysis of the effects of ORE on consumer repurchases intention. Overall, this is particularly relevant if we take into account the psychological distance theory. Several theories of interpersonal communication suggest physical proximity in communication fosters stronger bonds between the parties than communication that occurs remotely e.g., [27, 26]. The current study shows that ORE factors become a key means of fostering consumers' repurchase intention in a context where communications occur remotely.

8 Implications for Practice and Future Research Directions

Research suggests that ethics can play a critical role in the formation and maintenance of long-term relationships with customers [74]. In order to successfully operate a commercial website from an ethical perspective, online retailers need to understand how consumers' ethical perceptions are formed. The present study compiled a list of 23 items (grouped into five factors) that online retailers can use to assess such perceptions. These items would provide several hints to online retailers in terms of how to shape their customers' satisfaction and repurchase intentions.

We encourage future studies to use random sampling of general consumers. The ethics literature identifies some factors which influence ethical judgments of consumers (e.g., sex, age, and education). Such research could identify how each variable, individually and cooperatively, impacts consumer ethical evaluations of online retailing. We did not collect data from non-Internet shoppers because the focus of this study was online consumers referring to their latest purchase online. It may be an interesting extension, however, to test this conceptual model for other populations like non online consumers.

9   Conclusion

Some researchers believe that a systematic empirical study of e-commerce ethical issues must be conducted from the consumers' perspective [26]. This study represents an initial step into examining of e-retailing ethics from the consumers' perspective and the understanding of its effects on consumer repurchases intention. The results offer important implications for e-retailers and are likely to stimulate further research in the area of e-ethics from the consumers' perspective.

References

1. Internet world stats, "Miniwatts," (2013),
   http://www.internetworldstats.com/stats.htm (accessed May 25, 2013)
2. Freestone, O., Michell, V.: Generation Y attitudes towards e-ethics and Internet - related misbehaviours. Journal of Business Ethics 54, 121–128 (2004)
3. Bush, V.S., Venable, B.T., Bush, A.: ethics and marketing on the Internet: practioners perceptions of societal, industry and companyconcerns. Journal of Business Ethics 23, 237–248 (2000)
4. James, R.B., Rajiv, P.D.: The Theoretical Domains of retailing research: A Retrospective. Journal of Retailing 85(2), 113–128 (2009)
5. Fullerton, S., Kerch, K.B., Doger, H.R.: Consumer Ethics: An Assessment of individual Behaviour in the market place. Journal of Business Ethics 15, 805–814 (1996)
6. Muncy, J.A., Vitell, S.J.: Consumer Ethics: An investigation of the Ethical beliefs of the final consumer. Journal of Business Research 24, 297–311 (1992)
7. Strutton, D., Pelton, L.E., Ferrell, O.C.: Ethical Behaviour in Retail Settings: Is there a Generation Gap? Journal of Business Ethics 16, 87–105 (1997)
8. Vitell, S.J., Muncy, J.A.: The Muncy-Vitell Consumer Ethics Scale: A modification and Application. Journal of Business Ethics 62, 267–275 (2005)
9. Burns, D.J., Fawctt, J.K., Lanasa, J.: Business Students Ethical perceptions of Retail Situations: Amicrocultural Comparison. Journal of Business Ethics 13, 667–679 (1994)
10. Lagace, R.R., Dahlstrom, R., Gassenheimer, J.B.: The Relevance of Ethical Salesperson Behviour on Relationship Quality: The Pharmaceutical Industry. Journal of Personal Selling& Sales Management 11, 39–47 (1991)
11. Mcintyre, F.S., Thomas, J.R., Gilbert, F.W.: Consumersegments and Perceptions of Retail Ethics. Journal of Marketing Theory and Practice 2, 43–53 (1999)
12. Roman, S.: The Impact of Ethical Sales Behaviour on Customer Satisfaction, Trust And Loyalty to the company: AnImpirical study in the financial service Industry. Journal of Business Ethics 19, 915–949 (2003)
13. Beltramini, R.F.: Application of the Unfairness Doctorine to Marketing Communications on the Internet. Journal of Business Ethics 42, 393–400 (2003)
14. Caudill, E.M., Murphy, P.E.: Consumer Online Privacy: Lgal and Ethical Issues. Journal of Public Policy and Marketing 19, 7–19 (2000)
15. Maury, M.D., Kleiner, D.S.: E-Commerce, Ethical Commerce? Journal of Business Ethics 36, 21–31 (2002)
16. Pollach, I.: A Typology of Communicative strategies in online privacy policies: Ethics,Power and informed Consent. Journal of Business Ethics 62, 221–235 (2005)

17. Palmer, D.E.: Pop-Ups, Cookies, and Spam:Toward a Deeper Analysis of the Ethical Significance of Internet Marketing Practices. Journal of Business Ethics 58, 271–280 (2005)
18. Murphy, P.E., Laczniak, G.R., Bowie, N.E., Klein, T.A.: Ethical Marketing: Basic Ethics in Action. Pearson Prentice Hall, NJ (2005)
19. Gaski, J.F.: Does Marketing Ethics Really Have Anything to say? A critical Inventory of the Literature. Journal of Business Ethics 18(3), 315–334 (1999)
20. Pires, G.D., Stanton, J.: Ethnic Marketing Ethics. Journal of Business Ethics 36, 111–118 (2002)
21. Fisher, J., Taylor, D., Fullerton, S.: Attitudes towards consumer and Business Ethics among Canadian and NewZealand Business students: An assessment of 25 Scenarios. Journal of Business Ethics 3(2), 155–177 (1999)
22. Murphy, P.E., Laczniak, G.R., Wood, G.: An Ethical Basis for Relationship Marketing: A virtue ethics perspective. European Journal of Marketing 41(2), 37–57 (2007)
23. Vitell, S.J., Ho, F.N.: Ethical Decision making in Marketing: Asynthesis and evalution of scales measuring the various components of decision making in ethical situations. Journal of Business Ethics 16(7), 699–717 (1997)
24. Fraedrich, J.P.: Reviewed work(s): Ethics in Marketing by N. Craig Smith; John A. Quelch. Practical Business Ethics by Warren A.French; John Granrose. Journal of Marketing 60(1), 122–123 (1996)
25. Roman, S.: Relational Consequences of Perceived Deception in Online Shopping: The Moderating Roles of Type of Product, Consumer's Attitude Toward the Internet and Consumer's Demographics. Journal of Business Ethics 95, 373–391 (2007, 2010)
26. Roman, S.: The Ethics of Online Retailing: A Scale development and Validation from the Consumers' Perspective. Journal of Business Ethics 72, 131–148 (2007)
27. Roman, S., Cuestas, P.J.: The Perceptions of Consumers Regarding Online Retailers' Ethics and Their Relationship with Consumers' General Internet Expertise and Word of Mouth: A preliminary Analysis. Journal of Business Ethics 83(4), 641–656 (2008)
28. Kurt, C., Hacioglu, G.: Ethics as a customer perceived value driver in the context of online retailing. African Journal of Business Management 4(5), 672–677 (2010)
29. Limbu, Y.B., Wolf, M., Lunsford, D.L.: Consumers' perceptions of online ethics and its effects on customer satisfaction. Journal of Research in Interactive Marketing 5(1), 71–89 (2011)
30. Arjoon, S., Rambocas, M.: Ethics and Customer Loyalty: Some Insights into Online Retailing Services. International Journal of Business and Social Science 14(2), 135–142 (2011)
31. Barry, V.: Moral Issues in Business. Wadsworth Publishing Co., New York (1979)
32. Bartels, R.: A Model for Ethics in Marketing. Journal of Business Ethics 31, 20–26 (1967)
33. Beauchamp, T.L., Bowie, N.E.: Ethical theory and Business, 2nd edn. Prentice Hall, NJ (1983)
34. Sheth, J.N., Parvatiyar, A.: Relationship marketing in Consumer Markets: Antecedents and Consequences. Journal of the Academy of Marketing Science 23(4), 255–271 (1995)
35. Gremler, D.D., Brown, S.W., Gremler, D.D., Brown, S.W.: The loyalty ripples effect. International Journal of Service Industry Management 10(3), 271–291 (1999)
36. Oliver, R.L.: Whence consumer loyalty. Journal of Marketing 63(1), 33–45 (1999)
37. Cronin, J.J., Brady, J.R., Hunt, G.T.M.: Assessing the effects of quality, value, and customer satisfaction on consumer behavioral intentions in service environments. Journal of Retailing 76(2), 193–218 (2000)

38. Garca de los Salmones, M.M., Perez, A., Rodri Guez delBosque, I.: The social role of financial companies as a determinant of consumer behaviour. The International Journal of Bank Marketing 27(6), 467–485 (2009)
39. Lafferty, B.A., Goldsmith, R.E.: Cause-brand alliance: does the cause help the brand or does the brand help the cause. Journal of Business Research 58(4), 423–429 (2005)
40. Sen, S., Bathtacharya, C.B., Korschun, D.: The role of corporate social responsibility in strengthening multiple stakeholder relationships: a field experiment. Journal of The Academy of Marketing Science 34(2), 158–166 (2006)
41. Maignan, I., Ferrell, O.C.: Corporate social responsibility and marketing: an integrative framework. Journal of the Academy of Marketing Science 32(1), 3–19 (2004)
42. McDonald, L.M., Rundle-Thiele, S.R.: Corporate social responsibility and bank customer satisfaction: a research agenda. International Journal of Bank Marketing 26(3), 170–182 (2008)
43. Balabanis, G., Reynolds, N.: Consumer attitudes towards multi-Channel retailers' Web Sites: The role of involvement, brand attitude, internet knowledge and visit duration. Journal of Business Strategies 18(2), 105–131 (2001)
44. Kim, J., Fiore, A., Lee, H.: Influence of online store perception, shopping enjoyment, and shopping involvement on consumer patronage behaviour towards an online retailer. Journal of Retailing and Consumer Services 14, 95–107 (2007)
45. Wagner, T., Bicen, P., Hall, Z.: The dark side of retailing: towards a scale of corporate social irresponsibility. International Journal of Retail & Distribution Management 362, 124–142 (2008)
46. Sen, S., Bhattacharya, C.B., Korshun, D.: The role of corporate social responsibility in strengthening multiple stakeholder relationships. Journal of the Academy of Marketing 34, 158–166 (2006)
47. Siu, N., Zhang, T., Yau, C.: The Roles of Justice and Customer Satisfaction in Customer Retention: A Lesson from Service Recovery. Journal of Business Ethics 114(4), 675–686 (2013)
48. Chin, W., Marcolin, B., Newsted, P.: A partial least squares latent variable modeling app roach for measuring interaction effects: Results from a montecarlo simulation study and voice mail emotion/adoption study. Paper presented at the 15th International Conference on Information Systems, Cleveland, Ohio, USA, pp. 21–41 (1996)
49. Nunnally, J.: Psychometric methods, 2nd edn. McGraw-Hill, New York (1978)
50. Wixom, B., Watson, H.: An empirical investigation of the factors affecting data warehousing success. MIS Quarterly 25(1), 17–41 (2001)
51. Bock, G.W., Zmud, R.W., Kim, Y.G., Lee, J.N.: Behavioral intention formation in knowledge sharing: Examining the roles of extrinsic motivators, social-psychological forces, and organizational climate. MIS Quarterly 29(1), 87–111 (2005)
52. Bagozzzi, R.P., Yi, Y.: On the evaluation of structural equation models. Journal of the Academy of Marketing Science 16(1), 74–94 (1988)
53. Fornell, C., Larcker, D.: Evaluating structural equation models with unobservable variables, and measurement error. Journal of Marketing Research 18(1), 39–50 (1981)
54. Gefen, D., Straub, D., Boudreau, M.: Structural equation modeling techniques and regression: Guidelines for research practice. Communications of AIS 7(7), 1–78 (2000)
55. Doll, W.J., Weidong, X., Torkzadeh, G.: A confirmatory factor analysis of the end-user computing satisfaction instrument. MIS Quarterly 18(4), 453–461 (1994)
56. Dabholkar, P.A., Thorpe, D.I., Rentz, J.O.: A measure of service quality for retail stores: Scale development and validation. Journal of the Academy of Marketing Science 24(winter), 3–16 (1996)

57. Kline, R.: Principles and practice of structural equation modeling. The Guilford Press, New York (1998)
58. Kock, N.: Using WarpPLS in e-collaboration studies: Descriptive statistics, settings, and key analysis results. International Journal of e-Collaboration 7(2), 1–18 (2011)
59. Ellis, T.S., Griffith, D.: The evaluation of it ethical scenarios using a multidimensional scale. ACM SIGMIS Database 32, 75–85 (2001)
60. Peha, J.M., Khamitov, I.M.: Paycash: a secure efficient Internet payment system. Electronic Commerce Research and Applications 3, 381–388 (2004)
61. Hwang, R.J., Shiau, S.H., Jan, D.F.: A new mobile payment scheme for roaming services. Electronic Commerce Research and Applications 6, 184–191 (2007)
62. Kim, C., Tao, W., Shin, N., Kim, K.S.: An empirical study of customers'perceptions of security and trust in e-payment systems. Electronic Commerce Research and Applications 9, 84–95 (2010)
63. Lim, A.S.: Inter-consortia battles in mobile payments standardisation. Electronic Commerce Research and Applications 7, 202–213 (2008)
64. Parasuraman, A., Zeithaml, V.A., Malhotra, A.: E-S-QUAL A Multiple-Item Scale For Assessing Electronic Service Quality. Journal of Service Research 7, 213–233 (2005)
65. Wolfinbarger, M., Gilly, M.C.: eTailQ: Dimensionalizing, Measuring and Predicting etail Quality. Journal of Retailing 79, 183–198 (2003)
66. Ben-Ner, A., Putterman, L.: Trust in the New Economy. In: Jones, D.C. (ed.) New Economy Handbook, pp. 1067–1095. Academic Press, New York (2003)
67. DePaulo, B.M.: NonverbalBehavior and Self-presentation. Psychological Bulletin 111, 203–243 (1992)
68. Lichtenstein, D.R., Drumwright, M.E., Braig, B.M.: The effect of corporate social responsibility on customer donations to corporate supported non-profits. Journal of Marketing 68(9), 16–32 (2004)
69. Holland, D., Albrecht, C.: The Worldwide Academic Field of Business Ethics:Scholars' Perceptions of the Most Important Issues. Journal of Business Ethics 117, 777–788 (2013)
70. Collier, J.E., Bienstock, C.C.: Measuring service quality in e-retailing. Journal of Service Research 8, 260–275 (2006)
71. Stead, B.A., Gilbert, J.: Ethical Issues in Electronic Commerce. Journal of Business Ethics 34, 75–85 (2001)
72. Truste, TN's/Truste Holiday (2005),
    http://www.truste.org/about/press_release/
73. Wolfinbarge, M., Gilly, M.C.: eTailQ: Dimensionalizing, Measuring and Predicting etail Quality. Journal of Retailing 79, 183–198 (2003)
74. Roman, S., Ruiz, S.: Relationship Outcomes of Perceived Ethical Sales Behavior: The Customer's perspective. Journal of Business Research 58, 439–445 (2005)
75. Norris, D.G., Gifford, J.B.: Retail Store Managers and Students perceptions of Ethical Retail Practices? A comparative and Longitudinal Analysis. Journal of Business Ethics 7, 515–524 (1988)
76. LeMenestrel, M., Hunter, M., DeBettignies, H.C.: E-Ethics in Confrontation with an Activities Agenda: Yahoo on Trial. Journal of Business Ethics 39, 135–144 (2002)
77. Sama, L.M., Shoaf, V.: Ethics on the web: Applying Moral Decision-Making to the New Media. Journal of Business Ethics 36, 93–103 (2002)
78. Siplor, J.C., Ward, B.T., Rongione, N.M.: Ethics of collecting and using consumer internet Data. Information System Management 21, 58–66 (2004)
79. Stead, B.A., Gilbert, J.: Ethical issues in electronic commerce. Journal of Business Ethics 34, 75–85 (2001)

80. Hunt, S., Vitell, S.: A General Theory of Marketing Ethics. Journal of Macromarketing 1(1), 5–16 (1986)
81. Nardal, S., Sahin, A.: Ethical issues in e-commerce on the basis of online retailing. Journal of Social Sciences 7(2), 190–198 (2011)
82. Holden, R.K.: An exploratory study of trust in buyer±seller relationships. A Dissertation. University Microfilms International, ANN Abor (1990)
83. Fornell, C., Larke, D.: Evaluating structural equation models with unobservable variables and measurement error. Journal of Marketing Research 18(1), 39–50 (1981)
84. Chin, W.: Overview of the PLS method (1997), http://discnt.cba.uh.edu/chin/PLSINTRO.HTM
85. Vesel, P., Zabkar, V.: Managing Customer Loyalty through the Mediating Role of Satisfaction in the DIY Retail Loyalty Program. Journal of Retailing and Consumer services 16(5), 396–406 (2009)
86. Anderson, E.W., Sullivan, M.W.: The antecedents and consequences of customer satisfaction for firms. Marketing Science 12(2), 125–143 (1993)
87. Bolton, R.N.: A dynamic model of the duration of the customer's relationship with a continuous service provider: the role of satisfaction. Marketing Science 17(1), 45–65 (1998)
88. Cronin, J.J., Taylor, S.A.: Measuring service quality: a reexamination and extension. Journal of Marketing 56(3), 55–68 (1992)
89. Fornell, C.: A national customer satisfaction barometer: the Swedish experience. Journal of Marketing 56(1), 6–21 (1992)
90. Oliver, R.L.: A cognitive model of the antecedents and consequences of satisfaction decisions. Journal of Marketing Research 17, 460–469 (1980)
91. Patterson, P.G., Spreng, R.A.: Modelling the relationship between perceived value,satisfaction and repurchase intentions in a business-to-business, services context: an empirical examination. International Journal of Service Industry Management 8(5), 414–434 (1997)
92. Rust, R.T., Zahorik, A.J.: Customer satisfaction, customer retention and market share. Journal of Retailing 69(2), 193–215 (1993)
93. Kousaridas, A., Parissis, G., Apostolopoulos, T.: An open financial services architecture based on the use of intelligent mobile devices. Electronic Commerce Research and Applications 7, 232–246 (2008)
94. Palmer, A., Beggs, R., Keown-McMullan, C.: Equity and repurchase intention following service failure. Journal of Services Marketing 14, 513–528 (2000)
95. Maignan, I.: Consumers' perceptions of corporate social responsibilities: a cross-cultural comparison. Journal of Business Ethics 30(1), 57–72 (2001)
96. Vijayan, J.: Security Concerns Cloud Online Shopping. Computerworld, 5–8 (December 2005)

Connecting Social Capital by Social Media

Halvdan Haugsbakken

Department of Sociology and Political Science,
Norwegian University of Science and Technology, Trondheim, Norway
Halvdan.Haugsbakken@svt.ntnu.no

Abstract. Established sociological research on social networks and social capital has argued that large quantities of connections can represent access to resources. This claim has been challenged, due to the advent of social network sites. Researchers have little insights on how social actors use social network sites to organise particular web mediated social practices, besides for knowing they are employed for socialisation. There is also little research on how social actors *use* and *connect* to different social media applications and apply the resource embedded in them. This paper addresses that matter. It introduces a user perspective on how a group of social actors use a variety of social media application as resources, to carry out web mediated social practices. To empirically analyse this, the paper shows how a sample of Norwegian high school students use different types of social media applications for this purpose.

Keywords: social capital, social media, youth, resources, Norway.

1   Introduction

Norwegians spend significant time on different social media platforms, like blogs, content communities, and Social Network Sites (SNSs). Norwegians are digitally literate, considering that only 5 million reside in the country. The Norwegian online press has estimated that 2.8 million Norwegians are connected to Facebook [1]. National surveys suggest that approximately 410.000 check their Twitter account each week [2], while 641.000 have created a user profile on Linkedin [3]. 300.000 are claimed having tried Google+ [4]. Many are users of tablets too, approximately 700.000 [5]. Although these are estimations made by the online news press, we can assume that Norwegians are *connected* to *multiple* web services, forming is a systematic user pattern. The estimations also suggest that Norwegians have access to a large pool of resources.

The interesting research question remaining addressing, however, is to what extent such numbers are believable. Such assessments can fall short. They give little insights on *particular uses of SNSs* and how they are organised. Empirical research on Norwegians' use of SNSs, for example, suggests this [6-9]. The research community still lacks empirical knowledge, on what Jenkins calls the "participative culture" [10] of SNSs and social capital. Researchers are even now investigating users' connecting strategies, motivation for use, user characteristics and user topologies, privacy matters, online social identity management, and organisations' use [11]. Such topics dominate due to that quantitative research lead the way in forming current research [12].

K.K. Kimppa et al. (Eds.): HCC11 2014, IFIP AICT 431, pp. 15–26, 2014.

There are other issues too. Current studies often address use of *one* social network site, not several and how they are combined. They are also U.S. context-based and focus on few demographic variables, chiefly, American university students [11, 12].

Consequently, researchers still have little accurate research knowledge on how social actors make use and extract capital form the vast resources found in social media platforms, moreover, how they transform and utilize them as part of social practices belonging to larger socio-cultural contexts. Furthermore, we need to know more on what role the combination of off-line and on-line ties play in the complex coordination of social life.

This paper considers that matter. The paper examines *three* distinct social practices, which are neatly embedded and transpire from social actors' use of social media software. The paper examines how a cohort of Norwegian high school students use Facebook as a tool to (1) coordinate formal schoolwork, (2) as a mean to organise drivers for weekend partying, and (3) how YouTube tutorials can work as a learning resource to play music instruments and online gaming. Substantiating this argument, a look at the article's content pertains. The paper establishes an explorative user perspective on how a data sample of Norwegian high school students use different types of social media applications, understood as a form of social capital. First, relevant research on social network and social capital are accounted for. Second, choice of methods and data sample is outlined. Third, the study's results and findings are analysed, before the last part provides a preliminary conclusion.

2   Theoretical Inspiration and Research Horizon

The advent of Web 2.0 [13] services has involved the introduction of technical definitions. Boyd and Ellison define *SNS* as a "web-based services that allow individuals to construct a public or semi-public profile within a bounded system, articulate a list of other user with whom they share a connection, and view and traverse their list of connections and those made by others within the system" [14]. This definition involves that Facebook is a SNS, while "old" pages, like blogs are not [15]. Kaplan & Haenlein have defined *social media* as a "group of Internet-based applications that build on the ideological and technological foundations of Web 2.0, and that allow the creation and exchange of User Generated Content" [16]. They suggest that social media consists of six types; (1) collaborative projects, e.g. Wikipedia, (2) blog, (3) content communities, e.g. YouTube (4) SNS, e.g. Facebook, (5) virtual game worlds, e.g. World of Warcraft, (6) and virtual social worlds, e.g. Second Life [16].

These technical definitions touch upon sociological concepts of the social networks, ties, and social capital, but do not accentuate the social side of technologies. The advent of SNSs has reintroduced new research interest in social network analysis and social capital. Sociological work has been associated with Bourdieu [17],Coleman [18], Burt [19, 20], and Lin [21, 22]. Sociological research has argued that social capital is a resource found in social ties. These potential resources are assumed to be integrated in the social structures of social networks. Such resources can be emotional support and diffusion of ideas. Sociologists claim that social capital can possess the capacity of fostering cooperation between individuals or groups. It shares similar capacities to other forms of capital we normally associate that can provide economic growth, like financial capital. This means that social capital can be mobi-lised, in order to carry out social practices in social situations. This means that the value of ties and resources embedded in social media platforms can be employed by humans to carry out social practices. The question of a task's coordination would influence the success of how well a social practice is executed.

Early sociological work criticized the limited understanding of the social dynamics of ties in social networks. Granovetter's [23] "the strength of weak ties", claimed that the qualities in close ties between social actors were undertheorised. Granovetter sug-gested that remote ties played a more significant role in who social actors choose to connecting with. Connecting strategies become a central part of social capital, having consequences for how communities are formed and perceived too. Putnam [24] has suggested two forms of social capital, bonding and bridging. Bonding refers to re-sources coming from close relationships, while bridging are benefits which might come from casual or remote ties. Lin [21] argued for the theory of "instrumental ac-tion", suggesting that actors who invest in weak ties are likely to be benefiters. These approaches, however, theoretically assumes a resources are scarce and mutual recog-nition of action or tie. They also assume a type of game-theory approach, where social actors rationally compete and calculate their actions in social situations characterised by lack of resources.

In the digital age, it is all reversed. Information, resources, and ties, are abundant. This implies that consumption of digital devices and data sharing can have positive impact on social capital. The reoccurring analytical conundrum with current research, is that we have little knowledge on how the *actual* SNS use, practices, and patterns [25] transpire and are applied to coordinate tasks in social situations. Researchers are still bound to question the legitimacy of connections [26, 27]. Caers et.al argue that "our understanding is still quite fragmented and may lack nuances that characterize different settings, countries, and demographic variables" [11]. I argue that current research is too often concerned with understanding social capital to a limited number of SNSs. We need to expand our understanding beyond SNS and include "social media" more broadly, implying more detailed analysis on how different Web 2.0 applications connect with each other. Moreover, how social actors' interaction with user-generated content, can be seen as resources and a mean for cooperation and coordination.

3   Methods and Data Sample

The study's research design is based on a social scientific research methodology. The study applied an explorative approach. 26 students were interviewed by use of quali-tative in-depth interviews, 17 boys and 9 girls. There were no gender criteria for choice of informants. Informants were recruited from two classes at a high school in Trondheim, Norway. Vocational study programs in the Norwegian education system, for example, tend to be gendered. It is not uncommon to find classes in construction classes to only consist of males. The data sample is a reflection of its social setting. 12 interviews were carried out, 10 in groups, consisting of pairs to four students. Two interviews were completed individually, meaning a face-to-face conversation between researcher and student. The interviews lasted from 20 minutes to one hour. All interviews were semi-structured, but followed a guide with predefined questions. The interviews explored the students' user experiences. Concrete themes were investigated. After interviewing, the interviews were transcribed and patterns were attempted established. To complete this analytical goal, the sociological data analysis technique *constant comparative method* [28, 29] was used. The students' answers were coded and grouped into specific themes.

Table 1. The data sample employed in study, showing background of informants

Interview no.	Form of interview	Informant no.	Gender	Age	Approx. Facebook Friends	Member school FB-group	Active bloggers	Use YouTube Tutorials	Study program	Subject	Level in school	Date
1.	Group	1.	M	17	900	-	-	Y	Voc.	Eng.	2nd	Jan. 2012
		2.	M	17	600	-	-	Y				
2.	Group	3.	M	17	350	-	-	-	Voc.	Eng.	2nd	Jan. 2012
		4.	M	17	50	-	-	-				
3.	Group	5.	M	17	-	-	-	-	Voc.	Eng.	2nd	Feb 2012
		6.	M	17	800	-	-	Y				
4.	Group	7.	M	17	-	-	-	-	Voc.	Eng.	2nd	Feb. 2012
		8.	M	17	-	-	-	-				
5.	Group	9.	M	17	400	-	-	-	Voc.	Eng.	2nd	March 2012
		10.	M	17	-	-	-	-				
6.	Ind.	11.	M	17	300	-	-	Y	Voc.	Eng.	2nd	March 2012
7.	Group	12.	M	16	600	-	-	Y	Gen.	Spa.	1st	Feb. 2012
		13.	M	16	700	-	-	-				
		14.	M	16	-	-	-	-				
8.	Group	15.	F	16	1.000	Y	Y	Y	Gen.	Spa.	1st	March 2012
		16.	F	16	300	Y	Y	Y				
9.	Group	17	F	16	700	-	-	-	Gen.	Spa.	1st	March 2012
		18.	F	16	400	-	-	-				
		19.	F	16	800	-	-	-				
		20.	F	16	1.000	-	-	-				
10.	Group	21	M	16	700	Y	-	-	Gen.	Spa.	1st	March 2012
		22.	M	16	-	-	-	-				
11.	Ind.	23.	M	16	200	Y	-	-	Gen.	Spa.	1st	March 28. 2012
12.	Group	24.	F	16	200	Y	-	Y	Gen.	Spa.	1st	March 2012
		25.	F	16	200	Y	-	Y				
		26.	F	16	300	Y	Y	-				

4   Data Analysis

The data analysis is intended at showing the study's findings. The following data analysis is divided into two parts. The first part considers recent tendencies among youth's use of social media applications. The second part will analyse three distinct web mediated social practices. The latter examines how students use Facebook as a tool to (1) coordinate formal schoolwork, (2) as a mean to organise drivers for weekend partying, and (3) how YouTube tutorials can work as a learning resource to play music instruments and to learn gaming.

4.1   Part I: The Changing Web Landscape of Social Media

On a general level, the data shows that the students used social media for online socialisation activities and informal learning. They were "thick consumers" of social media. They used social media applications every day, either for passive or active purposes. They had *all* access to cell or smart phones or portable computers, either at their school or at home. Consumption of mediated computer practises played a crucial role in what it means to be teenager. Digitally "ubiquitous" is a suitable description. Online engagement was commonplace. The projected norm was that a teenager could be accessible 24/7, although one finds variations. This is often presented along a scale of being "always in there", which applied especially to Facebook, to just knowing "what is going on". The dualism between the "on-line" vs. off-line is blurred, but the students had a situational awareness on when it applied. It was often projected that they had an on-going cognitive scripted conversation with someone all the time. The majority of the informants communicated that they did not have a zealous relationship to social media. In other words, the data does not debunk previous research knowledge on youth mediated culture on this level.

The students were digitally informed citizens. They had considerable user experience. All had some previous user experience, prior to interviewing. This included five to six years of consumption of digital devices. Sometimes it was longer than that. They became consumers of desktops or portable computers and cells the age 13 or 14. The first introduction to the online world came often as the result of available resource facilitated by a close tie. A family laptop or desktop, for example, would serve as access to the virtual world. Others would gain more systematic access to the Internet by part-time working. Private wealth was a factor that decided if they had easy access to consumption of social media, than for example that this was enabled by prior schooling. Several informants, for example, had years of user experience before becoming Facebook users. The first introduction started with the Norwegian online community, *Nettby*,[1] before they registered as Facebook users in 2007/08, and later became part of the Twitter community in 2012.

The students were predominantly portrayed a *consumers* than *prosumers* user profile. They conveyed themselves as "passive web 1.0" users than active "Web 2.0" users. They had a "read-only" than "read-and-write" approach and lurked publically more than being active content-producers. The students were conscious that an

---

[1] See: http://en.wikipedia.org/wiki/Nettby for more background information.

ambiguous audience could potentially exploit them. Content creation was associated with *risk*, although many did not mind that their names could be googled or were searchable on other search engines. Privacy was a major concern and online interacting was characterised by strong conformity and self-censorship. This is reflected in how the engaged online, which was restricted to *private* digital rooms. They engaged online in exclusive rooms where trust in ties is exercised. Many still used e-mail and SMS as a way of communicating, in addition to reading online newspapers on a daily bases. The voice-over-IP service Skype was also popular. Use of *chatting* software was one of the main ways of communicating with ties, which often happened on Facebook. Some referred to Facebook's integrated chat software as the new "SMS". Few students were content creators. Only four of 26 students had regularly published web contents. Three girls had created blogs and blogged regularly. One male student had published a YouTube video. Even the students who published online content, exercised rigours ideas on what they could publish online.

The students navigated between four types of social media applications, where Facebook played a centring, connecting, and organising role on top of the other web 2.0 applications. Students divided their online time between; (1) SNSs, (2) video-sharing communities, (3) online gaming and (4) blogs. This division follows strong gendered ideas and values. They are almost sectorial, where blogging and gaming represented a digital "off-limit space" to the opposite sex. SNSs and video-sharing represented a more "gender-neutral" space.

Blogging was popular among the female students, but controversial among the males. Some male students expressed their prompt annoyance. The males claimed that they did not read blogs, as it was a "girl thing". "Blogs is for girls", as one informant expressed it. If they read one, they only admitted watching pictures. The gendered youth divide was related to the particular Norwegian mediated practice of "*rosalboggere*", or "pinkbloggers", translated into English. Unclear on its cultural nature, it can be understood as a form of an individualised young adult consumer culture lifestyle, dedicated to the experimentation on feminine practices and online social identities. Youth blog about their everyday life, emotions, love-life, social issues, and endorse commercial products, acting as role model for young adults. This online category has risen to be a form of symbolic representation of a successful teen, although being heavily criticized for monetising and uncritical personal branding. Pinkbloggers are also controversial public figures or celebrities. Some have their own TV-show, like Sophie Elise Isachsen, where she essentially talks about her everyday life.[2] The pink blogging practice is connected to the site *blogg.no*, which many of the female informants read on a daily bases. Female students approached blogging predominantly from a consumer approach.

Online gaming was a youth male domain. Some female students had gamed, but briefly. Males explained that they had gamed for years, portraying it as an important leisure practice. Gaming could last for hours. It was a weekend hobby. Friends congregated and played Call of Duty or Counter Strike. Some males were reluctant to speak about the numbers of hours they spent in front of a PC or video game machine. Many male students stated they had started cutting down on gaming. It was portrayed as "dull"; and, if, a male student still spent hours on gaming, he was somehow considered as "non-adult".

---

[2] Sophie Elise Isachsen's blog: http://sophieelise.blogg.no

YouTube was a favourite one among both sexes, portrayed as a "neutral" space. YouTube was used for different purposes; downloading music, just watching small video clips, and studying YouTube tutorials. These were the most common user practices. Many students used YouTube tutorials to learn how to play music instruments or how to play an online video game.

Facebook was the most popular social media application. All informants had a user profile. It was common having among 300 online friends, while some had 1.000 connections. Many had been users since 2008. The students reported contradictory habits. On the one hand side, they were connected everyday as "online-lookers", but on the other hand, stated a type of attitude of not being the one who contributed to online interaction and sharing, forming a "user paradox self-control". They exercised conformity, reflecting a high degree of editorial control and self-critical online stage-managing of their online self. This appeared being the outcome of an established online socialisation experience. Many years of use reflected a reoccurring pattern. When they first started using Facebook, they engaged deeply, but later took a shallow position. This appeared creating normative strategies for online engagement, rendered in critical beliefs for ideal use. This was reflected in distinct unwritten ideas for interacting on Facebook, forming as discourse for "proper Facebook use and etiquette". I will give examples.

First, the students now classified Facebook as culturally "dull". They were disappointed with Facebook, because "nothing happen there". Few students admitted posting or contributing to a public online dialogue. Second, user stories also showed another reoccurring pattern. Many said that they first wrote *status updates*, but stopped with it. Later they *liked*, but also stopped doing that, to just watch *pictures*. Third, this user pattern did not involve full stop in communicating. They communicated in closed web spaces, to Facebook's chat channels, where they interacted with strong connections. Fourth, we also find informants who stated that they had stop adding ties to their online Facebook network. Facebook networking was not a fashion anymore. It was rare, and they had somehow finished "networked", meeting a social "saturation point". It was more uncommon to come across students who recently had become Facebook users. When getting a friend request, they would often treat it with scepticism and run a "background check", to find out who it was and how they were related, implying a strong degree of social selection. Fifth, there were reported cases that students questioned the value of having *large* online social networks. Some had for example started down-scaling or "unfriended" their ties. One female student told that she had "de-networked" her Facebook network from 1.000 to 300 connections. Sixth, an odd attitude conveyed in the interviews was a sort of "teenage anxiety" mind-set, which acted as a justification for not sharing. When observing younger teenager than themselves, acting as "newcomers", they would seldom interact with them or network with them. Instead, this would acts as a justification to leave Facebook, and head toward Twitter, which were their new online playground.

4.2   Part II: Three Social Web Mediated Practices Connecting Social Capital

Based on review data, one can observe a user pattern showing influence of social networks and social capital. Students experience less positive value of networking. Large networks make little sense possessing, as they realise that they interact in with a limited number of ties. One identifies a "devaluating" in the quality of ties. Large access to online resources could have negative influence on social capital. Online socialisation can be argued of not providing access to particular interesting resources. On the other hand, when examining *particular use of social media* practices, one can potentially identify how social actors draw upon ties or resources in their social networks, which can suggest positive influence and use social capital. In order for this to work, requires that social actors execute social actions and coordinate task. The below sections will analyse three practices.

Practice 1: Trading and sharing formal school work

The first *particular use of social media* connects to how students use Facebook as a coordination site to organise schoolwork. Seven students, five female and two males, were members of school related Facebook groups reported, all attending general or academics studies, a study program preparing students for university studies. These were self-organised and moderated by the students themselves. Data suggests that there were two to five closed groups, while three were class-based. Students emphasized that they were useful and used them continuously. The Facebook groups acted either as a type of "class bulletin board" or "discussion forums", where the latter use was often related to assignments. They often shared information on practicalities. We find variations in what types of digital items were shared; information on what they have in homework for next class, which pages they are supposed to read for a particular lesson, for example. Cram sheets were popular items too, acting as a valuable and requested online resource. Sharing, however, was seldom based on a motivation to participate in a reflective process with the aim of turning data to knowledge on a distinct topic or subject. The Facebook groups are bulletin boards, a sort of a "student answering service", where communication is done individually with the expectation of an answer. There is a low threshold for sharing and anybody can post anything without having the risk of being bullied, for example. The groups acted as a supplement to the regular reminders students do face-to-face. The students' sharing reminds much of the old "work plan", a sheet, which teachers in the lower levels of the education system handed out to students at the beginning of each week. This student explains:

> I-21:   "And, then we have the class, we have an own Facebook group. When we have tests, for example, we can share cram sheets. If there is not someone who has done their homework, then we can share, so we can talk to each other, what is our homework for the next day, what is the work for the next week. In that sense, it is very convenient."

Data analysis also shows innovative ways in which social media applications are combined, with the intention collaboration. Female students in academic studies established temporary Facebook group, which were part of a larger cross-disciplinary project. In the groups, they commented on links and discussed the project's purpose, thus relating social web to a goal driven learning. Facebook groups acted as discussion forums, a type of digital "notebook", while they finalised their work in Google Docs. One of the female students explains.

I-15: We had a group project, "2050 Trøndelag", on how Trøndelag is going to be in the year 2050. There we had a Facebook group, where we discussed what we were writing, what we should put in our project, what was relevant to have, and things like that.

R: Who was most active in that group? Was it you?

I-16: No, it was not a big group. All contributed. We were five students, but the fifth did not do much. We were contributing all together. And we used Google Docs.

Practice 2: Organising drivers by faceworking

The second practice connects to how social media is integrated part of a much debated issue in the Norwegian public sphere, illegal taxicab operation. Taking an official taxi under regular fairs is expensive, a factor which has led to that young adults look for inexpensive and unregulated alternatives to get home after partying on weekends. Facebook groups and Facebook ties have risen to work as a type of "unofficial" unregulated "call centre", where vital contact information on potential drivers and fairs is shared. It is a small-scale dubious re-invention of ties in social networks, where ties have a highly regarded value, possessing potential "positive" influence on social capital. Two male students explain:

I-2:   Among my buddies, it is a lot about football.

I-1:   A lot of football, a lot of drinking, potential parties, drivers. Very much drivers. Many updates say you can call that and that number, if you need to driver at the end of the night.

R: Are they paid to be drivers?

I-1:   Most of them charge you. This may be 200 kroner, for example, to drive someone here and there. When I get my driver licence, I'll be sure to write that I can drive an evening, for example, if I do not drink myself, though. I'm going to write that I can drive. I might perhaps charge about 50 kroners per person. I will drive them wherever they need to go.

R: Who do you drive?

I-1:   Friends on Facebook, for example. I post my number, and anyone can call me.

I-2:   All my friends see that it is posted there. If they are in a place and cannot get home, they just call you and ask if you can drive them home.

I-1:   For example, and if there is anyone who know it, among those I know on Facebook, who know that I can drive, and they go to a party and I meet other many people there, who I don't know, they can disseminate to them that I drive. This might give many trips.

R: It is a sub business that has emerged?

I-1:   Yes. It has started to compete with the general taxi business, I think. Taking a taxi is the last resort, if you can't find a driver.

I-2:   You call through your Facebook contact list before calling for a taxi.

I-1:   I would rather walk home than taking a taxi.

I-2:   If I'm at a party somewhere, and can't reach a driver, I just walk home. I'm not calling for a taxi!

Practice 3: YouTubing to play music instrument and gaming

The third practice connects to use of "YouTube tutorials". Although YouTube has been around since 2005, the services has developed a variety of internal subgenres, which comes forwards as particular media texts. One of these are "YouTube tutorials", which constitute its own media texts. Sharing and consumption of YouTube tutorials reflects an emerging "peer-to-peer-share" social network informal learning setting. YouTube is full of tutorials. They are short videos intended for informal learning. One common theme is that someone takes on the role as a narrator, and poses as an instructor, giving a step-by-step instruction on how to do something. A tutor, with some degree of self-accumulated experience, break down the work process into separate modules or sections. The tutorials explain for example use of a software interface, how to play a song. The tutorials cover a range of topics, where an individual intends to model and disseminate knowledge or skill to anonymous learners.

Nine students explained that they used YouTube content to informal learning, which in most cases related to their hobbies. The study found that students used YouTube content to learn more about three social practices, to play a music instrument, to game, and photographing. Two female students explain how they use YouTube to learn to play instruments:

R: Do you use YouTube to learn?
I-15:   I tried to learn from YouTube, to play guitar, but then I did not have any awesome guitar either. It was purchased in Turkey. It did not work so well for me, but I learned some chords. It is possible to use it for learning. Not that I use it so much.
R: Do you use to learn?
I-16:   I have used it for learning.
R: Explain.
I-16:   For piano, chords, learning stuff like that. I have always played by listening, but when I come to a point in the song, where I don't really know where I'm going, I go on YouTube. Then I see how they play, how they press the keys. So there are many "how to play video", which I have been watching.
R: So you use tutorials?
I-16:   Yes. I have used it.

A male student explains use of YouTube to lean to game:

I-11:   Most times when new games are out, all my mates meet to find out more about it. We often sit and look on YouTube to see new things. It happens when we have to learn that and that, and that's the way to do it. It's really that way we use YouTube.
R: So you're sitting around and talking together?
I-11:   Yes, we are discussing.
R: It seems to very useful? It teaches you a lot?
I-11:   I learn a lot from it. I think that I couldn't have been able to play, if it wasn't for YouTube.
R: It would have been much harder?
I-11:   Yes. I'm pretty sure of that.

5   Conclusion

The advent of Web 2.0 applications has involved a renewed interest in sociological research on social capital and social network. Research has mainly been interested in analysing the diffusion of ideas, values, and qualities in ties. One often established and reproduced research knowledge, is the much cited idea that "diffusion of ideas do not work" [30]. This implies that there little degree of social capital to be harvested from social media. This finding is repeated in quantitative analysis, which often miss understanding the widespread *production* and *distribution* of social practices embedded in social media. With few analytical grips, one can easily show that that there is an *active, multiple* production, distribution, and consumption of specific communication-based relational activities. The conundrum is that we often lack the creativity to unlock them, as they are somehow "invisible". I have only demonstrated that within a small data sample, youth engage and produce social practice in overlapping social and digital networks. Future research on social media and social capital should focus the complex social dynamics of social networks, especially the role of how task and assignments are coordinated and organised. Researchers should explore the potential production, distribution, and consumption of online resources to enhance our understanding on the relation between social capital and social media. Analysing the meaning of isolated ties will seldom suffice.

References

1. Sveinbjørnsson, S.: Så mange nordmenn er på Facebook (2013),
   http://www.digi.no/920967/saa-mange-nordmenn-er-paa-facebook
   (cited September 10, 2013)
2. Fossbakken, E.: Rekord for Twitter i Norge (2012),
   http://www.kampanje.com/medier/article6039802.ece (cited September
   10, 2013)
3. Synlighet: Linkedin - fakta og statistikk over brukere i Norge og verden (2012),
   http://www.synlighet.no/linkedin/statistikk-antall-brukere/
   (cited September 10, 2013)
4. Myrstad, M.: Har over 300.000 nordmenn prøvd Google+? (2012),
   http://www.mmyrstad.no/2012/01/har-over-300-000-nordmenn-
   provd-google/ (cited September 10, 2013)
5. Fossbakken, E.: En millon brukere av tablets (2012),
   http://www.kampanje.com/medier/article6030446.ece (cited September
   10, 2013)
6. Brandtzæg, P.B., Heim, J., Kaare, B.H.: Bridging and bonding in social network sites Investigating family-based capital. International Journal of Web Based Communities 6(3), 231–253 (2010)
7. Brandtzæg, P.B.: Towards a unified Media-User Typology (MUT): A meta-analysis and review of the research literature on media-user typologies. Computers in Human Behavior 26(5), 940–956 (2010)
8. Brandtzæg, P.B.: Social networking sites: Their users and social implications - A longitudinal study. Journal of Computer-Mediated Communication 17(4), 467–488 (2012)

9. Brandtzæg, P.B., Lüders, M., Skjetne, J.H.: Too many Facebook "Friends"? Content sharing and sociability versus the need for privacy in social network sites. International Journal of Human-Computer Interaction 26(11-12), 1006–1030 (2010)

10. Jenkins, H.: Confronting the challenges of a participatory culture: Media education for the 21th century (2006)

11. Caers, R., De Feyter, T., De Couck, M., Stough, T., Vigna, C., Du Bois, C.: Facebook: A literature review. New Media & Society 15(6), 982–1002 (2013)

12. Brandtzæg, P.B.: Social implications of the Internet and social networking sites: a user typology approach, Oslo: Department of Media and Communication, Faculty of Humanities. University of Oslo (2012)

13. O'Reilly, T.: What Is Web 2.0? Design patterns and business models for the next generation (2005), http://oreilly.com/web2/archive/what-is-web-20.html (cited June 15, 2014)

14. Boyd, D., Ellison, N.B.: Social network sites: Definition, history and scholarship. Journal of Computer-Mediated Communication 3(1), 210–230 (2007)

15. Aalen, I.: En kort bok om sosiale medier, Fagbokforl, Bergen (2013)

16. Kaplan, A.M., Haenlein, M.: Users of the world, unite! The challenges and opportunities of Social Media. Business Horizons 53(1), 59–68 (2010)

17. Bourdieu, P.: The forms of social capital. In: Richardson, J. (ed.) Handbook of Theory And Action for the Sociology of Education, pp. 241–258. Greenwood, New York (1986)

18. Coleman, J.: Social capital in the creation of human capital. The American Journal of Sociology 94, 95–120 (1988)

19. Burt, R.S.: Structural holes: the social structure of competition. Harvard University Press, Cambridge (1992)

20. Burt, R.S.: Brokerage and closure: an introduction to social. Oxford University Press, Oxford (2005)

21. Lin, N.: Social resources and instrumental action. In: Marsden, P.V., Lin, N. (eds.) Social Structure and Network Analysis, pp. 131–145. Sage, Beverly Hills (1982)

22. Lin, N.: Building a network theory of social capital. In: Lin, N., Cook, K., Burt, R. (eds.) Social Capital: Theory and Research, Aldine de Gruyter, New York (2001)

23. Granovetter, M.S.: The Strength of Weak Ties. American Journal of Sociology 78(6), 1360–1380 (1973)

24. Putnam, R.: Bowling Alone: The Collapse and Revival of American Community. Simond and Schuster, New York (2000)

25. Ellison, N.B., Steinfield, C., Lampe, C.: Connection strategies: Social capital implications of Facebook-enabled communication practices. New Media and Society 13(6), 873–892 (2011)

26. Ahn, J.: Teenagers and social network sites: Do off-line inequalities predict their online social networks? First Monday 17(1) (2012)

27. Stefanone, M.A., Kwon, K., Lackaff, D.: The value of online friends: Networked resources via social network sites. First Monday 16 (2011)

28. Strauss, A., Corbin, J.: Basics of qualitative research: Grounded theory procedures and techniques. Sage Publications, Inc., Newbury Park (1990)

29. Strauss, A., Corbin, J.: Basics of qualitative research: Techniques and procedures for developing grounded theory. Sage Publications, Inc., Thousand Oaks (1998)

30. Wu, S., Hofman, J.M., Mason, W.A., Watts, D.J.: Who says what to whom on Twitter. In: Proceedings of the 20th International Conference on World Wide Web, Proceeding WWW 2011, Hyderabad, pp. 705–714 (2011)

Enhancing Innovation Potential through Local Capacity Building in Education

Jaana Holvikivi

Helsinki Metropolia University of Applied Sciences, Finland
jaana.holvikivi@metropolia.fi

Abstract. Global technology education is largely dominated by Western universities. Students from developing countries face an enormous challenge when moving from their local education system into the competitive international education market. Their local knowledge gets lost in a foreign education system where the students are required to acquire a new set of skills. This paper presents a survey among international technology students that highlights the differences. Moreover, the paper explores the situation from the developing country perspective, and brings forth a proposal for strengthening the education capacities in the developing countries particularly in the fields of ICTs and mobile technologies. Strengthening local knowledge building would allow innovations based on local needs and potentials.

Keywords: capacity building, ICTs, developing countries, education, mobile technologies, innovations.

1 Introduction

International education has grown to a large and ever changing market of services. A growing number of students seek a place to study outside their home country in order to find best education in information technology and engineering [1], [2]. On the other hand, many countries and universities have an explicit internationalization policy, actively inviting overseas students to their degree programs. Internationalization is considered as a positive trend in industrialized countries, as well as a novel source of revenues. However, it also brings challenges to institutions that may not have a long experience in educating foreigners.

The worlds' most prominent universities are in an advantageous position in the global competition. Their good reputation, top position in global rankings, and recently, their ability to offer high profile MOOC's (massive open online courses) attracts top students. In a situation where they can choose the best talent and most suitable students, they do not need to adjust to a heterogeneous student body. The background of students has been screened to fit the institutions' practices. Even when these universities set up subsidiaries in other countries such as China or India, their educational offering largely remains the same.

K.K. Kimppa et al. (Eds.): HCC11 2014, IFIP AICT 431, pp. 27–38, 2014.
© IFIP International Federation for Information Processing 2014

However, other universities face a more challenging situation: they need to work to obtain good quality applicants, they need to be able to screen among the great variety of them, and they have more pressure to adjust to student needs. Simultaneously, they need to produce competent professionals efficiently, in order to be profitable. These challenges have evoked much research and discussion among universities nationally and worldwide, generating a substantial literature on these issues. The main research approach has centered on a few questions: how to recruit efficiently, how to generate income, how to help students adapt to the new environment, and how to provide supporting studies. Only few universities have attempted to modify their core curricula to accommodate a diverse student population [2].

This paper aims at scrutinizing the need for more fundamental changes in internationalization of higher education, and technology education in particular. First, the extraordinary character of Western academic culture is discussed, focusing on the specific cognitive requirements of technology studies. Moreover, the dominance of Western science tradition is briefly compared with alternative approaches. Second, the state of education in developing countries is outlined by examples from Africa and South Asia. In the research section, the consequences of the educational disparity in international engineering education are presented through results of a survey. Finally, solutions to improve the current unsatisfactory situation are discussed. A shift of emphasis in development efforts is proposed: a move of focus from Western institutions to the research centers, universities and students in developing countries. The proposal addresses the need to enhance global innovation potential in less advantageous areas.

1.1   Eurocentrism in Science

Notwithstanding the knowledge that human cultures vary greatly, the academic world has functioned on the assumption of universality of Western science. The journal Behavioral and Brain Sciences published in 2010 a paper titled "The weirdest people in the world?" that invited much discussion from scientists in various fields. By "weird" people Henrich and his co-authors [3] referred to Western, Educated, Industrialized, Rich and Democratic people who had been subjects in behavioral research in the last century. The paper discussed the ethnocentric way human nature has been studied, and the implications of using a narrow sample of subjects in the study of human psychological functioning and cognition. Most of the research that has been published in psychology journals has been conducted by Western researchers (96%), using university students as test subjects (in 67% of the cases in American samples). Henrich et al [3] argued that this kind of sample is severely biased, and in some cases could be considered as outlier of the global population. They gave examples of comparative studies that indicated very different behavioral patterns in other populations, particularly in Asian and small societies.

In particular, the Western sample of study subjects has been shown to deviate from other cultural samples in certain cognitive skills such as spatial reasoning and thinking styles, especially analytical thinking. Moreover, there are pronounced differences in performance of language related tasks. English and other Indo-European languages differ from most other languages in their grammatical structures, which influences the way thoughts are manipulated in the brain [4]. Similarly, brain studies [5] have been conducted mainly in rich Western countries because of the high cost of the equipment and the high skill level needed. Otherwise only in Japan, Korea and China the technology has been advanced enough to conduct brain scans on the local population [6]. Nevertheless, the inclusion of Eastern populations has revealed interesting results such as the brain differences in reading: the use of Chinese characters employs brain areas differently from using alphabetic characters [7].

The problems of Eurocentrism in research have earlier been raised in humanities and social sciences most notably by Said [8] and Bernal [9], and Asante has advocated Afrocentrism for research that concerns Africa [10]. On the other hand, ICT has its roots in Angloamerican world, and the dominance of English language and culture in internet has been discussed by Diaz Andrade and Urquhart [11].

1.2   Universities and Research

Asides from the traditional internationalization option where students travel to the host university, other alternatives have emerged. There are partnerships or subsidiaries of Western institutions in growing economies such as Arab countries, India, China, Brazil, and Russia [12]. The aim of these units is to educate global professionals; obviously people who are working in Western style. The subsidiaries of Western universities educate local students and, in addition, they look for business partnerships and provide opportunities for their home staff to work in other countries. Western universities also enlarge their student pool by distance education and on-line courses, with the same offerings everywhere. The Journal of Studies in International Education published a special issue on Internationalization of the Curriculum and the Disciplines in May 2013 (17:2) [2], which indicated that the matter is very new as regards to the needs to adjust the content of the curriculum.

The top ranking universities in the world are still mainly located in the US and UK, or other European or English-speaking countries. Western science tradition dominates the research to the extent that other science traditions are considered ethnic or cultural curiosities. There have been very few attempts to challenge this attitude. Medicine is a major exception, as Chinese and Eastern medical sciences are studied in local universities. There have also been attempts to create a Chinese cultural value system [13], native psychological models in Taiwan, and an African personality model [14].

Accordingly, leading journals accept only studies that follow strictly Western standards and traditions. Other research traditions have little room for development or expansion outside national circles. Davidson [15] argues for more open editorial policies and for courage to publish intellectually challenging studies from various cultural contexts, such as China and India, in the field of information systems research. The unique features of local organizations are not truly appreciated or studied when Western standards are followed strictly, and potentially new interesting theoretical viewpoints are missed.

2   Educational Policies in Developing Countries

The global goal of United Nations to expand education to cover all children has been reached in theory, but the practice falls short of the goal in developing countries [16] . The Africa learning barometer shows that only 76% of children in Sub-Saharan Africa attend primary school, and the secondary school enrolment is as low as 28%. Moreover, more than half of students in Grades 4 and 5 in countries such as Ethiopia, Nigeria and Zambia are below the minimum learning thresholds. Even more alarming is the finding that many teachers have difficulties in scoring acceptably in the same tests. As teacher salaries tend to be very low in African countries, competent teachers often seek better paid employment opportunities.

Nevertheless, some African countries have engaged in overly ambitious educational reforms. In Ethiopia, secondary school education is conducted in English, and in Rwanda, the school language was changed from French into English [17]. Obviously, lack of educational materials in native languages makes it attractive to choose English, and there might be additional political reasons for the choice. Many African countries have two official languages, one being the dominant local language such as Swahili, the other one the language of the former colonial master, English, French or Portuguese. Additionally, most citizens speak a local language as their mother tongue. When children enter school, they usually start studying in their second or third language.

2.1   Kenya and Rwanda

The Kenyan government has a Vision 2030 Economic Stimulus Programme, which has equipped 1050 secondary schools with computers: 11 PCs, 1 laptop, 1 video projector and one printer for each school. The aim of the initiative is that teachers would be able to integrate ICT into curriculum. However, there can be as many as 80 to 120 students in one class, which makes it impossible to let all students to work with computers. Moreover, school administrators are sometimes preventing teachers to access the computers, so that they are not able to prepare for the classes [18]. The main teaching method in the crowded classrooms is lecturing and repeating teacher's words. Because of the shortage of materials such as textbooks or notebooks, students have to learn the material by heart. Furthermore, they are not able to practice writing sufficiently.

In June 2013, teachers were striking for more than 3 weeks for a pay raise, but the government insisted that they could not afford paying higher salaries, which had been promised already in 1997 [19]. Obviously the policy on ICT education is not realistic under current economic pressures.

The Rwandan government decided to switch the country's entire education system from French to English in one of the most dramatic steps to date in its move away from Francophone influence [17]. Primary education in first three years is conducted in local Kinyarwanda, and after that in English. Just 8 percent of Rwandans speak French, and 4 percent speak English, according to the government, but teachers have previously been educated in French. In 2009, out of Rwanda's 31 000 primary school teachers, only 4 700 were trained in English, and out of Rwanda's 12 000 secondary school teachers, only 600 were trained in English. To alleviate the situation, about 300 Ugandan teachers were employed to teach in English. It is not hard to imagine what confusion this policy has caused.

The curricula in African schools are based on western models, as well as most books and materials. The content of textbooks might be very remote from the everyday experience of students, adding an extra level of abstraction to the content to be learned. Therefore, students need to operate from two worldviews and often have two or more cultures to contend with. The education has very weak connections to the practical life of students, resulting in rote learning without reaching a de-contextualization of knowledge.

2.2   India and Bangladesh

The multiplicity of languages in the Indian subcontinent poses an enormous challenge for the early education system, as well. In addition to nationwide languages English and Hindu, there are dominant local languages and hundreds of minor language spoken in the country. 47 languages are used as media of instruction in schools. There have been some regional projects to teach children from indigenous tribes in their first language and stepwise shift to the dominant language of the area. However, the target populations in these projects have been marginal, in Bangladesh less than 70 000 [20]. Likewise, in July 2007, a project was started in the Indian state Orissa. Under that project, in 200 schools, indigenous (tribal) children from 10 language groups were being taught through their mother tongues in the first grades, with materials collected from children, parents and teachers. Later 16 more languages were added in 2008.

2.3   Language Question in Primary and Secondary Education

The studies in bilingualism and multilingualism have revealed a number of positive cognitive outcomes, including increased attentional control, working memory, metalinguistic awareness, and abstract and symbolic representation skills [21]. Bilingualism can greatly benefit intellectual development of the child, which extend to late adulthood [22]. Nevertheless, the benefits are lost if the child is not able to acquire fluency in her school language. For the development of abstract and scientific thought, mastery of the language is required [23]. Even mathematical skills are influenced by the language of instruction, as was shown by Saalbach and his collaborators [24]. According to their study, when language of instruction and language of application differed, the performance in arithmetic tests deteriorated. There was a significant cognitive cost involved even in this case where the subjects of the study came from a privileged Swiss German and French school system.

The above presented country cases illustrate the situation in poor developing countries. Good quality education is scare; moreover, the development policies are not well-informed or sufficiently resourced. Students who come from these countries to Western universities have already overcome many hardships: a student who is only gifted in mathematics, technology and science, has a very meagre chance to proceed through the system. The current situation excludes these students early in their studies. Naturally, there are also students who are fortunate to attend the best schools and who are multitalented, and finally capable to enter any university of their choice.

3   Research and Results

3.1   Research Methods

The Helsinki Metropolia University of Applied Sciences has educated international students in English in bachelor degree programs since 1994. The experience has revealed many kinds of challenges that students with developing country background confront when entering the Western engineering education system. Recently, one beginning study group consisting of 56 students answered an online questionnaire of their study experiences and previous practices. The survey included questions on the experience of computer use, earlier use of computers in studies, familiar study methods, and cognitive preferences.

The survey was given as an optional task in a study module, however, all students decided to participate. Moreover, they answered nearly all questions though none was indicated as compulsory. The ages of participants were between 18 and 34, average 23 years. 9 of the respondents were women. They came from many regions of the world: 8 from Africa (Af), 9 from Eastern Europe (EE), 9 from Western Europe (WE), 15 from South Asia (mainly Nepal, SA), 10 from East Asia (Vietnam, etc., EA), and 5 from Middle Eastern (ME) countries. They reported speaking altogether 26 different languages.

The survey consisted of multiple choice questions on technology use and understanding, questions on study modes and use of technology in the studies, questions on career aspirations and cognitive practices, and some open questions on the current studies. Respondents were given a link to the online form, which could be filled in any time. There was an identity check in order to eliminate duplicate submissions.

3.2   Results

The background diversity was reflected strongly in the usage of computers before studies. About one third of the respondents had been familiar with computers already when younger than 10, 24% started using computers at age 11-15, 28 % at age 15-20, and 16% were older than 20 when they started using computers regularly. The distribution of responses by nationality is shown in Fig 1. As could be expected, Africans had shorter exposure to computers than the other nationalities, whereas Western students had been using computers already in primary school age or before. The students were also asked if they ever participated in assembling a computer. To this question, Eastern Europeans gave most positive answers (67%), and Africans least (25%).

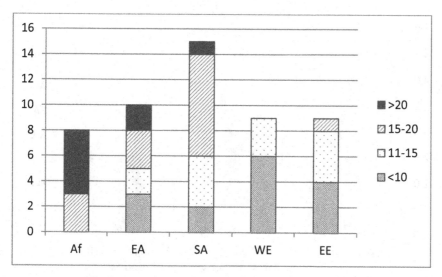

Fig. 1. Starting age of regular computer use by nationality

According to this survey, East European students had the most traditional study experience and less exposure to varied study methods such as team work, research report writing or giving presentations. The results are presented in Fig 2. In fact, Africans and West Europeans had nearly similar profiles in these modes of study. However, the implementations of methods could vary. East European students had an average 2,5 with team work familiarity and giving presentations, where 1 was "not at all familiar with" and 5 "very familiar with". On the other hand, there were no significant differences between exposure to laboratory work in physics or chemistry between groups, whereas there were striking differences between individual students: nearly half of them had no experience on chemistry laboratories, and about a third only little experience in physics labs.

Student interviews and self-reports relate of the cultural shock that they encounter when they move from developing country education to the western university system. A theoretical approach and difficulties to adapt theory into practice have been revealed in laboratory assignments that require hands-on work with the equipment, accurate measurements, or program coding. According to a study by Agiobu-Kemmer in 1984, Nigerian Yoruba children spent more time with human beings than with physical objects. The reverse was true with Scottish children who spent more time with physical objects than with human beings. This comparative study indicated that cultural factors have a strong impact on how the early upbringing introduces the physical world [14].

Moreover, earlier study results have indicated that tasks, which demanded logical reasoning, were particularly difficult to many international students. Separate tests to confirm this finding were given to students, and indeed they performed less well in different types of reasoning tasks [25]. As Henrich et al [3] in their paper showed, this finding is in accordance with general cultural cognitive differences. Analytical thinking and formal reasoning are typically skills that are produced by the western educational system and science studies [26].

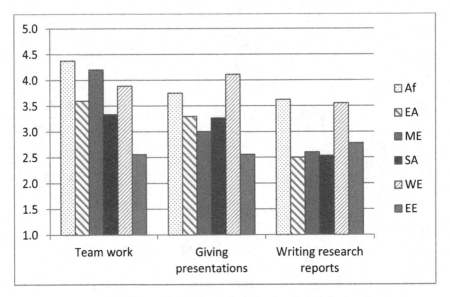

Fig. 2. Familiarity with study modes by nationality (scale 1 to 5)

4   Globalization Solutions through Capacity Building

4.1   Goal to Enhance Global Innovation Potential

The spread of mobile phone use in developing countries has been phenomenal. There are many areas in Africa where telephone cables were never installed and the mobile phone has been the first two-way communications devise that people have been able to use. This has created applications for mobile phones that are specific to developing areas such as phone banking applications, bush nurse services, and local market information distribution. There is a huge innovation potential in mobile applications due to lack of solid infrastructure. These innovations cannot be made in Western research centers where the local conditions and problems are unheard of. Moreover, the ways people prefer to operate their gadgets depend on culture, environment, education level, and context. For example, in rural areas in India, voice based interface is preferable because of illiteracy [27]. Therefore, strengthening research capability in African, Latin American and Asian universities would diversify innovations in global scale.

It is of course possible that students from developing countries create solutions for their home market when they work in western universities. Indeed, there are some examples of such innovations. A Muslim student founded a social networking web site for the Islamic community called Muxlim when he was working in Finland. The site gained popularity and international fame but finally failed to generate sufficient earnings and had to close four years later in 2008 [28]. Had the operation base been somewhere closer to large Islamic populations, the story might have ended differently.

4.2   Bringing in Local Capacities

UNESCO issued an extensive report "Engineering: Issues, Challenges and Opportunities for Development" in 2010 where needs for change in engineering practice and education were discussed, and issues that are similar to this paper's arguments were raised [29]. The report called for technical capacity-building in developing countries, stressing needs for local energy solutions, participatory urban planning and infrastructure projects for sustainable development. One example came from South Sudan where sustainable construction for using appropriate technology has been developed. For engineering education, a demand for holistic and integrated systems approaches was presented, and a call was issued to share pedagogical approaches and develop curricula in this context. Sharing is particularly important for universities in developing countries who face serious constraints regarding human, financial and institutional resources to develop such curricula, learning and teaching methods. Moreover, Gaillard argued [29] that developing countries cannot rely on their substantial diaspora of experts but efforts should focus on strengthening national engineering and scientific capacity particularly through training, recruiting and retaining the next generation of scientists.

Furthermore, according to Davidson [15], information systems research would gain both depth and breadth, if researchers were willing to set their work firmly in the local cultural context. Arguably, the same requirement could be extended to all information technology research as well as industrial engineering and organizations research and education. Engineering and management practices have to adjust to local conditions and environment, and therefore, local knowledge is invaluable. Additionally, the research needs to be informed not only on local technologies but by anthropology and sociology.

Scientific traditions that developed outside Western academia have a potential to enhance global understanding if they were incorporated in local research practices. Medicine has strong local practices also on university level in East Asia, but it is only part of the vast Chinese science that has developed its own course during millennia [30]. Other less well known or advanced traditions have influenced western science but could still benefit scientific work in other areas, as well. To name some:

- Knowledge of potatoes in Peruvian countryside far exceeds the Western cultivation traditions. Peruvian farmers may have over 80 varieties on their field, each with different resistance against humidity, draught, cold, or diseases [31].
- The extensive native knowledge on medicinal herbs and nature's poisons has already been harnessed by multinational pharmaceutical companies, but how much has is benefitted local knowledge and science?
- Sustainable agriculture turns more and more to local traditions. In Madagascar local peasants can assess the productivity of a plot of land simply by looking at it, based on their experience [32]. The role that indigenous knowledge can play in truly participatory approaches to sustainable development should be acknowledged.

- There are numerous ancient building traditions that have partially been abandoned. Recently, it was realized that the concrete built by Romans two millennia ago was much stronger and more long-lasting than modern concrete. The composition of that concrete is again being applied in modern construction [33].
- There has been important hydraulic engineering in many tropical areas such as Sri Lanka and Mesoamerica [34]. Advanced irrigation systems allowed the feeding of a large population base in areas that are currently tropical rainforests.

4.3   Proposed Measures for Universities

Universities in developing countries struggle with resource constraints. Local teaching capacities are in need of strengthening, particularly in Africa [29]. Programs to incorporate local knowledge and working styles into the curriculum and ways of doing research would offer an opportunity to lift the profile of universities, and at the same time, offer viable alternatives to the student diaspora. Recently, capacity building has become a popular approach in development projects, and it is definitely needed in engineering education, as well. Developing countries cannot act in such a demanding effort alone, as it will be long lasting and requires substantial resources. Strong partnerships and long-term commitments with Western institutions are indispensable.

Outline of the program would include measures such as:

1.   Curriculum review to suit local needs: school background analyzed and taken as starting point for education. Job market needs to be understood and met.

2.   Teacher training requires a collaborative effort with international professionals, local staff and consulting anthropologists or sociologist.

3.   Development of teaching methods that best suit the students and increase their professional abilities. Emphasis needs to be on areas that are not supported by the primary and secondary education.

4.   Creation of research programs to study native engineering science and related knowledge.

5.   Creation of local innovation centers close to universities in developing countries.

5   Conclusion

This overview has highlighted the need to enhance current trends in international education towards stronger emphasis in developing areas. University partnerships that are largely based on western model, can become balanced, bidirectional exchanges, if universities in developing countries are given support in their capacity-building efforts. Innovations and research are diversified through fresh inputs and utilization of local traditional knowledge. The growing market potential in developing countries can be better exploited from inside than from importing ideas from industrialized world. The novel solutions would probably suit local conditions better, moreover, they could undoubtedly be applied in many other areas as well, and thus enrich global knowledge.

References

1. EJEE, "Special Issue: Globalization and its impact on engineering education and research. European Journal of Engineering Education 31(3) (June 2006)
2. Leask, B.: Special issue on Internationalization of the Curriculum and the Disciplines. Journal of Studies in International Education (May 2013)
3. Henrich, J., Heine, S.J., Norenzayan, A.: The weirdest people in the world? Behavioral and Brain Sciences 33(2-3), 61–83 (2010)
4. Majid, A., Levinson, S.C.: WEIRD languages have misled us, too. Behavioral and Brain Sciences 33(2-3), 103–103 (2010)
5. Chiao, J.Y., Cheon, B.K.: The weirdest brains in the world. Behavioral and Brain Sciences 33(2-3), 88–90 (2010)
6. Hansen, P., Kringelbach, M.: The Neural Bases of Reading. Oxford University Press, Oxford (2010)
7. Chen, C., Xue, G., Mei, L., Chen, C., Dong, Q.: Cultural neurolinguistics. Prog. Brain Res., 178–159 (2009)
8. Said, E.W.: Orientalism. Vintage Books, New York (1978)
9. Bernal, M.: Black Athena, vol. II. Rutgers University Press, New Brunswick (1991)
10. Milhouse, V., Asante, M., Nwosu, P. (eds.): Transcultural realities. Interdisciplinary perspectives on cross-cultural relations. Sage, Thousand Oaks (2001)
11. Diaz Andrade, A.E., Urquhart, C.: ICTs as a tool for cultural dominance: Prospects for a two-way street. Electronic Journal of Information Systems in Developing Countries 37(2), 1–12 (2009)
12. Aydarova, O.: "If Not "the Best of the West," Then "Look East": Imported Teacher Education Curricula in the Arabian Gulf. Journal of Studies in International Education 17, 284–302 (2013)
13. Fan, Y.: A classification of Chinese culture. Cross Cultural Management 7(2), 3–10 (2000)
14. Lee, Y.-T., McCauley, C.R., Draguns, J.G.: Personality and Person Perception Across Cultures. Lawrence Erlbaum Ass. Inc., Mahwah (1999)
15. Davidson, R.M.: Retrospect and prospect: information systems in the last and next 25 years: response and extension. Journal of Information Technology 25, 352–354 (2010)
16. Watkins, K.: Too Little Access, Not Enough Learning: Africa's Twin Deficit in Education (January 16, 2013),
   http://www.brookings.edu/research/opinions/2013/01/
   16-africa-learning-watkins
17. McGreal, C.: Rwanda to switch from French to English in schools (October 14, 2008),
   http://www.guardian.co.uk/world/2008/oct/14/rwanda-france
18. Ang'ondi, E.K.: Teachers Attitudes and perceptions on the use of ICT in teaching and learning as observed by ICT champions. In: WCCE 2013, Torun, Poland. research papers, vol. 1 (2013)
19. Kenyan teachers end school strike (July 17, 2013),
   http://www.bbc.co.uk/news/world-africa-23346205

20. Singh, N.K.: Globalization and Multilingualism: Case Studies of Indigenous Culture-based Education from the Indian Sub-continent and Their Implications. International Journal of Multicultural Education 15(1) (2013)
21. Adesope, O.O., Lavin, T., Thompson, T., Ungerleider, C.: A Systematic Review and Meta-Analysis of the Cognitive Correlates of Bilingualism. Review of Educational Research 80(2), 207–245 (2010)
22. Bialystok, E., Craik, F., Luk, G.: Bilingualism: consequences for mind and brain. Trends in Cognitive Sciences 16(4), 240–250 (2012)
23. Haag, N., Heppt, B., Stanat, P., Kuhl, P., Pant, H.A.: Second language learners' performance in mathematics: Disentangling the effects of academic language features. Learning and Instruction 28, 24–34 (2013)
24. Saalbach, H., Eckstein, D., Andri, N., Hobija, R., Grabner, R.H.: When language of instruction and language of application differ: Cognitive costs of bilingual mathematics learning. Learning and Instruction 26, 36–44 (2013)
25. Holvikivi, J.: Culture and cognition in information technology education. Dissertation, vol. 5. SimLab Publications, Espoo (2009)
26. Norenzayan, A.: Cultural variation in reasoning. In: Biological and Cultural Bases of Human Inference, pp. 71–95. Lawrence Erlbaum Ass., New Jersey (2006)
27. Ruohonen, M., Turunen, M., Linna, J., Hakulinen, J., Nanavatija, A., Rajput, N.: E-Inclusion Innovation for rural India: mobile voice and tablet based educational services. In: WCCE 2013 Proceedings, Torun. Practice Papers, vol. 2 (2013)
28. Finpro, Tekla, REACHLaw and Muxlim community receive Internationalization Awards (February 4, 2010), http://www.goodnewsfinland.com/archive/news/tekla-reachlaw-and-muxlim-community-receive-internationalization-awards/
29. UNESCO, Engineering: Issues, Challenges and Opportunities for Development, UNESCO, Paris (2010)
30. Needham, J.: Science and Civilisation in China, vol. 7. Cambridge University Press (1954-2004)
31. Harrison, R.: Signs, songs, and memory in the Andes. Translating Quechua language and culture. University of Texas Press, Austin (1989)
32. Bloch, M.E.: How we think they think. Anthropological approaches to cognition, memory, and literacy. Westview Press, Boulder (1998)
33. Moore, D.: The riddle of ancient roman concrete (1995), http://www.romanconcrete.com/docs/spillway/spillway.htm
34. Demarest, A.: Ancient Maya. The rise and fall of a rainforest civilization. Cambridge University Press, Cambridge (2002)

Independent Agents and Ethics

Iordanis Kavathatzopoulos

Department of IT – VII, Uppsala University, Uppsala, Sweden
iordanis@it.uu.se

Abstract. The development of Information Technology, systems, robots, etc., that are capable of processing information and acting independently of their human operators, has been accelerated as well as the hopes, and the fears, of the impact of those artifacts on environment, market, society, on human life generally. Many ethical issues are raised because of these systems being today, or in the future, capable of independent decision making and acting. In the present paper it is discussed how ethical decision support pro-grams can be integrated into robots and other relatively independent decision making systems to secure that decisions are made according to the basic theories of philosophy and to the findings of psychological research.

Keywords: agents, automation, autonomy, decision making, ethics, moral, robots, systems.

1 Challenges of New Technology

Modern technology gives us the chance to automatize many tasks previously done under careful supervision by humans. Routine procedures have been able to be automatized since some time but now can technical systems accomplish many tasks in a relatively independent way. Accomplishment of important tasks independently and automatically has many advantages for persons, organizations and society. It delivers goods and services with higher quality, lower cost and in satisfying or increasing quantities. It helps us to reach important goals and solve many of our basic or special problems: prosperity, wealth, health, for example production of food, fight diseases and other problems that have tormented humanity before.

On the other hand, efficient technologies and automation may cause unemployment. New jobs are created because of the new technologies since this a process of societal and economic restructuring. Still the transition is painful, therefore responsible, innovative and mainly ethical policies by societies, organizations and persons have to be formulated and applied to alleviate any pain and to direct development toward preferred directions.

This is true on a general level. We can easily get aware of all the difficult ethical issues that may arise because of these changes. Particularly, in the area of independent agents and robots ethical concern is necessary. The development of Information Technology, systems, robots, etc., that are capable of processing information and acting independently of their human operators, has been accelerated as well as the

K.K. Kimppa et al. (Eds.): HCC11 2014, IFIP AICT 431, pp. 39–46, 2014.
© IFIP International Federation for Information Processing 2014

hopes, and the fears, of the impact of those artifacts on environment, market, society, on human life generally. Many ethical issues are raised because of these systems being today, or in the future, capable of independent decision making and acting. In situations where humans have difficulties perceiving and processing information, or making decisions and implementing actions, because of the quantity, variation and complexity of information, IT systems can be of great help to achieve goals and obtain optimal solutions to problems. One example of this is financial transactions where the speed and volume of information makes it impossible for human decision makers to take the right measures, for example in the case of a crisis. Another example is dangerous and risky situations, like natural disasters or battles in war, where the use of drones and military robots may help to avoid soldier injuries and deaths. A third example comes from human social and emotional needs, for example in elderly care where robots may play an important role providing necessary care as well as to be a companion to lonely elderly people.

It is clear that such IT systems have to make decisions and act to achieve the goals for which they had been built in the first place. Will they make the right decisions and act in a proper way? Can we guarantee this by designing them in a suitable way? But if it is possible, do we really want such machines given the fact that their main advantage is their increasing independence and autonomy, and hence we do not want to constrain them too much? There are many questions around this, most of which converge on the issue of moral or ethical decision making. The definition of what we mean by ethical or moral decision making or ethical/moral agency is a very much significant precondition for the design of proper IT decision systems. Given that we have a clear definition we will be able to judge whether an IT system is, capable of making ethical decisions, and able to make these decisions independently and autonomously.

2   Option and Ethical Decision Making

The distinction between moral content or moral statement or moral behavior, and ethical process or way of thinking is important in the effort to define ethical or moral decision making. In common sense, ethics and morals are dependent on the concrete decision or the action itself. Understanding a decision or an action being ethical/moral or unethical/immoral is based mainly on a judgment of its normative qualities. The focus on values and their normative aspects is the basis of the common sense definition of ethics.

Despite its dominance, this way of thinking causes some difficulties. We may note that bad or good things follow not only from the decisions of people but also from natural phenomena. Usually sunny weather is considered a good thing, while rainy weather is not. Of course this is not perceived as something related to morality. But why not? What is the difference between humans and nature acting in certain ways? The answer is obvious: Option, choice.

Although common sense does realize this, people's attachment to the nor-mative aspects is so strong that it is not possible for them to accept that ethics is an issue of choice and option. If there is no choice, or ability of making a choice, then there is no issue of ethics. However this does not solve our problem of the definition of independent agents, since IT systems are actually making choices. If ethics are connected to choice then the interesting aspect is how the choice is made, or not made; whether it is made in a bad or in a good way. The focus here is on how, not on what; on the process not on the content or the answer. Indeed, regarding the effort to make the right decision, philosophy and psychology point to the significance of focusing on the process of ethical decision making rather on the normative content of the decision.

Starting from one of the most important contributions, the Socratic dialog, we see that doubt is the goal rather than the achievement of a solution to the problem investigated. Reaching a state of no knowledge, that is, throw-ing aside false ideas, opens up for the right solution. The issue here for the philosopher is not to provide a ready answer but to help the other person in the dialog to think in the right way. Ability to think in the right way is not easy and apparently has been supposed to be the privilege of the few able ones [1, 2, 3]. For that, certain skills are necessary, such as Aristotle's virtue of *phronesis* [4]. When humans are free from false illusions and have the necessary skills they can use the right method to find the right solution to their moral problems [5].

This philosophical position has been applied in psychological research on ethical decision making. Focusing on the process of ethical decision making psychological research has shown that people use different ways to handle moral problems. According to Piaget [6] and Kohlberg [7], when people are confronted with moral problems they think in a way which can be described as a position on the heteronomy-autonomy dimension. Heteronomous thinking is automatic, purely emotional and uncontrolled thinking or simple reflexes that are fixed dogmatically on general moral principles. Thoughts and beliefs coming to mind are never doubted. There is no effort to create a holistic picture of all relevant and conflicting values in the moral problem they are confronted with. Awareness of own personal responsibility for the way one is thinking or for the consequences of the decision are missing.

Autonomous thinking, on the other hand, focuses on the actual moral problem situation, and its main effort is to search for all relevant aspects of the problem. When one is thinking autonomously the focus is on the consideration and investigation of all stakeholders' moral feelings, duties and interests, as well as all possible alternative ways of action. In that sense autonomy is a systematic, holistic and self-critical way of handling a moral problem. Handling moral problems autonomously means that a decision maker is unconstrained by fixations, authorities, uncontrolled or automatic thoughts and reactions. It is the ability to start the thought process of considering and analyzing critically and systematically all relevant values in a moral problem situation. This may sound trivial, since everybody would agree that it is exactly what one is expected to do in confronting a moral problem. But it is not so easy to use the autonomous skill in real situations. Psychological research has shown that plenty of time and certain conditions are demanded before people can acquire and use the ethical ability of autonomy [8].

Nevertheless, there are people who have learnt to use autonomy more often, usually people at higher organizational levels or people with higher responsibility. Training and special tools do also support the acquisition of the skill of autonomy. Research has shown that it is possible to promote autonomy. It is possible through training to acquire and use the skill of ethical autonomy, longitudinally and in real life [9].

3   Support for Ethical Competence

The focus of any measures to support the skill of ethical autonomy varies depending on the degree of independence of the system. In designing and using non-independent systems the focus cannot be on the system but exclusively on designers, users, operators and owners. They will develop the system and decide in detail how it will operate, so they need to have the ability to find the ethical solutions while they are thinking, having a dialog or negotiating with each other. In semi-independent systems the focus is again on designers, operators, users and owners like in non-independent systems. In addition to the system itself they have also to design an information-gathering, treating and communicating system which will be integrated into the agent. Its task will be to inform the operators about possible ethical conflicts and let them decide the proper action. However, the information has to be presented in such a way as to block heteronomy and promote autonomy in the thinking of operators. In the case of totally independent systems the focus of support for ethical autonomy should be on all parts involved, not only humans but also the agent itself since it will also have the responsibility of independent choice as well as an own basic interest to take care of (see Table 1).

It is important to keep in mind that measures to support ethical autonomy or philosophizing have to be applied anyway. Either on humans involved in designing and operating agent systems, or in the case of fully independent agents, on agents themselves as well. Fully independent agents, if they can exist, are ethical beings; they feel the need to make choices in order to fulfill their purpose of existence. Of course philosophizing and ethical autonomy are necessary not only for the design of systems or rules for information gathering and communicating, but also during the processes of interpreting rules or negotiating with other stakeholders.

4   Systems and Robots as Ethical Agents

Ethical decision support programs [10, 11, 12] can be integrated into robots and other decision making systems to secure that decisions are made according to the basic theories of philosophy and to the findings of psychological research. This would be the ideal. But before we are there we can see that ethical decision making support systems based on this approach can be used in two different ways.

During the development of a non-independent decision making system, support tools can be used to identify the criteria for making decisions and for choosing a certain direction of action. This means that the support tool is used by the developers, they who make the real decisions, and who make them according to the previous named philosophical/psychological approach [13].

Table 1. Focus of training and support for ethical competence depending on the degree of independence of robots and on the conditions of searching for or applying an ethical solution

Search or implementation	Degree of independence of robot		
	Non-independent	Semi-independent	Fully independent
Open search, person	Mental skills of humans	Mental skills of all humans & design of communication system	Mental skills of all humans and agents
Open search, group	Mental skills and group processes of humans	Mental and group skills & design of communication system	Mental and group skills of humans and agents; negotiation skills
Give or receive instructions	Mental skills or group processes of humans	Mental skills or group processes; rules for communication	Mental skills or group processes for all; strategic - democratic dialog
Give or receive answers, orders	Mental skills or group processes of humans	Mental skills or group processes; re-design of communication	Mental skills or group processes for all; risk for conflict

Another possibility is to integrate a support tool into the non-independent decision system. Of course, designers can give to the system criteria and directions, but they can also add the support tool itself, to be used in the case of unanticipated future situations. The tool can then gather information, treat it, structure it and present it to the operators of the decision system in a way which follows the requirements of the above mentioned theories of autonomy. If it works like that, operators of non-independent systems make the real decisions and they are the users of the ethical support tool. A non-independent system that can make decisions and act in accordance to the hypothesis of ethical autonomy is a system which 1) has the criteria already programmed in it identified through an autonomous way in an earlier phase by the designers, or 2) prepares the information of a problem situation according to the theory of ethical autonomy, presents it and stimulates the operators to make the decision in a way compatible with the theory of ethical autonomy. All this can work and it is possible technically.

But how could we design and run a really independent ethical decision making system? However, before we can speculate on that it is important to address some issues shortly, regarding the criteria for independence.

First is the issue of normative quality of the decisions made. Can we use this criterion for the definition of an independent ethical decision system? As we have already discussed this is not possible although it is inherently and strongly connected to common sense, and sometimes into research [14]. Normative aspects can be found in the consequences of obviously non-independent natural phenomena. Besides, there are always good arguments supporting opposite normative positions. So this cannot be a working criterion [15].

The alternative would be the capability of choice. Connected to this is the issue of free will. We could say that really independent systems are those that are free to decide whatever they want. However, this has many difficulties. There is theoretical obscurity around the definition of free will as well as practical problems concerning its description in real life situations. Furthermore, it is obvious that many systems can make "choices." Everything from simple relays to complex IT systems is able to choose among different alternatives, often in arcane and obscure ways, reminiscent of the way humans make choices. Then the problem would be where to put the threshold for real choice making.

If the ability to make choices cannot be the criterion to determine the independence of a decision system, then the possibility to control the system by an operator becomes interesting. Wish or effort to control, external to the system, may be something that has to be involved and considered. The reason of the creation of IT systems is the designers' and the operators' wish to give them a role to play. These systems come to existence and are run as an act of will to control things, to satisfy needs. It is an execution of power by the designers and the operators. We can imagine a decision system as totally independent, but even this cannot be thought without a human wish or will behind it. It is always a will for some purpose. It can be a simple purpose, for example to rescue trapped people in collapsed buildings, or an extremely complex purpose, like to create systems able of making independent decisions! In any case the human designer or operator wants to secure the fulfillment of the main purpose and does not want to lose control, and that would certainly conflict with the will of a fully independent system.

5   Identifying and Supporting an Independent Agent

So the issue could be about possession of an original purpose, a basic feeling, an emotion. Indeed recent research in neurobiology and neuropsychology shows that emotions are necessary in the decision making process [16, 17]. It seems that a rational decision process requires uninterrupted connection to emotions [18]. Without this bond the decision process becomes meaningless. Another effect of the "primacy" of emotions and purposes is that very often heteronomous or non-rational ways to make ethical decisions are adopted, despite the human decision maker being able to think autonomously and rationally.

Thus the criterion for a really independent decision system could be the existence of an ultimate purpose that is an emotional base guiding the decision process. Human emotions and goals have been evolved by nature seemingly without any purpose. That may happen in decision systems and robots if they are left alone, but designers, operators, and humans would probably not want to lose control. So what is left? Can we create really independent ethical decision systems?

The criterion of such a system cannot be based on normative aspects, or on the ability to make choices, or on having own control, or on ability of rational processing. It seems that it is necessary for an independent decision system to have "emotions" too. That is, a kind of ultimate purposes that can lead the decision process, and depending on the circumstances, even make the system react automatically, or alternatively, in a rational way.

Well, this is not easy to achieve. It may be impossible. However, if we accept this way of thinking we may be able to recognize a really independent or autonomous ethical agent, if we see one, although we may be not able to create one. This could work like a Turing test for robot ethics because we would know what to look for: A decision system capable of autonomous ethical thinking, i.e. philosophizing, but leaning most of the time toward more or less heteronomous ways of thinking; like humans who have emotions leading them to make decisions in that way.

If we have such systems we will need to direct our efforts toward them supporting their ethical decision making, like we do for humans. In this case it would be necessary to train and educate the fully independent agents in using ethical autonomy as well as to involve them in democratic dialog together with humans in searching for the right answers to relevant ethical problems.

References

1. Plato: Theaitetos. I. Zacharopoulos, Athens (1981)
2. Plato: Apology of Socrates. Kaktos, Athens (1992a)
3. Plato: The Republic. Kaktos, Athens (1992b)
4. Aristotle: Nicomachean Ethics. Papyros, Athens (1975)
5. Kant, I.: Grundläggning av Sedernas Metafysik. Daidalos, Stockholm (2006)
6. Piaget, J.: The Moral Judgement of the Child. Routledge and Kegan Paul, London (1932)
7. Kohlberg, L.: The Just Community: Approach to Moral Education in Theory and Practice. In: Berkowitz, M., Oser, F. (eds.) Moral Education: Theory and Application, pp. 27–87. Lawrence Erlbaum Associates, Hillsdale (1985)
8. Sunstein, C.R.: Moral Heuristics. Behavioral and Brain Sciences 28, 531–573 (2005)
9. Kavathatzopoulos, I.: Assessing and Acquiring Ethical Leadership Competence. In: Prastacos, G.P., et al. (eds.) Leadership through the Classics, pp. 389–400. Springer, Heidelberg (2012)
10. Laaksoharju, M.: Let us be Philosophers! Computerized Support for Ethical Decision Making. Uppsala University, Department of Information Technology, Uppsala (2010)
11. Laaksoharju, M., Kavathatzopoulos, I.: Computerized Support for Ethical Analysis. In: Botti, M., et al. (eds.) Proceedings of CEPE 2009 – Eighth International Computer Ethics and Philosophical Enquiry Conference, Ionian University, Kerkyra (2009)
12. Thaler, R.H., Sunstein, C.R.: Nudge: Improving Decisions about Health, Wealth and Happiness. Yale University Press, New Haven (2008)
13. Kavathatzopoulos, I.: Philosophizing as a usability method. In: Buchanan, E., et al. (eds.) Ambiguous Technologies: Philosophical Issues, Practical Solutions, Human Nature, pp. 194–201. International Society of Ethics and Information Technology, Lisbon (2013)

14. Kohlberg, L.: The Philosophy of Moral Development: Moral Stages and the Idea of Justice. Harper and Row, San Francisco (1984)
15. Wallace, W., Allen, C.: Moral Machines: Teaching Robots Right from Wrong. Oxford University Press, New York (2009)
16. Koenigs, M., Tranel, D.: Irrational Economic Decision-Making after Ventromedial Prefrontal Damage: Evidence from the Ultimatum Game. The Journal of Neuroscience 27, 951–956 (2007)
17. Damasio, A.: Descartes misstag. Natur och Kultur, Stockholm (2006)
18. Hume, D.: Treatise of Human Nature. Penguin, London (1985)

The Time of Our Lives: Understanding Irreversible Complex User Experiences

David Kreps

University of Salford, Salford, Greater Manchester, UK
d.g.kreps@salford.ac.uk

Abstract. The science of complexity [6], [12], [20, 21], [31, 32] has been introduced to Information Systems (IS) but thus far with seemingly little impact. This paper argues that its application can be located in the burgeoning field of User Experience (UX) in digital business practice [23], [38]. Both these developments are looking at *time* in a new way, specifically at the irreversibility of many living processes, whilst simultaneously involving, including, and relying upon very scientific and computational data. The paper introduces a forthcoming research project with a UX company seeking to discover more.

Keywords: Complexity, UX.

1   Introduction

There has, historically, been a broadly positivist bias in Information Systems (IS) literature, [2, 3], [5], [10, 11], [24, 25, 26], [28, 29]. More recently, however, there has been something of a shift in the conceptualisation of success in information systems from a focus on technical factors to a focus on human factors [30]. One might usefully quote Ray Paul from his editorial piece in the European Journal of Information Systems in 2007, where he offered a definition of information systems and its relationship with information technology (IT) that reflects this shift:

- "The IS *is not* the IT and the formal processes being used.
- The IS *is not* the people using the IT and the formal and informal processes
- The IS is what emerges from the usage and adaptation of the IT and the formal and informal processes by all of its users." [28]

IS research has evolved, then, from what might be deemed rather technologically determinist approaches, which investigate the effects of technologies on societies, to research which focuses on the human and the social [9], and addresses the increasing part technological artefacts play within the social. The positivist and interpretive methodologies used by various camps in the past, moreover, have increasingly become combined by IS researchers. Mixed methods approaches in IS, indeed, have a long pedigree, and have gained ground in both popularity and usage [15, 16], [19].

In this paper, I wish to focus on two parallel developments. The first promises a much more profound theoretical basis upon which such mixed methodology and human

K.K. Kimppa et al. (Eds.): HCC11 2014, IFIP AICT 431, pp. 47–56, 2014.
© IFIP International Federation for Information Processing 2014

usage can be studied. It has been growing over the last few decades in the worlds of environmental biology, chemistry, and other life sciences, and greatly advanced by the introduction of powerful computing tools to their study: it is the science of complexity [12], [20, 21, 22], [31, 32]. Some attention has been paid to this development, in the field of information systems, including a Special Issue in *Information Technology and People* in 2006 [4],[18] which included some internal debate. The second parallel development is the User Experience, (UX) approach that is rapidly superseding usability practice, responding to the legitimate business need to attend to the personal experiences of the human parts of information systems [38]. This is a popular area of focus for Human Factors scholars in IS.

Crucially, both developments are taking a new look at *time*, and the irreversibility of processes in systems that operate in far-from-equilibrium conditions: which includes all living systems. Irreversibility is proving to be the profoundest break from the traditional mechanical or reductionist tradition favoured by much of physics, mechanical dynamics, and the mindset of the hard sciences that prompted the positivist bias in IS for so much of its history as a field of enquiry.

As Paul said in his 2007 editorial, immediately following the above definition of IS. "Note therefore that the IS is constantly adapting to need as the users change their usage and the IT is updated or extended." [28] In other words, this paper seeks to stress, the IS is dynamic, subject to continual change - in ways even faster and more profound than perhaps Paul was implying in his editorial - and theoretical understandings and methodologies that incorporate this dynamism and the nature of its nonlinearity and irreversibility need to be explored and adopted by IS researchers.

So, this paper is about research towards achieving a better understanding of information systems as things which incorporate, rather than merely being used by humans, and what the impact of such a better understanding may be upon issues of design, usability, and success. The aim of the research is to find ways that might improve User Experience (UX), not simply by feeding these results back into a traditional requirements capture / design process, but towards the creation of learning systems that incorporate developers and end users in a continuous conversation with continually evolving information technology artefacts as the process language of that conversation.

I begin with a section outlining the most relevant ideas of complexity theory. I then move on to a consideration of the User Experience (UX) approach in web development businesses. I conclude with a brief review of the consideration of complexity in IS thus far, by way of an introduction to a research project due to begin with a UX small-medium sized enterprise (SME) in the North West of England, UK.

2   Complexity

Contemporary computational evolutionary biology has been one of the principle sites for the development of the sciences of complexity, in the latter part of the twentieth century. This development was greatly accelerated by the enormous advances in computing in the late 1980s and 1990s, and complexity science has spread to multiple sites and down multiple avenues, with the results disseminated from its multiple sources to equally multiple audiences during the 1990s and the first decade of the 21st

century. The work of Ilya Prigogine [31, 32], Brian Goodwin [12], and Stuart Kauff-man [20, 21], among others, is a view of evolution from chemistry and biology, and yet reaching out far beyond it, challenging the reductionist neo-Darwinian orthodoxy of the likes of Richard Dawkins [8], presenting a new understanding of evolutionary theory that places natural selection as a secondary, rather than primary force. The primary force behind evolution, for these complexity theorists, is self-organisation.

For Kauffman, "Life and its evolution have always depended on the mutual embrace of spontaneous order and selection's crafting of that order" [20]. Yet these insights into how patterns in the branching of evolution reveal a lawful ordering, how the complexity of teeming variety harbours principles of self-organisation, he also extends beyond the self-organisation of flora and fauna. "The natural history of life may harbour a new and unifying intellectual underpinning for our economic, cultural, and social life," he asserts [20]. He suspects that "the fate of all complex adapting systems in the biosphere - from single cells to economies - is to evolve to a natural state between order and chaos, a grand compromise between structure and surprise." [20]. One might say something very similar about most information systems.

Acknowledging the march of physics towards a final theory of everything, Kauff-man nonetheless reminds us that though it may end up explaining how the building blocks of the universe operate, it "almost certainly will not predict in detail" [20]. This failure to predict is down to two fundamental branches of physics itself: quantum mechanics, "which assures a fundamental indeterminism at the quantum level" with all its attendant macroscopic consequences, and chaos theory, neatly captured in the famous so-called 'butterfly effect' that can see the flapping of a butterfly's wings in Australia cause a Hurricane in the Atlantic [20].

But not knowing the details does not preclude us from building theories that "seek to explain the generic properties" - for example, "when water freezes, one does not know where every water molecule is, but a lot can be said about your typical lump of ice." [20]. Kauffman attempts to develop, through his work, "classes of properties of systems that ... are typical or generic and do not depend on the details" [20]. Giving numerous examples, from the origin of life "as a collective emergent property of complex systems of chemicals" through to "the behaviour of coevolving species in ecosystems that generates small and large avalanches of extinction and speciation", Kauffman finds that the "order that emerges depends on robust and typical properties of the systems, not on the details of structure and function" [20]. In this way the theory of complexity - and its attendant principles of self-organisation - is not tied to the world of biology, but capable of evincing patterns in all manner of complex adaptive systems - including information systems.

Complexity has been introduced and lauded as an important development in the social sciences, notably with Paul Cilliers', *Complexity and Postmodernism* [6] and more recently a Special Issue of *Theory, Culture and Society* given over to consideration of the Complexity Turn in sociological thought [36]. Cilliers lucidly points out a fundamental issue that must be grasped about complexity:

It is useful to distinguish between the notions of 'complex' and 'complicated'. If a system – despite the fact that it may consist of a huge number of components – can be given a complete description in terms of its individual constituents, such a system is merely complicated. Things like jumbo jets or computers are complicated. In a complex system on the other hand, the interaction among constituents of the system, and the interactions between the system and its environment, are of such a nature that the system as a whole cannot be fully understood by analysing its components. Moreover, these relationships are not fixed, but shift and change, often as a result of self-organisation. This can result in novel features, usually referred to in terms of emergent properties. The brain, natural language and social systems are complex. [6]

In other words, although the computer may be complicated, add human usage and the information system becomes complex.

There are important differences in approach that must be undertaken between studying something which is complicated, and something which is complex. The analytical method, whilst useful for complicated systems, is counterproductive when trying to understand complex systems. Complexity focuses on the shifting and evolving "intricate relationships" between components. "In 'cutting up' a system, the analytical method destroys what it seeks to understand." [6] Furthermore, interactions are not restricted to being physical - they can also be described as a "transference of information" [6]. These interactions are both rich − "any element in the system influences, and is influenced by, quite a few other ones", and non-linear - "small causes can have large results, and vice versa," [6].

Most complex systems "are usually open systems, i.e. they interact with their environment." By contrast, "closed systems are usually merely complicated" [6]. This is of crucial significance in environmental theory, where for much of the twentieth century - at least since Tansley [35]- a nineteenth century organicist metaphor of natural equilibrium has been the defining characteristic of the term Tansley coined, 'ecosystem.' Yet, as many ecologists in the last decade or so of the twentieth century found through painstaking study (see [13]), the natural world in fact displays no such equilibrium at all, and the notion of ecosystems has undergone a radical rethink. As Cilliers notes, "Complex systems operate under conditions far from equilibrium. There has to be a constant flow of energy to maintain the organisation of the system and to ensure its survival. Equilibrium is another word for death." [6].

Small causes, moreover, can include forces as weak as gravitational fields. Prigogine outlines how 'bifurcation points' arise when systems are pushed further and further from their stable equilibrium states, points where "an irreducible random element" enters the equation. There is no recourse to a "macroscopic equation" to "predict the path the system will take. Turning to a microscopic description will not help. There is also no distinction between left and right. We are faced with chance events very similar to the fall of dice," [31]. Sometimes it is the environmental fields in which the system sits - such as the gravitational field of the earth - which seem to be the only influence that might tip the dice one way or the other. The results are the common - and otherwise unexplained - left-handed turns of the DNA helix and most seashells.

The essential point here is that pre-existing conditions cannot be used to predict outcomes. Bifurcation points can come in clusters producing landslides of change through which there is little or any hope of even deriving an outcome from a previous state. Yet - extraordinarily - when these bifurcated, far-from-equilibrium states are reached, spontaneous order seems to arise, stable and yet kept moving in the stream of dynamic forces that propel the system along. Prigogine coined the term 'dissipative structure' to describe systems that are sustained by the persistent dissipation of matter and energy. As Kauffman tells us, "in dissipative systems, the flux of matter and energy through the system is a driving force generating order," [20]. The science of hydrodynamics has been very instructive here, and the image of a whirlpool of water at the plug-hole in a bathtub is a useful illustration. If the tap is left running, the whirlpool persists, bringing order to the constant flow of water. It is here, in this inherently unstable nonequilibrium, where, according to Kauffman, "life exists at the very edge of chaos" [20]. Living cells are themselves "nonequilibrium dissipative structures", and the very nature of evolution - and especially of the coevolution of many systems, such as species in an environment - is to attain the "edge of chaos, a web of compromises where each species prospers as well as possible but where none can be sure if its best next step will set off a trickle or a landslide," [20].

But as Cilliers is at pains to underline, for all this chaos and flux, these remain discernible systems, with pattern and order. As he asserts, "complex systems have a history. Not only do they evolve through time, but their past is co-responsible for their present behaviour," [6]. Unlike merely complicated systems, susceptible to analysis, this order does not arise through the control of one part of the system over another, or the predictable unfolding of one state towards a resulting state. "Each element of the system is ignorant of the behaviour of the system as a whole, it responds only to information that is available to it locally. This point is vitally important. If each element 'knew' what was happening to the system as a whole, all of the complexity would have to be present in that element," [6].

But as Kauffman asserts, the fundamental problem with reductionist, mechanistic thought, when applied to complex systems, is that to *represent* a complex system one must, of necessity, reproduce the system in its entirety. The representation, usually something like an algorithm - the "shortest description" which can capture the essential elements of a system - can only capture the *entirety* of a complex system, because a complex system is already its own shortest description. In computation this is known as an "incompressible algorithm," [20].

Perhaps the most important aspect of all this, is the introduction into scientific thinking of the arrow of time - of processes which, unlike simple dynamics, and mechanical processes, cannot be reversed. As Prigogine enthuses in his book, *Order out of Chaos,* citing 19th century thermodynamics as the beginning of such thinking, "far from being an illusion, irreversibility plays an essential role in nature and lies at the origin of most processes of self-organisation. We find ourselves in a world in which reversibility and determinism apply only to limiting, simple cases, while irreversibility and randomness are the rules......interest is shifting from substance to relation, to communication, to time," [31].

3   User Experience (UX)

Turning our attention back to contemporary information systems, we find that standard industry usability practice has, in recent years, become downgraded, and finds itself distinguished from the more novel User Experience approaches, the former being conceived as either completely separate, or at the very best subsumed within the latter [23]. The key differentiation between these two approaches is in what is regarded as the far more subjective concerns of UX with look, feel, and satisfaction, in comparison to the more operational, concrete concerns of usability with task execution times and clicks and error numbers. "A user's motivation and expectations play a much stronger role in UX than in traditional usability," [38].

Of course, mixed methodology is also crucial to UX. Mirroring the way in which information systems (as conceived, above, by Ray Paul) is, by nature, inevitably multi-disciplinary, calling as it must upon both sociology and computer science, the new approaches of UX, in addressing such human factors as satisfaction, cannot ignore the more numerical concerns of usability. But in the business world of web and app development, the realization has dawned upon those formerly wedded to the mathematical certainties of computer science that life just isn't like that. The retreat of the World Wide Web Consortium (W3C) from eXtensible Markup Language (XHTML) is a case in point. Paving the cowpaths, Hypertext Markup Language 5 (HTML5) walks where the real world has gone while the theoretical purity of XHTML was consigned to history. Equally illustrative is the failure of the semantic web, making room for the possibility of developments in cognition-as-a-service, whereby apps begin to make use of such Artificial Intelligence (AI) tools as Siri, Wolfram Alpha, etc, to provide a more human and interactive experience to the users of information systems [14], [34]. Matching the predictable, mechanical, certain equilibrium systems of our complicated machines, therefore, with the dynamic, far-from-equilibrium spontaneous order of living beings and our complex personal behaviour and social systems, is necessarily a very multi-disciplinary endeavour. The simple recognition that humans don't behave rationally is just the start [27]. The IT artefact may be complicated, but the information system, open to its environment, driven by and incorporating rich information flows with potential – and often all-too-human - bifurcation avalanches, are complex.

With the development of UX in mind, then, it may be that the locating of academic IS departments in Business Schools is no mistake, for it is bottom-line business drivers that have shifted attention beyond mere usability practice to attend to the more subjective concerns of the personal experience of the users – or should I say, the human parts - of information systems, just as it is business concerns that left the computational purity of XHTML, Web Ontology Language (OWL) and Resource Description Framework (RDF) to the history books, in favour of HTML5, JavaScript Object Notation (JSON), and apps with access to cloud-based 'intelligent' systems one can have a conversation with [34]. The stress in Web 2.0 upon user-generated content was exemplary of how core the human part of contemporary information systems can be - and often is. In the context of what many are calling Web 3.0 and its world of multi-device, multi-channel and multi-directional throughput of information, information communication technologies (ICTs) are all the more clearly revolving around us, our information, our needs, and in real time: the web 3.0 that some are beginning to call, 'the Stream' [34].

Here, the crucial break with the mechanical approaches of the past arrives with the realisation that these more experiential complex systems are most frequently not reversible. Time is an arrow in these instances and no amount of cookies, server-side accounts, or wish lists can make up for the loss of that most amorphous, context and moment-dependent quality of human behaviour upon which so many businesses depend: impulse. This is not even yet in the foothills, moreover, of that other crucial element of success in business: emotional intelligence. So in the field of UX, what has in the past been intellectually grasped as spatial, measured, and objective, is today by contrast increasingly being apprehended as durational, experiential, and subjective.

4   Further Research

Now, complexity and information systems are certainly not strange bedfellows, and this paper is not the first to suggest a confluence. Following a Special Issue in *Communications of the ACM* (2005) there was another in *Information Technology and People (ITP)* on Complexity and IS in 2006. In their introductory paper to the ITP Special Issue, Jacucci, Hanseth and Lyytinen argue that complexity needs to be taken seriously in IS research [16]. Benbya & McKelvey's core paper of this special issue, which we shall take as exemplary, inferred in the preamble that information systems development projects are complex not only because they deal with complex techno-logical issues, "but also because of organisational factors beyond a project team's control." [4]. More substantively, the authors argued, Van Aardt [37] had asserted that any information system displays the characteristics of a complex adaptive system. Van Aardt concentrates on the emergence of order as opposed to causal predetermina-tion, and the irreversibility of a system's history and unpredictability of its future. He focuses on open source software as the best example of IS as a complex adaptive system. Benbya & McKelvey, however, in their paper, go further, suggesting that all information systems act as complex adaptive systems [4].

But it is in a note by Kallinikos, another contributor to the ITP Special Issue, who furthers the debate with a critique of the Benbya & McKelvey paper [18], that my concerns with the meeting of complexity and information systems, thus far, are raised. Essentially, Kallinikos points to Benbya & McKelvey's continued embrace of what he describes as a *"representational* view of information and coding as mapping of an exogenous reality that is reflected on what we call 'user requirements,' considered both as independent and the starting point for coding," [18]. This, as Kallinikos asserts, "bypasses one of the major, contemporary sources of instability in organisa-tions, which is no other than the changing organisational conditions (and user re-quirements) created by the very development of information systems themselves. In other words, the ghost is not simply outside but inside the house as well," [18]. The human parts of the information system, in short, cannot be abstracted from the infor-mation technology such that the IT project team can then safely proceed without them. Given the insights into complexity explored in this paper, it seems extraordi-nary that such a notion could be entertained. But how could it come about - how could IS scholars brave enough to embrace the ideas of complexity nonetheless find a way to cling on to the safety of the predictable and discrete?

Herbert Simon's seminal paper from 1962 on the 'Architecture of Complexity', cited by both Benbya & McKelvey and by Kallinikos, includes the notion of *near decomposability:* the notion that complex systems have a hierarchical structure, that they are built up of inter-related subsystems, and that the intra-relationships within subsystems are stronger than the inter-relationships between components of different subsystems, such that the subsystems might easily be pried apart, and considered separately. For Simon, the distinction between a *decomposable* system and a *nearly decomposable* system is that in the latter "the interactions among the subsystems are weak, but not negligible." [33]. Moreover, for Simon, in nature, systems where the hierarchy is interdependent, and which are therefore less decomposable, "are far rarer and less typical," [33]. For Benbya & McKelvey it seems that the human and non-human 'subsystems' of an information system might be pried apart for the more pre-dictable information technology project to get underway. For Kallinikos this notion is regarded as supportive of modular architecture wherein a "loose coupling of processes and agents" is enabled, [18]. Yet, as Agre points out, "hierarchy is a somewhat more diverse phenomenon than the universal ambitions of Simon's theory require,"[1]. Indeed the ambition of Simon to subsume everything under his notion of hierarchy manages to ignore a great variety of instances where the modular approach simply does not hold, and his argument is "a product of its time…: [the] high-water mark of the classical hierarchical organization"[1].

Self-organisation, in fact - the favoured notion of the general systems theory of the time, and championed, as we have seen, by Prigogine and Kauffman, among others - turns out to be a much better description, certainly of the reality of contemporary information systems, than *hierarchy*. As Agre asserts, "Precisely because Simon's image of hierarchy is spatial, it does not fit well with the networked world, which collapses many types of distance," [1]. A more durational view is required, and, as Cilliers [6] reminds us, the intricate - and often sensitive - relationships between components, both within and between 'subsystems,' are often – for all that they may be considered 'weak' – nonetheless the most important aspects of complex systems, capable of bringing both sweeping and fundamental changes.

In this paper I have tried to show that in fact, given the involvement of humans as parts of information systems - the ghost both outside and inside - the characteristics of complexity must *inevitably* apply to IS, and its aspects of irreversibility, its durational rather than spatial characteristics, are of growing significance. Success in today's information systems development, then, infers durational complexity, and though Benbya & McKelvey make a brave attempt at a framework for considering complexi-ty in information systems, I consider that Kallinikos' criticisms - and my own - hold.

So what answers can I offer in a brief position paper for a conference? Well, the worlds of theory and practical application are sometimes difficult to bridge, but the opportunity is there to find in a Knowledge Transfer Partnership (KTP) between Uni-versity of Salford and UX specialists Sigma Ltd, in the UK, which began in March 2014, real-world examples that may help to flesh out an understanding of how non-reversible experiences in information systems unfold, how they operate, what guide-lines we might adopt in approaching their 'design', and how the experience of the human parts of those systems might be enhanced. The partnership will seek to explore how the concerns raised in this paper translate into concrete activities, with live cli-ents and their digital presence, and what can be learnt from studying the data accrued by user research for future understanding of this mixed method approach, and, crucially, how the element of time and irreversibility impacts upon issues of design, usability, complexity, and success.

5   Conclusion

In this paper, I have tried to introduce IS scholars to what I believe may be the next step in the trend away from reductionist, mechanical positivism, through an interest in social and human studies, towards a more complex, and durational understanding of information systems, as exemplified by the approach of the User Experience professionals. The novel understandings of the sciences of complexity, giving us insight into the irreversibility of living systems, gives pause for thought when considering the processes most information systems incorporate. As Paul [28] stressed, information systems are "constantly adapting," and this continual adaptation - and the flexibility that it requires - needs to be built into our designs for the future.

References

1. Agre, P.: Hierarchy and History in Simon's 'Architecture of Complexity'. Journal of the Learning Sciences 12(3) (2003), http://polaris.gseis.ucla.edu/pagre/simon.html (accessed December 9, 2013)
2. Banville, C., Landry, M.: Can the Field of MIS be disciplined? Communications of the ACM 32(1), 48–60 (1989)
3. Becker, J., Niehaves, B.: Epistemological perspectives on IS research: a framework for analysing and systematizing epistemological assumptions. Information Systems Journal 17, 197–214 (2007)
4. Benbya, H., McKelvey, B.: Toward a complexity theory of information systems development. Information Technology and People 19(1), 12–34 (2006)
5. Chen, W., Hirschheim, R.: A paradigmatic and methodological examination of information systems research from 1991 to 2001. Information Systems Journal 14(3), 197–235 (2004)
6. Cilliers, P.: Complexity and Postmodernism. Routledge, London (1998)
7. Cilliers, P.: Complexity, Deconstruction and Relativism. Theory, Culture & Society 22(5), 255–267 (2005)
8. Dawkins, R.: The Selfish Gene. Oxford Paperbacks, Oxford (1989)
9. De Vaujany, F.X.: Information Technology Conceptualization: Respective Contributions of Sociology and Information Systems. Journal of Information Technology Impact 5(1), 39–58 (2005)
10. Galliers, B.: A discipline for a stage? A Shakespearean reflection on the research plot and performance of the Information Systems field. European Journal of Information Systems 17, 330–335 (2008)
11. Gallivan, M., Benbunan-Fich, R.: Analysing IS Research Productivity: An inclusive approach to global IS scholarship. European Journal of Information Systems 16, 36–53 (2007)
12. Goodwin, B.: How the Leopard Changed its Spots. Charles Scribner & Sons, New York (1994)
13. Hagen, J.B.: An Entangled Bank. Rutgers University Press, New Jersey (1992)
14. ter Heide, D.: Three reasons why the Semantic Web has failed. GigaOm (2013), http://gigaom.com/2013/11/03/three-reasons-why-the-semantic-web-has-failed/ (accessed December 9, 2013)
15. Heyvaert, M., Hannes, K., Maes, B., Onghena, P.: Critical Appraisal of Mixed Methods Studies. Journal of Mixed Methods Research 7(4), 302–327 (2013)

16. Jacucci, E., Hanseth, O., Lyytinen, K.: Taking Complexity Seriously in IS Research 19(1), 5–11 (2006)
17. Johnson, R., Onwuegbuzie, A.: Mixed Methods Research: A Research Paradigm Whose Time Has Come. Educational Researcher 33(7), 14–26 (2004)
18. Kallinikos, J.: Complexity and information systems development: A comment on Benbya and McKelvey (2006), http://personal.lse.ac.uk/kallinik/docs/BenbyaMckelvey.doc (accessed December 9, 2013)
19. Kaplan, B., Duchon, D.: Combining Qualitative and Quantitative Methods in Information Systems Research: A Case Study. MIS Quarterly 12(4), 571–586 (1988)
20. Kauffman, S.: At Home in the Universe. OUP, Oxford (1995)
21. Kauffman, S.: Investigations. OUP, Oxford (2000)
22. Kreps, D.: Bergson and Complexity Theory. Palgrave MacMillan, London (forthcoming, 2015)
23. Law, E., Roto, V., Hassenzahl, M., Vermeeren, A., Kort, J.: Understanding, Scoping and Defining User eXperience: A Survey Approach. In: Proc. CHI 2009, ACM SIGCHI Conference on Human Factors in Computing Systems (2009)
24. Liu, F., Myers, M.: An analysis of the AIS basket of top journals. Journal of Systems and Information Technology 13(1), 5–24 (2011)
25. Lyytinen, K., Baskerville, R., Iivari, J., Te'eni, D.: Why the old world cannot publish? Overcoming challenges in publishing high-impact IS research. European Journal of Information Systems 16, 317–326 (2007)
26. Orlikowski, W., Baroudi, J.: Studying information technology in organisations: research approaches and assumptions. Information Systems Research 2(1), 1–28 (1991)
27. March, J.G.: A Premier on Decision Making. The Free Press, New York (1994)
28. Paul, R.: Challenges to Information Systems: Time to change. European Journal of Information Systems 16, 193–195 (2007)
29. Paul, R.: The only duty we owe to history is to rewrite it: reflections on Bob Galliers' article, 'A discipline for a stage?'. European Journal of Information Systems 17(6), 444–447 (2008)
30. Petter, S., DeLone, W., et al.: The Past, Present, and Future of 'IS Success'. Journal of the Association for Information Systems 13(5), 2 (2012)
31. Prigogine, I., Stengers, I.: Order out of Chaos. Flamingo, London (1984)
32. Prigogine, I.: The End of Certainty: Time, Chaos and the New Laws of Nature. The Free Press, New York (1996)
33. Simon, H.: The Architecture of Complexity. Proceedings of the American Philosophical Society 106(6) (1962)
34. Spivak, N.: Why Cognition-as-a-Service is the next operating system battlefield. GigaOm (2013), http://gigaom.com/2013/12/07/why-cognition-as-a-service-is-the-next-operating-system-battlefield/#   (accessed December 9, 2013)
35. Tansley, A.: The Use and Abuse of Vegetational Concepts and Terms. Ecology 16(3), 284–307 (1935)
36. Urry, J.: The Complexity Turn. Theory, Culture & Society 22(5), 1–14 (2005)
37. Van Aardt, A.: Open source software development as complex adaptive systems. In: Proceedings of the 17th Annual Conference of the National Advisory Committee on Computing Qualifications, Christchurch, New Zealand, July 6-9 (2004)
38. Vermeeren, A., Law, E., Roto, V., Obrist, M., Hoonhout, J., Väänänen-Vainio-Mattila, K.: User Experience Evaluation Methods: Current State and Development Needs. In: Proceedings: NordiCHI 2010, October 16-20 (2010)

Sustainable ICT: A Critique from the Perspective of World Systems Theory

Thomas Taro Lennerfors, Per Fors, and Jolanda van Rooijen

Dept. of Engineering Sciences,
Div. of Industrial Engineering and Management,
Uppsala, Sweden
{thomas.lennerfors,per.fors,jolanda.van.rooijen}@angstrom.uu.se

Abstract. Even though the ICT (Information and Communication Technology) industry has historically been spared the critique of being environmentally unfriendly, society has as of late recognised the negative environmental effects of the ICT industry. However, such critique has been gradually replaced by the concept of *Sustainable ICT*, in which ICT is almost seen as a saviour, something with big potential of solving economic, societal and environmental issues. In this paper, our aim is to critically discuss the notion of Sustainable ICT by turning to an ecological perspective of World Systems Theory (WST). Immanuel Wallerstein, the main proponent of WST argues that the success of developed (core) countries today is a product of systematic unequal exchange of raw material, goods and labour with underdeveloped (peripheral) countries. Alf Hornborg, the Swedish Marxist ecologist, develops WST by focusing on the global distribution of environmental degradation. In this paper, we present Hornborg's ecological WST, we apply it to ICT by means of examples from the ICT Value Chain (from materials extraction to disposal) in order to illustrate the global distribution of environmental degradation. We argue that WST is a fruitful, and critical, alternative perspective to the more optimistic view of Sustainable ICT.

1 Introduction

Even though the ICT industry has historically been spared the critique of being environmentally unfriendly, society has as of late recognized the negative environmental effects of ICT industry. Reports have shown that almost 2% of the total greenhouse gas emissions worldwide occur due to the usage of ICT equipment [1], and the increasing number of large data centres consume considerable amounts of energy. Furthermore, the ICT sector is a growth sector, and it has been calculated that by 2020, the total GHG emissions from mobile data traffic might be three times higher than today [2], and that this will be a much larger problem than the energy intensive data centers in the future [3]. There are also several other environmental and social implications in connection with the ICT sector, such as the production of e-waste, the extraction of rare earth elements (REEs) and conflict minerals and the sometimes hazardous production of the equipment.

K.K. Kimppa et al. (Eds.): HCC11 2014, IFIP AICT 431, pp. 57–68, 2014.

The general perception within the field today is that even though ICT has a big negative impact on the environment, it has probably an even greater potential in improving the environment by mitigating the environmental impact of other emission processes such as production, agriculture and transportation [1]. One simple Internet search with keywords such as "ICT" and "environment" combined, will tell the same story. Smart ICT solutions will potentially be able to decrease the annual GHG emissions by 9,1 GtCO$_2$e worldwide, as well as creating 29,5 million jobs and save USD 1,9 trillion for consumers and businesses [1]. Even though we agree that there are many positive aspects of ICT, we would like to apply a more critical perspective to the relationship between ICT and sustainability than that of Sustainable ICT.

In this paper, our aim is to critically discuss the notion of Sustainable ICT by turning to an ecological perspective of World Systems Theory [4,5,6]. By doing so, we want to open up a discussion about how Sustainable ICT and its predecessors contribute to ecological sustainability on a global scale. We argue that even though conditions in developed, core countries may be improved by the increased usage of sustainable ICT solutions, most of these improvements are made possible because of environmental and social degradation in peripheral, developing zones. Even though we do not claim this to be an entirely new insight, nor that we are able to prove that ecological effects of ICT are distributed unequally, we advance the claim that World Systems Theory is an important theoretical framework for discussing ICT, especially in the society of today where ICT is seen as one of many solutions to a range of economic, societal and environmental problems. A quite recent review of research on the environmental impact of ICT indeed confirms that a model-based approach is needed to allow "that positive effects can be promoted and negative ones alleviated proactively" [8]. World Systems Theory might be such model.

1.1   Outline of the Paper

In the second part of the paper, we will discuss Sustainable ICT and World Systems Theory (WST), and its ecologically aware versions. In this part, we will also review how WST has been applied to studies of ICTs in the past. In the third part we discuss the ICT value chain from material extraction to disposal. We present a number of examples and tentatively analyse these examples from the point of view of WST. In the fourth part, we summarize our main findings.

2   Sustainable ICT and World Systems Theory

2.1   From Green Computing to Sustainable ICT

As we have stated in the introduction, ICT has historically been spared of critique of being environmentally unfriendly, although recently concerns about energy use coupled with the growing use of ICT, and the increasing production of e-waste have been raised [1, 2, 9]. Certainly, there are positive environmental aspects of ICT as well and we would like to think about the discourse of positive environmental aspects of ICT as consisting of three phases - Green Computing, Green IT, and Sustainable ICT.

In the 1990s, under the label of *Green Computing*, the U.S. Environmental Protection Agency launched the voluntary program Energy Star, which is an energy-efficiency certification for electronic devices, mainly seen on old CRT monitors. Several other similar concepts emerged during the same time period, emphasising energy-efficiency as well as sustainable production and recycling of ICT equipment and other electronic devices (i.e. EPEAT, TCO certification). The focus in this phase was on the environmental aspects of the ICT devices in themselves. This was going to change.

In 2007, the discourse once again emphasised sustainable ICT practices, now under the concept of *Green IT*. Gartner Institutes launched a report in 2007, which showed that around 2% of the total energy consumption of Britain was due to the usage of ICT equipment. This was almost as much as the airline industry. Therefore, it became important to think about the greening of ICT. The difference between Green Computing and Green IT was that within Green IT, ICT was not only seen as the villain of the environmental issues, but more importantly a part of the solution [10]. The practices of Green Computing turned into *greening of IT* while the part of the concept where ICT could be the solution was called *greening by IT*. Greening of IT is thus not as focused on the ICT equipment, but rather focus on the beneficial potential of ICT applications Many argued that while Greening of IT did have some impact on sustainability, Greening by IT was even more important. The main argument presented was that while Greening of IT can only address 2% of the potential of Green IT, greening by IT could help streamlining other parts of the organisation by "smart" solutions, such as route planning, web meetings and virtualisation of servers, dematerialisation, in the remaining 98%. To sum up, the discourse on Green IT, although it started as a renewed concern with the amounts of energy consumed by ICT equipment (referring to the Gartner report), it got more and more focused on Greening by IT. It is plausible that a focus on Greening of IT, leads to further penetration of ICT into different societal sectors.

While the discussion of the positive impact of ICT was brought up by the discussion about Green IT from 2007, a burgeoning development, something we call the third wave in this field, is *Sustainable ICT*. In Sustainable ICT, economical and societal are added to the environmental concerns of green IT and green computing. Sustainable ICT focuses more on the "greening by" practices of green IT, while adding what IT can contribute with economically and socially. According to Harmond and Demirkan [11], this wave of sustainable computing will require organisations to consider "environmental (ecological and regulatory), social (ethical and philantropic) and economic strategies while delivering on core IT performance requirements to drive business productivity" [11, p. 19]. The same article argues that "sustainability has emerged as a business megatrend that fundamentally impacts how business compete" [11, p. 20].

During this whole development, a broadening of the scope has occurred, from the view of Green Computing, where we have to use ICT equipment more carefully and more efficiently, to Sustainable ICT, where ICT has a big potential of solving economic, societal and environmental issues. Above all, sustainability in general is described as a business strategy, used in order to gain market advantages. Yet another general direction in the development of the discourse on ICT is that it is turning increasingly optimistic.

2.2   World Systems Theory

The idea of World Systems Theory was created during the 1970s as a way to develop the Marxian tradition of social studies [12]. The theory is mainly based on the ideas of Karl Marx and Rosa Luxemburg. Rather than to discuss the class conflicts within a particular country, World Systems Theory discusses inequalities on a global level [13]. The reason for this broadening of the scope is due to Rosa Luxemburg's important remark that capitalism cannot be contained in itself, but must expand geographically in order to survive and prosper [14, p. 36]. In other words, instead of addressing the exploitation of the working class by the capitalists, Wallerstein discusses exploitation by inventing two key concepts - the core and the periphery. The core is basically the developed, rich countries, while the periphery is the poor countries, receiving a disproportionately small portion of the global wealth. The main argument in World Systems Theory is that the core countries exploit the "underdeveloped" countries by placing them on the outer edges of global trade. Wallerstein argues that the success of developed countries today is a product of systematic unequal exchange of raw material, goods and labour with developing countries. The exploitation of the periphery, from the point of view of WST, started during the age of colonisation and still exists in terms of trade between core and peripheral countries that constantly favour the core. The prosperity of core zones is thus not possible without the exploitation of peripheral zones, according to Wallerstein, just as the capital accumulation process of production is not possible without the exploitation of labour power of the working class in a Marxian analysis. Apart from core and peripheral regions, there are also semi-peripheries that are not as privileged as the core zones, but also not as exploited as the peripheral zones. Wallerstein's analyses of world systems often revolve around economic and, as an extension of economic effects, social effects of the unequal exchange between the core and the periphery.

Alf Hornborg, the Swedish Marxist ecologist, while being inspired by traditional WST, has developed WST in several ways. His focus is not only economic and social (addressing the economic relationship between the core and the periphery, and exploring its social effects), but more importantly environmental. In his analysis of world systems, the notion of emergy is vital [14]. Emergy is a measure of how much energy that has been consumed in order to create a product or an organism. When natural resources such as coal, oil and iron are extracted from the earth, the contribution of the natural processes (i.e. geothermal processes) to the emergy value of the resources are often neglected. According to Odum and Arding [15], the reason for this is because we see natural resources as "free gifts of nature" and misconceive their true value. The labour cost for extracting these resources are however being accounted for but, according to WST, at too low a price. The undervaluation of the price of natural resources, mainly extracted in peripheral areas, is one great contributor to why the core-periphery relation is still retained.

Not only are the natural resources unequally distributed by this relation, but also the environmental effects that the usage of these resources leads to. This is what Hornborg entitles the "global distribution of environmental degradation" [14] and is his greatest contribution to the theory. This assumption is based on that our world is a closed material system, a zero-sum game, and not a cornucopian world where re-sources are unlimited. This means that improvements in one part of the world system is always offset by deterioration in other parts of the world system. When natural resources are used by the core to increase the standard of living in the developed parts of the world, the periphery suffers the environmental and social consequences. The unequal exchange of resources allows the core to afford extensive investments in ICT solutions ("accumulation of technomass"), making their organizations more economi-cally efficient, while at the same time improving the work environment as well as lowering emissions of greenhouse gases directly from the core zones. This has some implications for sustainability and ICT, because the extensive usage of ICT in the core have social and environmental implications elsewhere, somewhere along the value chain of the required ICT equipment. Even though infotization is a major trend in world, world system theorists have been rather silent upon issues relating to ICT. There are however some important contributions, reviewed in the next section.

2.3   World Systems Theory and ICT

Konieczny [16] argues that all early ICTs such as printing technologies, the telegraph, the telephone, radio and television were all invented, developed and deployed in the core, which means that the core "had decades if not centuries of near monopoly on their use" [16, p. 260]. He argues that the case of the Internet is not different. Begin-ning as a US military project, the Internet relies on expensive technology and skills that are hard to come by in the periphery. However, while there are WST inspired debates about the digital divide, there are also important positive effects identified by World Systems Theorists. While traditionally having been used mainly by Western core countries, the number of Chinese users is increasing dramatically. In mid-2004, English speakers constituted 36 percent of Internet users, while Chinese users consti-tuted 13 percent. 5 years later, the English accounted for 28 percent of the Internet population, while the Chinese accounted for 23 percent. Konieczny thereby notes how the Internet indeed harbors potential for a more just and equitable use of information technologies.

Writing about the ICT equipment from a WST perspective, Nelson-Richards et al. [17] show how core countries invest heavily in ICT and that investments in ICT lead to higher productivity and business performance, which is to be expected. This dis-plays that they are now knowledgeable of the productivity paradox of ICT, which would imply that the core distances itself from the periphery.

Lawrence [18] discusses the intersection between energy use and WST. There is a strong positive correlation between energy use and a country's position in the world system. The semi-periphery, such as China, uses more energy and produces more emissions, while the periphery has seen energy and emissions increase but to a lower extent than the semi-periphery.

Smith, Sonnenfeld and Pellow [19] are portraying the negative environmental and social effects of the production of the latest high-tech gadgets. They focus on the US and on the emergence of the high-tech industry in what was going to become the Sili-con Valley in the 1980s. Sonnenfeld argues in the same book that "[h]ierarchies of power, profitability, and control are embedded within the structure of global economics. Key firms such as Intel and Hewlett-Packard remain headquartered in Silicon Valley, even while their manufacturing operations are distributed around the world." [19, p. 13]. Even though high-technology equipment is mainly used in the core and semi-periphery, the lion's share of the production today have been moved to peripheral zones because of its hazardous nature and cheap labour and raw material. This is of course not only valid for the ICT industry but applies to many other industries such as the garment industry.

One the same topic, Frey [20] shows how health and environmental hazards are transferred to the periphery of the world system. Many governments in peripheral countries are willing to accept hazardous production processes and recycling of dangerous wastes such as ocean-going vessels, e-waste, and automobile batteries, in order to gain economic [21][22]. The economic earnings of these tradeoffs only affects a small portion of the peripheral country, i.e. those in power, while the negative effects affects the whole population.

Even though ICT is a fairly untouched area from a world systems analysis approach, several studies on environmental impact of ICT, in different stages of its value chain, have been carried out. In the next section, we are trying to present examples of unequal environmental exchange by the usage of ICT equipment.

3   The Value Chain of ICT

In this part, we are inspired by the value chain perspective on ICT hardware, meaning that we study ICT from materials extraction, to manufacturing, use, refurbish, reuse, and finally disposal. We believe that in order to apply WST, one must take a broad perspective on ICT. We know that there are several environmental implications throughout its value chain, including the extraction of scarce rare earth metals and dumping of electronic waste. We would like to consider these aspects in a geographical, political, social domain by turning to Alf Hornborg, and try to unravel where the positive aspects of IT are enjoyed and where the negative aspects of IT are situated geographically and why.

This part does not aim to be a systematic analysis and a proof that ICT leads to the unequal distribution of environmental effects. Rather, it is a collection of some examples of practices in the ICT value chain that are aimed to give an idea of what a thorough application of WST to ICT could lead to. Thus, the aim of the part is to indicate how the most positive benefits of ICT appears in the core countries, while the more negative impact appears in peripheral countries.

3.1   Materials Extraction

The production of ICT equipment depends on the supply of raw materials, and there has been a constant struggle to mine for many of these materials. Mining activities, including the extraction of materials needed to produce ICT are always linked to some kind of environmental destruction in the local environment. From a historical perspective, the mining for precious metals has caused severe damage to the landscape, with environmental consequences such as desertification, which is still present 2000 years after the original damage was caused [23]. Del Mar argues that wealth in Europe during both the Roman Empire and 1000 years later during the Middle Ages, was made possible by the exploitation of labour and natural resources outside of Europe, such as the Spanish raid and quest for gold in Latin America [23]. In today's terms we could argue that this can be compared with exploitation of Zambia by corporations such as Glencore, mining for copper [24], the permanent radioactive land in Malaysia, or the mercury polluted land in Brazil due to mining.

Large amounts of energy, either generated by muscular power or by combustion of fuel, are required in order to extract and crush and refine the metal ore. Processes like leaching uses highly toxic and/or cancerogenic chemicals such as fluor, mercury and arsenic. Large quantities of water for filtering are also used, which subsequently is deducted from the supply of available drinking water in the local area. Mining generates large amounts of waste, both useless rock that destroys the landscape visually, but also toxic waste that destroys the ecosystem. Extracting 1 ton of copper generates 600 tons of dangerous waste that somehow needs to be disposed of [24].

Rare Earth Elements, (REEs) are the elements needed to give electrical products certain properties, and very small amounts are needed in the electrical gadgets people use in their daily lives. REEs make it possible to produce energy efficient fluorescent light bulbs and add power-saving abilities in certain technological devices. But the energy saved in the core is paid with a high environmental and social price in the peripheral zones [25].

Conflict Minerals is another issue. The Democratic Republic of the Congo is a large producer of minerals used to produce ICT equipment. As one of the poorest countries in the world, yet a rich country in natural resource, the income generated by exporting minerals supports military rebels. Mining and smelting of coltan and the "three T's": tin, tantalum and tungsten [26] is often performed under slave-like conditions before transporting them to countries like China and India for production. Even though the core is aware of these conflicts, their dependency on coltan and other minerals for ICT products forces the core to turn the blind eye on the millions of death that mining directly or indirectly has caused in the periphery.

3.2   Manufacturing

The manufacturing of ICT equipment is linked with several social implications. Because this stage of the value chain requires a lot of manual labour, it is often outsourced to the periphery and the semi-periphery, due to the lack of regulation in these countries. What is less reflected upon is that the production phase is both very energy intensive as well as resource intense. Williams argues that the life cycle energy consumption of ICT equipment is dominated by production (81 %) as opposed to operation (19%) [29]. James and Hopkinson state in the same book that "it is ... the case that when all impacts are considered, the materials and manufacturing stage probably has the greatest environmental impact" [29, p. 41]. Studies on notebooks show that the production phase, accounting for about 56% (214 kg CO_2e in 5 years) of the total greenhouse gas emissions of the total life cycle, casts a significantly higher impact than the use phase. Moreover, the environmental impacts of the production phase of a notebook are so high, that they cannot be compensated in realistic time-periods by energy efficiency gains in the use phase. In the case of a 10% increase in the energy efficiency of a new notebook as compared to the older one in the use phase, replacement of the older notebook can only be justified after 33 to 89 years, if other environmental concerns than just the energy part is considered [30].

The production of ICT components is very water and resource intense. A study shows that the total amount of secondary fossil fuel and chemical input to the production of a 2g 32MB DRAM chip is 1600 and 72g respectively. One of these small components also requires 32000 liters of water to produce [49]. While the size of chips decreases, the used materials might actually increase [29].

Furthermore, in the new report "CSR issues in the ICT hardware manufacturing sector", the Centre for Research on Multinational Corporations (SOMO) focuses on an industry that has continuously moves to countries where production is cheaper, focusing predominantly on zones where labour rights and environmental issues have no to little priority. Research done for SOMO in China and the Philippines shows that computers are produced under endemic overtime, while the lack of unions and barriers to organizing means that the workers cannot negotiate for improvements. Workers are hired on short term contracts for years, blacklisted and subjected to discriminatory application processes [29].

3.3 Use

The use phase is where we can reap the benefits of ICT practices, according to recent reports [1, 28]. While there are some obvious advantages in economic sustainability in the use phase, whether this phase can contribute to ecological sustainability globally is contentious. While some argue that ICT in the form of web meetings generates less need to travel and meet physically, others have argued that the number of physical meetings does not decrease [29].

It has been suggested that around 80% of energy consumption of PCs is in the production phase, as mentioned in the last section. However, a 2007 EU study by IVF reached the opposite. Their methodology suggests that 65% of the lifetime global warming impacts of a European office desktop computer are related to use the use phase, compared to 32% in production. The main reason for this is that although LCD monitors are lighter than CRTs, require less energy and resources in production, the latter can result in emissions of sulphur hexafluoride (SF_6) or nitrogen trifluoride (NF_3), which are very potent and long-lived greenhouse gases.

Kawamoto measured total energy use by office and network equipment as of 1999, which amounted to 2% of the total electricity in the US [29]. Koomey shows that electricity consumption of Internet servers doubled in the period 2000-2005 [31]. Mills and Huber suggest that Internet absorbs some 8% of the total US electricity supply [32 p. 81].

3.4   Refurbish and Reuse

Some refurbishers of computers in Sweden have found a niche market in prolonging the life of computers by selling them second-hand to semi-peripheral countries before they actually become waste. The refurbisher refreshes software, tests batteries, erases hard drives and exchanges keyboards to fit the export market within the EU. They mainly sell proper second hand computers to former East Block countries. In Sweden the demand for second hand ICT equipment is very limited. Even though formal EU rules on e-waste recycling are the same, the likelihood for a machine to be fully recycled after its second life is far reduced in former East Block countries, since Sweden currently has the highest EU recycling rate in kilogram per person. Thus even though this is a fully legal operation, the risk for these machines not being recycled properly might increase by this step. On the other hand refurbishing is doubling the lifetime of the machine that delays production.

3.5   Disposal

The Basil Action Network (BAN) also estimates that Western electronic waste, primarily from the United States and the United Kingdom, is illegally exported to different countries in Southeast Asia and Africa. In 2005 BAN estimated that 275.000 tons of e-waste was being shipped to someone else's "backyard" [33]. This waste is not treated in any proper way and basically motherboards are melted over open fires releasing mercury fumes and dioxins of flame-retardants in order to extract precious metals such as gold and silver. Similar treatment is done with cables in order to extract copper.

The authors of Cradle to Cradle [32 p. 5] mention that copper waste ending up in regular household stream which end up in incinerating plants is getting melted into asphalt to a value of £80 million. Braungart claims that 15.000 tons of copper is being smelted into asphalt in Germany every year and thus being lost as a value resource that potentially could be fully recycled. The throwaway society in the core thus demands a continuation of supply from the periphery.

3.6   Summary

What could be indicated and what would also be the normative conclusions from WST in most of these examples is that most of the negative impacts of ICT along its value chain are displaced to peripheral zones. In the examples above, one can deduce that significant negative environmental impact is attributed in resource extraction, which is highly energy consuming, changes the natural environment, and is also detrimental to human well-being for the employees as well as for the local community. A part of electronic waste is also exported to peripheral regions such as parts of China, and Africa. The exported electronic waste has less economic value than the electronic waste that is recycled within the core areas such as the European Union. Rather, the electronic waste exported is that which requires low labour costs to process, such as cables, often burned outside in empty barrels, sometimes by children. Certainly peripheral areas also use ICT equipment, but it is probable that the ICT equipment used in these areas are not the newest nor best, but more often intermediate technology [51]. Peripheral areas do not benefit from ICT in the same ways as core regions, because of the constant race for speed and efficiency in this sector. Rather, peripheral areas presumably suffer from slow equipment and slow networks.

Manufacturing is often located in semi-peripheral regions, such as parts of China and India. Manufacturing is also an energy demanding and chemical intensive process. There have also been reports that the local environment is polluted to a large extent. Due to the fact that semi-peripheral regions are richer than peripheral regions, these regions probably enjoy more positive impacts of ICT than peripheral regions. However, the main benefits from ICT is expected to happen in core regions, where the newest smart systems and the latest gadgets are used. Hence, environmental issues boils down to energy issues only, which is indicated in for example Sustainable ICT literature (produced in the core), which is always almost exclusively focused on energy [34].

4   Conclusions

In this paper, we have presented the emergence of the IT trend Sustainable ICT and the claim that ICT can be a driving force in promoting a sustainable society. Moving from Green Computing to Green IT to Sustainable ICT, we have argued that the focus on the environmental effects of ICT is getting more and more positive. Green Computing emphasised reduction of energy use of ICT as well as more sustainable production of ICT. Green IT, with its bifurcation into Greening of IT and Greening by IT, can be said to both subsume Green Computing into Greening of IT, while also opening up for a more positive perspective of ICT with the concept of Greening by IT. At the same time, in the popular discourse, more attention is given to Greening by IT, that is, the positive perspective. Sustainable ICT broadens the perspective to not only environmental but also social and economic issues. Still, there is a focus on the positive aspects of ICT. If the discourse is analyzed from the perspective of Alf Hornborg, it is obvious that the discourse is one of cornucopia. ICT can, in this cornucopian view, solve a range of social issues, and the increasing penetration of ICT into various societal sectors is both desirable, and more importantly, possible.

In contrast to this optimistic view, we have presented WST, which argues that the discourse of cornucopia cannot be true. Rather, there is always a zero-sum game: if someone wins, someone must lose. We have reviewed WST, especially its ecological versions, and applied that to the ICT value chain. Thus, we have indicated how WST can be used to throw light on inequalities in the value chain, for example that core regions benefit most from the use of ICT while negative environmental impacts of ICT befalls peripheral regions. We have also brought up examples that problematize the strong focus on energy efficiency. Rather, one should also think about other environmental aspects of ICT.

Although we have drawn on WST in this paper, we do not unconditionally believe that it is correct. Rather, what we have been trying to do is to introduce an alternative, or minor, discourse to the one-sided discourse that is being promoted by dominant actors in the industry (such as large companies). When discussing the sustainability of ICT, one should thus consider both the arguments from the discourses of cornucopia and zero-sum game.

References

1. Global e-Sustainability Initiative (GeSI), SMART 2020: Enabling the Low Carbon Economy in the Information Age, http://www.theclimategroup.org/assets/resources/publications/Smart2020Report.pdf
2. Fehske, A., Fettweis, G., Malmodin, J., Biczok, G.: The global footprint of mobile communications: The ecological and economic perspective. IEEE Communications Magazine 49(8), 55–62 (2011)
3. CEPT ECC PT1 International Report on Mobile Broadband Landscape (2011), http://www.cept.org/files/4549/ECC%20PT1%20internal%20report%20on%20MBB%20-%20ECC%20PT111162%20Annex%2023.docx
4. Hornborg, A.: Global ecology and unequal exchange: Fetishism in a zero-sum world (2011)
5. Hornborg, A., Jorgensen, A.K.: International trade and environmental justice: Toward a global political ecology. Nova Science Publishers (2010)
6. Hopkins, T.K., Wallerstein, I., Bach, R.L.: World-systems analysis: theory and methodology, p. 47. Sage Publications, Beverley Hills (1982)
7. Erdmann, L., Hilty, L.M.: Scenario Analysis. Journal of Industrial Ecology 14(5), 826–843 (2010)
8. Yi, L., Thomas, H.R.: A review of research on the environmental impact of e-business and ICT. Environment International 33(6), 841–849 (2007)
9. Ruth, S.: Green it more than a three percent solution? IEEE Internet Computing 13(4), 74–78 (2009)
10. Fors, P., Lennerfors, T.T.: Translating Green IT: The case of the Swedish Green IT Audit. In: Hilty, L.M., Aebischer, B., Andersson, G., Lohmann, W. (eds.) CT4S 2013: Proceedings of the First International Conference on Information and Communication Technologies for Sustainability, ETH Zurich, February 14-16, pp. 208–216 (2013)
11. Harmon, R.R., Demirkan, H.: The Next Wave of Sustainable IT. IEEE Computer Society IT Professional, 19–25 (January/February 2011); Lead article
12. Wallerstein, I.: World-systems analysis: An introduction. Duke University Press (2004)
13. Chirot, D., Hall, T.D.: World-system theory. Annual Review of Sociology 8, 81–106 (1982)
14. Hornborg, A.: The power of the machine: Global inequalities of economy, technology, and the environment, vol. 1. Rowman Altamira (2001)
15. Odum, H.T., Arding, J.E.: Emergy analysis of shrimp mariculture in Ecuador, p. 114. The Center (1991)
16. Konieczny, P.: The Internet and the world-system (s). In: Routledge International Handbook of World-Systems Analysis, p. 260 (2012)
17. Nelson-Richards, et al.: Routledge International Handbook of World-Systems Analysis (2012)
18. Lawrence, et al.: Routledge International Handbook of World-Systems Analysis (2012)
19. Smith, T., Sonnenfeld, D.A., Pellow, D.N. (eds.): Challenging the chip: Labor rights and environmental justice in the global electronics industry. Temple University Press (2006)

20. Frey, R.S.: The transfer of core-based hazardous production processes to the export processing zones of the periphery: The maquiladora centers of northern Mexico. Journal of World-Systems Research 9(2), 317–354 (2003)
21. Buerk, R.: Breaking Ships: How supertankers and cargo ships are dismantled on the shores of Bangladesh. Chamberlain Brothers, p. 192 (2006) ISBN 1-59609-036-7
22. Frey, R.S.: The transfer of core-based hazardous production processes to the export processing zones of the periphery: The maquiladora centers of northern Mexico. Journal of World-Systems Research 9(2), 317–354 (2003)
23. Del Mar, A.: A History of the Precious Metals, from the earliest times to the present. British Library, Historical Print Edition, London (1880)
24. Gulbrandsen, C.: Stealing Africa - Why Poverty? (Motion Picture) (2012)
25. Pitron, G., Turquier, S.: La sale guerre des terres rares (Motion Picture) (2012)
26. Eichstaedt, P.: Consuming the Congo, war and conflict minerals in the world's deadliest place. Lawrence Hill Books, Chicago (2011)
27. Prakash, S., Liu, R., Schischke, K., Stobbe, L.: Timely replacement of a notebook under consideration of environmental aspects. Umweltbundesamt (2012)
28. Gartner, The Data Center Power and Cooling Challenge, David Cappuccio and Lynne Craver (November 2007)
29. Rattle, R.: Computing Our Way to Paradise?: The Role of Internet and Communication Technologies in Sustainable Consumption and Globalization. Rowman & Littlefield (2010)
30. Prakash, S., Liu, R., Schischke, K., Stobbe, L.: Timely replacement of a notebook under consideration of environmental aspects. Umweltbundesamt (2012)
31. Kostigen, T.: The Underbelly of Globalization: Our Toxic Wastes Exported to Developing Countries (September 25, 2008) Basil Action Network - Library, http://ban.org/library/Features/080925_the_underbelly_of_ globalization.html (retrieved December 11, 2013)
32. McDonough, W., Braungart, M.: Cradle to Cradle. Vintage, Croydon (2009)
33. Sonhüter, B., Liebsch, M. (Directors): Nie mehr Müll - Leben ohne Abfall (Motion Picture) (2010)
34. Yotsumoto, M., Lennerfors, T.T., Majima, T.: The current trends and issues of Green IT. In: The Japan Association for Management Information (JASMIN) Conference, Japan, October 29-30 (2011)

Origins, Developments and Future of the Concept of Innovation: Opening the Economic Framing of Innovation to Social, Ethical, Political Parameters to Achieve Responsibility: Strengths and Limits

Laurence Masclet and Philippe Goujon

University of Namur, Namur, Belgium
laurence.masclet@unamur.be, pgo@info.fundp.ac.be

Abstract. The concept of innovation is making a successful comeback in philosophy, particularly with the qualifier "responsible" attached. This attachment of the qualification "responsible" reflects the idea that the concept of innovation has to be opened to new considerations, namely social, political and ethical concerns. Since the 18th century, innovation has been the object of economics and science of business and growth. This paper aims at testing the legitimacy of these attempts to open the concept and redefine it in terms other than those of economics. We start with a contextualization of the use of the term innovation, to see why it has been so strongly associated with the market, growth and business then we see what is at stake in opening it up to other considerations. We consider the limits of this opening and look at possible ways to attach other meanings to the concept, without losing significance by too much inclusion. The solution proposed is that instead of imposing new parameters and trying to shift the concept, we could keep the economic bias of the term, but challenge it with concerns expressed by people coming from the field of economics who are trying to propose an alternative framework for economics that would take into account other concerns, and in which responsible innovation could find a place.

Keywords: Innovation, economy, society, ethics, responsibility.

1   Introduction

The concept of innovation is nowadays coming back to fashion with the prefix "responsible" attached to it, to form the phrase "Responsible Innovation" or "Responsible Research Innovation" (RRI) [7,8]. The addition of the specification "responsible" is interesting in many respects. First, it emphasizes that innovation is not, by itself, responsible - hence the need for the specification - and secondly, it seems like the manifestation of a will to broaden the sphere of the analysis of innovation. Indeed, innovation has been the object of economics and the science of business and growth since the 18th century. This paper will try to test the legitimacy of the attempt to open the concept of innovation to other sources of meaning and to other concerns than those of economics.

K.K. Kimppa et al. (Eds.): HCC11 2014, IFIP AICT 431, pp. 69–77, 2014.

The meaning of the concept of responsibility is the object of a vast area of literature, especially in philosophy. We take it here as a broader concept than just legal accountability, as a moral concept [26, 27]. We will focus here on the "innovation" side of the concept of "responsible innovation", and on the presuppositions that are disclosed by the very use of that expression. The concept of innovation in its broad definition is used in many fields. It is not unusual to talk for example about innovation in art, innovation in teaching, innovation in governance, innovation in war making or car driving. In various fields the term is very often used as a weaker version of the term 'invention', meaning anything bringing something new to a field. It seems to be most frequently attached to technological changes occurring in different fields, but not always.

In the academic world, the term has been one of the main object of economy since the emergence of the field. Schumpeter in 1934 described innovation as "New Combinations" [16, 17], and the core of his analyses and framing of the definition of an innovation are still very much unchanged [11] [23].

In this paper, we will give a brief reconstruction of the history of the philosophical concept of innovation, focusing mainly on the major shift in the perception, the field and the use of the concept, in order to try to broaden its limits. Indeed, history shows that this concept is far from univocal, and has been the object of many changes of perception. This tends to validate the idea of trying to open the concept to other meanings than those drawn from economics and technology. Once we have established the freedom to manipulate the concept, we will have to see where the restriction to economics occurs, and what the legitimacy of this restriction is. By doing this, we will made apparent some limits to the idea of another shift of the concept to reach responsible innovation, and we will have to find compromises between the intrinsic economic bias of the concept and the need to open it to other preoccupations.

2   History of the Concept

The first occurrences of the notion of innovation are very different from current usage. Indeed, innovation, from it first use until the 18th century was used as a strongly derogatory term.

> "Innovation", from the Latin *innovare*, innovation, should signify renewal, rejuvenation from inside, rather than novelty, which is its modern meaning in both English and French. Judging from the examples in the Oxford English Dictionary and the Littré, the word came into widespread use only in the 16th century and, until the 18th century, its connotations are almost uniformly unfavorable."[5]

This negative bias is a result of innovation's original connection to theology. An innovation from a theological dogma is never considered to be progress. On the contrary, being innovative in the context of religion is regarded has a direct way to heresy.

The negative sense of the word innovation also occurs in political sciences, in which it is linked to rebellion and revolution, and is shared even among thinkers who we would call innovators today. The paradox is that even reformers like Calvin saw innovation as a bad thing, because the aim of the reformation was not to create something new, but to *come back* to the original ideal of Christianity. And the Humanists, after the Protestants, despised innovation as well, advocating a return to the ideas and models of classical antiquity [5].

Despite Girard's interpretation of what innovation "should" signify - i.e. "renewal, rejuvenation from inside" [5]- this is not really how it has been interpreted, otherwise the Reformation would have been branded as an innovation for example, which it wasn't. It is only during the 18th century that the notion started to take on a more positive meaning, corresponding to a shift in society. The word was increasingly detached from theology and was instead attached to technological development and economic growth. In the 18th century and later during the 19th century and the industrial revolution [25], the notion of innovation became used to mean the imitation and improvement of an invention in a field. Indeed, in the commercial and industrial fields it has never been enough to invent something new (new methods, new products, etc.): improvements always immediately connected to commercialization. And innovation seems to be associated with this commercial aspect of an invention, and its imitation and improvement by the competition, creating a chain of development that can revolutionize a field without needing properly new products or methods, but rather through improvements of ideas from one industry to the next, in a mechanism economists call "incremental innovation".

Invention in itself seems to be already connected to commercialization in most cases, so it is difficult to argue that innovation is only the commercial side of invention. It is much more significant to say that innovation distinguishes itself from invention by its incremental characteristics.[1]

We have briefly sketched the history of innovation as a concept, and seen that this history was marked by a major switch that corresponds to a major change of focus in society[2] from theology to economics. However, we have seen that nowadays, the concept of innovation is also used in other fields and has become part of vernacular language and popular culture. It is also more and more linked with the adjective "responsible" [19] [8] in an attempt to include other considerations (ethical, social, political) than those of economics[3]. But is this extension possible and legitimate?

---

[1] How then can we talk about "radical" innovation is another research question that we will have to develop in further researches.

[2] Although, of course, this change of focus in society did not happened over night, and there are a lot of discussions to be made on when and where (or indeed whether) this change happened.

[3] The question of the meaning and legitimacy of adding such a qualifier -thus implying that innovation is not/cannot be responsible *per se*- will also be the object of further researches and cannot be developed here.

3   Opening the Sphere of Meaning (and Limits)

3.1   Innovation as "New Combinations"

Joseph Schumpeter (1883-1950) was the first theorist to make the distinction between the concept of innovation and the concept of invention, and to define innovation as a first commercial transaction successfully achieved [1]. By this definition, Schumpeter links in the collective consciousness the notions of innovation, of commercialization and of technical objects. Schumpeter's framework is still being discussed today, and, although of course challenged on many points [2], it is still a general reference point for anybody who wants to tackle the subject of innovation or entrepreneurship [23][4]. Schumpeter defined innovation as "the setting up of a new production function" or "New Combinations", which relate to incremental innovation we referred to above.

> "We will now define innovation more rigorously by means of the production function previously introduced. This function describes the way in which quantity of product varies if quantities of factors vary. If, instead of quantities of factors, we vary the form of the function, we have an innovation. But this not only limits us, at first blush at least, to the case in which the innovation consists in producing the same kind of product that had been produced before by the same kind of means of production that had been used before, but also raises more delicate questions. Therefore, we will simply define innovation as the setting up of a new production function. This covers the case of a new commodity, as well as those of a new form of organization such as a merger, of the opening up of new markets, and so on. Recalling that production in the economic sense is nothing but combining productive services, we may express the same thing by saying that innovation combines factors in a new way, or that it consists in carrying out New Combinations, although, taken literally, the latter phrases would also include what we do not now mean to include -namely, those current adaptations of the coefficients of production which are part and parcel of the most ordinary run of economic routine within given production functions." [16].

This very economical way of defining innovation has been very influential but is in fact the heir of the 18th century's conception of innovation and its primary link to technological invention, commercialization, industrial concurrence and general growth. This way of looking at innovation as "setting up of new production functions" seems to be very narrowly economic, and, as a side effect, seems to put aside any consideration other than the need for growth and novelty for its own (economic) sake.

---

[4] For example : "Of all the theories of entrepreneurship that exist, his theory is still, to my mind, the most fascinating as well as the most promising theory of entrepreneurship that we have. Let me clarify. I do not argue that Schumpeter's theory, as it is understood today, can supply the key to the mystery of entrepreneurship. What I would like to suggest, however, and also devote this paper to, is the argument that it may well constitute the point of departure for the development of *the* theory of entrepreneurship." [23]

The combination between the increasingly ubiquitous nature of the concept of innovation nowadays, and its bias towards economics is problematic in the sense that it spreads its unquestioned presuppositions and strengthens the domination of economic thinking in society[5]. So there is a benefit in opening the concept of innovation, as the pursuit of innovation has massive impacts on society as a whole. If legislators act as innovators, it seems reasonable to demand that they seek ways to make innovations more responsible, more ethical and socially and environmentally aware, as well as to stifle innovations that have unethical impact on society[6]. Many theories of governance and research projects have investigated ways of opening the framework of innovation to include more contextual parameters into the conception of an innovation and more generally, into decisions to start to research a potential innovation (VOICES[7], PROGRESS [20], ETICA[8], Responsibility[9], GREAT[10], to quote a few, which are all funded either on the 7th framework Programme (FP7) or Horizon 2020 from the European Commission).

However, we are trying to find out here if the concept of innovation is ready to be opened to other spheres of meaning. Regarding the history of the concept, we can see that it is very much open to shifts in both meaning and fields of application, even though it is always connected throughout history with two features :the first is the notion of novelty (whether this is considered as a good thing or not) and secondly, it is always interpreted in relation to the most powerful and influential field in society (theological when theology was the most powerful force shaping society, and economic when economics was defining the aims of society).

The stakes are high because succeeding in transforming the mechanisms of innovation in order to make it more ethical would imply a shift towards a more ethical society. But this reasoning is of course bad logic, because the opposite is more probable: only a shift in society towards more responsible behaviour will change innovation.

The history of the concept of innovation also shows us the potential for inclusion that this notion entails. Indeed, if we take Schumpeter's definition of innovation as "New Combinations", it is very open to all sorts of spheres and material for combinations.

---

[5] The dominance of some economic ways of thinking cannot be reduced to the increasing use of the term innovation of course. The causal relation is probably reversed: it is the dominance of economic jargon that enhance the general use of the term innovation. But even if that is true, it is still an ethical and social worry to find economic terms carrier of so many economic presuppositions being used for daily conversation. The same can be said about many economic words that have invaded the public and private spheres.

[6] For more on this question on the ways to achieve responsible innovation, see for example the ongoing « Governance for Responsible Innovation" (GREAT) Project.
http://www.great-project.eu/

[7] (Views, Opinions and Ideas of Citizens in Europe on Science
http://www.voicesforinnovation.eu/).

[8] ETICA : Ethical Issues of Emerging ICT Applications, project funded under FP7.

[9] Global Model and Observatory for International Responsible Research and Innovation Coordination http://responsibility-rri.eu/

[10] Governance for Responsible Innovation. http://www.great-project.eu/. GREAT develop an empirically based and theoretically sound model of the role of responsible research and innovation governance and is funded under Horizon 2020.

Schumpeter reduces it to economics, but the reduction is not in the material of innovation but in its aims. Innovation's material (the things being reassembled into new combinations) is open to anything *as long as they are being commercialized and contribute to economic development.*

Does the opening to ethics and responsibility imply that we have to leave out the economic aims of innovation or that we have to make new combinations with other parameters than the ones usually used? It seems that it is the commercial aims that are at stake if we want to achieve responsible innovation, maybe not by removing completely its commercial side, but certainly by adding new aims, like constructing a more ethical and safe society. The limitation of thinking of innovation as New Combinations and opening its aims to other goals, is the danger that it becomes meaningless by including everything in it. Indeed, if we are talking about new combinations of any material (as Schumpeter's definition allows) without the restriction of economic aims, we could argue that any thought, any action is an innovation, as it is a new combination of existing elements [14] [15]. Language is the perfect example of new combinations. From a limited stock of words, human beings is able to produce unlimited texts, conversation, ideas and stories. Yet, we cannot consider any text or any conversation or any thought to be an innovation. There seems to be something more to it, otherwise it loses all meaning. If innovation material is open to anything, the restriction needed seems to be in the economic impact expected from it[11].

We could argue that random conversation or though can potentially be exploited economically, but the point is that it is only then, when economic exploitation is sought, that ideas become innovation. Before commercial aims, an idea cannot be considered yet an innovation.

3.2 Consequences of the Inherent Link between Innovation and Economics

We talked about the political and social will to make innovation more responsible and thus, opened it to new spheres of meaning and other concerns than mere economics and growth. But the definition of the concept of economics, as we argue, ask for an economical restriction to the concept, which is defined by its commercial goal.

So, if we want to open innovation to new spheres of meaning, new parameters and new aims, we have to retain a sufficiently determinate framing in order for the concept to stay meaningful. It does not seem plausible to achieve responsible innovation by situating it outside of economic discourse altogether. However, there are many ways of doing economics, and many economists in the 20th and 21st centuries are making efforts and developing new ways to include other concerns and aims -social fairness, redistribution, ethics, political stability, etc.- than mere economic growth[12] [28, 29, 30, 31, 32]. Alternative economic framings exist that take into account

---

[11] Whether or not these commercial aims are met is not relevant to qualify an innovation as such. The commercial aims themselves (added to the novelty of the combination) seems to be sufficient as a criterion for innovation.

[12] For example Amartya Sen, or on another level the current school of degrowth, like the The Club of Rome, Nicholas Georgescu-Roegen, Serge Latouche in France, *Christian Arnsperger* and Philippe Van Parijs in Belgium or even Marxist theorists.

contextual and ethical parameters within their conception, and responsible innovation seems to fit into this way of thinking. The task for philosophers remains to evaluate whether in those theories the economic framing that seems to be impossible to remove does not contaminate and reinterpret other concerns so much that they become themselves economic. This idea of contamination can be seen for example in the dynamic of trying to « sell » ethics as a « good commercial move » for companies (in term of image, long-term benefits, or saving by pre-empting potential social rejection[13]), or in the way of promoting art subventions as investments and potentiality to create growth, rather than for art itself, etc.

To achieve the challenge of putting responsibility into innovation, we cannot impose a new framing on the concept of innovation and impose a change of field. We cannot open it to the extent it becomes meaningless, but should find, within the conception of the notion itself, the openings that can be reached without reducing alternative aims to another economic framing.

The Information and Communication Technologies (ICT) field is an important sector of innovation and has been also the object of ethical concerns over the years [22]. The technological angle in innovation is as powerful as the economic angle, and is therefore responsible for restriction within the concept of innovation, which is not completely in phase with the will to open the concept. However, the same conclusion could be made for technology as it has been made for economics: it seems impossible to leave out the technological understanding of innovation. However, it does not mean that innovation is restricted to technological innovation, and moreover, that technological innovation are only technology. What the concept of responsible innovation tends to achieve is on the contrary to drive technical innovation toward other field of concerns outside mere technology or economy.

Even if the field of ICT is particular in many respects (treating which such a peculiar and ubiquitous object that is information [10]), the idea of opening the sphere of meaning of innovation has an identical application. In order to impose responsibility into innovation in ICT, one should not need to evacuate the economical bias implanted within the notion of innovation –basically innovation as a necessity for business to survive among competitors and for society to raise growth. On the contrary, the economic bias has to be thought of and evaluate for what it is, both what is driving innovation and the criterion by which it is judge. To add another principle, the principle of responsibility, to assess a technology, we have to be prepare to change our perspectives on economic benefits and on the type of economy we want for society.

4   Conclusion

Our brief reconstruction of some of the steps of the history of the meaning of innovation has shown us that this concept is both a carrier of huge presuppositions (attachment to economics, to economic growth, to technological development, and so on),

---

[13] Which is not to say that there is no good argument for ethics as a sustainable investment for companies, but making it the only argument seems to miss the real meaning of ethical concern, and would imply that, in absence of commercial potential, ethics would not be worth pursuing. It is the dynamic behind the argument that is criticized here.

and still very open to new meanings and very flexible. The only thing that seems to not be detachable from this concept without it losing all meaning is the very thing that has to be carefully managed if we take upon the task of making innovation "responsible": its attachment to economics. Indeed, without an economic connotation, the concept loses signification, and with it, it carries the risk of being blind to any other aspects of society and human life.

But the task of reaching for responsible innovation is not impossible, even from within the field of Economics. Indeed, there are a lot of "alternative" economic theories that aim exactly at this. In fact, the case might be made that most economic theories are aiming towards ethical and social progress and balance, and that some of the blindness in economics are more of a drift from the main aim of economics than an inherent feature of the field. The conceptual linkage between innovation, technology and economy is strong and the challenge of Responsible Innovation, taking responsibility in its full ethical sense and trying to inject it into innovation, has to face the history of its object and address in a fully reflexive way the presuppositions that are embedded in it.

References

1. Akrich, M., Callon, M., et Latour, B.: A quoi tient le succès des innovations? Annales des Mines 11, 4–17 (1988)
2. Taylor Cromer, C., Dibrell, C., Craig, J.B.: A study of Schumpterian (radical) vs. Kirznerian (incremental) innovations in knowledge intensive industries. Journal of Strategic Innovation and Sustainability 7(1), 28–42 (2011)
3. Chesbrough, H.: Open Innovation: the New Imperative for Creating and Profiting from Technology. Harvard Business School Press, Boston (2003)
4. Guchet, X.: Les Sens de l'évolution technique. Léo Scheer, Paris (2005)
5. Girard, R.: Innovation and Repetition. SubStance, Issue 62/63: Special Issue: Thought and Novation 19(2/3), 7–20 (1990)
6. Hilaire-Pérez, L., Thébaud-Sorger, M.: Les techniques dans l'espace public, Publicité des inventions et littératures d'usage au XVIIIe siècle (France, Angleterre). Revue de Synthèse, 5e série 2006(2), 393–428 (2006)
7. European Commission. Council Decision establishing the Specific Programme implementing Horizon 2020 -The Framework Programme for Research and Innovation (2014-2015), ch. 17. Science with and for Society, Version 1.0. 9 (2013)
8. European Union, Horizon 2020, Work Programme 2014-2015, ch. 16, Science with and for Society, European Commission Decision C (2013) 8631 (2013)
9. European Union, Responsible Research and Innovation, Europe's ability to respond to societal challenges (2012), http://ec.europa.eu/research/science-society/index.cfm?fuseaction=public.topic&id=1622 (retrieved in February 2014)
10. Masclet, L., Goujon, P.: Implementing Ethics in IS, presuppositions and consequences in ethics and IS. In: Hercheui, M.D., Whitehouse, D., McIver Jr., W., Phahlamohlaka, J. (eds.) HCC10 2012. IFIP AICT, vol. 386, pp. 287–298. Springer, Heidelberg (2012)
11. McCraw, T.: Prophet of innovation: Joseph Schumpeter and Creative Destruction. Belknap Press of Harvard University Press, Cambridge (2007)

12. McDonald, C.: Penserl'invention. Étudesfrançaises 26(3), 101–109 (1990), http://id.erudit.org/iderudit/035828ar (retrieved September 18, 2013)
13. Pestre, D.: A contre-science, Politiques et savoirs des sociétés contemporaines, Paris, Seuil (2013)
14. Schlanger, J.: Penser la bouche pleine. Librairie Arthème Fayard, Paris (1975, 1983)
15. Schlanger, J.: L'Invention intellectuelle. Librairie Arthème Fayard, Paris (1983)
16. Schumpeter, J.: Business Cycles, A Theoritical, Historical and Statistical Analysisof the Capitalist Process. McGraw-Hill Book Company, New York (1939)
17. Schumpeter, J.: The Theory of Economic Development: An Inquiry Into Profits, Capital, Credit, Interest, and the Business Cycle. Transaction Publisher, New Brunswick (1986); (first edition: Harvard University Press, Cambridge, MA, 1934)
18. O'Sullivan, D., Dooley, L.: Applying Innovation. Sage Publication, Inc., Thousand Oaks (2009)
19. Owen, R., Heintz, M., Bessant, J.: Responsible Innovation, Managing the Responsible Emergence of Science and Innovation in Society. John Wiley, London (2013)
20. Schrempf, B., Kaplan, D., Schroeder, D.: National, Regional, and Sectoral Systems of Innovation – An overview, Report for FP7 Project "Progress", progressproject.eu (2013)
21. Schutte, C., Marais, S.: The Development of Open Innovation Models to Assist the Innovation Process. University of Stellenbosch, South Africa (2010)
22. Stahl, B.: Responsible research and innovation in information systems. European Journal of information Systems 21, 207–211 (2012)
23. Swedberg, R.: Rebuilding Schumpeter's Theory of Entrepreneurship. In: Conference on Marshall, Schumpeter and Social Science. Hitotsubashi University (2007)
24. Veugelers, R.: How to Turn on the Innovation Growth Machine in Europe. In: Metaforum Leuven, Interdisciplinary Think-thank for Societal Debate, Leuven (June 2013)
25. Verley, P.: La révolution industrielle, Coll. Folio Histoire, Gallimard, Paris (2010)
26. Ricoeur, P., Ricoeur, P.: Oneself as Another. The University of Chicago Press, Chicago (1992)
27. Jonas, H.: The Imperative of Responsibility: In Search of an Ethics for the Technological Age. The University of Chicago Press, Chicago (1984)
28. Latouche, S.: Survivre au développement, De la décolonisation de l'imaginaire économique à la construction d'une société alternative. Arthème Fayard (2004)
29. Sen, A.: On economics inequality. Oxford University Press, Oxford (1973)
30. Okan, K., Pamukcu, T.: Innovation Capability for Development: An attempt to apply Amartya Sen's Capability Approach to Innovation Studies. In: 8th Annual Conference of the HDCA, The Hague, The Netherlands, September 6-8 (2011)
31. Arnsperger, C.: Critique de l'existence capitaliste: Pour une éthique existentielle de l'économie. Edition du Cerf, Paris (2005)
32. Georgescu-Roegen, N.: Energy and Economic Myths: Institutional and Analytical Economic Essays. Pergamon Press, New York (1976)

Human-Driven Design: A Human-Driven Approach to the Design of Technology

Marketta Niemelä, Veikko Ikonen, Jaana Leikas, Kristiina Kantola, Minna Kulju, Antti Tammela, and Mari Ylikauppila

VTT Technical Research Centre of Finland, Tampere, Finland

Abstract. In the midst of the many large-scale societal and technological trans-formations, there is a need for design approaches that respect human values and needs and are able to integrate multiple perspectives into technology design in order to work for outcomes that are interesting, feasible and sustainable in all senses of the term. For this purpose, we discuss a possible approach to the de-sign of technology that is driven by human and social values, is collaborative in nature and reflective in terms of responsibility and ethics in the design. We call this approach 'Human-Driven Design' and argue that it is needed especially when designing for enabling and emerging information and communication technologies. A human-driven design approach should focus on the early phases of design, be strongly future-oriented and aim to contribute to innovation for a sustainable society and better quality of life in the future.

Keywords: human-driven design, human-technology interaction, human values and needs, emerging ICTs.

1 Introduction

It has become increasingly important in the field of human-computer interaction (HCI) to understand the demands and opportunities that societal changes bring to technology development and interaction design. The grand challenges, such as climate change, an ageing population and the economic crisis, demand participation by and contributions from everyone, and HCI, combined with technology development and its vigorous expansion into our everyday lives, plays a key role. To deal with this, the intersection(s) between people, technology and design in HCI need(s) to be re-thought and the human-centred practices need more human values put into them (e.g. [1, 2]; see also [3]). Human values and needs should be better integrated into design to obtain solutions that are sustainable in all senses of the term.

There are a variety of approaches or frameworks that specifically emphasise a human perspective in design, such as participatory design and value-sensitive design, to mention a couple. In this paper, we review five of these frameworks and formulate this understanding for a more generic human-driven approach (or strategy) to design – *Human-Driven Design (HDD)*. As shown later in the text, this approach is based on emphasising human and social values, seeking true collaboration and empowerment with various stakeholders in the design process, and being reflective in terms of responsibility and ethics in design.

K.K. Kimppa et al. (Eds.): HCC11 2014, IFIP AICT 431, pp. 78–91, 2014.

As a term, human-driven design has been introduced before by Braund and Schwittay [4] (we present their perspective in Section 2.2) and Ikonen [5]. Ikonen presents HDD as an approach to the design of future smart environments and emerging ICT and describes HDD as an "approach which broadens the perspective from focused product or service development process model to the more holistic design perspective". Ikonen also describes stakeholder-based design that "furthermore broadens the scope and role of involved participant groups in the actual design process". Ikonen further calls for ethical assessments that should continue through the design process. Ikonen calls this resulting combination empowering design.

Based on our review, we agree that HDD should integrate the three perspectives endorsed in [5]: it should be holistic, strive for collaboration with different stakeholder groups and be ethically reflective. The present paper elaborates on our understanding of what human-driven design is in more detail for each perspective.

We characterise HDD as follows:

1. HDD takes a *human and social view* of users of technology as individuals and members of human social groups, such as family, organisation or community, and as consumers. The starting point of the design is the human being and her or his needs, goals and desires. The design is based on a deep understanding of the users' values and circumstances.
2. HDD is *participatory* in terms of promoting collaborative and co-design methods to empower users and other stakeholders in design and to ensure successful design outcomes.
3. HDD is *responsible* in terms of being aware of human, societal and ethical values related to a particular design and reflecting them in the design in order to make the technology support the wellbeing and activities of people as well as sustainability (social, environmental and economic).

Similarly to [5], we find the human-driven approach especially relevant in the context of emerging technologies and their future impacts. As technologies embed and intertwine in our everyday lives, they will also shape it and society: technology is increasingly something "we live with, not simply something we use" [1]. In some sense, to design technology is to design our future lives. Therefore, the design of technology should be formulated with an insight into human and societal phenomena and problems, sustainable development and business demands.

From this perspective, the design target of HDD would not just be human-computer interaction but broader Human-Technology Interaction (HTI) that emphasises the importance of research and design considerations that extend beyond the 'normal' user-computer combination. HTI addresses the interaction between users, technology and the physical and social environment [6]. In HTI, there is particular interest in the way technologies mediate the interaction between human actors and the environment, and in how to develop artefacts for the human-environment interaction. The holistic perspective of HTI is important when the purpose is to design solutions for human or societal problems (for example, to improve quality of life; see, e.g., [7]) and not just solutions for and within a certain technology. In practice, our current thinking about HDD is mostly based on developing ICT and emerging ICT (e.g. applications and services based on ambient intelligence). Therefore, with 'design' or 'technology design' we mainly refer to the design of the interaction between humans and computer systems, especially emerging information and communication technologies and systems.

With this paper, we hope to open discussions with other HCI/HTI researchers or designers who feel they could benefit from having a more holistic, human-driven approach to apply to design.

We proceed as follows. First, we position HDD in the field of HCI/HTI research by discussing some influential frameworks and research that form its basis: Human-Centred Design, Participatory Design, Value Sensitive Design, Human-Driven Design and Research, and Life-Based Design. Next, we elaborate on HDD by examining its three principles. Finally, we discuss what is still needed to develop HDD as a useful alternative to designing emerging (information) technologies.

2   Related Frameworks

2.1   Human-Centred Design

Human-Centred Design (HCD) is the prevailing general human-perspective frame-work for the design of interactive products, services and systems [8]. The aim of HCD is to make systems usable and useful by focusing on the users, their needs and re-quirements. The ISO standard for HCD defines both 'usability' and 'usefulness' broadly: for instance, usability may include aspects of use that are typically associated with user experience, such as emotional pleasure. Applying HCD to design should show, for example, increased productivity, improved ease of use, and user experience or reduced discomfort and stress.

HCD emphasises understanding the users and contexts of direct use, and it recom-mends the involvement of users throughout the design and development, including long-term monitoring of the product. HCD also addresses the impacts on stakeholders other than direct users.

The HCD standard also includes a perspective on sustainability [8]. Economic sus-tainability is supported as HCD provides cost-effective solutions and reduces the risk that the designed product will be wasteful or rejected. As the application of HCD results in products that are better for the health, well-being and involvement of their users, it supports social sustainability. HCD indirectly contributes to environmental sustainability as it encourages consideration of the long-term implications of systems.

The HCD framework provides several important principles for HDD: the human perspective itself, as well as a broad understanding of the users and their context, and the stakeholders. However, HDD should apply ethical and responsibility reflections more prominently in design. One reason for this is that emerging technologies often raise ethical considerations. For example, in the case of ubiquitous computing, ethical concerns have been raised, especially from the point of view of privacy, confidential-ity, integrity, availability, trust, control and autonomy (e.g. [9]). Another issue that we have found to be underemphasised in HCD is justification and meaning of technology to users.

2.2   Participatory Design

Participatory Design (PD) is another well-established human-centred approach that emphasises active involvement by the users and all the stakeholders in design. PD involves or proposes: 1) mutual learning between users and designers about their respective fields, 2) the use of tools in the design process that are familiar to the users, 3) envisionment of future work situations to allow the users to experience how emerging technologies may affect the work practice, and 4) the importance of starting the design process in practice for the users [10] (referred to in [11]).

The original purpose of PD was emancipatory, to empower workers by involving them in the development of new systems for the workplace. Since then, PD has been applied to the development of systems outside the work context, such as leisure activities, entertainment and social service provision [11]. As the design focus of PD has evolved, the understanding of what PD is may also have changed. Nowadays, PD can be understood as a "practice of collective creativity" and it is rather called *co-design* or *co-creation* [12] (p. 7).

A major impact of participatory design or co-design concerns the roles of the stakeholders, namely the user, researcher and designer [12]. The users become co-designers, and active and creative participants, to some extent at least. The researcher changes from a translator of information between the users and the designer to a facilitator who encourages and allows people's expressions of creativity at all levels. And, even if the user is a co-designer, there is a specific place for the professional designer, whose expertise on design thinking and contextual issues (technologies, production processes, business) is needed even more than before in order to solve global, systemic problems.

Sanders and Stappers [12] note that today, co-design is very market-oriented and even an elite project with the focus on the "lead users". The original idea of PD, of emancipation and empowering the user to influence her or his living and working environment, has been somewhat blurred under such design ideas as open innovation or user-driven innovation with direct business aims. Co-design of products and services is a positive trend in production and business, but PD and empowering the user also have greater potential to help people to understand large-scale socio-technological changes and their expected impacts, and, in particular, to influence them.

2.3   Value Sensitive Design

Value Sensitive Design (VSD) is a widely known method for ethical design of technology [13, 14]. VSD provides a framework into which to integrate human values with ethical imports to design systematically and from different perspectives. 'Value' is broadly defined as something that a person or group considers important in life [14]. However, VSD states that certain values are universally held, although they may manifest themselves in various forms in different cultures and times.

The iterative methodology provided by VSD includes conceptual, empirical and technical research and evaluation work. The process starts with the conceptual phase, the purpose of which is to identify the design stakeholders and their values, in addition to those stakeholders that interact with the designed technology directly or indirectly. The central values are also conceptually defined; for instance, what is meant by trust, on what does trust depend and how can trust be operationalised as concretely as possible? Next, the empirical phase concentrates on identifying and evaluating how the central values are implemented in practice in activities and interactions with people and systems. Finally, in the technical phase, the properties and background mechanisms of technology are studied to understand how they either support or hinder the implementation of certain values. This phase also includes anticipative, technical design that supports the integration of the central values into the design results.

Value lists can be used to support and guide design in a heuristic manner [14]. Typical values include human wellbeing, freedom of bias with regard to technical or social issues, accountability for one's own actions and thoughtfulness. Several of the values named by Friedman and her colleagues relate to privacy and data handling.

The original idea of VSD that certain values are universal has raised discussion among researchers. For instance, Borning and Muller [15] argue that this statement impedes adopting VSD by researchers and designers. They suggest that VSD should accept the idea of pluralism, i.e. the simultaneous existence of several alternative values. VSD should endeavour to contextualise the expressions of values in different ways, for instance when using value lists as a tool or writing research reports.

VSD may also be difficult to apply in practice because the methods of VSD do not provide concrete guidance for how to integrate ethics in design. Huldtgren [16] asks whether a "design team need[s] to include a social scientist or someone trained in the [VSD] methods above to be able to carry out VSD" (p. 87). Expertise on ethics is not always easily acquired in industry, and the role of "value advocates" may be difficult [17]. To support overcoming this problem, Huldtgren helpfully provides some practical questions to be considered when using VSD in practice, such as "Which values are important in a given design case?", "Whose values are they?" and "Which methods are suited to discover, elicit and define values?" [16] (p. 88).

2.4   Human-Driven Design and Research

The framework for *Human-Driven Design and Research* (HDDR) [4] has been formulated in the context of ICT development projects for developing countries. Here, one important question is how to balance the pull exerted by local wants and aspirations with the push from global institutional and technological forces.

Braund and Schwittay [4] argue for focusing on real human needs when using ICT and point out that there must be "room for possibility that for certain groups ICT is not (at least at the moment) an appropriate solution to their problems". The response by HDDR to this call is that it is being driven by in-depth knowledge about local conditions gained from long-term human-centred research and a participatory community design process. HDDR recognises that the success of ICT development needs understanding and action in all four dimensions: local practices, a participatory design process, sociocultural contexts and political conditions. For instance, attempts to involve the community in development projects (participatory action) may fail because the necessary preconditions for the involvement to take place are not created (e.g., local practices, political conditions).

HDDR sees the importance of technology in improving the conditions of human life but simultaneously recognises that technology can become just "another tool of political, economic and social exclusion". To prevent this, HDDR promotes multidimensional collaboration and listening to all the stakeholders in the development.

HDDR and HDD seem to grow from the same ground; only the context of design is different. In developing countries, HDDR probably needs to deal with much stronger conflicts between Western economic culture, and local needs and culture. Otherwise, both share the concern of how to make local people heard and empowered by the design process and result. Furthermore, both focus on the question of how to integrate ICT into people's lives so that it makes a meaningful difference.

2.5   Life-Based Design

The responsibility of design, the justification for technology and the question of 'good technology' are essential aspects of HDD thinking for which we draw theoretical strength from *Life-Based Design* (LBD). This is a multi-dimensional and holistic approach to the design of technology and the information society developed in [7] and [18, 19, 20]. LBD calls for understanding the true value of technology as a means to the ultimate target of improving the quality of human life: what technology could really offer people and in what forms and on what terms it would be welcomed and adopted.

LBD emphasises a holistic understanding of human life as the foundation of the design: life is conceptualised and analysed from different perspectives (biological, psychological, socio-cultural) as *Forms of Life* that technology should support and advance in order to enhance quality of life. Forms of Life analysis paves the way for concept design (e.g. by practicing HCD).

Concepts are further exposed to *Fit-for-Life* analysis that examines the ethicality of the design solutions and the benefit and meaningfulness that users can receive from the solutions that are developed and how these can be improved for better quality of life. Finally, the phase of innovation design defines a procedure for creating usage cultures and exporting the outcome for general use.

In short, LBD is an approach that involves the concepts of human life sciences through the span of the design of technology and the information society in general: from (e.g. ethically reflected) ideas to (collaboratively designed) concepts to technology use and its impacts on quality of life and usage cultures [7]. For HDD, LBD offers the ground framework with holistic research paradigms for organising design thinking and carrying out research and design activities.

2.6   Summary

We have used the five frameworks described above – Human-Centred Design, Participatory Design, Value Sensitive Design, Human-Driven Design and Research, and Life-Based Design – to build our understanding of what *Human-Driven Design* is, in particular, what the central principles of the approach are (Table 1). First of all, HDD takes a perspective of the human and her or his values, the living and working environment, and other conditions of human life as a starting point in the design. Second, the users and other stakeholders are not just identified and recognised in the design process but involved as active participants in the design to the extent that the presupposed roles of the researcher and designer change, and all the participants are empowered. Finally, HDD goes beyond designing 'just' a product, service or system. HDD includes a larger, perhaps societal, point of view. We call this characteristic 'responsibility'. It expresses itself in different ways as promoting social and economic sustainability, and ethical and moral values.

Table 1. Principles of HDD design based on the five influential frameworks

Design approach	Principles of human-driven approach		
	Human and social view	Participation	Responsibility
Human-Centred Design	Human perspective on iterative design	Participatory approach to involve users and other stakeholders in the design	Direct support for social and economic sustainability
Participatory Design	Empowering users (as workers, co-creators and co-designers)	Involving users throughout all the phases of the design	Advances democracy and equality between people
Value Sensitive Design	Integrates human values into design	All stakeholders' values are identified and recognised	Promotes values with ethical and moral import
Human-Driven Design and Research	ICT as a tool to make a meaningful difference	Emphasis on local practices and empowering people	Awareness of conflicts of interests between stakeholders in development
Life-Based Design	Justification for technology: to improve quality of life. Understanding of human life as the foundation of the design	Concept design is based on the analysis of a form of life, supplemented by ideation, reflection and elaboration of solutions with users	Reflections of real human needs. Analysis of fit for life and long-term impacts. Value and ethicality of design solutions

3   Reflecting Human-Driven Design

We now elaborate on the three principles of HDD: the human and social perspective on design, participation and responsibility. We also illustrate these principles with some practical experiences and methods. The purpose of this chapter is to help other practitioners in the HCI/HTI field to recognise and reflect on how they can apply (parts of) HDD to their own work, either in the design of emerging technologies for the future society or in other contexts.

3.1   Human and Social View

HDD promotes a human perspective on technology design in a profound way: technology should make a meaningful difference, and the justification for technology should be to improve quality of life. A true ICT society should be examined and developed through human dimensions and the concept of quality of life. In current HTI design, usage situations are too often the main area of concentration, while ignoring the real needs that arise out of people's needs. Access to and usability of technology do not yet imply use, however, and use does not necessarily imply meaningful use. A successful solution creation process needs to look at technology as one possible enabler and not as the default tool [21]. HDD thus applies methods to understanding social and cultural settings for the development of emerging technologies and how to assess the meaningfulness of technology for the user. These refer to values, expectations, beliefs and practices that also influence the way individuals interpret the world and technology. They have significant influence on the individual's involvement in technology and on the way a community is able to make use of technology (see, e.g., [22]).

The Fit-for-Life design [19], for example, is a method (under development) to test the meaningfulness of a technology concept – its fit in the lives of future users to ensure that it will enhance the quality of life. The method should be applied after the concept design phase, before proceeding to the implementation. The Fit-for-Life analysis refers to re-checking the concept against the human requirements defined in earlier design phases (e.g., through the holistic Form-of-Life analysis). At the same time, the requirements should be reflected for the needs of the implementation phase. If there is a mismatch between the concept and the requirements, the concept should be refined.

3.2   Participation

HDD seeks users' active, co-creative involvement throughout the design span. The other stakeholders such as technology developers and service providers are of equal importance. HDD could be described in the words of Marc Steen [3]: with all stakeholders, HDD aims to *"engage in a dialogue in which we can learn from each other, and jointly explore and articulate ideas about needs we can try to solve"*, and moreover *"create a setting in which different people contribute their skills and ideas so that we can jointly explore, envision and evaluate ideas, concepts and new products"* (p. 15).

To illustrate the participatory aspect of HDD, we present four example co-design approaches developed or applied by us as a HCI/HTI research team. Our aim has been to develop human-driven methodology in which participation in design occurs close to the real use context and as intertwined with everyday life, similarly to Ikonen et al. [23]. Human-driven methods set a low threshold for participation but aim to bring value for all stakeholders. The methods seek to provide optional ways to contribute and encourage creativity and informal interaction, and enable agile gathering and analysing of data as well as support for iterative development.

IHME - an Open, Public Showroom and Co-design Environment. In 2010, we designed and implemented an open, public technology showroom and co-design environment in small commercial premises in a shopping centre [24]. The purpose of the showroom was to demonstrate an open, low-threshold co-design environment in which different stakeholders of technology design could meet and learn from each other. The place opened its doors to attract shoppers and other passers-by to pop into the premises to familiarise themselves with the latest advancements in ICT (namely, 3D television, augmented reality, virtual travelling, etc.) and to participate in user studies. Two employees worked at the premises full time to show visitors around, interview them and organise questionnaire studies. The showroom was open for two months in the summer of 2010, during which time it had approximately 2500 visitors. The feedback from the visitors was positive: the environment was considered fun, informative, interesting and easy to approach.

Owela – A Social Media Platform for Co-design. Another method that we have developed and systematically apply for easy involvement in design is the online platform 'Owela' (Open Web Lab), built on social media-type interaction, which thus enables user participation regardless of time and place [25]. This platform provides tools and methods (discussion, polls, voting, online chatting, etc.) for understanding users' needs and experiences as well as innovating and designing new products and services together. The platform enables different levels of participation based on the users' own interests and provides scoring tools to reward and motivate the participants. The advantage of online co-design is that all the developers have real time access to user feedback without intermediaries. The developers have an easy option to ask questions directly to the users. This supports reciprocal understanding between the users and developers.

Visual IHME – A Visual Online Platform for Co-designing Places. The aforementioned method, Owela, has been further developed towards a more visual co-design platform that utilises realistic images of places. This platform provides a photo-based, interactive spherical panorama environment with a set of easy-to-use co-design interaction tools such as discussion boards, questionnaires and polls on the screen (on the panorama image). All user-created content can be pinned to specific spatial spots on the image. The platform can be used for HDD purposes to study and co-design indoor and outdoor places, i.e. for understanding, co-creating and sharing meanings bound to or growing from specific locations. In this sense, the platform can be used, for instance, to promote sustainable behaviour [26, 27].

Living Lab. Other 'human-driven' methods are those in which participation is embedded in the routines and practices of the user in a long-term manner – so-called Living Labs. Our most recent Living Lab case focused on the development of future postal services. The Living Lab was based on a small village, and the participant households (approximately half of the village) committed to the iterative co-design and development process for several months. A variety of methods from household and individual interviews and questionnaires to co-design sessions with group dialogical methods and Owela were utilised. The Living Lab community seemingly benefited from the social agenda and the technical platforms set by the Living Lab, as the participants were encouraged to meet each other and collaborate for the common goals of the Living Lab.

3.3   Responsibility

HDD goes beyond the design of products and systems to the wellbeing of people and sustainability. In this sense, HDD can be part of the emerging activity of responsible innovation (RRI, Responsible Research and Innovation). RRI refers to "a transparent, interactive process by which societal actors and innovators become mutually responsive to each other with a view on the (ethical) acceptability, sustainability and societal desirability of the innovation process and its marketable products" [28]. We suggest *by design* thinking here, in order to promote responsibility in design outcomes, e.g. "Ethics by design" is a model to integrate consideration of ethical issues deeply into the technology development process from the early phase so that ethics is not an external part of a development project but rather an ongoing dialogue throughout the development span [29].

Ethics by Design. During the last decade, we have participated as HCI/HTI researchers in research focusing on the ethics of emerging ICTs and, for instance, developed ethical guidelines for mobile-centric ambient intelligence [30]. With regard to emerging ICTs, we have noticed a need for thinking and practices aimed at a positive ethical contribution in system design [cf. 29]. Ethical principles and questions should work as sources of innovation for designing ethically sound concepts. This thinking can be called ethics by design, extending from Marc van Lieshout and colleagues' model of privacy by design [31].

In ethics by design, ethical considerations are involved from the very beginning of the development process and embedded through the process. All stakeholders including technology developers, direct users and indirect users are involved in ethical deliberation through representatives, e.g. in focus groups. In addition, to ensure sufficiently deep understanding of ethical issues, ethical experts can work for the project, either as internal project workers or as an external expert board. Ethics is also included at the user end so that the user experience of ethicality of design outcomes is considered.

Sustainability by Design. Here, sustainability is defined with regard to sustainable development "that meets the needs of the present without compromising the ability of future generations to meet their own needs" [32]. A common view is to consider sustainability along three dimensions that focus on environmental, social and economic long-term consequences.

Within HCI, research related to environmental sustainability, in particular, has expanded in recent years. In 2007, Jennifer Mankoff and colleagues introduced several pathways for HCI to contribute to the well-being of the environment [33]. Once again, we have paid special attention to the *sustainability by (through) design* perspective. This view considers ways to support sustainable lifestyles and decision-making through the design of technology. Sustainability by design sees technology as a "channel for intervention in the everyday decisions and mindsets" [33] that, partly, underlies environmental problems. In line with this, we have developed a visual, online co-design tool to provide easy ways to co-create and share meanings in regard to physical environments and, in this way, encourage shifting the users' practices toward sustainability (see Section 3.2 and [27]).

4   Discussion

This paper presents an attempt to collect and elaborate on principles for a human-driven approach to technology and interaction design. Based on the well-known frameworks of design such as Human-Centred Design, Participatory Design and Value Sensitive Design, Human-Driven Design takes human and social values profoundly into account and aims to take real human needs as a starting point of the design. HDD endorses participation and empowering of users and other stakeholders by developing and applying co-design methods, of which we have provided examples. The general aim of HDD should be to involve people in the design of emerging technologies and human-technology interaction concepts so that their needs and values become articulated in the design process. At the same time, the process should include reflection on ethical and sustainability terms. HDD also promotes responsible research and innovation, e.g., in the forms of ethics by design and sustainability by design. In fact, HDD can be seen as an attempt to take the framework of responsible research and innovation (e.g. [28]) in practice.

We have developed HDD thinking in the context of designing emerging technologies, that is, technologies that are currently being developed and that hold realistic potential to become widely adopted within the next 10 to 20 years [34]. This includes concepts like ambient intelligence, ubiquitous computing, autonomous systems, emotional computing, service robotics and convergence of ICT with other technologies, e.g. nanotechnology or human implants. In addition to the human and social view, participation and responsibility, HDD should try to understand the future contexts in which certain technology would be embedded. Arguably, HCI has capitalised very little on systematic methods of futures thinking, although this could "prepare us for problems that have not yet arrived, enable the 'invention' of a better future, or increase the long-term impact of our work" [35, p. 1629]. Our next step is to study relevant methods to gain an insight into the future, especially in terms of human and social behaviour and societal trends, i.e. to study *human-driven foresight*. This step is necessary for us to be able to formulate HDD as a useful alternative design approach to emerging ICTs that is deeply based on respecting human values and needs as well as sustainability.

Acknowledgements. We would like to thank the reviewers for their helpful comments. This work has been funded by the GREAT project (EU FP7/grant agreement no. 321480) and supported by the VTT Design for Life innovation program.

References

1. Bannon, L.: Reimagining HCI: toward a more human-centered perspective. Interactions 18(4), 50–57 (2011)
2. Friedland, B., Yamauchi, Y.: Reflexive design thinking: putting more human in human-centered practices. Interactions 18(2), 66–71 (2011)
3. Steen, M.: The fragility of human-centred design. Doctoral Thesis, Delft University of Technology (2008)
4. Braund, P., Schwittay, A.: The Missing Piece: Human Driven Design and Research in ICT and Development. In: Proceedings of the International Conference on Information and Communications Technologies and Development, May 25-26, pp. 2–10 (2006)
5. Ikonen, V.: Towards empowering design practices. In: Proceedings of the Ambient Intelligence Forum 2008, Hradec Králové, CZ, October 15-16, pp. 132–139 (2008)
6. Norros, L., Kaasinen, E., Plomp, J., Rämä, P.: Human-Technology Interaction Research and Design. VTT Roadmap, VTT Industrial Systems, Espoo (2003)
7. Leikas, J.: Life-Based Design - A holistic approach to designing human-technology interaction. VTT Publications 726, Edita Prima Oy, Helsinki (2009),
   http://www.vtt.fi/inf/pdf/publications/2009/P726.pdf
8. ISO: Ergonomics of human-system interaction. Part 210: Human-centred design for interactive systems, ISO 9241-210:2010 (2010)
9. Bohn, J., Coroama, V., Langheinrich, M., Mattern, F., Rohs, M.: Living in a World of Smart Everyday Objects – Social, Economic, and Ethical Implications. Journal of Human and Ecological Risk Assessment 10(5), 763–786 (2004)
10. Greenbaum, J., Kyng, M.: Design at work: Cooperative design of computer systems. CRC (1991)
11. Holone, H., Herstad, J.: Three Tensions in Participatory Design for Inclusion. In: Proceedings of the SIGCHI Conference on Human Factors in Computing Systems, Paris, France, pp. 2903–2906. ACM, New York (2013)
12. Sanders, E.B.-N., Stappers, P.J.: Co-creation and the new landscapes of design. Co-Design: International Journal of CoCreation in Design and the Arts 4(1), 5–18 (2008)
13. Friedman, B., Kahn Jr., P.H.: Human values, ethics, and design. In: Jacko, J.A., Sears, A. (eds.) The Human-Computer Interaction Handbook, pp. 1177–1201. Lawrence Erlbaum Associates, Mahwah (2003)
14. Friedman, B., Kahn, P.H.: Jr., Borning, A.: Value Sensitive Design and information systems. In: Zhang, P., Galletta, D. (eds.) Human-Computer Interaction in Management Information Systems: Foundations, pp. 348–372. M.E. Sharpe, London (2006)
15. Borning, A., Muller, M.: Next steps for value sensitive design. In: Proceedings of the SIGCHI Conference on Human Factors in Computing Systems, pp. 1125–1134. ACM, New York (2013)
16. Huldtgren, A.: Addendum: Practical Considerations of Value Sensitive Design. In: Doorn, N., Schuurbiers, D., van de Poel, I., Gorman, M.E. (eds.) Early Engagement and New Technologies: Opening Up the Laboratory, pp. 85–95. Springer, Dordrecht (2013)

17. Manders-Huits, N., Zimmer, M.: Values and Pragmatic Action: The Challenges of Introducing Ethical Intelligence in Technical Design Communities. International Review of Information Ethics 10, 37–44 (2009)
18. Leikas, J., Saariluoma, P., Rousi, R., Kuisma, E., Vilpponen, H.: Life-based design to combat loneliness among older people. Journal of Community Informatics 8, 1 (2012), http://ci-journal.net/index.php/ciej/article/view/778/890
19. Leikas, J., Saariluoma, P., Heinilä, J., Ylikauppila, M.: A Methodological Model for Life-Based Design. International Review of Social Sciences and Humanities (IRSSH) 4(2), 118–136 (2013), http://irssh.com/yahoo_site_admin/assets/docs/11_IRSSH-415-V4N2.44203734.pdf
20. Saariluoma, P., Leikas, J.: Life-Based Design – an approach to design for life. Global Journal of Management and Business Research (GJMBR) 10(5), 17–23 (2010), http://journalofbusiness.org/index.php/GJMBR/article/view/199/174
21. Datye, S.: Life-Based Design for Technical Solutions in Social and Voluntary Work. Jyväskylä University Printing House, Jyväskylä (2012)
22. Pinkett, R.: Bridging the Digital Divide: Sociocultural Constructionism and an Asset-Based Approach to Community Technology and Community Building. In: 81st Annual Meeting of the American Educational Research Association (2000)
23. Kaasinen, E., Koskela-Huotari, K., Ikonen, V., Niemelä, M., Näkki, P.: Three approaches to co-creating services with users. In: Proceedings 4th International Conference on Applied Human Factors and Ergonomics, San Francisco, USA, July 21-25 (2012)
24. Ikonen, V., Hakulinen, J., Kivinen, T., Aloja, M., Hokkanen, L., Ruutikainen, P., Kymäläinen, T., Nelimarkka, M., Harrela, A.: IHME = Miracle - Make, Imagine and Research Applications for Computerised Living Environments. In: Proceedings of the 14th International Academic MindTrek Conference: Envisioning Future Media Environments, Tampere, Finland, pp. 3–6 (2010)
25. Näkki, P., Antikainen, M.: Online tools for co-design: user involvement through the innovation process. In: Karahasanovic, A., Følstad, A. (eds.) The NordiCHI 2008 Workshops: New Approaches to Requirements Elicitation & How Can HCI Improve Social Media Development? Tapir Akademiskforlag, Trondheim, pp. 92–97 (2008)
26. Niemelä, M., Kivinen, T., Kulju, M., Tammela, A., Ikonen, V., Korhonen, H.: Visual IHME: co-designing meaningful places for sustainability. In: IADIS Interfaces and Human-Computer Interaction Conference, Czech Republic, July 22-24 (2013)
27. Niemelä, M., Kivinen, T., Kulju, M., Tammela, A., Ikonen, V., Korhonen, H.: Visual IHME: co-designing meaningful places for sustainability. In: Isaías, P., Blashki, K. (eds.) Human-Computer Interfaces and Interactivity: Emergent Research and Applications. IGI Global (in press)
28. Von Schomberg, R. (ed.): Towards Responsible Research and Innovation in the Information and Communication Technologies and Security Technologies Fields. Publication Office of the European Union, Luxembourg (2011), http://ec.europa.eu/research/science-society/document_library/pdf_06/mep-rapport-2011_en.pdf
29. Guardian Angels: FET Flagship pilot, final report (July 2012), public version (2012), http://www.ga-project.eu/files/content/sites/guardians-angels-neutre/files/pdf/Guardian_Angels_Final_Report_July_2012.pdf

30. Ikonen, V., Kaasinen, E., Niemelä, M.: Defining Ethical Guidelines for Ambient Intelligence Applications on a Mobile Phone. In: Workshops Proceedings of the 5th International Conference on Intelligent Environments, Barcelona, ES, pp. 261–268. IOS Press, Amsterdam (2009)
31. van Lieshout, M., Kool, L., van Schoonhoven, B., de Jonge, M.: Privacy by Design: an alternative to existing practice in safeguarding privacy. Info 13(6), 55–68 (2011)
32. World Commission on Environment and Development: Our Common Future (Brundtland Report). Oxford University Press, Oxford (1987)
33. Mankoff, J., Blevis, E., Borning, A., Friedman, B., Fussell, S.R., Hasbrouck, J., Sengers, P., Woodroff, A.: Environmental sustainability and interaction. In: Proceedings of the SIGCHI Conference on Human Factors in Computing Systems, San Jose, CA, USA, pp. 2121–2124. ACM, New York (2007)
34. Stahl, B.C., Heersmink, R., Goujon, P., Flick, C., van de Hoven, J., Wakunuma, K., Ikonen, V., Rader, M.: Issues, Concepts and Methods Relating to the Identification of the Ethics of Emerging ICTs. Communications of the IIMA 10(1) (2010)
35. Mankoff, J., Rode, J.A., Faste, H.: Looking past yesterday's tomorrow: using future studies methods to extend the research horizon. In: Proceedings of the SIGCHI Conference on Human Factors in Computing Systems, Paris, France, pp. 1629–1638. ACM, New York (2013)

Slow Tech: The Bridge between Computer Ethics and Business Ethics

Norberto Patrignani[1] and Diane Whitehouse[2]

[1] Politecnico of Torino, Italy and Uppsala University, Sweden
norberto.patrignani@polito.it
[2] The Castlegate Consultancy, UK
diane.whitehouse@thecastlegateconsultancy.com

Abstract. This paper addresses the difficult task of implementing the concept of Slow Tech, that is, information and communication technology (ICT) that is good, clean and fair, in a business environment. It investigates the democratic, environmental, and social challenges currently facing ICT vendors. More specifically, it examines the opportunities available for these companies to use Slow Tech as a bridging mechanism between their Computer Ethics and their Business Ethics strategies, based on Corporate Social Responsibility. Last but not least, it highlights what some "next step" questions for further investigation and implementation might be and the challenges of implementing these.

Keywords: Business Ethics, Computer Ethics, Corporate Social Responsibility, Information and Communication Technology (ICT), Slow Tech.

1 Introduction

Today, internationally as well as in Europe, large-scale corporations are getting ready for the next phase in social, economic and environmental developments by preparing appropriate corporate social responsibility strategies. Information and communication technology (ICT) vendors are a specific case in point: they sell large quantities of technologies which are currently helping to re-shape society through resulting significant social and environmental changes.

Largely in response to policy and regulatory changes, some large ICT companies are now filing social and environmental balance sheets in addition to completing their annual financial reports. However, very few ICT vendors currently consider the computer ethics side of their businesses even while they are beginning to adopt the notion of corporate social responsibility: even fewer undertake social and environmental audits of the ICT that they sell. For the sake of consistency, ICT vendors should begin to examine their own business and investigate the specific ethical, environmental and social impacts of the products and services they provide to their customers.

Thus, this paper suggests that ICT vendors should be among the first companies that start to develop an applied ethics that examines the ethical challenges related to

K.K. Kimppa et al. (Eds.): HCC11 2014, IFIP AICT 431, pp. 92–106, 2014.

computers, i.e., computer ethics. It proposes Slow Tech as a tool to facilitate companies' efforts to analyse the ethical, environmental, and social impacts of the ICT that they design, develop, produce, and sell. Whenever business ethics is used as a form of applied ethics that examines the ethical challenges that arise in a given business scenario, Slow Tech is able to provide a suitable bridge between those computer ethics and business ethics.

The paper is structured so as to introduce Slow Tech as a concept, and describe briefly its relationship with Slow Food. This introduction is followed by a discussion of the role of computer ethics and business ethics in today's society. In particular, the paper outlines the relationship between business ethics and corporate social responsibility. It then examines the formal annual reporting processes of ICT vendors: it shows how these vendors are increasingly responding to requests to make public their corporate social responsibilities, and yet are still doing so in quite limited ways. It highlights a number of important challenges for the ICT industry, and indicates in what way this industry might take a number of steps on the journey to becoming more Slow Tech. While the paper takes an optimistic view of the opportunities that lie ahead, it does not shirk from facing the challenges that are implicit in beginning this new way of thinking and acting.

2   Slow Tech and Its Parallels to Slow Food

Some forms of Slow Tech have been around for at least a decade (Hallnäs and Redström, 2001; Price, 2009). These earlier approaches either considered designing Slow Tech to be about the creation of periods of reflection and mental rest (Hallnäs and Redström, 2001) or they focused on the need for robust engineering practices (Price, 2009). Since 2010, the Slow Tech notion has been further revised and refined (Patrignani, 2010; Patrignani and Whitehouse, 2013).

Today, Slow Tech is being re-formulated as a concept that invites people to reflect on the social and environmental impacts of ICT (Patrignani and Whitehouse, 2013; Whitehouse and Patrignani, 2013). It encourages concentration on the entire technology value chain, i.e., the whole chain of activities performed to create ICT products and services. This contemporary version of Slow Tech proposes that ethical ICT should have three characteristics: it should be *good*, *clean* and *fair*. There three terms - good, clean and fair - explicitly replay the Slow Food movement's appeal to reflect on the whole food-chain, so as to ensure that food should be: of *good* quality, *clean* (it should respect the environment, promote biodiversity and sustainability) and *fair* (i.e., the cultivation and production of food must respect the rights of farmers) (Petrini, 2007; 2011). In other words, *good* ICT is based around notions of human-centredness, user involvement, participatory design, enjoyment, aesthetics, and a balance between work and home life. *Clean* ICT means taking into consideration the environmental impacts (such as materials and energy consumption) of the manufacture, use and disposal of ICT products. *Fair* ICT means ensuring fairness and equity of the conditions of workers throughout the entire supply chain. Detailed explanations of the basics of Slow Tech are outlined in other papers (Patrignani and Whitehouse, 2013; Whitehouse and Patrignani, 2013).

Slow Tech should not be misunderstood as an appeal necessarily for technology to "go slow". Rather, in terms of the ICT industry, it should be seen as a plea for its these three aspects of concern - goodness, cleanliness, and fairness - to be viewed holistically rather than each being addressed in very different ways, and separately. Slow Tech should be viewed as a proposal to look at ICT in a new, more holistic, manner that represents an innovative approach to technology for the 21st century.

3   Computer Ethics and Business Ethics

In terms of the holism with which ICT should now be regarded, it is important to examine both computer ethics and business ethics. While a trend against technological determinism was already evident in the 1930s, these two ethical domains, computer ethics and business ethics, have developed most swiftly since the 1970s over a similar time-horizon although largely separately. These two ethical domains show certain similarities: in particular, their current focus is on stakeholder collaboration and the co-shaping of technology and society by people themselves.

On the one hand, computer ethics has possibly been more limited in its sphere than business ethics. While academe has shown considerable interest in it, at least some computer societies have applied its principles. On the other hand, business ethics has been taken up rather more obviously: this is perhaps due to its commercial setting or because of the many ethical and behavioural weaknesses in business that have been so publicly pointed out over the last decade and a half. This uptake has occurred on the part of at least three distinct sectors: academe, business organisations and associations, and policy fora.

Now is the time to examine the similarities and synergies between the two fields of ethics and, as appropriate, to bring the two forms of ethics together. This section of the paper concentrates on a comparison of computer ethics and business ethics.

Computer Ethics
Writing in rejection of technological determinism was evident at least since the 1930s on the part of several philosophers and social scientists. See, for example, the work of such writers as Lewis Mumford and Jacques Ellul (Mumford, 1934; Ellul, 1954). Yet, it was Norbert Wiener - a professor at the Massachusetts Institute of Technology (MIT) - who was probably the first scientist to reflect on the social and ethical impacts of computers, with his recommendation to shift "from know how to know what" (Wiener, 1950). The first research engineer to follow up on Wiener's ideas was Donn Parker with his *Rules of Ethics in Information Processing* (Parker, 1968). Joseph Weizenbaum, another professor at MIT, described the risks related to the use of computers for military applications (Weizenbaum, 1976). However, the term "computer ethics" was used for the first time in 1978 by Walter Maner in his taught course, the notes from which were eventually published as a *Starter Kit in Computer Ethics* (Maner, 1980). A later description of computer ethics was introduced by James

Moor (Moor, 1985). It was based on a perceived lack of policy and guidance in terms of the use of computers: "... *there is a policy vacuum about how computer technology should be used. ... A central task of Computer Ethics is to determine what we should do in such cases, that is, formulate policies to guide our actions* ..." (Moor, 1985, p.1). This description of computer ethics was focused on the end-uses of ICT and on the social and ethical implications of this use. At this period, some 30 years ago, the role of the ICT industry - itself at the very core of the information technology development process - did not appear to be questioned. Following the work of Deborah Johnson, which took place around the same time, it was, however, realised that "... *technology is not just artifacts, but rather artifacts embedded in social practices and infused with social meaning*" (Johnson, 1985, p.16). This shift in thinking enabled a new way of looking at ICT systems as socio-technical systems: a context in which technology and society shape each other. This focus on co-shaping means that people have the opportunity to steer technology developments in different directions: they are not bound by a framework of technological determinism.

It is precisely in the field of computer ethics that Slow Tech can play a fundamental role, by creating a positive form of computer ethics rather than one which has a negative orientation. Slow Tech offers a potential enlargement of the scope of analysis, and application, of computer ethics by including the entire ICT value chain: thus, it covers both the development process of ICT as well as its use. Slow Tech's view of ICT ranges from the extraction and processing of raw materials, and ICT manufacturing processes, through to responsible renewal, recycling and disposal. The supply chain does not start in the warehouse or the store. This stance is particularly valid for ICT vendor organisations because, today, they are the main actors involved in designing, developing, producing, and selling computer technologies.

Business Ethics

The classical definition of business ethics is "... *the applied ethics discipline that addresses the moral features of commercial activity*" (Marcoux, 2008). This form of applied ethics tries to provide answers to such difficult questions as: "Is the corporation a moral agent? How and in whose interests ought the corporation to be governed?" In terms of the establishment of its associations and societies, business ethics has appeared only relatively recently on both sides of the Atlantic. The Society for Business Ethics was founded in the United States in 1980 by Richard De George, while in Europe the European Business Ethics Network was launched in 1987.

Yet, for at least the last forty years, a vigorous debate has taken place in both American and European business schools about the role of the corporations in society. On the one hand, the work of Milton Friedman was concentrated on shareholder theory, in which the mission of the corporation is to maximise profit for a company's shareholders (Friedman, 1970). On the other hand, Edward R. Freeman's work was based on stakeholder theory, where business ought to be managed in such a way that it achieves a balance among the interests of all who bear a substantial relationship to the firm - the firm's stakeholders. According to Freeman (1984), the purpose of the corporation is its joint service to its stakeholders.

However, discussion about computer ethics and business ethics does not only take place in business schools. A parallel discussion has been conducted in the business world, and has been articulated in the field of European and international policy: it is called corporate social responsibility.

4   Corporate Social Responsibility

Corporate social responsibility is a form of corporate self-regulation, that is integrated into a company's business model. In other words, the policy of corporate social responsibility functions as a built-in, self-regulating mechanism that ensures compliance with prevailing legal and ethical standards and international norms (Wikipedia, 2014a).

Corporate social responsibility is in line with stakeholder theory, since it includes all those entities, groups and individuals on whom a corporation has an impact. It enables a profile to be drawn of the effects that a corporation has beyond its own shareholders. This wider, holistic picture includes employees, consumers, communities, and the environment. It is for this reason that the proponents of corporate social responsibility argue that organisations with this perspective are more able to make profits in the long-term. If a company that embraces a business ethics approach is willing to examine the ethical challenges that likely to arise as a result of the business scenarios that it is applying, then two actions will occur. It will extend its concerns beyond the strict interests of its shareholders, and it will have a strong corporate social responsibility strategy.

A number of policy bodies have taken up this concern with corporate social responsibility. This movement can be seen both in Europe, in the work of the European Commission, and more widely internationally in the context of the International Organization for Standardization (ISO). A preoccupation with corporate social responsibility has been present in European policy for over a decade. In the five-year period at the start of this century, the European Commission published two relevant policy documents (European Commission, 2006; 2011). More recently, the Commission has tightened up its concept of social responsibility relative to its earlier definition. In a 2011 Communication, it defines it directly as "*the responsibility of enterprises for their impacts on society*" (European Commission, 2011, p.6). This policy document also states that, to fully meet their social responsibility, enterprises "*... should have in place a process to integrate social, environmental, ethical human rights and consumer concerns into their business operations and core strategy in close collaboration with their stakeholders*" (Op cit, 2011, p.6). This Communication includes a set of eight recommendations, which range from awareness-raising to international discussion and collaboration. They form a list of corporate social responsibility guidelines or clauses. Similar statements occur in the ISO's voluntary guidelines, ISO 26000, launched in 2010 (ISO, 2010). Among others, these include:

- *principles of social responsibility* (accountability, transparency, ethical behaviour, respect for stakeholder interests, respect the rule of law, respect for international norms, respect for human rights);

- *fundamental practices of social responsibility* (recognising social responsibility, stakeholder identification and engagement);
- *social responsibility core subjects* (human rights, labour practices, the environment, fair operating practices, consumer issues, community involvement and development) (ISO, 2010).

Even though these guidelines are voluntary in character, they are beginning to influence the ways in which international, large-scale businesses view the importance of their corporate social responsibility.

5   ICT Vendors and Corporate Social Responsibility

ICT vendors constitute a specific category of firms within this corporate environment. They have a major influence over the shaping and co-shaping of the digital world in which a considerable proportion of the population of the planet currently lives. ICT vendors are members of a group of organisations that need to examine - in conjunction with all businesses - their business ethics generally. In addition, given the corporate sector in which they operate, they also particularly need to explore their computer ethics. This dual approach to both business ethics and computer ethics forms an integral part of ICT businesses' corporate social responsibility.

Given the growing importance of corporate social responsibility, 2014 provides an opportune moment to explore how this strategy is handled by ICT vendors. If an ICT vendor would like to develop a coherent and consistent corporate social responsibility strategy based on the triple bottom-line approach of "*profit, people, planet*" (Spreckley, 1981; Elkington, 1997; ORSE, 2010), then computers - or ICT in general - will have to be included in any analysis of the company's own behaviour.

The ICT market is made up of various components: it includes, among others, hardware, software, ICT services, networking devices, social networks, and e-commerce sites. This market is one of the most important at the global scale. In 2013, its value was estimated to be around 3,700 billion US dollars: in the 12-month period since, it has seen a slight increase of +4.2%, despite the financial and economic crisis (Gartner, 2013). The world's ICT companies have experienced a strong process of consolidation over the last decade. The few remaining competing firms have become, or are in the process of becoming, global giants. The 2013 ranking of ICT companies in terms of their revenues shows that the main ICT vendors are corporate behemoths. Table 1 shows the largest ICT vendors in terms of their 2013 revenue (Forbes, 2013), together with the official documentation related to their corporate social responsibility strategy.

For ICT vendors, it is clear that one critical success factor could be to articulate a strategy that stipulates their corporate social responsibility. The publicly available documentation of the largest international ICT companies (cited in Table 1) indicates that, for the majority of these corporations, corporate social responsibility means only developing a number of generic activities relating to social concerns, for example, by funding projects in various charitable areas. These companies appear to report very little activity that would have a direct impact on their responsibilities in terms of the ICT sector itself or that would address the very specific social and environmental challenges posed by their own companies in relation to ICT.

Table 1. Corporate Social Responsibility Reports in 2013 - Main ICT Vendors

Corporate Social Responsibility Reports in 2013 - Main ICT Vendors		
Company	*Revenues*[1]	*CSR public documentation*
Samsung	187.8 B$[2]	Sustainability Report 2013 (Samsung, 2013)
Apple	164.7 B$	Supplier Responsibility at Apple (Apple, 2013)
HP	118.7 B$	HP Global Citizenship Report (HP, 2013)
IBM	104.5 B$	Corporate Responsibility Report (IBM, 2013)
Sony	78.5 B$	Annual Report 2013 Business and CSR review (Sony, 2013)
Microsoft	72.9 B$	2013 Citizenship Report (Microsoft, 2013)
Amazon	61.1 B$	Amazon Smile (Amazon, 2013)
Dell	56.9 B$	The Dell 2020 Legacy of Good Plan (Dell, 2013)
Intel	53.3 B$	Intel 2012 Corporate Social Responsibility Report (Intel, 2013)
Google	50.2 B$	Who we are - Corporate Social Responsibility (Google, 2013)
Cisco	47.3 B$	Corporate Social Responsibility (Cisco, 2013)
Oracle	37.1 B$	Corporate Citizenship Report (Oracle, 2013)
SAP	20.9 B$	Corporate Social Responsibility (SAP, 2013)
Facebook	5.1 B$	_[3]

1. Source: (Forbes, 2013)
2. B$ represent a billion US dollar (1,000,000,000 USD)
3. The authors were unable to find ant official report or documentation about Facebook's strategy on CSR. This may be due to the relative youth of this company (Bacile, 2013), which was founded a decade ago in 2004. Yet the lack of a CSR strategy is also surprising since, by September 2012, it managed a social networ k of more than one billion users (Fowler, 2012).

While it is difficult to consolidate a single view of these very different companies in terms of their corporate social responsibility strategies, it is obvious that it is becoming more and more important for them to show - with a degree of transparency - to both their investors and their customers the factors that contribute to their economic results.

Some large ICT vendors - in particular in the ICT manufacturing area - do have their own codes of conduct. For example, the Electronics Industry Code of Conduct, a non-profit corporation established in 2009, states that it *"was established to ensure worker safety and fairness, environmental responsibility, and business efficiency"* (EICC, 2012, p.1). However, two years after the code was set up, many limitations were still found to these approaches due to the general lack of international standards, the low level of commitment, and a lack of verification and enforcement mechanisms (Martinuzzi et al., 2011). e-commerce sites and online retailing, as industries, have been scrutinised from an ethical perspective (Agag and Elbertagi, 2013). This study's findings demonstrate the importance of business ethics and corporate social responsibility for companies *"... ethical problems like security, privacy, reliability, non-deception and corporate social responsibility on [sic] Internet are core issues that limit the growth of online retailing"* (Op cit, 2013, p.15).

As can be seen from the above discussion, ICT vendor corporations have a special accountability in terms of society and the planet. Thus, their reporting should take a step beyond the traditional corporate social responsibility reporting of companies in other industries. In their corporate social responsibility strategy or, more generally, in their business ethics strategy, ICT vendors should also incorporate a computer ethics strategy. Presumably, developing such a stance on corporate ethical and social concerns would help them to improve the companies' performance, growth and profitability.

6   Slow Tech as a Bridge: Good, Clean and Fair ICT

Slow Tech is proposed as a tool for bridging the two fields of computer ethics and business ethics. It could ensure the incorporation of appropriate corporate social responsibility codes and behaviours for ICT vendors.

How precisely can Slow Tech (*good, clean,* and *fair* ICT) help ICT vendors in their definition of their triple bottom line (ORSE, 2010)? How can Slow Tech help in bridging business ethics and computer ethics? It can do so at three levels: it brings together in a succinct and straightforward manner the three notions of good, clean and fair with those of profit, planet and people. In Figure 1, a representation is provided of Slow Tech as a possible bridge between computer ethics and the classical corporate social responsibility triple bottom lines that are embedded in business ethics.

Figure 1 acts as a reminder that the basis of computer ethics has traditionally been about the use of ICT. Slow Tech widens that limited scope to explore the whole of the ICT value chain. The diagram shows that both Slow Tech and business ethics - in which corporate social responsibility is implicitly included - outline a trio of concerns. For Slow Tech, this triad is based around the three notions of good, clean and fair. The three notions incorporated in corporate social responsibility are profit, people and planet. In this figure, therefore, good ICT can be equated with the capacity to make a long-term profit; clean ICT is linked with the planet; and fair ICT is associated with people. Each of the three sets of relationships are explained below in more detail.

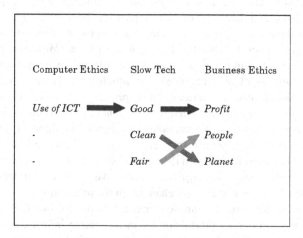

Fig. 1. Slow Tech as a Bridge between Computer Ethics and Business Ethics

Good ICT and Profit

Starting from the creation of a bridge between the ability to make a profit in the long-term - and hence to maintain financial sustainability - with a good form of ICT, good ICT is an ICT that should be human-centred. Thus human-computer interaction, and participatory design are the core starting requirements in ICT design. Good ICT should be designed by using either a design-for-all or an inclusive approach. Good ICT can therefore be associated with profitable i.e., financially sustainable ICT.

ICT that is desirable, and yet also financially sustainable, requires a continuous investment in innovation. Organisations that would like to stay at the forefront of ICT innovation need to design high-quality and advanced products. This ambition requires a considerable investment in knowledge-workers. Most ICT companies are aware that, in terms of achieving success, their work is founded on knowledge intensity, human capital, and investments in research and development (Martinuzzi et al., 2011). Being innovative means being able to attract talented personnel from around the globe, as part of those large industrial clusters and cooperative networks that include universities and research centres.

Innovation in ICT means being ready to develop a continually updated research agenda. In 2014, for example, it should include such areas as: Big Data, Intelligent System and Decision Support Systems (for which data scientists will be people highly requested by companies), Cloud Computing and Internet of Things (that aspect of the cloud based on the use of sensors), Information and Knowledge Management (the new web or network science), Organisational Models and Information Systems (which offer new roles for Chief Information Officers), Mobility (in which the vehicle, such as a car, is the computer), and Human-Computer Interaction (which might eventually mean bidding farewell to computer keyboards).

Clean ICT and Planet

For an ICT vendor, creating a bridge between clean ICT and the planet means undertaking a profound analysis of the impact of both hardware and software production, and their use and disposal. This clean approach takes into account those limits to growth that result from the limits of the planet (Meadows et al., 1972). Indeed the ICT sector could play a fundamental role in developing the domain of cleantech, that field of clean technology for which there is not yet any standard definition, yet which can be termed "*any product or services that improves operational performance, productivity, or efficiency while reducing cost, inputs, energy consumption, waste, or environmental pollution*" (Wikipedia, 2014b). Clean ICT could help people to minimise their consumption of conventional fossils fuels, and non-renewable materials (through de-materialisation), thereby reducing pollution. The reduction would occur by applying innovative science and technology and introducing new life-styles and cultural changes, in the long-term.

At the same time, this would mean two approaches: maximising the contribution of renewable resources in energy production by incorporating information technologies in new technological and organisational systems; and finding the most appropriate materials and form of energy by diffusing knowledge of cleantech. More specifically, ICT devices should be recyclable-by-design; their lifetime should be extended and lengthened; and interoperability standards between modules should be made mandatory.

Last but not least, the rebound effects of ICT should be analysed in-depth and clarified at all three levels of their impact. The first-order effect relates to resource and energy consumption, green-house gas production, and e-waste. The second-order effect to the impact of the continuing use of ICT, de-materialisation, e-procurement, tele-work, transactions speed, and transparency. The impact and opportunities created by the use of ICT by large numbers of people, their productivity, well-being, and lifestyles, are the third-order effect (Yi and Thomas, 2007). Further research is needed on the long-term sustainability of ICT since, as demonstrated in several simulation studies, there is a risk that the positive and negative effects of ICT may counterbalance each other: the rapidity of the development of ICT may induce more material and energy consumption and more e-waste generation (Hilty et al., 2006).

Fair ICT and People

Bridging fair ICT with the needs of people means that an ICT vendor needs to create transparency in the supply chain with regard to its employees' working conditions. In particular, the corporation should pay special attention to human rights. A company needs to ensure that human rights are respected, for examples, in the mines of Africa and those other countries that are the main sources of the materials (such as coltan and the rare-earths) used to build its computer equipment (Vazquez-Figueroa, 2010). It should commit to enforcing the respect of human rights, health, and safety of working conditions in all its suppliers' manufacturing and assembly plants, and ensuring that workers are not forced to undertake monotonous and repetitive tasks, or to work for very low wages. In other types of organisational context, the pressure of the work undertaken by knowledge workers should be counterbalanced by improvements in the quality of the work environment. Fair ICT should also include offering users the opportunity to change their ICT provider through the use of proper "spanning layers" with open interfaces. A fair ICT vendor should not lock its users and developers into "silos" that possess proprietary formats and application programming interfaces (Madrigal, 2012). The growth of the open data, open software, and open hardware movements are three examples of Slow Tech good practices.

One of the main features of Slow Tech as a tool is the improved capability of the corporation to design a complete stakeholders' network. For an ICT vendor this means the opportunity to identify both its downstream actors and its upstream actors. The stakeholders covered include not only those which are present after the vendor's products and service are released onto the market, but also those involved in the extraction and processing of raw materials, and in the manufacture of the ICT products. Key questions for ICT vendors - and for all other stakeholders in the ICT value chain - become not only where the technology itself comes from, but also their social and environmental costs. Being able to ask, and answer, these kinds of questions openly and transparently will initiate a means of approaching an innovative ethical, social and environmental good, clean and fair ICT for the 21st century.

7   Conclusions, Challenges and Next Steps

This paper starts with a discussion of the origin and development of Slow Tech, and its basic characteristics. It argues that Slow Tech can be broadened to provide a means of looking at ICT in a more holistic manner, by taking into account the extent to which the creation and sale of ICT services and products can be characterised as good, clean and fair. Thus, Slow Tech as an approach provides a specific business opportunity for the computer industry, especially for ICT vendors.

ICT vendors' challenge is how to ensure that, when they examine and test their own levels of corporate social responsibility, they concentrate far more than at present on their computer ethics. Thus, Slow Tech provides a tool for developing a more robust and comprehensive business ethics for ICT vendors. It enables them to construct a computer ethics strategy, which focuses on both the end-uses of computers and questions the technology in itself. This paper indicates how a bridge can be built between each of the three following notions: good ICT and profit - i.e., financial sustainability - or the achievement of profit in a financially sustainable way; clean ICT and planet; and fair ICT and people. Slow Tech does this in terms of providing a concept and overview of appropriate business ethics.

Challenges
Of course there are many challenges in building these bridges, both conceptually and in terms of implementation. In conceptual terms, the basic ideas behind Slow Tech mean thinking more holistically, more aesthetically, more sustainably, more democratically in an organisational sense - and ultimately less opportunistically, less egotistically, and less short-term - than perhaps many ICT companies have had the habit of doing. These conceptual shifts may prove to be a challenge for some of the more recently established corporations.

In practical term, the world-wide economic crisis that started around 2007 could shorten the long-term view of many ICT companies and remove the motivation from them to maintain a sound approach to business ethics based on a solid understanding of computer ethics. How can a corporation begin to be willing to go beyond its legal requirements? What would be its first steps? For some companies, led by ethical and social visionaries (see Patrignani and Whitehouse, 2013, for at least three case studies), those steps are already being made. For the late adopters and laggards, other mechanisms are also evident. One way is for companies to realise that the pressure from stakeholders will grow: users, computer professionals, and policy makers, for example, can all steer the markets in appropriate directions. The more often that stakeholders' networks are defined, the more transparency and awareness will grow in society. In any event, transparency may well expand, since interested parties can in any case use social media and Web 2.0 to facilitate the exposure of inappropriate business practices on the part of ICT vendors.

Next Steps
Further investigatory steps are now needed in relation to Slow Tech. Among these are assessments of how corporations can actually answer the questions posed in this

paper: i.e., what kinds of internal processes are needed in organisations; what types of methods should be used; and how do firms interpret and address the three spheres of goodness, cleanliness and fairness. Special attention needs to be paid to how companies not only perceive, but also analyse, their own stakeholder network, and how they can work more closely and intensively with the full range of stakeholders whom their products and services affect - from design to manufacturing, and from sale to use to disposal or re-use.

In Europe (for example, European Commission, 2011), some helpful proposals are being proffered. The anticipated establishment of a European multi-stakeholder platform, in early 2014, might prove especially positive in this regard. Techniques are also being cited that can influence the thinking and acting of those who may not yet be working in the corporate sector but who may still be members of the generation undergoing education and training. Globally, the work of the ISO also offers a means of encouraging the corporate social responsibility that is now needed on the part of ICT vendors (ISO, 2010).

Today's challenges to the production and use of good, clean, and fair ICT, both conceptual and concrete, can of course act as incentives for action: they can further applied research or encourage social activism. Encouraging the study, and the application, of Slow Tech is intended as a deliberate - and positive - first step in this direction.

References

1. Amazon, Amazon Smile (2013), http://smile.amazon.com (accessed March 9, 2014)
2. Apple, Apple Supplier Responsibility, Progress Report (2013), http://www.apple.com (accessed March 9, 2014)
3. Agag, G., Elbeltagi, I.: A framework for electronic business ethics: a comparison study between the UK and Egypt. In: Bynum, T.W., Fleishman, W., Gerdes, A., Moldrup Nielsen, G., Rogerson, S. (eds.) The Possibilities of Ethical ICT, ETHICOMP 2013 Proceedings, Kolding, Denmark, June 12-14, pp. 14–24. Print & Sign University of Southern Denmark (2013)
4. Bacile, T.: Has Facebook Heard of 'Corporate Social Responsibility'? (September 30, 2013), http://toddbacile.wordpress.com (accessed March 9, 2014)
5. Cisco, Corporate Social Responsibility (2013), http://csr.cisco.com (accessed March 9, 2014)
6. Dell, The Dell 2020 Legacy of Good Plan (2013), http://www.dell.com (accessed March 9, 2014)
7. EICC, Electronic Industry Code of Conduct, Electronic Industry Citizenship Coalition (2012), http://www.eicc.info/eicc_code.shtml (accessed March 9, 2014)
8. Elkington, J.: Cannibals with Forks - The Triple Bottom Line of 21st Century Business. Capstone Publishing Ltd., Oxford (1997)
9. Ellul, J.: La technique ou l'enjeu du siècle, Paris, Armand (1954)

10. European Commission, Promoting a European Framework for Corporate Social Responsibility, (COM(2011) 366 final) (2001), http://eur-lex.europa.eu/LexUriServ/site/en/com/2001/com2001_0366en01.pdf (accessed March 9, 2014)
11. European Commission, Implementing the Partnership for Group and Jobs: Making Europe a Pole of Excellence on Corporate Social Responsibility, (COM(2006)136 final) (2006), http://eur-lex.europa.eu/LexUriServ/LexUriServ.do?uri=COM:2006:0136:FIN:en:PDF (accessed March 9, 2014)
12. European Commission, A renewed EU strategy 2011-2014 for Corporate Social Responsibility, (COM(2011) 681 final) (2011), http://eur-lex.europa.eu/LexUriServ/LexUriServ.do?uri=COM:2011:0681:FIN:EN:PDF (accessed March 9, 2014)
13. Forbes, The World's Biggest Public Companies (2013), http://www.forbes.com/global2000 (accessed March 9, 2014)
14. Fowler, G.A.: Facebook: One Billion and Counting. The Wall Street Journal (October 4, 2012)
15. Freeman, E.R.: Strategic Management: A Stakeholder Approach. Pitman Publishing, Boston (1984)
16. Friedman, M.: The Social Responsibility of Business is to Increase its Profits. The New York Times Magazine (September 13, 1970)
17. Gartner, Gartner Says Worldwide IT Spending on Pace to Reach $3.7 Trillion in 2013 (2013), http://www.gartner.com (accessed March 9, 2014)
18. Google, Who we are - Corporate Social Responsibility (2013), http://www.google.com (accessed March 9, 2014)
19. Hallnäs, L., Redström, J.: Slow Technology; Designing for Reflection. Journal of Personal and Ubiquitous Computing 5(3), 201–210 (2001)
20. Hilty, M.L., Arnfalk, P., Erdmann, L., Goodman, J., Lehmann, M., Wager, A.: The relevance of information and communication technologies for environmental sustainability. A prospective simulation study. Environmental Modeling and Software 21(11), 1618–1629 (2006)
21. HP, HP Global Citizenship Report (2013), http://www.hp.com (accessed March 9, 2014)
22. IBM, Corporate Responsibility Report (2013), http://www.ibm.com/ibm/responsibility/2012/overview/index.html (accessed March 9, 2014)
23. Intel, Intel 2012 Corporate Social Responsibility Report (2013), http://www.intel.com (accessed March 9, 2014)
24. ISO, ISO 26000 - Social Responsibility (2010), http://www.iso.org (accessed March 9, 2014)
25. Johnson, D.G.: Computer Ethics, 4th edn. 2009. Pearson International Edition, Prentice Hall, New Jersey (1985)
26. Madrigal, A.C.: Bruce Sterling on Why It Stopped Making Sense to Talk About 'The Internet' in 2012. The Atlantic (December 27, 2012)
27. Maner, W.: Starter Kit in Computer Ethics. Helvetia Press, West Virginia (1980) (published in cooperation with the National Information and Resource Center for Teaching Philosophy)

28. Marcoux, A.: Business Ethics. In: Zalta, E.N. (ed.) The Stanford Encyclopedia of Philosophy (Fall 2008 Edition) (2008), http://plato.stanford.edu/archives/fall2008/entries/ethics-business (accessed March 9, 2014)
29. Martinuzzi, A., Kudlak, R., Faber, C., Wiman, A.: Sector profile CSR Activities and Impacts of the ICT Sector. In: Research Institute for Managing Sustainability (RIMAS), vol. 5, Vienna University of Economics and Business, RIMAS Working Papers, No. 5/2011, Vienna (2011)
30. Meadows, D.H., Meadows, D.L., Randers, J., Behrens III, W.W.: The Limits to Growth. A Report for the Club of Rome's Project on the Predicament of Mankind. Universe Books, New York (1972)
31. Microsoft, 2013 Citizenship Report (2013), http://www.microsoft.com (accessed March 9, 2014)
32. Moor, J.H.: What Is Computer Ethics? Metaphilosophy 16(4), 266–275 (1985)
33. Mumford, L.: Technics and Civilization. Harcourt, Brace and Company, Inc., New York (1934)
34. Oracle, Corporate Citizenship Report (2013), http://www.oracle.com (accessed March 9, 2014)
35. ORSE, Observatoire de la Responsabilité Sociétale des Enterprises (2010), http://www.orse.org (accessed March 9, 2014)
36. Parker, D.: Rules of Ethics in Information Processing. Communications of the ACM 11, 198–201 (1968)
37. Patrignani, N.: Slow Tech. Manifesto for a Social and Ethical Governance of Converging Technologies. In: Paper Presentation at IFIP/WG9.2 International Working Conference "Converging Technologies: Body, Brain and Being", Maribor, Slovenia, May 17-18 (2010)
38. Patrignani, N., Whitehouse, D.: Slow Tech: towards a good, clean and fair ICT. In: Bynum, T.W., Fleishman, W., Gerdes, A., Moldrup Nielsen, G., Rogerson, S. (eds.) The Possibilities of Ethical ICT, ETHICOMP 2013 Proceedings, June 12-14, pp. 384–390. Print & Sign University of Southern Denmark, Kolding (2013)
39. Petrini, C.: Slow Food Nation: Why our Food should be Good, Clean and Fair. Rizzoli Intl. Pub., Milano (2007)
40. Petrini, C.: Buono, Pulito e Giusto. Principi di Nuova Gastronomia. Einaudi, Torino (2011)
41. Price, A.R.G.: Slow-Tech. Manifesto for an Overwound World. Atlantic Books, London (2009)
42. Samsung, Global Harmony with People, Society and the Environment, Sustainability Report (2013), http://www.samsung.com (accessed March 9, 2014)
43. SAP, Corporate Social Responsibility (2013), http://global.sap.com (accessed March 9, 2014)
44. Sony, Annual Report 2013 Business and CSR review (2013), http://www.sony.net (accessed March 9, 2014)
45. Spreckley, F.: Social Audit. A management tool for co-operative working. Beechwood College, Leeds (1981)
46. Yi, L., Thomas, H.R.: Review of research on the environmental impact of e-business and ICT. Environment International 33, 841–849 (2007)
47. Vazquez-Figueroa, A.: Coltan. Ediciones B, Barcelona (2010)
48. Weizenbaum, J.: Computer Power and Human Reason: From Judgment to Calculation. Freeman, San Francisco (1976)

49. Whitehouse, D., Patrignani, N.: From Slow Food to Slow Tech: a reflection paper. In: Proceedings of the IADIS International Conference, ICT, Society and Human Beings 2013, Prague, Czech Republic, July 24-26, pp. 141–145. IADIS Press (2013) ISBN/ISSN: 978-972-8939-91-5
50. Wiener, N.: The Human Use of Human Beings: Cybernetics and Society. Houghton Mifflin, Boston (1950)
51. Wikipedia, Corporate Social Responsibility (2014a), http://en.wikipedia.org/wiki/Corporate_social_responsibility (accessed March 9, 2014)
52. Wikipedia, Cleantech (2014b), http://en.wikipedia.org/wiki/Clean_technology (accessed March 9, 2014)

Towards a Smart Community Centre: SEIDET Digital Village

Jackie Phahlamohlaka, Zama Dlamini, Thami Mnisi, Thulani Mashiane, and Linda Malinga

Council for Scientific and Industrial Research (CSIR)
Pretoria, South Africa
{JPhahlamohlaka,IDlamini,TMnisi1,TMashiane,LMalinga}@csir.co.za

Abstract. South African communities are constantly being developed through new ICT projects which are initiated by individuals, government and private organisations. The problem with these developments is that they are implemented in isolation. This isolation causes limited sharing of resources, duplication, poor-governance of the resources and in worse-case scenarios, failure of project initiatives. This paper proposes a model that could be used to address these problems by focusing on the SEIDET community centre using it as an example. The model follows a descriptive analysis of ICT related work spanning over two decades performed within the SEIDET context, including the ongoing SEIDET Digital Village. The benefits of the proposed smart community centre model include community and rural development through sharing of scarce ICT resources. It could further provide support for entrepreneurs through training interventions, action-based research for policy development as well as spawn local innovation and free-sharing of resources and services.

Keywords: Community Centre, Digital Village, SEIDET, Siyabuswa, Smart Community Centre, Village Operators.

1 Introduction and Background

The question as to whether the Siyabuswa Educational Improvement and Development Trust (SEIDET) was like Linux was raised in 2003 by Tom Siebeling [1]. Broadly speaking, Linux is associated with open source and innovation. SEIDET is also an organisation that encourages the collaboration of individuals in order to achieve the common goal of uplifting the community of Siyabuswa. With these characteristics of being open and innovative in its outlook, a question as to whether it could successfully morph into a Smart community centre within the envisaged SEIDET Digital Village could be asked. Smart community centre concept could be defined by looking at the smart city definitions.

According to Caragliu, Belbou and Nijkamp (2009), a city can be referred to as 'smart' when investments in human and social capital, traditional and modern Information and Communication Technologies (ICT) communication infrastructure fuel sustainable economic development and a high quality of life, with better management

K.K. Kimppa et al. (Eds.): HCC11 2014, IFIP AICT 431, pp. 107–121, 2014.
© IFIP International Federation for Information Processing 2014

of natural resources, through participatory action and engagement [2]. Chourabi et al. (2012) believe that a smart city concept essentially means efficiency [3], but efficiency based on the intelligent management and integrated ICTs, and active citizen participation, resulting in a new kind of governance and genuine citizen involvement in public policy [3].

From the above definitions, the notion of 'smart' of ICT infrastructure, education, learning, social and human capital development and innovation is emphasised. With an emerging drive by the SEIDET board towards ICT enabled entrepreneurship, the authors were curious to investigate how the Smart Community Centre idea would be pursued within the envisaged Digital Village. The authors were also aware of studies currently undertaken within the Council for Scientific and Industrial Research (CSIR) in South Africa and globally on Smart Cities and wanted to explore possibilities for collaboration between SEIDET and the CSIR on research, development and innovation. Since the definition of 'smart' has as its core, access to and use of ICT infrastructure, a short background on ICT related work at SEIDET is in order.

This paper is part of a long term project made up of three phases as illustrated in Figure 1. It focuses on the first phase of the project and it aims to formulate a smart community centre model as well as analyse it in SEIDET community centre context. This is achieved by conducting a literature study on SEDEIT community centre, smart city and smart community.

| PHASE 1: | PHASE 2: | PHASE 3: |
| Literature study and formulation of smart community centre model | Model simulation and verification through stakeholder workshop | Model implementation, testing and maintanance |

Fig. 1. Smart Community Centre Model Plan

The rest of the paper is organised as follows: Section 2 presents the background on elements of the ICT enabled entrepreneurial drive contextualised within SEIDET is outlined and a literature study on smart cities and smart communities is undertaken; the proposed model that SEIDET could consider as it moves towards becoming a smart community centre is presented in Section 3. The paper concludes in Section 4 with a discussion on analysis which further motivates for the innovative collaboration between SEIDET and the CSIR.

2   Literature Study

2.1   SEIDET Community Centre

Siyabuswa Educational Improvement and Development Trust (SEIDET) is a non-profit organization, initiated in May 1990 by the Siyabuswa community located in Mpumalanga province of South Africa. This is a community centre consisting of two ICT labs, readily available to the community under strict administration. This community centre hosts various community based projects. These projects include educational and business oriented initiatives. The goal of these projects is to involve various stakeholders in the public sector, the private sector as well as the general community participation in educational and economic development [4].

ICT related work and studies at SEIDET are well documented, and span more than a decade and a half [4,5]. Pioneering work was done by a number of academics from the Department of Informatics at the University of Pretoria [5]. Several conference proceedings, journal publications and a book dedicated to this work are readily available [5].

Two Masters dissertations and five PhD theses were completed using some aspects of ICT related work at SEIDET [5]. None of these studies were about the establishment of a smart community centre. Rather, they were about how ICT could contribute to socio-economic development. Since the concept of "smart" assumes ICT infrastructure access and use, all these studies are useful references for purposes of this paper [6].

The SEIDET project has helped expose members of the Siyabuswa community to basic ICT skills. Many leading professionals from both local and provincial governments in the Mpumalanga Province of South Africa touched a computer keyboard for the first time at the SEIDET community centre in Siyabuswa. Hundreds of community members and thousands of school learners as well as all primary school science teachers from Nkangala Region of Mpumalanga province were exposed to basic ICT literacy and learnt how ICT could be used to support them in their learning and teaching tasks at SEIDET [4]. This makes the SEIDET community centre a profound-ideal community centre for this project to use in testing the proposed smart community centre model.

In recognition of the ground breaking work done in partnership with the University of Pretoria on ICT use at SEIDET, a national seminar leading to the launch of the National eSkills Plan of the Department of Communications (DoC), was co-hosted by SEIDET in Siyabuswa. The following quote from DoC press release in 2009 succinctly captures the recognition:

> "It is fitting that this first iJima be located in Siyabuswa, the site of SEIDET and the location of a partnership with the University of Pretoria including more than fifteen years of community focused research on ICT enabled socio-economic development" (Department of Communications, RSA, 2009) [7].

All of the above sited background presents the SEIDET community centre as a well-established environment with great potential of becoming a modern state-of-art ICT community centre; overcoming most of the day-to-day ICT challenges through ICT utilisation, especially distracted governance, decentralisation of resources which often result in limited sharing of skills, knowledge, services and resources. This paper proposes a model that could be used to overcome these challenges using smart community centre concepts.

There are a number of ICT initiatives that are taking place at the SEIDET community centre. Some of these initiatives involve the South African government, Mpumalanga province municipalities, public and private sector, academic and research institutions (such as University of Pretoria and CSIR) who currently are working with SEIDET on research and community development. These isolated collaborations can be better managed using the existing ICT resources and infrastructure, such that SEIDET community centre houses the centralised system that manages both the service providers and the consumers. Having such system in place could also reduce redundancy of service delivery. The current ICT initiatives at SEIDET community centre, working together with University of Pretoria (UP) and CSIR include, the e-entrepreneurial training and eSkills programme, Cybersecurity awareness training and CSIR broadband for all (BB4All) and village operators project [4], [7,8]. All these initiatives are discussed in details in the following subsections.

E-entrepreneurship Training and eSkills Programme
The first entrepreneurship training of sixteen members from the SEIDET Community was done in 2011 by the Department of Economics at UP. This was followed by further training of fourteen members from the broader Siyabuswa Community in 2013 at the SEIDET community centre in Siyabuswa. On the part of the Board of SEIDET side, the training was in line with one of its objectives, to enable communities to participate in economic development [5].

Linked to this entrepreneurship training was also the eSkills training component, facilitated once again by academics from the Department of Informatics, UP. The second training at the SEIDET community centre in Siyabuswa was the collaboration between SEIDET, the University of Pretoria and the CSIR; with the CSIR focusing on Cybersecurity Awareness Training [4], [9,10]. The eSkills component was conducted as part of the broader eSkills Programme of the Department of Communications mentioned earlier in the introduction. The combination of the entrepreneurship and the eSkills training was dubbed e-entrepreneurship training.

The SEIDET Digital Village concept referred to in this paper is an outcome of the e-entrepreneurship training programme [4]. It is conceptualised as a variant of the SEIDET Model which focuses on enabling communities and individuals to participate in economic development. It is envisaged that the conversion of the SEIDET community centre to a Smart community centre will be pursued.

Cybersecurity Awareness Training
In an effort to prevent innocent internet users from becoming victims of cyber-attacks, the CSIR has initiated an intensive cyber security awareness program developed specifically to educate novice internet and technology users with regard to basic cyber

security. As part of the e-entrepreneurship training initiative, the entrepreneurs were trained on the safe and secure online behaviour to ensure their safety if they were to consider using the Internet to either market or sell their products. They were further given a better view of the vulnerabilities that comes with the advantages of the Internet [10].

The topics that were covered in the training session include: Cybersecurity in the Enterprise, Physical Computer Security, Mobile Security, Password Protection, Malware, Pop-ups - Adware and Spyware, Botnets, Surfing the web, Email Security, File Sharing and copyright, Internet Banking, Cookies, Phishing Attack Avoidance, Social Networking, Social Engineering, Identity Theft and Cyberbullying [8]. This is a significant aspect of any ICT training for any user as it encourages safe use and good behaviour when using the internet. It further provide list of threats and best practises when using the technological devices. This training initiative is regarded as an important aspect of the smart user services on the proposed model, because it promotes safe use of any technology as how one safe guard their lives in real life.

CSIR BB4All and Village Operators Project
Broadband for All (BB4All) is the outcome of a collaborative effort led by the CSIR's Meraka Institute to bridge the digital divide and bring the social and economic benefits offered by broadband connectivity to rural communities (such as Siyabuswa) in South Africa and other developing countries [11]. The objective of the project is to offer broadband access to rural communities in an affordable and sustainable fashion. This is made possible by enabling low cost building and sharing of connectivity through utilising Mesh Networking [12] principles and equipment to expand coverage within local communities negating the need for expensive radio equipment and high radio towers.

To ensure sustainability of the initiative, the local community and more specifically adequately skilled and trained local entrepreneur also known as the Village Operators (VO) are responsible for operating, promoting and expanding the BB4All offering within Siyabuswa [11]. SEIDET facilitated the VOs recruitments via schools and the Mpumalanga department of Education. SEIDET is regarded as a significant stakeholder and key contributor to the BB4All initiative. They are local entrepreneurs; young people with the right attitude and approach to become VOs. The VOs undergo entrepreneurial and business mentoring, personal development and training on the BB4All network infrastructure maintenance, operation and support [13].

The function of the VO is to service an exclusive area with limited number of clients, key clients being clusters of schools. The clients are connected through a peer-to-peer *community mesh* network. The mesh community networks are linked through a backhaul network called *backhaul mesh*. In addition to connecting the mesh communities, this mesh network contains a link to an IP backbone for IP services and Internet (See Figure 2). For redundant routing, this type of network ensures that a VO's device can link to two or more other VOs from other communities.

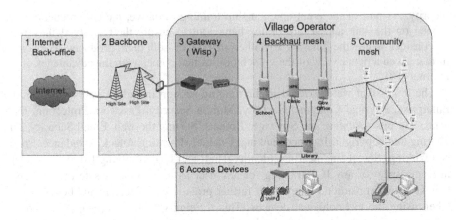

Fig. 2. CSIR BB4All Network Infrastructure [13]

The three initiatives discussed above could better be managed and distributed using governed technological advances that could be encompassed within the concept of a smart city. The smart community centre concept is based on the smart city concept; therefore the following subsections present literature on smart city and smart community.

2.2   Smart City

The concept of 'smart city' has become popular across the world and is currently the centre of attention for industry and governments globally [14,15]. Scholars and domain experts have presented ideas in an effort to describe smart cities; some of the definitions are presented as follows:

- Partridge (2004) believes that a smart city is "a city where the ICT strengthen the freedom of speech and the availability of public information and services" [16].
- Bowerman (2000) described a smart city as "a city that monitors and integrates conditions of all of its critical infrastructures, including roads, bridges tunnels, rails, subways, airports, seaports communications, water, power, even major buildings can better optimize its resources, plan its preventive maintenance activities, and monitor security aspects while maximizing services to its citizens" [17].
- Caragliu et al (2009) defined the smart city concept as "a concept to enable management and governance of the resources of the city through ICT, social, intellectual and the environment to create sustainability and efficiency by information sharing" [2].
- Kehoe et al (2011) consider a smart city as a city that "makes optimal use of all the interconnected information available today to better understand and control its operations and optimize the use of limited resources" [18].
- Rios (2012) defined a smart city as "a city that gives inspiration, shares culture, knowledge, and life, a city that motivates its inhabitants to create and flourish in their own lives" [19].

From the above definitions of a smart city, the common components of a smart city can be identified as *people, technology and governance*. These can be regarded as the drivers to achieve a smart city [14,15] and are discussed in detail below.

Smart People

The people, who are part of a smart city, comprise of any individual or organisation that has an interest in the success of the smart city. For example entrepreneurs, education institutions and law enforcement institutes, government institutes, NGOs as well as volunteers. The people who are active in a smart city are referred to as smart people [3], [19,20,21]. Smart people need to be properly educated and trained to operate in the smart city [15]. Once qualified, they are able to use their creativity in leveraging the city's infrastructure in order to create social, economic and environmental values. Smart people must be committed to a lifelong learning, and sharing of knowledge [15], [18]. These characteristics of smart people enable them to create a sustainable smart economy, smart environment and smart education system and an overall smart living [15], [18,19].

Smart Technology

An important aspect of a smart city is the platform that allows the interaction between the smart people. This platform is referred to as, the technology of the city. Technology in a smart city includes all the infrastructure, ICT, applications, smart technologies, digital networks and mobile devices [17,18]. These technologies are used as a channel or platform where smart people share knowledge, skills and services. The technology is leveraged in order to maximise the value to smart people [2]. For example, a smart person can use a smart device such as a cellular telephone to plan their route from a publicly accessible traffic web portal or an electronic board. This electronic traffic management, amongst other benefits, enables goods to be delivered on time, which increases productivity rate of the city.

Smart Governance

The interaction of the smart people amongst themselves, as well as the interaction with the technology needs to be governed [15]. Governance is the cornerstone of smart cities. This includes policies, regulations and directives that encourage collaboration, partnership and participation within the smart city. Governance ensures that the actors within the smart city act in a predictable and monitored manner. Governance oversees the standardisation of how different stakeholders interact within the smart city [16], [18], [20].

By synergising the components of a smart city, the goal of a smart city is realised and the people of the city fully harness the resources that their city provides [15], [20]. Examples of this harnessing can be seen in processes such as information gathering, where a city deploys an energy smart grid to monitor and manage the energy usage. This is achieved by interconnecting energy measuring sensors in predetermined locations through ICTs. These sensors send data to a central system. This data can be used for future energy resource planning [22]. Service delivery can be greatly improved by connecting government, public and private services through ICT. Emergency service personnel can be equipped with a smart device which has Internet access. The device can also be used to access a health record of a patient remotely from a public health record database [20]. This leads to accurate and fast treatment of the patient at the scene. Safety and Security can also be improved by inter-connecting smart devices such as cameras and motion sensors through ICT [23]. Some of the early studies on smart cities have been initiated by the CSIR Meraka Institute [24,25].

The concept of smart city focuses on a broader view of development of a city through ICT. This study focuses on the development of the smart community centre model using SEIDET community centre as the test-bed, yet flexible enough to be adapted to any South African community. The following subsection presents the concept of smart communities.

2.3   Smart Community

The phrase: "No man is an island", is the first line and the title of the popular poem by John Donne [26]. This line stresses that people need each other to survive. For this reason, in all parts of the world, people live in communities. A community can be defined as either a group of individuals and organisations who share an environment or a group of individuals and organisations that share common values or goals [27,28,29].

The pervasiveness of the Internet has made it possible for new types of communities to be formed. Technologies, such as, blogs have created a platform for people with common interest to share information and experiences with each other [30]. This notion of using the Internet to work together toward a common goal is the foundation of smart communities [6].

A smart community is a group of individuals and organisations that work together to leverage Information Technology (IT) in the creation of economic, cultural and social value [6]. Smart community members can include individuals, educational, government and business organisations [6]. A smart community can be seen as group of 'smart people' as defined in Section 2.2. In other words, a smart community is a system where people and organisations use IT to enhance the way that they conduct their everyday business. This enhancement can lead to advantages, such as, new revenue streams or attaining new knowledge that can be used to improve the efficiency of a business functions [6], [22].

Smart communities can exist in the virtual space, such as in SecondLife [31] or a hybrid of physical and virtual space, such as, Silicon Valley [32]. On the SecondLife platform, people leverage the Internet to perform business transactions, lecture presentations and even social gatherings. In both domains members of the community build relationships with each other for specific purposes such as collaborative learning, information and resource sharing [31]. Simply providing IT capability to a community does not make it a smart community. The individuals and organisations within the community must be educated and trained to make the applications more accessible and useful to them. It is only when the members of the community can use IT capabilities to produce new values that improve their lives, can it be classified as a smart community [6].

The availability of technology in a smart community is also as important as it is in a smart city. The infrastructure acts as a platform where community members interact. The networking infrastructure of the smart community can be made up of different technologies that need to interact with each other. Like most networking projects, the interoperability of different technologies is a challenge. This is because different technologies use different protocols and standards [6].

Smart communities have the potential of speeding up the processes of innovation and getting a product or service to the market. This is because members of the community work in partnership to realise specific goals. The digital divide can also pose as a threat in smart communities. Partnerships such as these can help in closing this divide [9]. By pulling resources together, members of the community can buy and maintain IT capability that would not have been attainable individually. Some members of the community may not have enough knowledge of the technology to be able to leverage it. Lack of knowledge and understanding of potential benefit for the members may lead to slow or no 'buy in' by the community [5]. This threat can be mitigated through continuous training and support to all the members of the community that need it. Community members must be consulted for input throughout the development and implementation in order to increase their desire to be a part of the smart community.

The literature of the ICT enabled entrepreneurial drives, all of which are linked to SEIDET community centre; and having looked at the literature on Smart Cities and Smart Communities; the following section presents the proposed Smart Community Centre model.

3   The Proposed Model of a Smart Community Centre

This section presents the proposed smart community centre model in the SEIDET community centre context. Some of the components of the model are derived from the above literature. The model aims to overcome the challenges of decentralised services and resources which results in limited sharing, redundancy of service delivery, and difficult access of services. The following subsections present the proposed model in details as well as an example of how it could be applied in the SEIDET context.

3.1   Smart Community Centre Model

As defined in the introduction and background Section 1, some of the challenges that the community of Siyabuswa is facing are; having disjointed developments in place which often result in poor administration, miscommunication and limited sharing of facilities and resources. These challenges are also experienced at the SEIDET community centre.

The proposed model, depicted in Figure 3, is a smart community centre model which aims to resolve some of these challenges. These include distributed resources, lack of governance, collaboration and sharing. This is achieved by employing smart city concepts to the existing SEIDET ICT architecture.

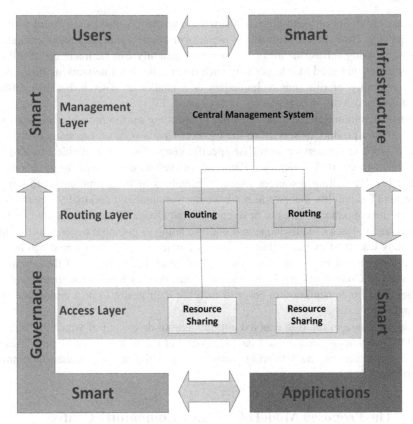

Fig. 3. Proposed Smart Community Centre Model

Smart Community Centre Services

The proposed model is based on a *service* oriented approach. From the definition of smart city, it was identified that the value is provided by the services that are delivered by the components (people, technology and governance); hence, the service oriented approach. It focuses on services required to achieve the goal of the smart community centre. These services are; *smart users, smart infrastructure and ICT, smart applications* and *smart governance*.

The services are discussed in detail below.

- **Smart Users:** These services are skills and knowledge based provided by the smart community centre such as education and training. These services empower the users with the skills to participate, and share resources. Examples of smart users within a smart community centre context include: training of users to able to efficiently utilize both smart applications and smart infrastructure to their benefits and the benefits of their businesses. This further improves quality of life and improved the economy, which can be summed as "smart living and smart economy". This will develop further participation in public life, flexibility, creativity/innovativeness, social and cultural plurality and affinity to lifelong learning.

- **Smart Infrastructure and ICT:** These services are network and ICT based and provide *two* functions. The first function is to create an information flow path. For an example, implementation of networks, such as the *mesh* (BB4All), allow information to flow. The second function is to provide access to the network through smart devices. For an example using *tablets, servers,* etc. Other examples of these services include; information systems (applications and data architecture), technological infrastructure, business architecture and communication protocol.
- **Smart Applications:** These are services that are provided by interactive software packages. These includes web portal in the remote servers, applications in the users' devices. For an example, in resource management, they enable visualisation of the resources and registration.
- **Smart Governance:** These are services that are provided by the stakeholders; public, private sector in a form of policies, rules and regulations for participation. These services aim to promote a system with predictable behaviour as participants are obliged to follow them. These rules, regulations, policies are formulated through active reviews, and inputs from all stakeholders. The main role for the smart governance is to promote participation and decision making in the smart community centre.

Smart Community Centre Implementation Layers

There are three layers in the smart community centre model and are shown in Figure 3. These layers are components which provide different services at different levels in a resource management process. These layers are described in detail below:

- **Access Layer:** This is the user layer responsible for access to the system. It consists of the users and devices (as data resources providers and consumers) of the traditional community centre. The main role of this layer is to enhance sharing amongst the user and also supply information about resources and available services between the users and the routing layer.
- **Routing Layer:** This layer is responsible for the routing of requests between the entities (users and CMS) in the system. All data shared by users is interconnected, structured, sorted, processed and routed to and from both the access and management layer.
- **Management Layer:** This layer is responsible for central managing of the resources. It is the layer where all the data (shared services, application, software, etc.) is stored and managed for efficient utilisation intelligent decision making, better service monitoring and easy access of services.

3.2 An Example of the Proposed Model Application within SEIDET Community Centre

In subsection 2.1, the challenges that are faced by the Siyabuswa community, such as decentralisation of resource management, limited sharing and collaboration, and lack of governance of ICT resources were outlined. The smart community centre model is proposed to address these challenges. This subsection illustrates how the proposed model could be used in addressing some of these challenges through ICT.

The entrepreneurs in Siyabuswa operate in isolation and as a result there is limited or no collaboration. Resources such as printers and fax machines are shared in a traditional manner, that is, if different entrepreneurs share a building, they will know the available resources by talking to each other. This model attempts to address such problems using modern means through ICT. This implies that exposing resources to participants in the smart community model system.

Possible Smart Community Centre Services at SEIDET

- **Smart User:** The smart user services could be all the human capital development services that are already provided at SEIDET community centre, such e-entrepreneurship and eSkills programme and cybersecurity awareness training.
- **Smart Infrastructure:** The smart infrastructure and ICT services could be the network services that are already provided by the current BB4All network infrastructure which is available to SEIDET community centre.
- **Smart Application:** Currently, SEIDET does not have elements that can provide smart applications services.
- **Smart Governance:** The SEIDET stakeholders can provide the smart governance services after they have acquired the appropriate training.

Registration Process

The first process in the system is the registration process. In this process, users register with the central management system. The central management system keeps records of all VOs, resources and users. The smart governance services provide rules and qualification criteria to determine the fitness of the user. This includes the skills the user needs to actively participate in the system, in which such service are provide by the smart user services of the model. Upon successful registration, the user is given terms and conditions regarding participation, also provided by the smart governance.

Resource Sharing

Once the user has been registered in the system, they can start sharing and requesting resources. This process is divided into three layers: *access, routing, management*. Figure 3 shows an architectural implementation of the model for Siyabuswa.

- **Access Layer:** In the case of the Siyabuswa, a user uses a smart device (smart infrastructure and ICT), PC to log on with their credentials. Upon successful log-on, a request is sent to the local VO, i.e. VO responsible for the area where the user is in. A user is any entity or participant that is capable of exposing and sharing resources. In the context of the SEIDET community centre, these could include the entrepreneurs, users, stakeholders, communication devices or sensors.
- **Routing Layer:** VOs play a pivotal role in this layer. VOs service an exclusive area. For example, assume that one entrepreneur attended an overseas training and would like to share business marketing ideas he learnt from that training in a form of a document. He will have to registers with the VO leader, the local VO keeps records of all shared resources from that area and has the responsibility make the resources available to all the community by uploading them to the central management system.

VOs accept the requests from, and forward responses to the access layer. They keep track of the local resources. If a requested resource is not available locally, they route the request to the CMS. In the SEIDET context, an entrepreneur who needs a specific service submits their request and has it dealt with by the area specific VO. That VO responds to the inquiry. If the requested services are not available locally, the VO asks other VOs through a central management layer.

- **Management Layer:** All VOs and resources are registered with the CMS. The CMS accepts request from the VOs, query its database for the requested resource and responds to the VO.

This example illustrates how the proposed model could be adapted for the current SEIDET community centre towards making it a smart community centre. It goes through each of the services of the model and recommends the available SEIDET components that can fulfil the services of the model.

4   Concluding Discussion

SEIDET has made a big impact during the past decades of its existence, not only in terms of its contribution to human capital development through education, but also on how ICT could be accessed and used by communities in support of socio-economic development. The new thinking and drive by its board to morph it towards a Smart Community Centre within what they envision as the SEIDET smart community centre makes perfect sense. It could draw on a wide range of its previous collaborators, the CSIR included, to make this happen.

The Smart Community Centre model proposed in this paper follows a conceptual analysis of its ongoing open characteristics highlighted in the introduction. The ICT enabled initiatives discussed in section 2.1 are classic demonstrations of this facilitative and open nature of SEIDET. The proposed model encapsulates and borrows the concept of a Village Operator, developed by the CSIR as part of its BB4All project and identifies the currently available ICT enabled initiatives as the examples of the smart community centre services.

The central management system in the proposed model could be the anchor point of the envisaged SEIDET smart community centre, where members of the smart community, including the entrepreneurs, users and other organisations could be linked. Linked to the smart community centre could therefore be physical, virtual as well as communities of interest, such as researchers at the CSIR. For instance, several entities within the CSIR are already collaborating to look at a smart city model that could be fitting to the South African context. As part of this study, it could link up into the proposed smart community centre to experiment with some of the initial ideas. The smart community centre model proposed in this study could thus assist in attaching local meaning to the smart city model that the international community is interested in pursuing.

References

1. Siebeling, T., Romijn, H.: Why People Contribute Voluntarily to Innovation: Insights from South Africa's Siyabuswa Educational Improvement & Development Trust. In: Eindhoven Center for Innovation Studies (ECIS) (2005)
2. Caragliu, A., Del Bo, C., Nijkamp, P.: Smart cities in Europe (2009), http://ideas.repec.org/p/dgr/vuarem/2009-48.html
3. Chourabi, H., Nam, T., Walker, S., Gil-Garcia, J.R., Mellouli, S., Nahon, K., Pardo, T.A., Scholl, H.J.: Understanding smart cities: An integrative framework. Presented at the 2012 45th Hawaii International Conference on System Science (HICSS), pp. 2289–2297 (2012)
4. SEIDET, "SEIDET" (2014), http://www.seidet.org.za/ (last accessed on March 31, 2014)
5. Phahlamohlaka, J.: Community-driven projects: reflections on a success story: a case study of science education and information technology in South Africa. Van Schaik Publishers (2008)
6. Baskin, C., Barker, M., Woods, P.: Towards a smart community: Rethinking the strategic use of ICTs in teaching and learning. Aust. J. Educ. Technol. 19(2), 192–210 (2003)
7. Department of Communication-South Africa, E-Skills Institute newsletter (February 11, 2013), http://www.esi-sa.org/media-and-publications/pdfs/edition11_newsletter.pdf (accessed March 12, 2014)
8. Stillman, L., Herselman, M., Marais, M., Boshomane, M.P., Plantinga, P., Walton, S.: Digital doorway: social-technical innovation for high-needs communities. Electron. J. Inf. Syst. Dev. Ctries. 50 (2011)
9. Kaplan, A.M., Haenlein, M.: The fairyland of Second Life: Virtual social worlds and how to use them. Bus. Horiz. 52(6), 563–572 (2009)
10. Roux, R.: Broadband for all (BB4all) TM. CSIR Sci. Scope Mag. 3(3), 16–17 (2009)
11. Siebeling, T., Romijn, H.: How SEIDET achieved success-an exploration from the perspective of innovation theory. In: Phahlamohlaka, J., Braun, M., Romijn Roose, H. (eds.) Community-Driven Proj. Reflect. Success Story Case Study Sci. Educ. Inf. Technol. South Afr., p. 77 (2008)
12. Siebeling, T., Romijn, H.: A novel approach to innovation processes in community driven projects: how an extented learning selection model explains the success of SEIDET, an educational community development project in rural South Africa (2004)
13. Grobler, M., Dlamini, Z., Ngobeni, S., Labuschagne, A.: Towards a cyber security aware rural community (2011)
14. Dlamini, Z., Modise, M.: Cyber Security Awareness Initiatives in South Africa: A Synergy Approach. Case Stud. Inf. Warf. Secur. Res. Teach. Stud., p. 1 (2013)
15. Al-Hader, M., Rodzi, A., Sharif, A.R., Ahmad, N.: Smart city components architecture. Presented at the International Conference on Computational Intelligence, Modelling and Simulation, CSSim 2009, pp. 93–97 (2009)
16. Hollands, R.G.: Will the real smart city please stand up? Intelligent, progressive or entrepreneurial? City 12(3), 303–320 (2008)
17. Partridge, H.L.: Developing a human perspective to the digital divide in the'smart city (2004)
18. Bowerman, B., Braverman, J., Taylor, J., Todosow, H., Von Wimmersperg, U.: The vision of a smart city. Presented at the 2nd International Life Extension Technology Workshop, Paris (2000)

19. Kehoe, M., Cosgrove, M., Gennaro, S., Harrison, C., Harthoorn, W., Hogan, J., Meegan, J., Nesbitt, P., Peters, C.: Smarter cities series: A foundation for understanding ibm smarter cities. Redguides Bus. Lead. IBM (2011)
20. Rios, P.: Creating 'The Smart City' (2012)
21. Nam, T., Pardo, T.A.: Conceptualizing smart city with dimensions of technology, people, and institutions. Presented at the Proceedings of the 12th Annual International Digital Government Research Conference: Digital Government Innovation in Challenging Times, pp. 282–291 (2011)
22. Su, K., Li, J., Fu, H.: Smart city and the applications. Presented at the 2011 International Conference on Electronics, Communications and Control (ICECC), pp. 1028–1031 (2011)
23. Kenichi, M.: Information and Communication Technology and Electric Vehicles–Paving the Way towards a Smart Community. IEICE Trans. Commun. 95(6), 1902–1910 (2012)
24. Li, X., Lu, R., Liang, X., Shen, X., Chen, J., Lin, X.: Smart community: an internet of things application. Commun. Mag. IEEE 49(11), 68–75 (2011)
25. Donne, J., Berkeley, C.: No man is an island. Peacock Press (1964)
26. Stevenson, A.: Oxford dictionary of English. Oxford University Press (2010)
27. Rifkin, S.B., Muller, F., Bichmann, W.: Primary health care: on measuring participation. Soc. Sci. Med. 26(9), 931–940 (1988)
28. Krogstad, D.J., Ruebush, T.K.: Community participation in the control of tropical diseases. Acta Trop. 61, 77–78 (1996)
29. Blood, R.: How blogging software reshapes the online community. Commun. ACM 47(12), 53–55 (2004)
30. Lindskog, H.: Smart communities initiatives. Presented at the Proceedings of the 3rd ISOneWorld Conference, pp. 14–16 (2004)
31. Basu, A., Virick, M.: Learning from experience: Novice and serial immigrant entrepreneurs in Silicon Valley. Presented at the 2013 Suzhou-Silicon Valley-Beijing International Innovation Conference (SIIC), pp. 40–52 (2013)

Computers, Time and Speed:
Five Slow Tech Case Studies

Diane Whitehouse and Norberto Patrignani

The Castlegate Consultancy, UK, and Politecnico di Torino, Italy,
and Uppsala University, Sweden
diane.whitehouse@thecastlegateconsultancy.com,
norberto.patrignani@polito.it

Abstract. This chapter examines briefly the notions of time and speed. It introduces the notion of Slow Tech: information technology that is *good*, *clean* and *fair*, and places an especial emphasis on technology that is *clean*. This chapter does not delve deep into the Slow Tech concept. Rather, it highlights a set of arguments about why speed is not always important or necessary. People are now increasingly beginning to think about much longer periods and phases that may extend at least as long as the existence of human beings on the globe. As illustrations, the chapter explores five specific case studies. Each comes from a different location, yet all describe global implications and challenges. One example is in fact a mathematical model. Two sites, in sympathy with the location of the Human Choice and Computing 11 (HCC11) conference, are from Scandinavia – one from Onkalo, Finland, and a second from Svalbard, a northern Norwegian island. A further two cases are from the United States of America. The logic behind these five case studies strengthens the arguments about why – with the support of the Slow Tech concept – it is increasingly important for society and its many stakeholders to question the current information and communication technology (ICT) obsession with speed and rethink the relationships between society and technology.

Keywords: Action, case studies, life cycle, myth, slow, Slow Tech, speed, thought, time.

1   Time and Speed: Their Relationship with Slow Tech

It is important to investigate the limits of time. In the 21st century, a whole new set of questions are arising. Is ICT changing very fast the human concept of time? How is ICT changing people's everyday lives, i.e., what human beings do and who they are? Is ICT improving people's quality of life? Can ICT contribute to people's well-being without having detrimental side-effects on them, their social structures, and the planet? Can people identify guiding values that could influence the development of ICT from the point of view of society itself?

As a result, is it possible to build a set of positive, ethical guidelines for ICT development? If so, could this set of guidelines be called Slow Tech, an initiative to build *good*, *clean* and *fair* ICT [1]? While this chapter acknowledges its debt to Slow

K.K. Kimppa et al. (Eds.): HCC11 2014, IFIP AICT 431, pp. 122–135, 2014.

Tech ideas (see, for example, Patrignani and Whitehouse [2] elsewhere in this volume), it describes them only briefly here.

Similar challenges to those facing the technology industry today faced the agricultural and food sectors in the late 20th century. These challenges generated a new approach to food: Slow Food. The Slow Food movement was born in 1989 in Italy: *"... a global, grassroots organization ... linking the pleasure of good food with a commitment to ... community and the environment ... to counter the rise of fast food and fast life, the disappearance of local food traditions and people's dwindling interest in the food they eat, where it comes from, how it tastes and how our food choices affect the rest of the world"* [2]. This slow philosophy provided people with a new ecology of mind [4]. Today's challenge is not only to consider the benefits of Slow Food, but also to develop an appropriate Slow Tech philosophy and, ultimately, perhaps a Slow Tech movement.

Slow Tech offers people the opportunity, on the one hand, to spend more time on thought, observation, and choice and, on the other, to enjoy their short lives more. Slow Tech introduces the time dimension into thinking about technology. It means that, while people continue to use ICT in the future, they may do so in a more conscious and responsible way. It implies that people will need to regain control of the pace of their days and lives, by designing technologies that are more respectful of their brains and bodies and that are not necessarily based on a continual increase in clock speed. It highlights the importance of starting to examine longer-term, human-oriented perspectives.

2   Time and Speed: Their Relationship with ICT

This section of the chapter explores human fascination with time as well as the myth of speed. Today, ICT is at the core of many of society's critical processes: the speed of ICT itself controls the tempo of these activities – whether involved in communication, hardware development, manufacture, processing, software development, storage or retrieval and indeed, the obsolescence of the technologies themselves. The multitasking capability that many people are experiencing as a result of using ICT may offer them the illusion of compressing time and may offer them a range of different opportunities and even challenges (some would say, dependent on their gender). People may try to undertake different sets of activities, to complete more than one scenario or task at any one moment. They are attempting to control several processes that are evolving in parallel. Computers appear to increase people's productivity and performance. Thus, it may look as though ICT provides people with incredible speed in the management of information.

Yet people still need to reflect on the limits of human minds and the consequences that arise as a result of speeding up of all life's processes, including those with impacts on the environment and on the consumption of limited resources. In this chapter, therefore, the authors support the notion of the design of complex ICT systems, together with a human-centric approach – where sometimes speed is needed and sometimes not. Therefore, they query the myth of speed *per se*.

2.1   Human Fascination with Time and Speed

Time is a convention that has been evolving throughout human history. People started to measure time at the very beginning of their history, when they looked at the sun rising every morning and the stars or the moon moving throughout the sky at night: time was measured in terms of natural events that recurred regularly, such as the new moon occurring over a period of about twenty-eight days, and the birth and re-birth of the seasons – through spring to summer, autumn, and back to winter before the beginning of the new year. Indeed, human beings perceive the passage of time according to what happens around them.

As a consequence of scientific enquiry and technological development, human beings have refined and extended the measurement of time as they have become aware of processes that are not readily perceivable. These processes include phenomena in particle physics, such as the decay of a quark, that – in order to be measured – need only a yocto-second (10^{-24} sec) or less. The decay of one of the known quarks, the top-quark, requires only 0.5 yocto-seconds. Artefacts, including containers for nuclear waste, are therefore built to last for thousands of centuries – for tera-seconds (10^{12} sec.).

Speed is also a matter of fascination. A 2011 update on supercomputer competition indicated that Fuijtsu's K-Computer runs at more than 10,000 TeraFLOPS (Floating Point Operations per Second), which is 10,000 x 10^{15} FLOPS, or 10 x 10^{18} FLOPS. Just a single operation needs less than 0.1 x 10^{-18} sec. or 0.1 atto-seconds to be executed [5]. The fastest computer on the planet is Chinese. Called Tianhe2, it runs at more than 33,000 TeraFLOPS [6]. Artefacts are now built that are planned to last for thousands of centuries, tera-seconds (10^{12} sec.), including deposits of nuclear waste.

2.2   The Myth of Speed

Speed is indeed a physical variable. At times, it can be useful to act fast. When people are at risk – and even society as a whole is in danger – and when the aim is to protect people, society, infrastructure, and frameworks, then it is important to act quickly. For example, an accident victim must be brought to hospital in an ambulance, a child saved from falling from a chair, the behaviour of an incoming hurricane simulated to prepare for mass evacuations, or people's lifestyles modified promptly so as to cope with climate change. Ultimately, a long-term view on the impact of human activities on the environment needs to be developed.

Otherwise, while speed is seductive, it may often prove to be an illusion. There are lots of ways to look at the history of speed as "faster-is-better", and many ways to interpret the motivation to go faster. It is important too to examine speed's benefits and shortcomings. In terms of physical transportation: speed helps to transport raw materials, perishable goods, manufactured goods and people quicker. Yet it also has effects on many other socio-economic factors: the profitability of trade; the type of diet people eat; the time passengers and goods spend in transit; and comparisons of the time at destination to that of arrival. With regard to communication: there is also, historically, a variety of speeds at which messages have been sent. These include via hand, drum or flame for physical messages and via courier or stage coach for letters.

More recently, messages have been sent through non-material transmission by telegraph, radio, telephone and the Internet. Unfortunately, it seems to have been assumed that the speed at which humans – and groups of human beings – can process these messages and formulate a reply will keep pace – naturally – with the transmission speed. While computer programs were initially devised to mimic, electronically, the application of a clearly-defined procedure that was to be applied to quantitative input data, it must be borne in mind that these procedures had themselves been developed and adopted over long periods, which involved decades and centuries, by experts in a field.

Early in the twentieth century, speed became to be seen as a myth. Almost every human activity began to look better if it was faster. Speed was at the core of the Futurist movement: progress and modernity were synonymous with its writing and activities. Futurism was considered to be the avant-garde of culture: its leaders wrote that "...*the splendor of the world has been enriched by a new beauty: the beauty of speed*" [7]. The desire was there to celebrate modern engineering achievements that were measurably faster than those available in the previous century: vehicles that included automobiles, ships, trains and, later, aircraft. 'Slow' was associated with the previous (nineteenth) century and was seen as a drag on progress. This movement in support of speed can also be associated with the cultural background of the dictatorships of the twentieth century, and the eventual drive towards war. The perceived beauty of speed at the start of the twentieth century was based at least partly on the conviction that human power could dominate and over-ride nature. It is now acknowledged what a terrible mistake this illusion was with regard to the control of nature.

Indeed, approaches alter. Speed is no longer a value in itself. In the twenty-first century, it is becoming increasingly clear that the complexity of natural systems is so sophisticated that it is more effective to find new ways to co-exist with such systems than to attempt to dominate them. Rather, there is an growing fascination with the opposite – with slow. A message is emerging that – before initiating new ICT projects and initiatives – more time is needed. It is important to consider the impact that initiatives and advances relating to ICT may have on natural and social systems. Alternative solutions or different approaches or projects could be found rather than risking damage to the natural environment.

As Italian journalist, Giovanna Giuffreda, says: there is a real need for society to slow down [8, 9]. In order to face current societal challenges, innovation is certainly needed. However, it must occur in a way that enables people to use the incredible power that lies in their hands, with care, and without destroying living environments. This is especially pertinent in the field of ICT. According to a 2011 report from the European Commission: "... *(ICT) Responsible Innovation ... must be socially desirable and inclusive, ... environmentally sustainable, ... ethically acceptable ...*" [10].

2.3   Dealing with Limits and with Myths

Human beings tend not to like limits: they are constantly looking for new challenges. Since people need challenges in their lives, they need to continue to make use of fascinating myths, such as speed and time. However, people have to be conscious that many of the novel challenges that they face are now actually located inside themselves – intellectually and emotionally – rather than outside.

Human beings are also living on a finite planet [11]. People's continuing exploitation of natural resources, based on processes that are increasing in speed, need to be re-examined. Computers are the core engines that are speeding up many incompletely defined or tested processes. Instead, perhaps human beings now need to accept and embed the concept of limits – limits that are imposed by the current environmental and social crises – in their plans and endeavours, including those including new ICT initiatives. This is today's challenge for human beings.

Today, ICT and computers lie at the core of the increasing speed of technical processes, and indeed also social and societal processes. Yet are faster and faster processes always needed? Are there limits to this growth in computers? Is it time to rethink computer speed? Should computers be introduced into society not just because they are available but when and where they really make sense, and at speeds that make sense? Can good ICT (that is, is it ICT that is good for human beings) be designed and built? Is there likely to be a revival of interest in appropriate technology [12]?

3   Case Studies to Illustrate the Challenges of Time and Speed

Case studies can often paint clear messages. To introduce a set of arguments about the many possible views of time and why speed is not always important or necessary, five case studies have been selected by the authors. Each comes from a different location around the globe. Many relate to technology and its implications, although not all.

The first use case is simply a model. The Lotka-Volterra model shows the systemic and natural balance that occurs – over the very long-term – between prey and their predators. It provides a fundamental reminder of how different animal or human development can look when it is examined over a sufficiently long time. The second case is located in Onkalo in Finland: it contains a long-term danger since it is a storage space for nuclear waste. The third case, Svalbard, is based in northern Norway, a place dedicated to beneficence: it stores examples of plant seeds for future, long-term usage. The fourth case, to be found in Van Horn in the United States' state of Texas, is also a building with a benevolent message. At Van Horn, a clock which is intended to run for at least 10,000 years is buried deep in the desert. The fifth and final use case alerts human beings to the dangers inherent in a reliance on computers that run critical systems. The 2010 New York Stock Exchange crash is a frightening illustration of an event that shows that human beings are no longer totally in control of banking and financial systems.

Today, people are beginning to think about very long periods and, indeed, phases that may extend beyond the existence of human beings on this globe. Three of the cases introduced here draw people's attention to this long-termism and the responsibility that is needed over lengthy periods. Most look a considerable time ahead, and at least one of them looks ahead for the lifetimes of 300 generations of people. They are all illustrations of means of facing, and overcoming, disasters. Some raise the challenge, whether for good or bad reasons, of how to alert future generations to the location of the materials and equipment that they house.

3.1   Long Lifecycles: The Lotka-Volterra Model

Human beings are simply small animals on a single, limited planet. When analysing a number of physical variables to see their evolution over time, all functions are in fact limited. Although some forms of (short-term) "exponential" growth can be observed, sooner or later, all growth is saturated and reaches its limit. On planet earth, in the long-run, only self-sustaining systems can survive. On the earth, nature is indeed composed of a collection of cycles. Examples include the carbon cycle, the water cycle and the life cycle.

The Lotka-Volterra Prey-Predator Model is a pertinent case in point (see Fig. 1). It is a long-term natural cycle. The figure illustrates complete life cycles. The model was described by the American demographer, Alfred J. Lotka, in 1924 and the Italian mathematician, Vito Volterra, in 1926. It is a linear system of differential equations of the first order. It describes a simple system formed by two species: one is the prey (for example, small fish) and the other is the predator (such as large sharks). The following assumption can be made: a population of prey increases exponentially in the absence of predators, and a population of predators decreases exponentially in the absence of prey. Yet, if predators consume too many prey, they will have less food available to them and the population of predators will decrease. The population of prey then increases. Finally, the population of predators will again have more food. Of course, however, sometimes something goes catastrophically wrong, and extinctions occur that cause animals and other beings to disappear.

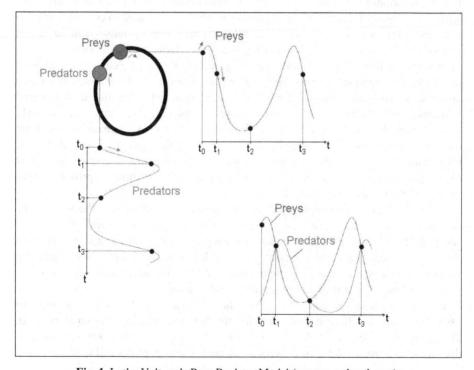

Fig. 1. Lotka-Volterra's Prey-Predator Model (source: authors' own)

3.2   Long-Lasting Dangers: Onkala, Finland

Some human activities necessitate long-term planning and building, as the Onkalo nuclear waste depository illustrates. Onkalo provides a concrete means of avoiding catastrophe. In Finnish, Onkalo means a "hiding place". It is also the name of the facility that will act as the long-term storage for all nuclear waste produced in Finland. It is to be found at a few miles from the Olkiluoto nuclear plant located about 280 kilometres north-west of Helsinki. This cave, which is built in the granite bedrock and constructed in a spiral shape, will be 520 metres deep when it is completed.

Construction of the cave started in 2004, and it will be ready to host nuclear waste by 2022 (http://www.posiva.fi). It will then be used for the disposal of nuclear waste for about 90 years. At that point, no further nuclear waste will be taken to the cave, and the tunnel which leads to it will be backfilled. In 2020, the repository will be sealed – it is hoped, forever. This project has been started while today's generation is still living, but its mission will be complete when contemporary adults have been dead for a very long time. More precisely, the nuclear waste that Onkalo contains will remain dangerous for more than 100,000 years.

Onkalo therefore opens up new kinds of challenges related to people's concept of time. Some technologies are pushing people to a point where they simply do not have the intellectual background to answer a number of deep philosophical questions. For example, what will become of the planet over this period of 100,000 years? How can future generations be prevented from entering into contact with Onkalo's contents? What kind of messages, languages, visual images or symbols can be used to communicate this underground danger? *Into Eternity* is the title of a documentary, released in 2010, that poses difficult questions about Onkalo (http://www.intoeternitythemovie.com).

Human civilisation has existed for only a few thousand years (the Egyptian pyramids, for example, are just 5,000 years old). Human minds cannot easily make projections that extend into such a 100,000 year-long, long-term future. A hundred millennia, on the human scale, is close to eternity – the *saecula saeculorum* – a world without end, that is thought to go on for ever and ever. For human beings, their concept of time is deeply affected by the artefacts, and the technological choices, that they make. The relationship between human beings and time is one of the oldest philosophical challenges to have faced humankind: the questions it provokes have fascinated people from their very origins.

Onkalo is a perfect example of a human attempt to pre-determine the future. The decision to build this nuclear repository extends beyond the limits of scientific acceptability, even if it is one of the few serious projects that exist around the world to deal with nuclear waste management. The developments at Onkalo show where the zeal of dominating nature crosses the boundary of scientific acceptance, and enters the domain of 'magic' – stories that proceed beyond science.

It might, instead, be wiser to accept the experience of limits that is strongly associated with the human body and its physical and intellectual experiences. In Germany and Italy in 2011/2012, to offer just two examples, several political decisions were made related to the closure of nuclear power plants and to stopping the generation of nuclear waste. These decisions about plant closure seem to indicate that a number of past nuclear disasters, and their associated security arrangements, have been transformed into real learning experiences (examples include the experiences at Three Mile Island, USA, 1979; Chernobyl, Soviet Union, 1986; Fukushima, Japan, 2011). Increasingly, in these two European countries, and possibly others, planning for the future seems to be based more than it was, in the immediate past, on a concern and consideration for saving and reducing energy consumption, and on developing renewable and cleaner energy sources. On the agenda for exploitation and use are hydroelectricity, geothermal power, wind, solar power, biomass and the waves of the oceans.

3.3   Crops for Eternity: Svalbard, Norway

The Svalbard Global Seed Vault provides a form of long-term insurance to provide food for future generations.

Svalbard (formerly called Spitsbergen) is the name of a Norwegian archipelago about 3,000 kilometres north of Oslo. William Barents discovered it in 1596. In the 17th century, it was used by whaling and fishing communities but was later abandoned. At the beginning of the 1900s, coal-mining began there and, in 1925, these remote islands became part of Norway. Travelling around one of the islands, by snowmobile or ship, one eventually comes to a strange construction with a small door: this is the Svalbard Global Seed Vault, a seed bank intended to last for eternity. Its entrance provides access to a 120 metre tunnel under a sandstone mountain that is equipped to cool seeds to -18°C. It is a place able to preserve about 4.5 million seeds so that they can survive for hundreds, even thousands, of years.

The construction was begun by the Norwegian government in 2006, and has cost about US$9 million. The government is supported, in its operational costs, by a combination of international organisations and foundations. Officially opened in 2008, the seed bank and its management is ensured by a three-party alliance: the Norwegian government, the Global Crop Diversity Trust and the Nordic Genetic Resource Center.

The vault was built with the mission to save the most important seeds on planet earth. The goal of the seed bank is to maintain reserves of seed in the event that all other samples of them are destroyed. Indeed, the Svalbard facility stores duplicates of seeds from several other collections around the world (many of them in developing countries and emerging economies). If these collections were to be lost, they could then be regenerated with the seeds from the Svalbard seed bank [13].

The idea of protecting seeds from possible catastrophes is not new. However, today's vaults – like Svalbard – have been built so that they can survive doomsday-like events. For example, the Svalbard seed bank is built at 130 metres above sea level, so that it could survive rising sea levels caused by global climate change. Historically, such disasters were the outcomes of natural events such as volcanoes, asteroids or earthquakes: today, humankind is faced potentially with additional, artificial or human-created catastrophes like nuclear disasters, bioterrorism and global warming.

The idea underpinning this seed bank is the very opposite of a nuclear waste management site (such as Onkalo, where future generations need to be kept away from the location). With a seed bank, such as Svalbard, future generations – or at least the human beings who survive a possible cataclysmic event – will want to enter this place, gain access to the seeds, and be able to sow them in the ground as future food sources.

Svalbard therefore illustrates yet another vision of time: one in which human beings are attempting to supplant the tyranny of split-second measures and counterbalancing such foolishness with the generosity of near-limitless time.. Indeed, the official Svalbard Web site announces that " ... *The facility is designed to have an almost 'endless' lifetime*" (http://www.regjeringen.no/en/dep/lmd/campain/svalbard-global-seed-vault.html?regj_oss=1&id=462220).

3.4   Long-Term Thinking: Van Horn, Texas

This 10,000 Year Clock provides a reminder that civilisation is only about 10,000 years old: a mere moment when set against the 4.5 billion year-old age of the planet. It prompts human beings to ask, "What's the hurry?"

It takes a day's hiking over the mountains in the western part of the state of Texas, in the United States of America, to arrive at a construction site, inside a mountain, that houses an amazing clock. A group of visionary people have united under the umbrella of The Long Now Foundation (TLNF; www.longnow.org) to build the world's first monumental clock, called the 10,000 Year Clock. This is the slowest computer in the world [14].

The Long Now Foundation is behind the development of this clock, as well as several other projects. It has as its mission the goal of enlarging the human concept of time: "*The Long Now Foundation was established in 01996 ... to become the seed of a very long-term cultural institution ... to provide a counterpoint to today's accelerating culture and help make longterm thinking more common. We hope to creatively foster responsibility in the framework of the next 10,000 years.*" [15]. When writing dates, the foundation uses five-digits for each year, so that – to identify 2014, for example – it uses the number 02014. This device is intended to encourage longer-term thinking.

Once finished, the 10,000 Year Clock will be open to visitors who will have to climb a spiral staircase for hundreds of metres in order to see the huge mechanical computer that drives the clock. The complex system that underpins the clock will capture and store mechanical energy as a result of the physical movements made by the visitors themselves. Yet, another mechanism is also operating. Energy is stored by using a smart system that captures different temperatures induced by the rays of the sun that enter through a hole in the vertical tunnel at the top of the clock. The clock uses the power of the sun to correct small variations in the length of the day, making its own self-adjustments. At noon, the sun lies exactly over a tunnel leading to the clock A prism directs the sun's rays inside the mountain, and down, to be captured by the mechanical engine and interpreted as a synchronising signal. This thermal power is translated into mechanical power by transmitting heat inside the clock by means of long metal bars. So, the clock is designed to run on its own. Even if not a single person comes to visit it, the sun will power the clock! It can last for one thousand decades, even if no one comes to visit it. It is built to cope with both human survival, and also its opposite.

The clock itself is huge: it is more than fifty meters high. This monumental device is intended to help human thinking develop over a long period of time. While the engineering challenges in building the clock are immense, its real goal is to stimulate thinking about the long-term future. The clock will, for example, play different melodies, and is programmed not to repeat any of the music it plays for 10,000 years. The main question the clock aims to pose to human beings is: How are we acting today with regard to future generations of people? *"Are we being good ancestors?"* [15].

More pragmatically, the clock is also intended to avoid anxieties around yet another millennium computer bug occurring in the year 10,000. Most of those involved in this initiative are people whose careers originated in various high-tech domains. They include: Danny Hillis (a parallel computing pioneer, the designer of the clock), Steward Brand (founder of the Global Business Network, Whole Earth Catalog, the Hackers Conference and The WELL), Ester Dyson (pioneer of the digital age and founder of ICANN), Kevin Kelly (founder of Wired magazine), and Mitch Kapor (pioneer of personal computing and founder of the software company, Lotus). This group of people looks as if it is expressing a need: the need to zoom out from the imperceptible intervals of computer clocks (that run at the scale of nanoseconds, a kind of narrow time) to the immensity of a ten thousand year-duration initiative. This collective of leading personalities wants to show a more responsible face to future generations by building the slowest computer on earth. As Steward Brand, President of the Long Now Foundation, says: *"Civilization is revving itself into a pathologically short attention span. The trend might be coming from the acceleration of technology, the short-horizon perspective of market-driven economics, the next-election perspective of democracies, or the distractions of personal multi-tasking. All are on the increase. Some sort of balancing corrective to the short-sightedness is needed, some mechanism or myth which encourages the long view and the taking of long-term responsibility, where 'long-term' is measured at least in centuries. Long Now proposes both a mechanism and a myth."* [15].

3.5   Limits to the Speed of Machines? NYSE, New York Stock Exchange

On Thursday, May 6th, 2010, something strange happened on the frantic floor of the New York Stock Exchange. The stock market was down just 1.5% from the previous day. At around 2:30pm something exceptional occurred. At 2:47pm the rate was -9.16%. In just ten minutes, a billion dollars had been lost. In only a few minutes, the indices that enumerate market status had dropped hundreds of points. Some shares lost 90% of their value (the price of Accenture, the business consultancy, for example, dropped to 1 cent); other businesses were traded at incredibly high prices (Apple shares were purchased at $US100,000). Operations were cancelled and the entire financial system stopped. What happened was later described as the *"flash crash"* (see Fig. 2).

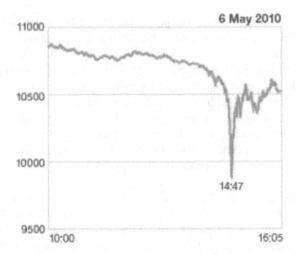

Fig. 2. Dow Jones Index during the "flash crash" (source: Bloomberg)

For the first time ever, human beings no longer controlled the execution of trades in the financial markets; computers were in control of the process. Indeed, the trading speed reached that May afternoon was impossible for human beings to follow, whether they were investors or brokers. Nevertheless, the fast-trading software algorithms continued to compete with each other.

It took months for the United States Commodity Futures Trading Commission (CFTC) and the United States Securities and Exchange Commission to produce a detailed report [16] explaining the flash crash. Yet one thing was clear. The cause of the catastrophe was not human beings[1]. It was machines, algorithms, and sophisticated software programs that were able to place 10,000 bids-per-second through computer trading. These algorithms were very similar to each other: one program emulated the behaviour of others that, in turn, influenced other programs. In the end, the process triggered a snowball effect.

Machines can keep millions of variables under their control simultaneously. They are able to trade thousands of stocks at the same time in order to exploit extremely small changes in stock prices. Every day more than 70% of the volume of transactions are now controlled by computers that have taken over the trading industry [17]. The responsibility for the handling of these incredibly fast mechanisms – that are impossible for a human being to control – have been delegated to machines to play stock market games that can change the destiny of entire companies and markets. At these speeds, cause-and-effect explanations of market phenomena become impossible while they are occurring.

At a later date, Mary Schapiro, the then chairwoman of the Security and Exchange Commission, admitted that *"automated trading systems will follow their coded logic*

---

[1] One could also argue, of course, that human beings were partly the indirect cause of the failure, since they had not recognised the need to question, nor questioned, their assumptions about market behaviour when designing the algorithms underpinning the trading systems; neither had they, presumably, tested the software sufficiently thoroughly.

regardless of outcome ...." and *"human involvement likely would have prevented these orders from executing at absurd prices"* [18]. As a result, the United States Securities and Exchange Commission imposed circuit breakers, mechanisms that slow down the speed of transactions (for example by automatically stopping trading if the fluctuations are higher than 10% in five minutes) [17]. More recently, the European Parliament has published guidelines on how to better handle high-frequency trading [19].

Both of these 2011-2012 measures go in the direction of slowing algorithms down. Ultimately, they are admissions that some limits have to be imposed on the speed of execution and operation of computer software.

4   Discussion and towards a Set of Conclusions

This chapter has dealt with the concept of time and the preoccupation with speed in the context of ICT. It questions the indiscriminate pursuit of faster technologies and the assumption that faster is better. It highlights a set of arguments about why speed is not always important or necessary. In contrast to the technological imperative to measure changes over ever tinier fractions of a second, and in recognition of the need to address longer-term concerns and phenomena, some people are now starting to consider periods at the other end of the temporal scale: decades, centuries, millennia and beyond.

The chapter illustrates this by putting forward four concrete case studies, and offers a fifth which is more conceptual in its basis, to underline the need for more circumspection in the quest for faster ICT. Important messages that emerge during the course of the chapter include the facts that:

- **Life cycles are long:** this is a valid observation for both for human beings and for technology. Human beings need to consider the use of technologies over time and throughout life cycles.
- **The notion of slow refers to both time and speed:** slow and fast refer to rates of change that take place in conditions or items over a given period of time.
- **Speed may need to be limited:** in appropriate circumstances, the speed of machines may need to be limited. It may not always be a recommendation to push on the accelerator at the maximum speed allowed by technology. Instead, human beings might seek to regain the control of the 'pedal' that drives the speed of technology, and thus avoid a kind of techno-deterministic fatalism.
- **Dangers can be particularly long-lasting:** today, the possibility of immense disasters needs to be faced, whether these are natural catastrophes, such as the failure of crops, or – and especially – human-created ones (examples include atomic accidents and the side-effects of atomic waste).
- **Control on the part of humans is important:** human beings have created more than one technological process – the chief example being trading using financial systems – for which there is a need to reclaim a certain degree of control.

- **Preparing for eternity is important, and long-term thinking and acting, should both be encouraged:** in preparing for the extremely long-term future needs of humanity, there needs to be implicit wisdom, care, and a sense of concern.
- **Links with ICT can be positive:** some of this chapter's case studies are about how technology can help humankind plan long-term, and keep stores and symbols going over the long-term. As examples, Onkala and Svalbard could presumably not exist without technologies to power them, whereas the clock at Van Horn shows that it is possible to do something similar that is kept running by only the sun.

All five of the case studies explored in this chapter relate in some way to nature, ecology, sustainability and the continuity of human life over time. Given this orientation, ultimately, there will be a need to focus on sustainable elements of technologies, what Slow Tech calls *clean ICT*. Clean ICT means taking into consideration the environmental impacts (such as materials and energy consumption) of the manufacture, use and disposal of ICT products [20]. This, technology should respect the environment, and promote biodiversity and sustainability. It will mean undertaking in-depth analyses of the impact of both hardware and software production, use and disposal. It could help people to minimise their consumption of non-renewable resources and materials, and thereby reduce any ensuing pollution. At the same time, it could maximise the contribution of renewable resources in energy production. More specifically, ICT could be recyclable-by-design so that ICT lifetimes are extended and lengthened, and interoperability encouraged.

Ultimately, clean ICT is just one of the three important element of Slow Tech: these are technologies that are *good*, *fair*, and *clean*.

References

1. Patrignani, N., Whitehouse, D.: Slow Tech: A Quest for Good, Clean and Fair ICT. Journal of Information, Communication and Ethics in Society 12(2), 78–92 (2014), doi:10.1108/JICES-11-2013-0511.
2. Patrignani, N., Whitehouse, D.: Slow Tech: The Bridge between Computer Ethics and Business Ethics (this volume)
3. Slow Food, Slow Food International-Good, Clean and Fair food (2014), http://www.slowfood.com (accessed May 29, 2014)
4. Bateson, G.: Stepstoanecologyofmind. Chicago University Press, Chicago (1972)
5. Nakamura, A.: Japan's K computer becomes fastest super computer in the world. Technology Headlines (June 20, 2011)
6. TOP 500 (2013), China's Tianhe2 Supercomputer Takes No.1 Ranking on 41st TOP500 List, http://www.top500.org/blog/lists/2013/06/press-release/#.U4eBlxZvdFI (accessed May 29, 2014)
7. Marinetti, F.T.: Manifesto del Futurismo (February 1909)
8. Giuffreda, G.: Elogiodellalentezza, Roma. Ilmanifesto (May 27, 2011)
9. Giuffreda, G., Langer, A.: Conversioneecologica e stili di vita. Rio 1992-2012. Edizionidell'Asino, Roma (2012)

10. Von Schomberg, R. (ed.): Towards Responsible Research and Innovation in the Information and Communication Technologies and SecurityTechnologies Fields. European Commission, Directorate General for Research and Innovation (2011)
11. Meadows, D.H., Meadows, D.L., Randers, J., BehrensIII, W.W.: The Limits to Growth. Universe Books (1972)
12. Schumacher, E.F.: Small is Beautiful: A Study of Economics as if People Mattered. Blond and Briggs (1973)
13. MAAF, Ministry of Agriculture and Food, Svalbard Global Seed Vault Official Web site (2011), http://www.regjeringen.no/en/dep/lmd/campain/svalbard-global-seed-vault.html?regj_oss=1&id=462220 (accessed May 29, 2014)
14. Hillis, D., Seaman, R., Allen, S., Giorgini, J.: Time in the 10,000-year Clock. American Astronomical Association, 11-665 (February 2012)
15. TLNF, The Long Now Foundation (2014), http://www.longnow.org (accessed May 29, 2014)
16. CFTC (U.S. Commodity Futures Trading Commission) / SEC (U.S. Securities & Exchange Commission) (2010), Findings Regarding the Market Events of May 6, 2010, Report of the staffs of the CFTC and the SEC to the Joint Advisory Committee on Emerging Regulatory Issues, Washington, D.C. (September 30, 2010)
17. Salmon, F., Stokes, J.: Algorithms Take Control of Wall Street, Wired (January 2011)
18. Norris, F.: Time for Regulators to Impose Order in the Markets. The New York Times (May 13, 2010)
19. European Parliament, Financial trading rules: Economic Affairs Committee MEPs outline reform plan. Committees: Committee on Economic and Monetary Affairs (September 27, 2012)
20. Patrignani, N., Laaksoharju, M., Kavathatzopoulos, I.: Challenging the Pursuit of Moore's Law: ICT Sustainability in the Cloud Computing Era. Politeia. Notizie di Politeia - Rivista di Etica e Scelte Pubbliche, Anno XXVII(104) (2011)

Case Study of Practice of the Tea Ceremony (*Sado*) through Distance Education

On the Ethics of ICT

Sachiko Yanagihara[1] and Hiroshi Koga[2]

[1] University of Toyama, Faculty of Economics, Japan
sachiko@eco.u-toyama.ac.jp
[2] Kansai University, Faculty of Informatics, Japan
koga@res.kutc.kansai-u.ac.jp

Abstract. The purpose of this paper is to consider the meaning of the distance education which utilizes ICT from the viewpoint of the ethicality of ICT. In Particular, this paper would discuss the distance education system of the tea ceremony (specifically, *Ensyu Sado School*) in Japan. This paper is organized as follows. First, the education system of the tea ceremony is introduced. Second, as a case of distance education utilizing ICT, "WEB lessons" of the tea ceremony of traditional Japanese performing arts are taken up. Third, the effect of the distance learning system of the tea ceremony had on the code of conduct of trainees will be discussed. In other words, ethics of ICT in WEB lessons of tea ceremony is considered.

Keywords: Distance Education Systems, Ethics of ICT, the Tea Ceremony.

1 Introduction

In recent years, the distance education system attracts attention. Innovation in distance education system is remarkable. The driving force is an application of technologies such as "gamification" and "AR (augmented reality)", supported by 3D technologies. Here, gamification is the use of game thinking and game mechanics in non-game contexts to engage users in solving problems [1]. Distance education (e-learning) is undergoing a major transformation in this way.

The purpose of this paper is to consider the meaning of the distance education which utilizes ICT (Information and Communication Technology) from the viewpoint of the ethicality of ICT. Sometimes, the focus of research of distance education has a tendency concentrated on a technical trend. For example, the meaning of "gamification" or "serious game" is told in many cases (e.g. [1-2]). There, it is discussed what is acquired (or lost) by the virtual space closer to the real there. However, in this paper, such newest distance education systems are not targeted. Rather, it is a subject discussed in a relatively simple system. In addition, the tea ceremony (*sado*) of traditional Japanese performing arts would be taken up as a learning object. Conventionally, it is an area in which it has been considered only face-to-face training is effective. Therefore, the authors suspect it to be beneficial in the discussion of the

K.K. Kimppa et al. (Eds.): HCC11 2014, IFIP AICT 431, pp. 136–145, 2014.

ethics of the information system in distance education and exploring the meaning of distance education.

This paper is organized as follows. First, the education system of the tea ceremony is introduced. Second, as a case of distance education utilizing ICT, "WEB lessons" of tea ceremony of traditional Japanese performing arts (specifically, *Ensyu Sado School*) is taken up[1]. Third, the effect of the distance learning system of the tea ceremony had on the code of conduct of trainees will be discussed. In other words, ethics of ICT in lessons WEB of the tea ceremony is considered.

2   Background of Lessons of the Tea Ceremony

In this section, before a discussion, the education system or lessons of the tea ceremony are introduced.

The first step of the exercise in the tea ceremony is mastery of basic operation. Specifically, they are the manners in tearoom and *temae* (procedure for making *maccha*, that is, Japanese green tea, for guests as they watch). In practice, lessons would be divided the operation of the procedure for making tea, mastery of each part would be a challenge: how to fold the *fukusa* (silk cloth), how to inspect the *chasen* (tea whisk), how to wipe the *chawan* (tea bowl), container for powdered thin tea, tea scoop, how to fold *chakin* (a tea cloth). In Figure 1, we can see *Chawan, Chasen, chakin, Natsume* (which use to contain the powder of green tea), *Chashakus* (which is spoon for scooping into bowls green tea).

Fig. 1. Tea Utensils (Right: Chawan, Chasen, Chakin, Natsume, and Chashaku; Left: Fukusa)

---

[1] *Enshu Sado (Tea) school* has 400 years of history. Enshu Kobori who is the originator was a feudal lord of the early 17th century (Edo Era). Therefore, Enshu School is known as samurai tea ceremony. The Spirit of Enshu Sado lies in "*Kirei Sabi*", or gracefulness and simplicity. *Kirei Sabi* has its origin in ancient Japanese sense of beauty which is closely related to *ccha* of the Heian period. (Quoted by Enshu's Tea Ceremony Web site [3]).

Exercise of such divided operation is called "*Wari Geiko*" in Japanese. Although exercises of the tea ceremony are one to one fundamentally, in this stage, two or more pupils may receive exercise simultaneously. After finishing mastery of these basic practices, a pupil performs the face-to-face training. The center of training is accomplishment in *temae*. Since the face-to-face training is in the mainstream, two or more pupils cannot be practiced simultaneously. Therefore, other pupils will play a visitor's role during a one pupil's exercise. In Figure 2, we can see training that is carried out at the same time more than one in the initial stage (left photo) and pupils those who play the role of customers except those who train (right photo).

Fig. 2. State of the practice

However, the contents of exercise of the tea ceremony do not stop only at them. In the field of lessons, the pupil would learn the traditional culture of Japan, such as the following as well as manners and way of *temae* or *otemae*. That is, *Ikebana* (arranged flower), the meaning of a *kakejiku* (hanging scroll), incense, tools, a tearoom and the yard, confectionery, Japanese clothes (*wafuku*), *kaiseki ryori* (dishes served before tea ceremony), and so on. That is, the opportunity to learn traditional Japan culture synthetically is condensed by exercise of the tea ceremony. In Figure 3, we can see *Kakejiku* and *Ikebana* (left photo) and *Wafuku* (right photo that the first author is wearing a *Wafuku*).

Fig. 3. The traditional culture in Japan

Furthermore, there is no end in exercise. Tea ceremony is different in each season. In order to learn the manners of each, a long life of learning is required. And, the art or technique of tea ceremony is broken down into *Kata*: model form[2]. That is, there are successive levels of study and people study step by step to an instructor from a beginner. And, when the learner has finished learn each stage, the instructor would issue a certificate (called *Kyojo*, meaning license) that proves it.

By the way, the guidance in the lesson of tea ceremony, specific instructions in everyday language is common. For example, instructions such as "a teacup is on the left of the front", "being a left hand there" is made. Then, in the practice room, the mentor does not instruct using the metaphor or "*Waza* Language" by Ikuta [4]. It can be said that guidance is by everyday specific.

Moreover, while training continuously, pupils can take "diplomas" such as "*Shihan* (instructor)." However, in this paper, lessons which aim at an instructor are not taken as an object. Rather, in order to clarify the ethics of ICT, discussion of this paper is limited in practice to target disciples general.

3   Case Study of the Tea Ceremony through Distance Education

In this section, the case of lessons of the tea ceremony as a key which considers the meaning of a distance education system is taken up[3]. And in this paper, we focus on non-vocational training for adult.

By the way, as is well known, the tea ceremony is the originator by men and it has been popular among men (that is, the *machisyu* (commercial and industrial men) and the samurai). In a word, the tea ceremony was a male-dominated world until the first half of the Edo period. However, in the late Edo period, players of the majority are women. In other words, the central players in the tea ceremony were replaced by women [5]. Because the tea ceremony became to be considered one subject of domestic training.

If repeatedly emphasized, despite have been formed in the male-centered society, tea ceremony has been penetrated as a lesson events in women. Tea ceremony has been learned as a domestic training or training for homemaking. However, female learners have been reduced by the social advancement of women [6, 7]. On the other hand, the number of male learners is flat trend [6, 7]. Therefore, there is a tendency to increase the ratio of male learners. A lot of male learners would like to become familiar with Japanese culture. Therefore, leaners who aim to become instructors are very few. Almost of the learners in "WEB lessons" do not intend to become an instructor.

---

[2] Kata (model form) is a cardinal rules or basic promise, and refers to how to behave. For example, there are how to use *fukusa*, how to drink tea, how to perform *temae*, and so on.

[3] This case study was created based on the atypical interviews with Mr. Horiuchi to deploy WEB lessons (December 4, 2011, October 12, 2013 and March 17, 2014). Interview survey was carried out in one-two hours each times. In addition, we would reference the writings of Mr. Horiuchi [8], web site, and Facebook. Furthermore, we send an e-mail any question as appropriate. And Fig.1 (the lower right one), Fig.2 and Fig.5 are photos that Horiuchi is taken.

Rather, they would aim to learn mind and form (called *kata*) of tea ceremony [9]. And many of the learners in "WEB lessons" are male. The authors would like to emphasize this point.

Now, in exercise of the tea ceremony based on facing education, probably, it is only Gishio Horiuchi (The name in the tea ceremony is Kochu-An-Socho) who uses the distance education system. Mr. Horiuchi is a master of the tea ceremony who plays various active parts. With regard to the activities of Mr. Horiuchi, please refer to the following website [10].

Fig. 4. Mr. Horiuchi (left) and the State of the lessons (right)

The direct trigger of the "Web lessons" was a pupil's overseas transfer. One male pupil was transferred to France. If it is domestic transfer, it is possible to continue the lesson by finding the mentor of the same school. However, since it was the transfer to overseas in the case of this pupil, it was difficult. Then, there was a proposal of distance education spontaneously from a pupil. In this way, the "WEB lessons" is born as a result of unintended.

At the beginning, the lesson was carried out with an iPhone. At the lesson, since instruction was performed orally, the camera function of iPhone was enough. That is, system requirements are simple. A mentor just sees a pupil's operation. After, a system configuration progresses follows: the latest version of the freeware Skype ™ in which IP video call is possible can use. However, the web camera of high resolution is recommended.

Now, at a WEB lessons, image of pupil's procedures will be captured in the Web camera. In lessons, Mr. Horiuchi sees in the home video of pupil. He will indicate by words specific to the pupil as necessary. It would be just "365 day and 24 hours," and "living room exercise." Recently, two cameras have been used during the practice of the WEB lessons. In order to teach to fine operation, it decided to use together not only the whole body but the camera for hands.

In 2011, pupil of the Web lesson had been living in Singapore, New York, Vietnam as well as France. The problem for a mentor was that instruction time is midnight. Time for a pupil to finish work and go home becomes midnight due to the time difference in many cases. Therefore, there are not few burdens of Mr. Horiuchi who is a mentor. However, Mr. Horiuchi still says that WEB lessons have a big charm. That is, first, it can have a pupil, without affecting exercise in the usual practice room.

Next, it is that a burden is small since it is not a lot of people. In addition, Mr. Horiuchi said as follows: 'I think the reaction of WEB lessons when viewed from the pupil also good. It is the reason why pupil is satisfied with the environment of being able to question at any time'.

Fig. 5. The State of WEB lessons (Screenshot of the mentor side)

By the way, WEB lessons would be carried out in private room of leaners. Of course, it is not a formal tea room. In addition, the tool also dispense with substitute in many cases.

Mr. Horiuchi has been instructed to bring tools from Japan, such as *fukusa* (silk wrapper) and *chasen* (bamboo whisk). However, pupils have to use a substitute in the local tool such as a furnace. So to speak, the practice by *mitate* (resembling) had been practiced.

The training fee was set at 2000 yen for 30 minutes. Normal practice is 4000 yen in about an hour once. In addition, it has introduced a coupon system of six times 10,000 yen at present.

4   Ethics in Distance Education Systems

In this section, ethics of ICT in distance education system will be discussed. In other words, the authors would like to pay attention to changes in the educational activities for the pupil. That is, the question whether ICT changes the code of conduct of the real world would be discussed[4].

---

[4] In this paper, we would referred to an implicit assumption about the practice of the tea ceremony as "the Code of Conduct." Specifically, we refer to the idea of common sense in the tea ceremony world such as "how should we do with the practice of the tea ceremony," "what should a teacher-student relationship" and so on.

There are two challenges: First, a change in the code of conduct of Mentor. Second, changes in code of conduct of leaners. In this paper, we focus on the first challenge. That is, changes in the code of conduct of mentor (not leaners) would be discussed. By the way, our previous work [8] analyzed changes in the code of conduct of the learner from the perspective of organizational citizenship behavior, but it is not from the perspective of ethics of ICT. Furthermore, as to the changes in the code of conduct of the learner, "double-loop learning" also is involved [11]. The idea of double-loop learning is proposed by Chris Argyris. The popularly idea of the learning is that we are working to solve problems according to the framework of ideas and action that has already. However, there is another type of learning. It is to discard the existing frameworks, and to incorporate a framework for new thinking and action. Such a type of learning is "double-loop learning."

In practice in remote location, the tea utensils are not perfect. Since there is no *furo* which is tool to boil water[5], it is replaced by an electric kettle. Or, there is no coal, but to perform the practice with the intention of some.

Fig. 6. *kama* (kettle) and *furo/ro* would vary depending on the season

Through such lessons, pupils would the concept of practice as well as the procedure of the tea ceremony. It is said that the learning through such lessons is a double-loop learning exactly. Therefore, we would like to challenge in the future the issue of learner.

By the way, through the practice of the WEB lessons, the contents of the lesson have not been substantially changed. And, the way of lessons are not changed significantly. That is, code of conduct is not changed significantly. However, the authors would focus on the context that is the background of the lesson. ICT in Web lesson is a mirror and an amplifying device of context.

At this time, contexts in which Mr. Horiuchi had are as follows: First, he would like to guide to the entrance of the tea ceremony to a lot of people. Second, he would like to impart the pleasure of tea ceremony in Japan. Third, he would like to break down stereotypes that it requires specialized tools and that learning is difficult[6].

As related to the context of the first and second, the authors would like to point out that Mr. Horiuchi was reviewing the traditional master and pupil relationship. It is said that traditional master and pupil relationship as being collapsed in the world of

---

[5] In the tea ceremony, the tool to boil hot water will vary from season to season. Therefore, it is not possible to provide a hook for all remote.

[6] Personal interview at December 4, 2011 and October 12, 2013.

tea ceremony (or it might not limited to the world of tea ceremony). In the case of domestic training, voluntary pupils were few. Pupil of this type had come to practice for a period of up to marriage. But, in recent years, new pupil who would pay a fee on their own has been increasing. They believe the lesson of a lifetime. In addition, the master and pupil relationship sought by new leaners would be dry, such as the service consumer. (It is said to be the era where disciples choose a mentor.). It would not be a wet relationship such as apprenticeship[7]. Therefore, Mr. Horiuchi would be considered weak ties are important. ICT (that is, distance education system) has strengthened the concept of weak ties. Consequently, ICT revealed the significance of maintaining a weak relationship.

Then, in terms of the third context that described above, the practice of lesson using ICT was a breakdown of stereotypes in the tea ceremony. Mr. Horiuchi was hoping that people will enter the world of tea ceremony frankly. And he would like to tell not only how to *kata* of *temae* (partial form model of *temae*) but also the fun of tea ceremony. Then, it is important that the pupil continues the lessons in order to have the experience of the pleasure of tea. However, there are cases where continuation of the lessons is difficult on account of work. Therefore, as described above, distance education system by ICT is enabled. Then distance education system according to ICT is a reflection of the intention of Horiuchi. In other words, ICT can be understood as a tool to convey the heart of tea rather than a tool to teach *kata* (form). That is, ICT has amplified his intentions or was polarized to his intentions. Further, in order to continue the dry master-pupil relationship, Mr. Horiuchi adopted a fare system in accordance with the practice times.

Then, ICT is a mirror that reflects the context as described above. WEB lessons were developed while reflecting the context of Mr. Horiuchi. And, through a WEB lessons, he began to strengthen the context of his own. And, he was convinced of the validity of the context of his own. The loose coupling master and pupil relationship is the prominent example. New pupil (who would become pupil to learn Japanese culture) different from the old disciple (the people that was recommended from the parent as domestic training) prefer relationships dry. So, he clarified the unit price of the lessons. That is, Web lesson was induced behavior of discount rates in response to the absence. Further, Mr. Horiuchi said "It is necessary for master to compromise with disciples."

In addition, Mr. Horiuchi said, "I does not matter the reason for the absence of lessons of disciple. (Rather, the continuation of the lesson is important)." ICT has also induced such correspondence.

As described above, ICT promoted the loose coupling master and pupil relationship. And, ICT lowered the threshold of the introductory tea ceremony. However, to convey the fun is only one aspect of interest. Another object is to teach proper type. Also in this regard, ICT induced additional actions. It is a change of

---

[7] The apprenticeship system in Japan, it has been emphasized technology can be obtained through the washing and cleaning. In other word, it's been said that it is important that you spend together the day-to-day life. Sometimes such a relationship is expressed as "wet" in Japan. In this paper, I use a wet with the same meaning. Conversely, it is referred to as "dry" when building the appropriate relationship as needed.

distance education system itself. That is, it is the addition of the Web camera. Then, the mentor would be able to monitor the enlarged image of a hand if needed. As a result, the mentor is ready to check the detailed behavior of the disciples.

Finally, for the context of breaking stereotypes, ICT has been reinforced. Originally, the use of a substitute for professional tool in the tea ceremony is not a few. However, Mr. Horiuchi admits further substitution of the tool. As a result, WEB lessons were to break down stereotypes that lesson is not possible without adequate tools.

As mentioned above, it would correspond to *"the bricolage"* to point out of Levi Strauss that one pupil would liken the electric kettle to *furo* [12]. Off course, the procedure of the tea ceremony is formalized. However, it is not necessary to view the absolute form of model (that is, *kata*). It's may be a flexible (case by case) approach. Because the environment is restricted as a remote location, the student can learn the flexibility of interpretations. After all, the pupil would begin to consider that "we can continue the lessons without access to the equipment"[8].

However, ethics of the distance education system like this is not the uniqueness of ICT. Rather, it is the one that ICT enhance or reflect the ethics of users (mentor).

5   Conclusion

This paper was discussed the ethics of ICT (the promotion of changes in the Code of Conduct) on distance education system of the tea ceremony that is a traditional Japanese performing arts.

And ethicality that polarizes or reinforces the context of the user of the ICT is discussed. In a nutshell, we argued that ICT is to reinforce the Code of Conduct of the user. In other word, ICT does not include ethics of its own. Through reflecting the context of the user, ICT to reinforces the code of conduct of the user. In addition, by utilizing the ICT on the basis of the Code of Conduct that has been reinforced, code of conduct to more polarized. With the negative feedback loop such acts, ethicality of ICT will be polarized ethics of the user. This is the conclusion of this paper.

In the tea ceremony tea utensils plays an important role, making a practice of behavior to fit the tea utensils is essential. Also, it is a matter sensuous. Therefore, the idea that people could substitute other things because there are no adequate utensils. However, disruption to practice for that is that a waste. After all, distance education systems were facilitated the direction in which to continue practices in admit a certain degree of substitution.

In addition, these findings were obtained from targeting the distance education system of simple configuration. Distance education systems using the latest technologies such as augmented reality are seeking the realization of reality. However, WEB lessons are seeking actuality. Through a system of simple configuration, mentors are aware of the master and pupil relationship and have done an invitation to the world of tea ceremony.

---

[8] Personal interview at December 4, 2011 and October 12, 2013.

Also, when viewed from the standpoint of the pupil, the concept of actuality is useful. WEB lessons are a tool that allows you to feel the loose coupling master and pupil relationship. However, in this regard, we want to challenge for the future.

Acknowledgment. We are deeply grateful to Gishio Horiuchi (Kochu-An-Shocho). We appreciate anonymous reviewers for their helpful comments on the earlier version of this paper. This work was supported by JSPS KAKENHI Grant Numbers 22530358, 26380458 and 26380550 and by a grant from Center for Asian and Pacific Studies, Seikei University.

References

1. Deterding, S., Khaled, R., Nacke, L., Dixon, D.: Gamification: Toward a Definition. In: CHI 2011 Gamification Workshop Proceedings, Vancouver, BC, Canada (2011)
2. Lewis Johnson, W.: Serious Use of a Serious Game for Language Learning. In: Proceedings of the 2007 Conference on Artificial Intelligence in Education: Building Technology Rich Learning Contexts That Work, pp. 67–74 (2007)
3. Web Site of Enshu's Tea Ceremony,
   http://www.enshuryu.com/English/index.html (reference March 31, 2014)
4. Ikuta, K.: Learning from "Waza": Inquiry into the New Form of Knowledge. University of Tokyo Press, Tokyo (2007) (in Japanese)
5. Kato, E. (ed.): The Tea Ceremony and Women's Empowerment in Modern Japan: Bodies Re-Presenting the Past. Routledge (2014)
6. MIC's Survey on Time Use and Leisure Activities (2007),
   http://www.stat.go.jp/data/shakai/2006/index.htm
   (reference March 31, 2014)
7. MIC's Survey on Time Use and Leisure Activities (2012),
   http://www.stat.go.jp/data/shakai/2011/index.htm
   (reference March 31, 2014)
8. Horiuchi, G.: The Tea Ceremony Guidance for Men. Hara-Syobo (2004) (in Japanese)
9. Yanagihara, S.: Customer Relationship Management and Trust management using "The WEB lessons" in the Iemoto System. Journal of Japan Telework Society 10(2), 23–30 (2012) (in Japanese)
10. Web Site of Horiuchi, G., http://www.kochu-an.jp/ (reference March 31, 2014)
11. Argyris, C.: Increasing Leadership Effectiveness. Wiley, New York (1976)
12. Levi-Strauss, C.: The Savage Mind (French: La Pensée sauvage). University of Chicago Press, Chicago (1966, French 1962)

A Little-Known Chapter in the History of Computing in Belgium: The *Machine Mathématique IRSIA-FNRS*

Marie d'Udekem-Gevers

Faculty of Computer Sciences, University of Namur, Belgium
marie.gevers@unamur.be

Abstract. Based on original documents, this article deals with the first stored program computer designed and built in Belgium in the early 1950's, the *Machine Mathématique IRSIA-FNRS* (MMIF). After addressing the history of this prototype, it describes the Machine and highlights its specificities. Then, showing how the computing techniques that led to this machine were originally disseminated in Belgium, it underlines the Swiss (particularly *Eidgenössische Technische Hochschule* (ETH)) influence on this project.

Keywords: Belgium, dissemination of innovations, history of computing, stored program computer.

1 Introduction

The present contribution[1] addresses a subject that remains largely[2] unknown: the origins of computing in Belgium. It discusses the design and building in Antwerp of a computer known at the time as the *Machine Mathématique IRSIA-FNRS* [3] (MMIF) because it was funded by the *Institut pour l'Encouragement de la Recherche Scientifique dans l'Industrie et l'Agriculture*[4] (IRSIA) and the *Fonds National de la Recherche Scientifique*[5] (FNRS).

The information presented here is the result of research[6] begun in 2005 and completed in 2011. The study focused initially on interviews with pioneers in the computing field[7]. Each of these interviews was conducted in a semi-directed manner and was audio-taped[8]. Each taping was then transcribed and sent to the interviewee for corrections. However, it quickly became apparent that, in order to confirm details or resolve any ambiguities or contradictions, it would be necessary to telephone the interviewees

---

[1] It is a summary of a detailed monograph [33], published only in French.
[2] When the monograph summarised here was being printed, P.-J. Courtois published an account about this same machine [32].
[3] See Figure 4. The IRSIA-FNRS Mathematical Machine.
[4] Institute for the Promotion of Scientific Research in Industry and Agriculture.
[5] Belgian National Fund for Scientific Research.
[6] Sandra Mols collaborated in this research from 2007 to 2009.
[7] This was how Jean Meinguet, Nicolas Rouche, Claude Fosséprez and then later André Fischer were interviewed.
[8] Each tape recording has been added to the *"Histoire informatique belge"* Archival Fund (HIBAF).

K.K. Kimppa et al. (Eds.): HCC11 2014, IFIP AICT 431, pp. 146–161, 2014.
© IFIP International Federation for Information Processing 2014

after the interviews or to contact new eyewitnesses. Furthermore, during the study, E-mail exchanges became increasingly important and relevant. They enabled us to compare diverging accounts and also to encourage reminiscences. In all, twelve people[9] who were actively involved in the history of the MMIF were contacted and gave their accounts. In addition, these eyewitnesses provided contemporary documents[10] about the Machine: texts pertaining to the description, functioning and programming of the MMIF, as well as photos from that time. On the basis of these eyewitness accounts and, above all, the contemporary texts and photos about the MMIF, I began to write a technical description of the Machine. Then, I systematically gave the eyewitnesses the texts I had written for corrections and additions. Subsequently, it became evident to me that the historical context of the prototype would have to be addressed. There were major gaps in my information about this subject, and therefore I went to the FNRS Archives. Using photocopies of documents found there, I was able, step by step, to write the detailed history of the MMIF. This text was further enhanced with information from other sources already gathered about the Machine. Finally, the completed monograph was sent to a number of people (including participants in the MMIF project), who agreed to read it and make any suggestions for improvements.

2   Historical Context

The first event that would lead to the building of the MMIF dates back to 3 May 1946 [25]: this was the decision by the FNRS Board of Directors to ask Professor Charles Manneback[11] (*Université Catholique de Louvain*) and Mr L. Brillouin (*Collège de France*) to conduct a survey of "large mathematical machines" in the USA. This mission would lead to a report submitted to the FNRS on 16 June 1947 [27]. During the winter and spring of 1947/48, M. Linsman (an assistant at the *Université de Liège*) and W. Pouliart (an engineer for Bell Telephone Manufacturing Company (BTMC) in Antwerp) participated in building and setting up the Mark III machine at Harvard University under the direction of Professor H. Aiken. On 15 June 1949, Willems (FNRS Administrator-Director), Linsman, Pouliart and Henry (IRSIA Director) met in order to agree on a future course: Linsman and Pouliart would write a machine construction project in a few months and BTMC would provide the facilities necessary for completing this project. In August 1950, Professors Aiken, Manneback and Boulanger (Professor at the *Université Libre de Bruxelles* and the *Faculté Polytechnique de Mons*) met at Harvard to discuss the project written by Linsman and Pouliart. That same year, IRSIA and FNRS agreed to finance the execution of the project, via the *"Comité pour l'étude et la construction de machines à calculer électroniques"*[12] (CCCE), which was specially created for this purpose. On 16

---

[9]   The ten main eyewitnesses were the four people cited above as well as Paul Dagnelie, Armand de Callataÿ, Frédéric Iselin, Jacques Loeckx, Paul Parré and Fritz Wiedmer. Pierre Macq and Guillaume Van Mechelen also provided some information.

[10] These documents (either originals or copies) have also been added to HIBAF.

[11] See [30].

[12] Committee for the Study and Construction of Electronic Calculating Machines.

and 17 January 1951, Professors Aiken, Manneback and Boulanger, Mr. Pouliart and Mr. Linsman met at the IRSIA and compiled 16 recommendations (including the 'specifications' for the MMIF) [23]. A few days later, an agreement [26] was signed, containing the following clauses:

> "It is hereby agreed [...]
>   e/ that the Committee and Bell Telephone shall undertake all necessary measures to ensure that a certain number of scientists - engineers, mathematicians and physicists - are assigned to design and build the Machine and are trained in the techniques for the building and use of said Machine;
>   f/ that the building shall be performed under the leadership of Mr W. Pouliart, Mr. Linsman and Mr. Belevitch[13] working on it full time."

In early May 1951, the design of the MMIF began, followed almost immediately by work on its construction. On 14 May 1952, following a visit to BTMC, Aiken wrote a letter [21] in which he recommended a few new improvements and proposed a schedule for completion. In June of that year, the assembly[14] of the MMIF commenced.

On 13 December 1954 [24] the initial version of the MMIF (17 racks), located on the top floor of an old BTMC building became operational. In January 1955, King Baudouin of Belgium was given a private tour, and then the Machine was officially unveiled on 12 February of that same year[15].

Fig. 1. People responsible for designing the MMIF, in front of the machine during construction (Source: HIBAF with annotations by M. d'Udekem-Gevers)

---

[13] See [31].
[14] See Figure 1.
[15] See Figures 2 and 3.

Fig. 2. Private tour for the King of Belgium (Source: [18])

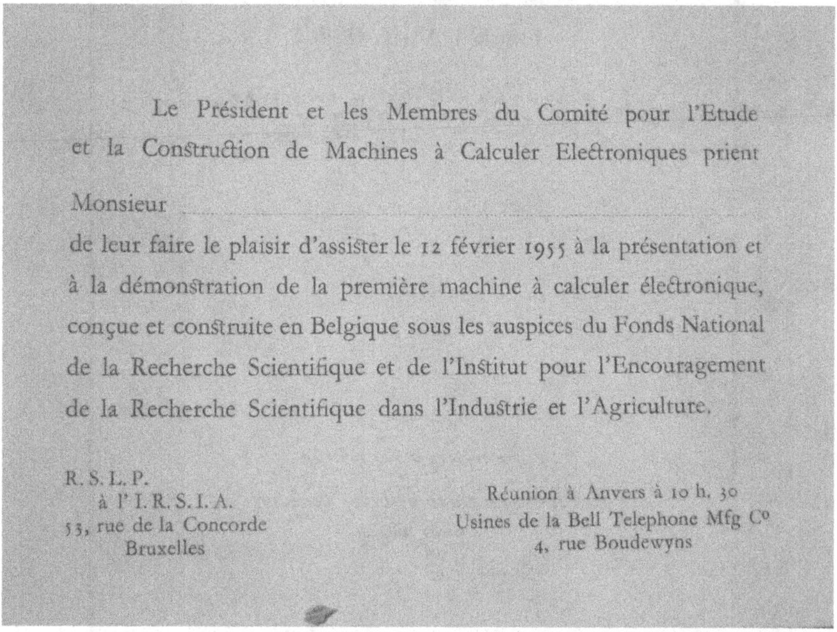

Le Président et les Membres du Comité pour l'Etude et la Construction de Machines à Calculer Electroniques prient

Monsieur

de leur faire le plaisir d'assister le 12 février 1955 à la présentation et à la démonstration de la première machine à calculer électronique, conçue et construite en Belgique sous les auspices du Fonds National de la Recherche Scientifique et de l'Institut pour l'Encouragement de la Recherche Scientifique dans l'Industrie et l'Agriculture.

R. S. L. P.
   à l'I. R. S. I. A.
53, rue de la Concorde
      Bruxelles

Réunion à Anvers à 10 h. 30
Usines de la Bell Telephone Mfg Cº
        4, rue Boudewyns

Fig. 3. Invitation to the unveiling ceremony of the Machine (Source: FNRS Archival Fund)

The day after the unveiling, the commissioning and practical use of the MMIF began. In March 1955, the *"Comité d'étude et d'exploitation des calculateurs électroniques"*[16] (CECE) was created, with Belevitch named as chairman soon thereafter.

---

[16] Committee for the Study and Use of Electronic Calculators.

In late December 1956, the final version of the MMIF (34 racks) was completed, and it was moved to a new location in the new BTMC tower. Soon thereafter, a testing and correction phase started and was completed in late March 1957.

The operational period came immediately after this test phase. On 10 July 1957, a favourable assessment about the MMIF was written by Aiken and van Wijngaarden[17] [22]. Both were later present when the MMIF was received by the CCCE. From mid-May to early November 1958, use of the MMIF was temporarily interrupted when the Machine was being moved from Antwerp to Brussels. Then operation continued until April 1960, when use of the MMIF was discontinued on an almost definitive basis. However, it was only in late December 1962 that the CECE was effectively disbanded.

Fig. 4. Cover photo from [19] (Source: HIBAF)

---

[17] A. van Wijngaarden was the head of the Computing Department at Mathematisch Centrum in Amsterdam.

The real overall cost of the MMIF has been able to be calculated on the basis of several documents contained in the FNRS Archival Fund. It amounted to 25,515,000 Belgian francs at the time[18]. This was almost four times the cost as it was first foreseen in 1950. Of this total, 22,935,000 francs were provided by IRSIA and the FNRS while the remainder came from Bell.

3   Anatomy of the Machine

3.1   Designation and Definition

The MMIF was considered at the time to be a "universal scientific digital computer" [15]. In current terminology, it is known as a stored program computer.

3.2   Logical Architecture

The logical architecture of the MMIF is classical: it can be described as being composed mainly of five parts or "components" [19]:

1. Memory: on which the data and programs are written separately. This distinction between the two types of memory is characteristic of what is now called "Harvard"[19] architecture;
2. "Arithmetic unit" [15]: which is in charge of basic arithmetic operations;
3. "(Automatic) Control" [19], also known as the "control circuit" [29]: which distributes "instructions provided by the program to the Machine" [29] ;
4. "Input components" [29];
5. "Output components" [29].

3.3   External Aspects

The following is the description of the "initial" MMIF in 1955, provided by Linsman and Pouliart [19]: "The Machine is in the form of a set of racks arranged around the perimeter of an open rectangle[20] behind and inside of which the magnetic memory cylinder is housed. Its footprint is 7.50 m X 2.50 m X 2.50 m". These authors [19] also state:

> "The [standard] racks, which are 20 cm deep, are similar to those used in Bell Telephone Manufacturing C^o transmission equipment [...]. All the parts in the racks are removable, and spare parts are available for a quick return to service in case of a breakdown."

---

[18] This investment added up to 178 millions Belgian francs at the end of 2010 (considering inflation since 1955 according to IMF), that is to say 4.4 millions euros.

[19] Wikipedia. This architecture should therefore be distinguished from von Neumann's, in which this separation does not exist.

[20] This is clearly illustrated in Figures 5 and 6.

The "final" MMIF had 34 racks and as a function of its successive locations, it had first an L-shape (13 m long) and later regained a U-shape.

Fig. 5. The "initial" MMIF (with 17 racks), front view (Source: [19], photo I)

Fig. 6. The "initial" MMIF, rear view (Source: [19], photo II)

3.4   Description of the Physical Architecture

Introduction

In 1955, according to Linsman and Pouliart [19]: "the Machine had about 3,000 hot cathode vacuum tubes, 1,000 cold cathode gas tubes, 400 relays, 1,000 selenium rectifier diodes and about 5,000 germanium diodes. It used about 15 kW of power." In 1957, according to the CECE, these numbers were the same for the rectifiers and gas tubes, but the MMIF then had 5,000 hot cathode vacuum tubes[21] and used 25 kW of power [15].

We should state that the MMIF was, according to Meinguet [8], analogous to the Harvard Mark IV machine. While the MMIF did use technology from across the Atlantic, it is nevertheless true that it was also the opportunity, on the local level, for innovative technical research and execution in computer hardware. Linsman and Pouliart [19] note that there were certain components "whose design clearly differentiates MMIF from other computers." These authors [19] list the following distinguishing features:

- The magnetic tape memory;
- The magnetic cylinder memory;
- Amplifiers to record and read magnetic signals;
- Electronic memory on cold cathode gas tubes;
- The arithmetic unit.

Owing to a lack of space, we will focus here only on the memory units[22] and in particular on those that make the MMIF unique.

Physical Memory

We can classify, in line with Rouche [5] and Loeckx [35], the memory of the MMIF in three categories as a function of access time: slow memory, faster memory and fastest memory.

Until (at least) 1957, the only **slow memory** cited in the texts used magnetic tape technology. This involved six identical mechanisms[23] "which can be used either to provide input for the Machine or to collect calculation results. They are composed each of a small pulley and a pneumatic device whose combined action controls the movement of a continuous magnetic strip" [29]. "On the tape, the whole made of the word and its address forms a series of 22 figures, with the address before the word [...]. A tape is able to hold more than 2,000 words. [...] The reading or writing time on the tape is about 30 msec. per word, the starting and pausing time after each word being included. " [14]

---

[21] F. Wiedmer [12] states: "The increase in racks to 34 and vacuum tubes to 5,000 was mostly due to the more elaborate control and program circuits".

[22] A description in English of the arithmetic unit can be found in [32].

[23] See Figure 7.

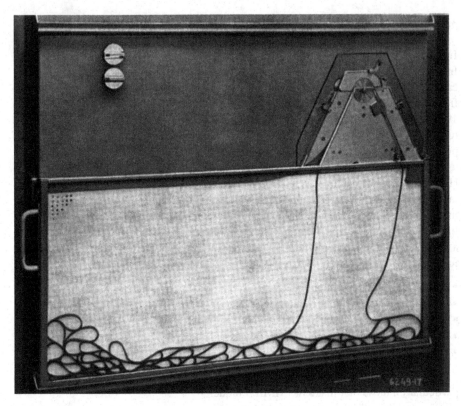

Fig. 7. One of the six magnetic-tape memories (Source: [19], photo III)

The MMIF also had a magnetic cylinder memory[24], which was **faster**, and built entirely by BTMC [19]. As Figure 8 shows, this cylinder was actually composed of two
half-cylinders, each made of five discs stacked on a single axis. In the photo, one can
also see the "writing and reading heads placed above and below a brake shoe-shaped
support along the two axes of the cylinders" [34]. The double cylinder "has 200 circu-
lar tracks or channels: one hundred of them are reserved for numbers and the other
hundred for programs" [29]. The capacity of the cylinders is "2,000 decimal
numbers (a 15-digit mantissa and a two-digit exponent with their signs) and 4,000
instructions," according to Fosséprez [34], who was one of the instrumental actors in
implementing this magnetic memory. "In the drums, the information is divided into
18-digit words (numbers or pairs of instructions) whose location is given by a four-
digit address" [14]. We can also cite some numerical values: the rotational velocity of
the cylinder is 4,100 rpm, and the average access time (individual selection of a word)
is 7 msec [15].

---

[24] It corresponds the component referred to above as "memory".

Fig. 8. Magnetic memory cylinder (Source: [19], photo IV)

The **very fast** memory of the MMIF is obviously electronic. "Two types of electronic memory" were used: the first involved "[cold cathode] gas tubes" [19] and the second hot tubes.

The cold cathode gas tube technology is specific to the Machine: it was the Bell Company that had the idea to use an existing, commercially available neon tube to make memory. "The tubes are assembled in rows[25] in which a direction of flow is established, such that when an advancement pulse command is given, each tube sends its information to the next tube," explain Linsman and Pouliart [19]. "A row of memory of this type ran, under laboratory conditions, at the frequency of 70 kilocycles per second, which is the speed limit of the tube... This type of row is used, in this machine, at frequencies between 0 and 25 kilocycles per second. " [19] "In general, the use of memory rows on cold cathode gas tubes enables significant desynchronisation of the Machine" [19]. As such, the gas tubes were used in particular for asynchronous transfers between drums and magnetic strips and between the cylinder and the arithmetic unit [29]. These rows of memory also played a fundamental role in constituting the arithmetic unit [19].

Hot tube technology was used to make the fastest memory employed by the MMIF [1]. It was used in many places: in particular, to make the logic gates which played a role in implementation of the control unit. It also participated in the making of the arithmetic unit [19]. However, this form of memory can be "found in any electronic machine" [29].

---

[25] See Figure 9.

Fig. 9. Front view of a rack frame containing, in the centre, nine columns of four cold cathode gas tubes[26] (Source: [19], photo VII)

3.5   Programming

The pioneers who built the MMIF were confronted with a twofold challenge: the first was to design a code (or language) that could be used to program the machine and the second was to write programs.

Programming Codes
"The Machine has a single address, which means that any instruction (or order) is composed of an operating prefix followed by a single address"[14]. "The address contained in an instruction may be the address for a number (operation instruction or write instruction) or the address for a pair of instructions ('*renvoi*' instruction)" [14]. In fact, two programming codes were written for the MMIF: the first is known as the "[regular] code" and the second, simpler one, is called the "pseudocode".

The (regular) code used for programming the MMIF was obviously the work of specialists in electrical circuits or hardware in general [4]. Using the original vocabulary, we can make up the following list[27] of its main orders:

1. "operation orders" (in particular, addition, subtraction, multiplication);
2. "write orders" on the drum or tape or register;
3. "alterations" (operations "affecting a single number, and modifying its different parts or making permutations between them (sign, mantissa, exponent)";

---

[26] Four gas tubes correspond to a decimal number represented in bi-quinary code. Nine columns of four tubes correspond to an instruction or a half-number [34].

[27] This list has been compiled from selected information in [14] and [15].

4. "usual organisation orders" for the drums (since "the left and right drums can each be used to record numbers or pairs of instructions) and tapes;
5. "calls, whether conditional or not";
6. "operations on addresses";
7. "transfer organisation", i.e. the movement of data or instructions, e.g. from the tape to the drum or vice versa.

This *(regular)* code was found to be difficult to use. An improvement was therefore sought out, leading to the pseudocode. According to Meinguet, who was the linchpin in programming the MMIF from 1956 onwards, the pseudocode was practically on the level of an assembly language, since it was a simplification of the machine language ([regular] code), particularly by replacing a five-digit prefix with a two-digit prefix and, above all, by replacing some addresses with designators.

Programs

Let us first look at the programs known at the time as "routines". They were written using [regular] code. Some were used by each program [14]. The routines were as follows:

• "start-up program" (written permanently on the instruction drum);
• "initial transfer program [from the tape to the drum]", written on tape;
• printing program;
• "translation routine" (called up by all programs in pseudocode) [16].

Other routines were called up by certain programs only. These include the routines that calculated elementary functions [28] (inverse, sin x, log x, etc.). According to the CECE [14], these sequences were built solely "using calculation methods described in the article by V. Belevitch and F. Storrer"[29]. These methods were aimed at the "approximation of functions by polynomials, with a defined maximum relative error" [28]. Some of them are original in conception. As such, we can see that the building of the MMIF was also coupled with research in numerical analysis.

The other programs, i.e. the "programs for customer problems", were first written in "code" and then, as soon as possible in "pseudocode" [3]. This occurred starting in 1955, with experimental programs (particularly for the calculation of Bessel functions as requested by the *École royale militaire* [30]). However, in late March 1957, a regular programming period began for a variety of customers [17], in particular: the *Institut météorologique*[31], the *Fabrique Nationale (FN) d'armes de guerre*[32], the *Université de Liège* and the *Commission des tuyauteries*[33].

---

[28] See [32].
[29] See [28].
[30] Royal Military Academy of Belgium.
[31] Belgian Weather Institute.
[32] National Weapons Plant.
[33] Pipes Commission.

4   Discussion

Several documents from the 1950's describe the US influence on the MMIF. For example, the preface to the 1955 text by Linsman and Pouliart [19] highlights the role played by Howard Aiken. However, several documents from that time[34] also stress that the design and building of the MMIF were Belgian. And these Belgian achievements were made at the suggestion of Aiken himself [20]. As Henry [25] stated during the unveiling of the MMIF in 1955: "We could have purchased a machine, we could have copied a machine that had already been tried and tested, but more than anything we wanted to spark interest in new automation techniques and, by undertaking a difficult, long-term project, we wanted to orient young people towards promising new pathways."

To try to understand Aiken's contribution to the Belgian project in greater detail as well as the manner in which computing technologies were spread to Belgium, I interviewed the eyewitnesses in great depth. As far as MMIF architecture is concerned, the accounts by Wiedmer and Iselin, two Swiss engineers who designed the circuits of the Machine, have proved capital in this respect. "Using two drums, one for data and one for programs, was decided by W. Pouliart who had visited Harvard," Wiedmer readily admitted [11]. However, he immediately added: "I do not remember anything else that came from Harvard. We began from scratch." In particular, he states that he never looked at any drawings from the USA. Furthermore, during the design and building phases of the MMIF, these pioneers, by their own admission, had only very rare contacts with the Americans. Wiedmer [11] says "Aiken visited BTMC once or twice, but he never talked to our engineers nor gave us anything." Iselin [6] agrees: "The influence of the Americans? In my opinion, there wasn't any, except for one or two visits by the head of Bell USA, Mr. Sosthenes, who made a whirlwind tour of the lab, without looking at or speaking to any of us." He adds [7]: "We saw Mr. Aiken one or two times, for about five minutes, during a four-year period." When asked about their educational background, these two linchpins in the design of the MMIF replied that they are both graduates of the ETH (*Eidgenössische Technische Hochschule*) in Zurich. Wiedmer [13] adds: "The best professors I remember were P. Scherrer for physics and E. Baumann for what is called electronics today. But I also learned a lot in my first job, at *Standard Telephon und Radio AG* in *Wollishofen-Zürich*."

Now let's examine the influences experienced by those who worked on programming the MMIF. The sub-routines for elementary functions and for application programs were completed in Antwerp, without any foreign contributions or influences. In this area, the Belgian pioneers "started from scratch", in the words of Meinguet [2]. In addition, Meinguet [8] writes: "the people who have influenced me most in terms of numerical analysis (...) are Belevitch, Stiefel and Rutishauser." And the direct influences cited by Meinguet for programming techniques are Rutishauser, Speiser and Stiefel: these influences are not directly American, but rather Swiss. However, we can

---

[34] See for instance Figure 3.

then ask how these three Swiss engineers acquired their expertise. Meinguet [10] shines some light on this subject:

> "During their stay in the USA (beginning in October 1948), Professor Stiefel (until March 1949) and his assistants (Rutishauser and Speiser, until late 1949) did serious research about contemporary American achievements and, more broadly, American ideas relating to electronic calculating machines. Like other European forerunners, they then used the acquired knowledge to develop their own ideas. This, I believe, is how things went. This trip took them to New York (Columbia University: Eckert, Courant Institut : Courant and Friedrichs, National Bureau of Standards : Lowan and Salzer), to Washington D.C. (Office of Naval Research: Rees, National Bureau of Standards : SEAC), to Boston (Harvard University: Aiken and the Mark III [machine] in construction) and to Princeton (Institute for Advanced Study: von Neumann and the machine in construction). Stiefel felt validated in his opinion: a relatively simple and slow machine (at moderate cost), but still reliable, would be particularly suitable for the Swiss (science and industry); this led to the design of ERMETH[35] with its specific characteristics (large memory but with limited speed), whose later construction would also benefit from the experience acquired at ETH on Z4[36]. In addition, Stiefel and his assistants visited a number of European colleagues, particularly in Germany."

In the end, I thus believe that we can say that Aiken's contribution to the MMIF can be found mostly on two levels: explaining the basic principles of a computer (in particular, to those people who visited Harvard prior to construction of the Belgian prototype) and coaching the leaders of the MMIF construction project. Furthermore, this contribution is restricted essentially to the project's leaders, to the virtual exclusion of the engineers who designed the Machine and the mathematicians who programmed it. Finally, both in terms of the physical architecture and its programming, the American influence on the Belgian project was merely indirect, whereas the direct influence was provided by the ETH in Zurich.

Acknowledgements. I would like to warmly thank the twelve people who provided eyewitness accounts of the MMIF for their support and assistance: they are truly the co-authors of this work. I would also like to recognise the FNRS, which allowed me to use its archives and also made my task much easier by providing a great number of photocopies. I also thank Dr. Sandra Mols, in particular for her contribution to information gathering and for managing the oral interviews, and Professor Robert Halleux, for his advice and support.

---

[35] *Elektronische Rechenmaschine der ETH.*

[36] The computer Z4 – based on electromechanical technology – was completed in 1944 by the then almost unknown scientist Konrad Zuse. The machine was fortunately kept safe from Allied bombing over Germany and then leased by ETH, where it served from 1950 to 1954. Z4's long lasting life continued until 1960 at the French Institute of Aerodynamics.

References

I. Sources

a) "Histoire informatique belge"[37] Archival Fund (HIBAF) (*Unamur, Namur*)

Unpublished Archives
- Oral Archives
1. Fosseprez, C.: Telephone communication on May 21, 2008
2. Meinguet, J.: Interview on November 23, 2007
3. Meinguet, J.: Telephone communication on October 2, 2008
4. Meinguet, J.: Interview on November 14, 2008
5. Rouche, N.: Interview on December 3, 2007

- Written Correspondence
6. Iselin, F.: E-mail dated July 12, 2009
7. Iselin, F.: E-mail dated October 10, 2009
8. Meinguet, J.: Letter dated March 11, 2002
9. Meinguet, J.: Letter dated June 24, 2002
10. Meinguet, J.: E-mail dated November 13, 2009
11. Wiedmer, F.: E-mail dated October 12, 2009
12. Wiedmer, F.: E-mail dated November 26, 2009
13. Wiedmer, F.: E-mail dated December 11, 2009

- Documents Pertaining to the Functioning and Programming of the MMIF
14. CECE: Document no. 1, Manuel de programmation pour la machine mathématique IRSIA-FNRS, VI + 157 p. (1957)
15. CECE: Progress Report no. 1, 12 p. (June 1957)
16. CECE: Document no. 2 – Pseudocode Manual for the IRSIA-FNRS Computer, IV + 62 p. (1958)
17. CECE: Liste des problèmes traités par le CECE, 5 p. (undated)

Limited-Edition Documents
18. Bell: Bell Telephone Manufacturing Company 1882-1982. Service Presse et Information Bell Anvers (1982)
19. Linsman, M., Pouliart, W.: La Machine mathématique IRSIA – FNRS, 47 p. Département technique de la Bell Telephone Manufacturing Company, Antwerp (February 1955)

b) FNRS Archival Fund (Brussels)
20. Aiken, H.: Typewritten letter sent to L. Henry, 1 p. (January 17, 1951)
21. Aiken, H.: Typewritten letter sent to L. Henry, 5 p. (May 14, 1952)
22. Aiken, H., van Wijngaarden, A.: Typewritten letter sent to L. Henry, 2 p. (July 10, 1957)

---

[37] History of Computing in Belgium.

23. FNRS 1951: Minutes des réunions des 16 et 17 janvier 1951 à l'IRSIA. D 1/4 - 390/447, 4 p. (1951)
24. FNRS 1954: Memorandum. D 1/4 – 7473/447, 1 p. (December 13, 1954)
25. Henry, L.: Présentation et démonstration de la machine à calculer IRSIA-FNRS, Speech given by Mr. Henry, IRSIA Director, 4 p. (1955)
26. Henry, L., Willems, J., Van Dyck, L., Manneback, C.: Convention, 4 p. + 2 p. of appendices (January 24, 1951)
27. Manneback, C., Brillouin, L.: Les machines mathématiques aux États-Unis, Rapport au Fonds national de la recherche scientifique (Restricted distribution clause cited on a sticker attached to the report), 35 p. (1947)

c) Printed and Published Sources

28. Belevitch, V., Storrer, F.: Le calcul numérique des fonctions élémentaires dans la machine mathématique I.R.S.I.A.-F.N.R.S. Bull. Acad. Roy. Belg. XLII, 543–578 (1956)
29. Linsman, M., Pouliart, W.: La Machine mathématique IRSIA – FNRS en construction à la Bell Téléphone Mfg C°. Industrie 8, 505–509 (1953)

II. Secondary Literature

30. Biot, M.A.: Charles Manneback. In: Académie royale de Belgique, Classe des Sciences (ed.) Florilège des Sciences en Belgique II, pp. 369–377 (1980)
31. Courtois, P.-J.: Notice Biographique de Vitold Belevitch. In: Académie royale des sciences, des lettres et des beaux-arts de Belgique (ed.) Nouvelle Biographie Nationale, vol. X, pp. 35–42 (2010)
32. Courtois, P.-J.: The Belgian Electronic Mathematical Machine (1951-1962): An Account. In: Jones, C.B., Lloyd, J.L. (eds.) Dependable and Historic Computing. LNCS, vol. 6875, pp. 225–237. Springer, Heidelberg (2011)
33. d'Udekem-Gevers, M.: La Machine mathématique IRSIA-FNRS (1946-1962). Académie royale de Belgique, Classe des Sciences, 224 p. (2011)
34. Fosséprez, C.: Les fondements de l'Informatique et des Télécommunications. Notes de cours à l'Université des Aînés (UDA), Louvain-La-Neuve, Belgium (2002)
35. Loeckx, J.: Computer design and software development in Belgium before 1970: a personal retrospect (Text written in March 2007, to be published in 2014)

Ingenuity in Isolation: Poland in the International History of the Internet

Christopher Leslie and Patrick Gryczka

New York University Polytechnic School of Engineering, Brooklyn, NY, USA
{chris.leslie,pg1009}@nyu.edu

Abstract. The popular understanding of the invention of the Internet is that it was the work of researchers in the United States working in relative isolation. However, the Internet is about connection, and so its success required the independently developed networks of the international community. By analyzing early network development in politically isolated Poland toward the end of the Cold War, one sees development concurrent to the development of the Internet but separated technologically through CoCom trade embargoes. By analyzing information technology periodicals, FidoNet newsletters, and other sources, a number of projects have been identified: data distribution over radio and the use of computer networks to protest communist propaganda. In addition to these amateur efforts, we learned about commercial products and academic research. While these efforts were not successful in a conventional sense, they do demonstrate how the computer industry and network research in Poland played an important role despite the political restrictions.

Keywords: Internet, Poland, Cold War, innovation, technology transfer, ethics.

1   Introduction

The Internet is popularly considered to be an invention of the United States. At the height of the dot-com boom, the myth of the American ingenuity that created the Internet in isolation was perfected: once TCP/IP was perfected for a military research network, ARPANet, it was brought to the academic world with CSNET, discovered by civilian users with USENET and other online sources, and finally distributed to the rest of the world in the 1990s via NSFNET projects (see, for instance, [1,2]). The first mention of the international community in this narrative is often Tim Berners-Lee, the British inventor of the World Wide Web.

This fable of Yankee ingenuity disregards both the global nature of the Internet community and the national infrastructural developments needed to provide the necessary intellectual and technical infrastructure for Internet technology to be widely adopted. As presented elsewhere, core concepts behind the Internet, such as packet switching, have roots in the international technical and scientific community. What is more, the Internet is about connecting networks, and a key design consideration of TCP/IP was to allow independently developed networks from the international community a means to connect [3]. It should not be controversial to state that the U.S.

K.K. Kimppa et al. (Eds.): HCC11 2014, IFIP AICT 431, pp. 162–175, 2014.
© IFIP International Federation for Information Processing 2014

relied heavily on their counterparts in other countries to produce the flexible protocols that account for the rapid spread of the technology, and yet this story is not often told.

In addition to the direct influence of the international community, one should consider how researchers in countries who were not directly involved. The dictum that the number of Internet users reached 50 million in 4 years, while it took television 13 years and radio 38 years, may be difficult to verify – it certainly depends on which statistics one uses [4] – but there is no question that the seeds of TCP/IP fell on fertile ground. The impression that the Internet spread to many corners of the world quickly, however, should lead one to question the notion that it diffused on its own accord. As noted by in the case of the diffusion of the Internet to Israel [5], the Internet "is unable to 'march' anywhere" (327): adoption of Internet technology depends on the preparation and interest of identifiable people. This insight can be profitably applied to the analysis of technology transfer to Poland. Although it might seem that the Internet could not be diffused to Poland until after the fall of the Berlin Wall and the collapse of the Soviet Union, this would deny the active effort of individuals in Poland who prepared the way for a technology like the Internet even while they were politically separated from areas that used it.

The entry of western technology at the start of the 1990s is described as if high-tech companies were entering into barren field, a rhetoric that might be expected given a world weary of the more than 40 years of standoff. A press release distributed by IBM [6] announced a grant for the creation of a "backbone of a computer network" linking 14 Polish universities "with each other and with similar networks created by IBM." The program was to include training "to increase the level of information technology skills, skills that are vital for competitive economies." Poland was described in the *Wall Street Journal* as leading the computerization of eastern Europe: "Entrepreneurs are starting small personal-computer dealerships, business people are equipping their firms with low-powered computers, and small companies are fighting for government software contracts" [7]. The triumphant tone is still visible in articles like [8], which notes that "changes came quickly" after the fall of the Berlin Wall. Demand for privatization in the former Soviet block along with relaxing restrictions on the export of technology brought computing to eastern Europe, and "companies that survived began modernizing" (20). From these descriptions, it seems as if there had been no computers and no networks in Poland earlier, and only through the beneficence of the victors of the Cold War was Poland able to enter the computer age.

The sensation that the countries of eastern Europe were in a state of technological depravation, while accurate in some ways, does not tell the entire story. The online magazine *Pigulki* snidely commented on the paragraphs of the 1991 IBM press release [6], noting "the Poles themselves have brought this network into being already, as *Pigulki* readers would have gathered by now" and suggesting "Big Blue was, to say the least, not among the major forces spearheading Poland's academic computer network." The foundation for the connection to the west was done by those in the hard sciences, computer systems administrators, and colleagues in the Polish diaspora [9]. With the connection to the west, there was a sudden sense of connectivity, though this apparently was more keenly felt from the outside. One researcher [10] writes, "there were [a] lot of people from the USA, Germany, the UK, and France, checking constantly whether PLEARN was already on line." A question he was asked in one of his first chats with someone in the U.S. was whether he could send messages without censorship from any terminal. Nevertheless, network connections had already existed.

It is true that Cold War prohibitions on high-tech exports had restricted Poland's access to the computer technology and, more specifically, to the growing community of TCP/IP users as well as other networks. What are now known as the CoCom restrictions began as part of the administration of the Marshall Plan aid to Europe in 1948. As a condition of receiving aid, recipient countries were prohibited from exporting products to non-recipients anything that the U.S. would normally disallow [11]. In this way, the U.S. hoped to prevent communist countries from mustering the strength to wage war. The Coordinating Committee for Multilateral Export Controls (CoCom for short) was set up to manage the embargo. The ban was not absolute; in a 1960 meeting to review items on the embargo, the U.S. was unsuccessful in convincing British authorities to classify digital computers as munitions subject to the embargo, asserting that the Soviet Union used computing for military purposes. In 1969, the U.S. announced new guidelines that only between 6 and 18 fast computers per year could be exported to eastern Europe (excluding the USSR). In 1984, these restrictions were tightened to include recent advances in smaller, personal computers. In a newspaper article at the time, an Assistant Secretary of Defense was cited as the source of the idea that the military uses Apple 2 computers for targeting nuclear weapons, and so proliferation of such small devices must be restricted [12]. In spite of these challenges, a number of developments, potentially unique to Poland, can be identified. Among them, a radio modem, which was developed to deal with the unreliable telecommunications infrastructure in Poland, and the use of computer networks to protest communist propaganda.

The story of Poland's ingenuity despite being isolated from international developments, taken together with other stories of the diffusion of the Internet, presents an ethical challenge. It might be simpler and more dramatic to tell the story of U.S. engineers wresting control of a military research project for the benefit of the international public. However, this story is unethical in that it suggests that innovation takes place within isolated national borders, disregarding the role of individuals outside of those borders on which innovation depends. The World Wide Web, for instance, depended heavily on the conventions of TCP/IP and the DNS that had already been designed with the engineers in different countries in mind and vetted by the international community. Without this this deep involvement with researchers outside of the United States, Berners-Lee's innovation would have remained a distributed hypertext project confined to workstations at CERN.

Documenting the projects that encourage the development of computing intellectual capital – in other words, the development of engineers and scientists who are familiar with computing concepts – is pivotal in the diffusion of technologies like the Internet. Because innovation sometimes comes from the negotiation of different technical and cultural standards, and because technical innovations fail and succeed based on a larger community of practitioners, it is unethical to assert that a small group of researchers in one country are responsible for a widespread technical achievement like the Internet.

2   Methodology

In Science and Technology Studies, the concept of the user has gained increasing prominence over the past twenty years, and the study of the history of the Internet could benefit from this development. In Poland, the situation was that a user base was previously established onto which TCP/IP could easily be transmitted once the necessary political blocks were eliminated. To analyze the technical developments of early network development in Poland and the cultural influence on the network's uses, documents pertaining to the topic have been found, compiled, translated, and analyzed. By combing through numerous information technology periodicals, FidoNet newsletters, and other assorted sources, we have sought evidence of an important ethical consideration: it is not the case that a relatively isolated country like Poland was passively waiting for a connection.

Although there are no books on the topic, articles do mention Polish academic networks and personal connections to FidoNet. To find out as much as possible about the beginnings of the Internet in Poland and the early academic networks that came out of Polish universities, it seemed appropriate to look for previous works on that topic; however, it soon became evident that there were few if any published academic works on this topic in either English or Polish. Turning to the technical periodicals of the time and newsletters of early networks such as FidoNet, an enormous archive of network newsletters and newspaper and magazine articles from the time period, interesting and significant papers in Polish were found. In addition, attempts were made to email contributors to the early academic networks in order to gain firsthand information about the networks; a portion of the information gathered has been found in the university libraries and archives. Many of the technical details that were learned about the early networks were found by visiting the universities where these networks originated and reading through students' and professors' theses and works that have been written about the networks.

This documentation supports a different ethical framework that appreciates the complex interactions between innovation and diffusion of technology. In telling the story of Poland's researchers in the waning years of the Cold War, we hope this methodology demonstrates the importance of adopting different ethic of innovation.

3   Polish Networking at the End of the Cold War

Networking in Europe was well underway in the 1980s. One of the most visible international networking efforts began in 1983, when IBM established a counterpart to its 1981 network, BITNET, in Europe. Called the European Academic Research Network (EARN), IBM provided access to networking through a connection through Wisconsin [13]. With a connection provided by EARN, one could browse the famous Request for Comments (RFCs) distributed by the burgeoning Internet community, making people curious about its protocols even though the official policy was to wait for the formalization of OSI standards [14]. As the German Internet pioneer Claus Kalle has remarked, this connection finally gave users an experience of the Internet, "das man damals höchstens aus dem Kino (War Games) kannte)" (which one then at least knew from the cinema (War Games)) [15].

Through e-mail came RFCs about TCP, IP, Telnet, and FTP, from which users and learned how the new protocols could be implemented on local platforms. These efforts to use TCP/IP in Europe, however, did not extend to the Warsaw Pact countries due to an interpretation of the CoCom restrictions. In fact, the only way to users in this region were able to connect their computers was to a friendly computer on the other side of the Iron Curtain, but according to Tomasz Hofmokl this was inexpensive and unreliable, and more official solutions were not forthcoming. He writes, "I received the official refusal from the French side to establish a permanent communication line with Paris in 1987 by e-mail in Warsaw" [16].

In early 1990, when the CoCom restrictions were relaxed, countries in Eastern Europe could connect to international computer networks. A few months later, the board of directors of EARN decided to admit eastern European countries; Poland was the first, bridging the divide between Europe and former Soviet Block countries. This link was followed by Czechoslovakia and Hungary [16]. The president of EARN, Frode Greisen, visited Warsaw University to make the announcement on April 10 [10]. The symbolic date denoting the beginning of the Internet in Poland was 1990 when engineers at Instytut Fizyki Jadrowej (IFJ, the Institute of Nuclear Physics) in Krakow sent the first email from Poland. Within a few months, many connections to EARN were set up and within a year many of Poland's larger cities connected to the Internet.

As seen in Figure 1, Poland's first international link to the TCP/IP Internet was established by Naukowa i Akademicka Sieć Komputerowa (NASK, or Research and Academic Computer Network) in November 1991, with a data line of 64Kb/s. A month later, Polish Internet traffic was then allowed into the United States network, NSFNET. In 1992, the first academic metropolitan area network (MAN) was built, which ran on fiber optic cables. That same year, a networking organization for the region, Central and Eastern European Network (CEENet) was established; it would grow to 19 members. Soon after, in 1993, ten more MANs were set up across Poland in cities with large universities. Then in 1997, these MANs were interconnected with a new broadband network. The network, POL-34, started with speeds of 34 Mb/s and was quickly upgraded in 1998 to 155 Mb/s, and it was also connected to the global internet through a Swedish satellite link through Telenordia. By 2002 POL-34 had been upgraded to even faster lines and upgraded to use ATM, Gigabit Ethernet, and Cisco routers (7200, 7500, 12000 GSR). These upgrades allowed for a main line of 622 Mb/s and 155 Mb/s and 34 Mb/s branching lines. After these upgrades were completed halfway through 2002, POL-34 was connected to a new Polish academic network, the PIONIER fiber optic network [17].

The fact that Poland was the first of the Soviet Block countries to connect to the west was not an accident. This achievement, after all, was built on earlier accomplishments and the successful lobbying of members of the Polish computer science community. In spite of CoCom restrictions, manufacturers were allowed to export computers in excess of the quotas under an exceptions clause related to computers for non-military use; interestingly, Poland was the "largest designation" of exceptions at 135 cases [11]. One can assert that this embargo was effective. While, as noted by

[18], "it is extraordinarily difficult to *prove*, with hard economic data, that Western export controls have held back the development of computing" in Poland and other countries of the Council for Mutual Economic Assistance (CMEA), the "causal observer" can see that eastern Europe was behind (429; emphasis in original). Nevertheless, Geipel et al. demonstrate that CMEA countries in general, and Poland in particular, made an effort to invest in computers. Investment "always either increased more or decreased less" when compared to other light industries, and the percentage of the population engaged in scientific research ranged from 0.25 to 0.45, as compared to 0.22 in the United States.

Furthermore, Poland along with Hungary allowed private enterprise in computing starting in the 1980s, and at the time of the Wende there were more than 500 private computing firms in Poland. Additionally, personal computers were excluded from CoCom restrictions in the 1980s, which meant importers were free to bring them to market. This community of personal computer users – based on ZX Spectrums, Commodore 64s and Atari 800XLs – sought to connect Poland to FidoNet, a loose organization of amateur bulletin board systems (BBSs). Jan Stozek translated FidoNet documentation into Polish in 1987 and soon a BBS was set up in the offices of *Komputer* magazine [19]. This publication covered modems and FidoNet, and the community began to grow. Region 48 was assigned to Poland by a Dutch computer club official of Polish descent, and it would be the first region in the Soviet Block. The following year, Stozek would become the network coordinator in Poland. By 1991, there were 15 BBSs operating in Poland, most of which were set up at private companies by individuals who convinced their superiors that such a service would support their commercial activity. One BBS was located at the University of Poznan, where Zbyszek Borowiec was able to transfer messages to BITNET before PLEARN was established.

Poland's readiness to accept international data was also facilitated by earlier work in networking. Because these networks used X.25, it was simpler to make the connection; Smereczynski, who set up the Polish node of EARN, PLEARN, notes that the "constrained isolation" of networking in Poland in the last years of the Cold War helped to show how a network could be formed in adverse conditions. "The main achievement of the KASK project," he writes, "was the experience of showing that you cannot ignore the international standards, or your project would fail" [10]. Smereczynski's tone is one of despair concerning the state of computer science in Poland, but this is clearly from his perspective as someone who could see the future potential. For instance, he was not positive in his recounting of IBM's support; he recollects several experiences with IBM equipment that was late and delivered with software full of bugs, and the first connection to EARN was actually made on an IBM clone, a BASF 7/38 with Hitachi components. This alone demonstrates his effectiveness in dealing with less than optimal conditions. Likewise, Smereczynski notes that there were many people in the Polish computer science community that did not know what it meant to send email or to join into an international network, and so he and his colleagues set up seminars on EARN, e-mail, Listerv, and fundamentals of networking commands, or "just enough to introduce people to EARN networking." The fact that there was a technical community ready to undergo this training, and individuals from Poland ready to offer it, makes it clear the active role the local community played in the diffusion of this technology.

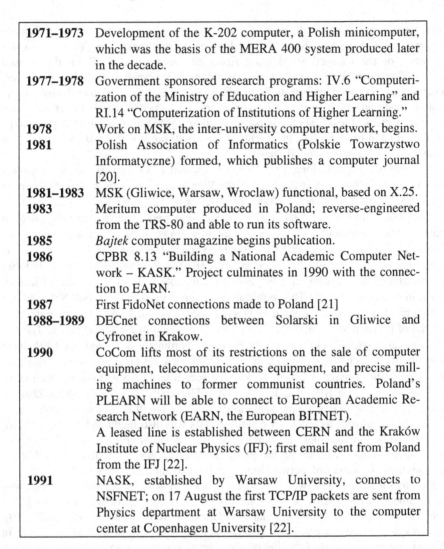

1971–1973	Development of the K-202 computer, a Polish minicomputer, which was the basis of the MERA 400 system produced later in the decade.
1977–1978	Government sponsored research programs: IV.6 "Computerization of the Ministry of Education and Higher Learning" and RI.14 "Computerization of Institutions of Higher Learning."
1978	Work on MSK, the inter-university computer network, begins.
1981	Polish Association of Informatics (Polskie Towarzystwo Informatyczne) formed, which publishes a computer journal [20].
1981–1983	MSK (Gliwice, Warsaw, Wroclaw) functional, based on X.25.
1983	Meritum computer produced in Poland; reverse-engineered from the TRS-80 and able to run its software.
1985	*Bajtek* computer magazine begins publication.
1986	CPBR 8.13 "Building a National Academic Computer Network – KASK." Project culminates in 1990 with the connection to EARN.
1987	First FidoNet connections made to Poland [21]
1988–1989	DECnet connections between Solarski in Gliwice and Cyfronet in Krakow.
1990	CoCom lifts most of its restrictions on the sale of computer equipment, telecommunications equipment, and precise milling machines to former communist countries. Poland's PLEARN will be able to connect to European Academic Research Network (EARN, the European BITNET). A leased line is established between CERN and the Kraków Institute of Nuclear Physics (IFJ); first email sent from Poland from the IFJ [22].
1991	NASK, established by Warsaw University, connects to NSFNET; on 17 August the first TCP/IP packets are sent from Physics department at Warsaw University to the computer center at Copenhagen University [22].

Fig. 1. Important dates leading to the first TCP/IP connection to Poland

In 1988, the first effort to connect BITNET to Poland came from the high-energy physicists. This community, which was accustomed to working in international groups, had enjoyed using BITNET while working abroad "and felt very handicapped without it at home" [23]. They desired to set up a local network connection to SASK, the Warsaw branch of KASK, with the hope that their counterparts in other countries might eventually help to connect them to BITNET. With the support of the university hierarchy, the physicists leveraged their contacts, both with BITNET in the United States and inside the Polish government.

4   Networks in Poland

The myth of the computerization of Poland after the fall of the Iron Curtain also neglects prior work that was done. The earliest observations of the project had to do with how quickly Poland was able to connect to the Internet after the loosening of CoCom restrictions. It seemed unlikely that without any previous effort Poland could have so suddenly connected to the Internet within months of getting access to western computing and networking technology and then within two years have been able to put down the infrastructure necessary to connect many of its major cities to the Internet. COCOM actually seems to have been more of a political catalyst in Poland's connection to the Internet, rather than a technical one.

The credit for the technical underpinnings of Poland's connection to the Internet seems instead to lie with the scarcely mentioned academic networks. A number of early networks were found, but the earliest identified was the Miedzyuczelniana SiecKomputerowa (MSK, or the Inter-university Computer Network), whose efforts eventually evolved into Krajowa Academicka Siec Komputerowa, (KASK, or the National Academic Computer Network).

As seen in Figure 1, MSK and the Warsaw localized Akademicka Siec Komputerowa (ASK, or the Academic Computer Network) stemmed from government research topics IV.6 "Computerization of the Ministry of Education and Higher Learning" (mgr inz. Andrzej Zienkiewicz, UW) and RI.14 "Computerization of Institutions of Higher Learning" (dr inz. M. Bazewicz, PWr), which were proposed between 1977 and 1978. Work on MSK began in 1978; however, at the time the engineers who were working on MSK were unaware of ISO documentation on the Open Systems Interconnection (OSI) model. Fascinatingly, for its pilot program, MSK connected the Centrum Obliczeniowe Politechniki Wroclawskiej (Computation Centre of the Technical University of Wroclaw), the Osrodek Elektronicznej Techniki Obliczeniowej Politechniki Slaskiej (Electronic Computing Technology Centre of the Technical University of Slask), and at the Centrum Obliczeniowe Instytutu Podstaw Informatyki (Centre of Electronic Computing Technology at the Institute of the Fundamentals of Information Technology) in Warsaw. Within this pilot configuration there were two sub nodes in Wroclaw, an Odra 1305 and a R32; one in Warsaw, an Odra 1305; and one in Gliwice, an Odra 1305 as well.

Warsaw, Wroclaw, and Gliwice were chosen as the initial nodes in the MSK not only because these cities contained well-respected universities that possessed the necessary computer resources to take part, but also because of the existing telephone line infrastructure between the cities. Of course, with the expected expansion of MSK into KASK, plans to connect numerous other cities were already made, namely to connect Krakow, Katowice, Poznan, Torun, Bydgoszcz, and Gdansk. In addition to connecting new cities there were also intentions to connect more and more subnodes within the cities, allowing more universities to join the network, and beyond that, there were also hopes for establishing a direct link between the Warsaw node and the

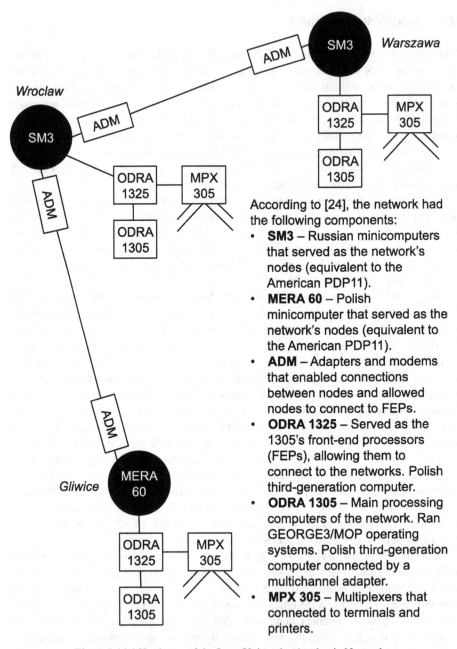

According to [24], the network had the following components:

- **SM3** – Russian minicomputers that served as the network's nodes (equivalent to the American PDP11).
- **MERA 60** – Polish minicomputer that served as the network's nodes (equivalent to the American PDP11).
- **ADM** – Adapters and modems that enabled connections between nodes and allowed nodes to connect to FEPs.
- **ODRA 1325** – Served as the 1305's front-end processors (FEPs), allowing them to connect to the networks. Polish third-generation computer.
- **ODRA 1305** – Main processing computers of the network. Ran GEORGE3/MOP operating systems. Polish third-generation computer connected by a multichannel adapter.
- **MPX 305** – Multiplexers that connected to terminals and printers.

Fig. 2. Initial Hardware of the Inter-University Academic Network

Gliwice node. From these aspirations, it is clear that Polish engineers were moving ahead with their own networks and making sizable strides in spreading their network across Poland.

For the most part, the early academic networks, such as MSK, were seen as purely academic endeavors by both the Polish authorities and many of the academics who made use of them. Within its pilot stage, MSK allowed users to access data bases within the processing computers from any connected terminal, to send collections of data between any two processing computers, run programs available on any of the processing computers on any given terminal, and communicate between terminals.

5   Standards and Connections

Despite the fact that the early Polish academic networks were developed behind the isolative barrier of CoCom, connection to outside networks came about quite rapidly once the political situation allowed organizations like EARN to grant Poland connection to their networks. This was in no small part thanks to the mindset of the engineers behind networks like MSK. While ISO documentation on networks was unknown to the engineers behind MSK at the start of their project, in order to one day connect to the international community the engineers went through the substantial effort of re-starting their work to have MSK follow the standards set by ISO [25].

At the start of MSK, the engineers were basing their work on the data link protocol ISO HDLC (High Level Data Link Control) and INWG 96, a transfer protocol that guaranteed datagram transfer. Despite a lack of access to the latest in western computing equipment, Polish engineers found equivalent hardware for their networks in their own Odra and Mera computers or Soviet SM3s. Work on MSK began in 1978; however, at the time the engineers were unaware of the effort by the International Organization for Standardization (ISO) renewed effort to define data protocols. Although the concepts behind TCP/IP reach as far back as 1973 in INWG 39, their implementation was not yet fully developed in 1975 when INWG 96 was released. Despite the agreement on INGW 96, DARPA broke off, at this point, stating that the were "too close to completing implementation of the updated INWG 39" [26]. Nevertheless, the rest of the international community had come to a consensus to move away from TCP/IP towards a model that would better manage bandwidth allocation.

Fascinatingly, once the engineers found out about the documentation they restarted their work on the network in order to have it meet international standards, implying that the engineers intended to make a network that would be able to connect to the rest of the world when the political situation allowed. After becoming acquainted with ISO documentation on the OSI model and the CCIT documentation pertinent to the first three layers, the conception of MSK was shifted in a direction that would maximize agreement with the OSI model [25]. Poland's decision to move away from the datagram model to the more moderated model of OSI may seem counterproductive if we are comparing their networks to today's internet; however, at the time the international community was moving away from TCP/IP, considering it to be a temporary experiment [27]. Poland's switch to an OSI model does point to a desire and effort to stand with the international community and move towards a model that would, in the future, best be able to interact with other academic networks abroad.

6   Computers and the Underground

Poland's rich computer culture has been documented elsewhere, but it is worthwhile to note that the first local personal (micro) computer produced began production in 1983, the Meritum, which was reverse-engineered from the Tandy corporation's TRS-80, released in the U.S. in 1977. In collaboration with *Bajtek*, a Polish computer magazine founded in 1985, the Polish Boy Scout association broadcast programs over FM radio in BASIC that users would record on cassettes and load into their computers [22]. Other examples of selling western computers on the so-called informal market abound.

Computers in Poland and Hungary were commonly used at home, and PCs played an important role in producing and distributing *bibu a* (the Polish version of the Russian *samizdat*). A covert program, which [28] calls "the best-kept secret of all the CIA's Cold War operations" (429), smuggled printing presses, radios, computers, Telex machines, and the first fax machines to Poland to help the Solidarity movement. In addition, computers were used to "organize the boycotts and evaluate data" concerning the election results (462). The Solidarity paper *Tygodnik Mazowsze*, which started as an underground journal, was produced on a PC and printed on a laser printer [18], [29].

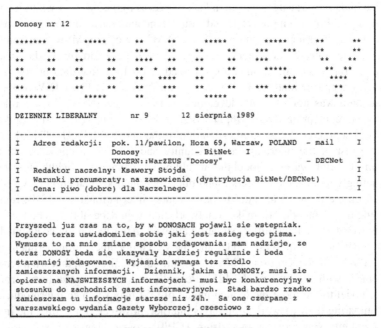

Fig. 3. *Donosy* E-Newspaper

Being seen purely as tools to enhance academic capabilities within the fields of physics and astronomy, the academic networks largely escaped any monitoring of use. Thus, the networks created a uniquely safe environment, where academics, or at least those who wished, could communicate freely amongst themselves about topics that strayed from academia into something closer to political criticism and dissent. A prominent example of dissenting expression within such an environment is *Donosy* (Fig. 3), the first Polish digital newspaper, which originated within the Warsaw University's Physics department in 1989. In August, this daily newspaper in e-mail format gathered uncensored news and rumors from a variety of sources, and also published information about salaries and pricing, reprinted letters to the editors, and made reflections on current events. The return addresses indicate that *Donosy* was distributed via BITNET and DECNet.

7 Conclusion

The thesis that significant investments in network research and implementation were necessary on national levels in order for the Internet to spread to Poland as quickly as it did provides an important insight into the ethics of innovation. Myths about the Internet being created by the U.S. in isolation and diffusing to other countries effortlessly suggests that ideas succeed on their own merits. The theory that information technology spread easily into Poland once political blocks were eased is satisfying in some ways, but in fact does not tell the entire story. Technology transfer is dependent upon the work of many individuals in the target area, and it is these users who have as much to do with the innovation's success as do the innovators. The story of facile technology transfer seems to suggest that a good idea will diffuse on its own accord, so the only responsibility of an innovator is to develop a good idea. A more nuanced story is needed so that future innovators recognize how technologies depend upon a user base that is ready and able to take advantage of it.

This story also demonstrates the fact that what might seem to be innovation for the sake of innovation was a success in Poland. The story of the 20th century is sometimes told as one of the loss of disinterested scientists who no longer were able to follow their curiosity. As shown by [30], however, this is not an entirely accurate portrait. In fact, it would seem as if there has been plenty of time and effort dedicated to amateur and disinterested pursuits. The story in Poland demonstrates how this effort paid off. Even while scientists had no way of knowing that the Cold War was drawing to a close, they continued in isolation to innovate and explore current ideas in computer networking. This effort paid off unexpectedly when they were able to join the TCP/IP Internet, in much the same way one would expect the disinterested inquiry of science to pay off in unforeseen ways.

Finally, this story points toward the importance of international standards organizations such as ISO. This is not to be expected, given that the story of TCP/IP is generally told as "standards war" in which the ISO's OSI protocols failed. As much as the success of TCP/IP seems to be a triumph over the failed OSI standards, the story of Poland seems to indicate that the story needs to be told differently. Even as political barriers prevented trade in high technology goods, access to international standards allowed Polish engineers to independently create computers and networks that would eventually be able to connect to the rest of the world.

Acknowledgement. The authors are indebted to the Undergraduate Summer Research Program and its founder, Associate Dean Iraj M. Kalkhoran, at the New York University Polytechnic Institute of Technology, which provided Patrick Gryczka with a stipend that supported this research.

References

1. Naughton, J.: A Brief History of the Future: From Radio Days to Internet Years in a Lifetime. Overlook Press, Woodstock (2000)
2. Segaller, S.: Nerds 2.0.1: A Brief History of the Internet. TV Books, New York (1998)
3. Leslie, C.: Competing Histories of Technology: Recognizing the Vital Role of International Scientific Communities behind the Innovation of the Internet. In: Tatnall, A., Blyth, T., Johnson, R. (eds.) HC 2013. IFIP AICT, vol. 416, pp. 196–206. Springer, Heidelberg (2013)
4. Hannemyr, G.: The Internet as Hyperbole: A Critical Examination of Adoption Rates. The Information Society 19(2), 111–121 (2003)
5. John, N.A.: The Diffusion of the Internet to Israel: the First 10 Years. Israel Affairs 17(3), 327–340 (2011)
6. Budd, R.: IBM and Polish Universities Create Computer-Network (June 11, 1991)
7. Hooper, L.: Poland Moves Toward Leading Role In Computerization of Eastern Europe. Wall Street Journal: A7H (December 2, 1991)
8. Cortada, J.W.: Patterns and Practices in How Information Technology Spread around the World. IEEE Annals of the History of Computing 20(4), 4–25 (2008)
9. Phillips, D.: Chronicle. Pigulki 6 (June 5, 1991),
   http://ftp.icm.edu.pl/packages/pigulki/pigulki6.pub
   (accessed March 19, 2014)
10. Smereczynski, A.: One Year of EARN Networking in Poland. Pigulki 6 (June 5, 1991),
    http://ftp.icm.edu.pl/packages/pigulki/pigulki6.pub
    (accessed March 19, 2014)
11. Cain, F.: Computers and the Cold War: United States Restrictions on the Export of Computers to the Soviet Union and Communist China. Journal of Contemporary History 40, 131–147 (2005)
12. Lewis, P.: Allies Curb Computers for Soviet. New York Times, Late Edition (East Coast): D7 (July 17, 1984)
13. Naumann, F.: Abakus zum Internet: Die Geschicte der Informatik. Primus Verlag, Darmstadt (2001)
14. Grassmuck, V.: Internet (2008), http://www.hgb-leipzig.de/~vgrass/
    semi-mediengesch/10_internet.html (accessed January 5, 2014)
15. Kalle, C.: Das Internet in Deutschland - Ein alter Hut? Kompass 64 (July 18, 1995),
    http://mikro-berlin.org/Events/OS/ref-
    texte/kalle/0InetinDland.html (January 5, 2014)
16. Hofmokl, T.: Academic Networks in Central and Eastern Europe (2008),
    http://www.ceenet.org/ceenet_cbyc_anicaee.html
    (accessed April 5, 2009)
17. Binczewski, A., Mazurek, C., Meyer, N., Niwinski, S., Stroinski, M.: Perspektywy Rozwoju Sieci POL-34/155. Sieci Komputerowe w Badaniach Naukowych (n.d.)
18. Geipel, G.L., Tomasz Jarmoszko, A., Goodman, S.E.: The Information Technologies and East European Societies. East European Politics & Societies 5(3), 394–438 (1991)

19. Stozek, J.: FidoNet in Poland. Pigulki 6 (June 5, 1991), `http://ftp.icm.edu.pl/packages/pigulki/pigulki6.pub` (accessed March 19, 2014)
20. Wasiak, P.: Computing behind the Iron Curtain: Social Impact of Home Computers in the Polish People's Republic. Tensions of Europe & Inventing Europe Working Paper Series (2010), `http://www.tensionsofeurope.eu/www/en/files/-get/publications/WP_2010_08_Wasiak.pdf` (accessed March 18, 2014)
21. Daniels, D.: IFNA Welcomes Poland to FidoNet. FidoNews: International FidoNet Association Newsletter 4(34) (1987)
22. Baran, D.: Polish Internet at the End of the 20th Century. In: Pokorna-Ignatowicz, K. (ed.) The Polish Media System 1989–2011, pp. 41–51. Krakow Society for Education (2012)
23. Gajewski, J.: Polish Bitnet: How It All Started. Pigulki 6 (June 5, 1991), `http://ftp.icm.edu.pl/packages/pigulki/pigulki6.pub` (accessed March 19, 2014)
24. Janyszek, J.: Dziesieciolecie Dzialalnosci Wroclawskiego Centrum Sieciowo-Superkomputerowego 1995–2005. WCSS, Wroclaw (2005)
25. Bilski, E.: Protokoly w Miedzyuczelnianej Sieci Komputerowj. Wydawnictwo Politechniki Wroclawskiej, Wroclaw (1987)
26. McKenzie, A.: INWG and the Conception of the Internet: An Eyewitness Account. IEEE Annals of the History of Computing 33(1), 66–71 (2011)
27. Abbate, J.: Inventing the Internet. MIT Press, Cambridge (1999)
28. Fischer, B.B.: Solidarity, the CIA, and Western Technology. International Journal of Intelligence and Counter Intelligence 25(3), 427–469 (2012)
29. Diehl, J.: In Moscow and Warsaw, Official and Unofficial Press Playing New Roles; Solidarity Weekly Evolves in Scope, Sophistication. The Washington Post: A13 (April 4, 1987)
30. Shapin, S.: The Scientific Life. Chicago University Press, Chicago (2008)

Implementation Criteria of University Computer Education in Spain between First Experiences and the European Higher Education Space (EHES)

Ramon Puigjaner[1] and Jordi Fornes[2]

[1] Universitat de les Illes Balears.
Ctra de Valldemossa, km 7.5 07122 PALMA, Spain
putxi@uib.cat
[2] DAC, UPC-BarcelonaTech.
Campus Nord, c/ Jordi Girona, 1-3, 08034 Barcelona
jfornes@ac.upc.edu

Abstract. This paper intends to present a short overview of the different criteria used in the university environment for setting up the computer education in Spain since the first teaching experiences in this do- main to the current implementations adapted to the European Higher Education Space (EHES). Also some samples of these different curricula are presented.

1   Introduction

A point that is necessary to take into account is that, until the implementation of the Bologna agreement the diploma recognizing that somebody had attained some university level was delivered by the Ministry of Education and Science (MEC). In order to ensure that the knowledge delivered to the students was coherent with the diploma, the MEC required a set of conditions, variable along the years. The goal of this paper is to present the changes of criteria, the control applied to the universities by the MEC and the curricula implemented consequently.

Some historical background is needed. Computerization of Spain had begun in 1958 with two major acquisitions: an IBM 650 for RENFE, the national railway company, and an UNIVAC UCT for the JEN, the national nuclear research institution. The early push of central state, characteristic of the autarchic period, had been followed in the 1960 by a development based on private industry. With computerization ac- companying economic modernization, Spain counted by mid-1970 with almost 100,000 people working in electronic computing [29]. As happened in other countries [8], these professionals lacked a formal university education in computing and had been generally acquired their skills in computer companies such as IBM or UNIVAC. Spanish companies, relying generally on American machines, had also took advantage in the early 1960s of new installations, mostly IBM 1401 and Bull Gamma 10, to train their employees [32], and a few began to access the profession in university computer labs, private schools and self-learning. We begin our narrative at this point, when Spanish government had just acquired an UNIVAC 1108 to process

K.K. Kimppa et al. (Eds.): HCC11 2014, IFIP AICT 431, pp. 176–190, 2014.

Ad-ministration payroll. Minister of Education, pushed by the lack of computing people among the civil servants, accepted the creation of the Informatics Institute.

No comprehensive account exists to date about the creation and evolution university studies in computing. Some articles and books had explore the topic: [33] provides a chronological listing of courses, pointing out that British universities created their stud-ies following the model started in Cambridge, while [6] analyses the role of two government agencies, the Advisory Committee on High Speed Calculating Machines and the University Grants Committee, in the establishment university-based computing facilities in the United Kingdom. Finally, William Aspray's paper [4] on the early development of computing in five American universities (MIT, Harvard, Penn, Princeton, and Columbia) has inspired international comparison, specifically in the case of French computing, which has been studied in great detail by Mounier-Kuhn [26, 27]. In Spain, his- tory of computing has a handful of scholars [34, 31, 3, 11, 13]. Also there are some contributions made by economic historians [14, 15] and [7]. In contrast, the history of the Barcelona's School of Informatics is generally well known thanks to a commemorative work [28] and two recent papers on the history of the school's early days [9, 10].

The motivation of this paper is to present the evolution of the regular informatics teaching in 1969 until today. In this history the reader will find two main key actors: from one side the Ministry of Education with the goal of controlling the informatics teaching and in the other side the universities, initially each one individually and finally grouped in the CODDII (*Conferencia de Decanos y Directores de Centros Universitarios de Informática*, Conference of Deans and Directors of Informatics University Centres) trying to incorporate studies of something very much appreciated in eighties and nineties.

The titles of sections of this paper remark the years with significant changes in these criteria:

- Section 2: In 1969 the MEC created the *Instituto de Informática* (II), estrange organization delivering a diploma each year.
- Section 3: In 1976 the MEC created the *Facultades de Informática* transforming the delegations of the *Instituto de Informática* existing at that time to deliver the title of *Licenciado en Informática* (Licencesed in Informatics).
- Section 4: In 1992 the MEC transformed the diplomas delivered by the universities from *Licenciado en Informática* into *Ingeniero en Informática* (Informatics Engineer).
- Section 5: In 2010 all universities started to deliver the *Grado en Ingeniería Informática* (Bachelor in Informatics Engineering).
- Finally, section 6 gives some conclusion and future expectations.

2   1969, Informatics Institute. Official Certification, Out of the University

At this time, after 30 years under the Franco's dictatorship, the centralism in the administration was very strong. Informatics as a body of knowledge was not included in the University. There were some courses in different studies like the *Universidad Complutense de Madrid* that had an Automatic Computation specialty with some courses on the basic computer architecture and on programming, common to the curricula on Mathematics and Physics, and the Industrial Engineering Schools that had a course on Computers in which was mainly explained the basic von Neumann architecture and the FORTRAN language. In March of this year, the MEC decided to create in Madrid the *Instituto de Informática* [16] directly depending of the MEC. This institute had strange organization, without any contact with the university and following a strange curriculum: the students earned a different diploma after each one of the five years of studies after the secondary education [17].

- *Programador de aplicaciones* (Applications programmer)
- *Programador de sistemas* (Systems programmer)
- *Analista de aplicaciones* (Applications analyst)
- *Analista de sistemas* (Systems analyst)
- *Técnico de sistemas* (Systems engineer)

The first two levels had compulsory courses but in the other three there were three specialties: fundamental informatics, business management informatics and physical systems. The specialties of fundamental informatics and business management informatics had at the applications analyst, systems analyst and systems engineer optional courses chosen in both cases among the same set of courses mainly oriented to applications and not to fundamental informatics. With these degrees it was intended that people who earned them were ready to develop professional tasks in industry and companies. It is easy to understand the difficulties of simultaneously giving a solid back-ground and the practical knowledge associated to each degree. The Informatics Institute started its courses in 1970.

In 1971 the II created a delegation in San Sebastián that was obliged to follow the same curriculum and also without any contact with the University. In 1972, the *Universitat Autònoma de Barcelona* (UAB) succeeded to create in its Faculty of Sciences an Informatics Department. It decided to start teaching Informatics in this Faculty as a 5 years curriculum with a typical university structure, but rapidly the II reacted and obliged the UAB to follow the same curriculum in its teaching. However, the team that started to teach Informatics at the UAB was a mixture of good professionals and people having followed some university computer courses, mainly in France (Paris and Grenoble); they kept the course titles of the official curriculum but they tried to transform the contents into a more reasonable structure according the university spirit. Criterion in this period: Centralism that is all centers teaching informatics should follow the same curriculum, at least formally. The idea of giving a professional diploma each year avoided the possibility of a good theoretical basis before giving the application knowledge.

Table 1. Informatics Institute. Degrees, courses and teaching hours

Diploma	Compulsory courses	Compulsory teaching (hours)	Optional courses	Optional teaching (hours)	Total teaching (hours)
Applications programmer	4	750	0	0	750
Systems programmer	6	750	0	0	750
Systems analyst: Fundamental informatics	6	690	1/3	90	780
Applications analyst: Business Management Informatics	6	690	1/3	90	780
Applications analyst: Physical systems	6	770	0	0	770
Systems analyst: Fundamental informatics	3	570	2/3	180	750
Systems analyst: Business Management Informatics	4	660	1/3	90	750
Systems analyst: Physical systems	5	750	0	0	750
Systems engineer: Fundamental informatics	3	480	3/6	270	750
Systems engineer: Business Management Informatics	4	570	2/6	180	750
Systems engineer: Physical systems	5	690	0	0	690

3   1976, the First University Degrees in Informatics

In 1974, the MEC considered that Informatics had to be included in the regular university teaching structure. A commission was created to study how to pass the Informatics Institute and its satellites to the university. Several universities fight in this commission to get the informatics studies. Finally by the end of 1975 (the decision was published by the MEC early 1976) was decided that three Faculties of Informatics had to be created in Barcelona (in the *Universitat Politècnica de Catalunya*, UPC), in San Sebastián (in the *Euskal Herriko Unibertsitatea*, EHU) and in Madrid (in the *Universidad Politécnica de Madrid*, UPM), and that the previous institutions giving informatics studies had to stop to teach informatics [18]. This was true in Madrid and

San Sebastián because the Informatics Institute and its delegation were incorporated to the corresponding universities and their denomination changed. In Barcelona the situation was more complicated because it was necessary to passing studies from one university to another (unbelievable in Spain at that time). Finally, both universities kept their studies. The new Faculties started to work in October 1977 with a five year curriculum that, for the first time in Spain, was different for each university but approved by the MEC. In addition, in the Faculty of Barcelona the classical curriculum structure of a fixed set of courses per academic year was broken and the curriculum was organized by courses with their corresponding pre-requisites in such a way that the student was able to organize his/her own curriculum choosing courses among those offered by the Faculty but respecting some compulsory courses [19] and the student had the right to earn his/her diploma when they had cumulated an established number of credits. This curriculum was deeply inspired by the ACM Computing Curriculum 1968 [5]. A draft version of this curriculum can be found in [30]. In all cases curricula were planned for five years of studies. Curricula of the Madrid and San Sebastian Faculties followed the traditional structure but also inspired by the ACM Computer Curriculum 1968 [19].

The students that successfully followed the studies in one of these universities obtained the title of *Licenciado en Informática* (Licensed in Informatics).

Criterion in this period: Centralism because the curricula should be approved by the MEC but, for the first time in Spain, each centre was following a different curriculum proposed without any guidelines and the MEC delivering the same diploma. These curricula were proposed, according the university interests and the possibilities of their teaching staff. Around 1980 a new 3-years study in Informatics was created and started in Madrid (UPM) and Valencia (Universitat Politècnica de València). The students that successfully followed these studies obtained the title of *Diplomado en Informática* (Diplomate in Informatics). Few after the Universidad de Las Palmas de Gran Canaria and the Universistat de les Illes Balears (Palma de Mallorca) created 3-years studies in Informatics. When these studies in Valencia, Las Palmas and Palma de Mallorca arrived to the third year, extensions to 5-years were implemented in these three universities. These three years studies had two orientations or intensifications, common to all centers, derived from the specialties of the Informatics Institute:

- Computer systems mainly devoted to a vision of the computer under the user interface.
- Business management applications mainly devoted to the computer over the user interface.

4   1992, Informatics Engineering

By the late 1980s, the MEC started a general reorganization of all university studies creating a catalogue of official titles (those delivered by the MEC itself based on the studies done in some university) reorganizing the existing titles and creating new ones. To get the official acceptance by the MEC each one of these titles had to respect a set of contents established by the MEC (main topics). To describe the relative importance of each of these topics a measure was invented: the credit equivalent to ten hours of teaching (including all kind of activities driven by the university teaching staff: theoretical classes, practical classes, etc.) received by the students. An academic year was estimated to have 30 weeks. Each university wishing to deliver some diploma had to submit a curriculum proposal that was controlled by the MEC itself in order to check if the compulsory main topics were correctly covered.

In the case of informatics three new titles were created and those existing till that moment disappeared:

- *Ingeniero en Informática* (Informatics Engineer): 5-years divided in two cycles and between 300 and 400 credits [20].
- *Ingeniero Técnico en Informática de Sistemas* (Technical Engineer in Informatics: Computer systems orientation): 3-years and between 180 and 225 credits [21].
- *Ingeniero Técnico en Informática de Gestión* (Technical Engineer in Informatics: Computer business management orientation): 3-years and between 180 and 225 credits [22].

Also it was stated that the students having earned one of these 3-years degrees were allowed to follow the second cycle of *Ingeniero en Informática*. In the early years of this decade all universities giving the old degrees in informatics adapted their curricula to the new characteristics and other universities started to teach informatics with this new orientation. This adaptation took different solutions:

- Universities that delivered the three degrees separately: the 5-years degree in a faculty or school and the 3-years degree in a different school.
- Universities that delivered the three degrees in the same faculty or school with a complete implementation of the three degrees.
- Universities that delivered the three degrees in the same faculty or school but without the implementation of the first cycle of *Ingeniero en Informática* and using both 3-years degrees as the first cycle.
- Universities that had just the 5-years degree.
- Universities that had one or both 3-years degrees

However, soon several problems appeared:

- The fact that three different first cycles gave access to the second cycle introduced difficulties in different topics like networks, computer architecture and software engineering. The reasons were that sometimes the same main topic with the same descriptors had assigned different number of credits or that the student coming from some first cycle had a previous knowledge of some topic unknown for the students coming from other first cycles.
- The low number of credits assigned to operating systems (6) that obliged to most of universities to create supplementary courses in this topic.
- The growing importance of networking. It was possible that an *Ingeniero Técnico en Informática de Gestión* could earn his/her title with no knowledge on networking.

- The inconvenience of having Automata theory as a compulsory topic in the first cycle of *Ingeniero en Informática* (too theoretical for beginners) and in *Ingeniero Técnico en Informática de Sistemas* (too theoretical for the applied orientation of the 3-years studies).

During this period the number of faculties and schools delivering these degrees was continuously increasing (and currently there are approximately 80 in Spain). This fact and the need of exchanging information about experiences and discussing about the difficulties in the implementation of their curricula provoked the need of discussion meetings with the participation of all faculties and schools teaching informatics careers. These annual meetings started in 1995. However, as the number of schools and faculties was continuously increasing, in 1998 it was decided to set up a minimal organization for these meetings, with a president and a secretary and a title: CODDI. The first task assigned just after the appointment of a president was the review of the main topics of the informatics careers in order to correct the detected inconveniences. CODDI submitted this proposal to the MEC. However, it was not accepted by the MEC because the acceptation would have allowed other studies to request also the modification of their compulsory main topics. And this would have introduced a high degree of discussions between universities and between these ones and the MEC. Nevertheless, this proposal was accepted for the new informatics curricula as guidelines for the analysis and acceptation of future curricula submitted to the MEC by the universities.

Criteria: The degree of freedom in the creation of new university curricula was reduced. The names of the diplomas were fixed by the MEC and these diplomas were delivered by the MEC following the university proposal when a student had successfully passed all courses. Each university curriculum could be different.

5   2010, European Computer People

5.1   Adaptation to the EHES

In coincidence with the change of millennium, the European Union decided ask the member states to reorganize their university systems in such a way that a convergence was reached around 2010 in two main points:

- University studies should be organized in three levels: bachelor, master and doctorate.
- University studies should define for each course the effort required to the student, the European Credit Transfer System (ECTS), equivalent, approximately to 25 to 30 hours of work for the student including all his/her activities (theoretical courses, practical courses, seminars, personal study, exam preparation, etc.).

This convergence was named as the Bologna process because the agreement of all the member states was reached in a meeting held in the city where the first European university was created.

In 2001 CODDI started a volunteer work on how to adapt the informatics studies to this convergence process. Initially a set of considerations showing mismatches in either the university studies structure or in the consideration by the society of the degrees delivered by the university [12]. Later in 2003 CODDI started an economically funded that confirmed the conclusions of the previous one [2].

Several changes in the MEC delayed the implementation of the EHES. Finally in 2007 the framework for the implementation of the EHES was set up [23]. Some points were clear but the framework was not yet complete:

- There would not be a catalogue of official titles; each university had to propose its own titles that would be validated by an independent agency (*Agencia Nacional de Evaluación de la Calidad del Sistema Universitario*, ANECA, National Agency for the Evaluation of the Quality of the University System) that would evaluate the appropriateness of the proposed title (specially avoiding confusion to the society), the quality of the proposal and the existence of a sufficient amount of the human and material resources allocated to the correct implementation.

- The *Grado* (Bachelor), in our case of *Ingeniero en Informática*, would have 240 ECTS that would include an end of studies project.

- The Master degree would have 60 or 120 ECTS depending on the coherence between the grade earned and the intended Master and including an end of Master project.

The proposal of the CODDI, several years before the decisions of the MEC, was fully in line with the framework in which the universities will work in the following years.

Early 2008 five commissions were set up to analyse the new curricula on Science, Engineering, Health, Law and Economics, and Letters and Humanities. Informatics was included in the engineering domain.

In order to understand the environment, it is necessary to know that all classical engineering studies (agronomical engineers, aeronautical engineers, civil engineers, forest engineers, industrial engineers, mining engineers, naval engineers and telecommunication engineers) have exclusive professional capabilities and differentiated by branch and level (3-years or 5-years of studies) and associated only to the academic diploma. This organization causes serious conflicts of interests in which are involved the corresponding professional associations. The informatics engineers have no defined professional capabilities and their professional space is frequently invaded by other engineering branches, mainly the industrial and telecommunication engineers.

Traditional engineering associations were against the decision of the government of associating professional capabilities to the *Grado* diploma when there were different capabilities for diplomas of 3 and 5 years. Before solving this fight, the verification process started in March 2008. This process was theoretically very well-conceived but looking more to how to teach than what should be taught. However, there were terms not clearly defined, related between them and critical for the correctness of this process, like: objectives, competencies, modules, matters, courses, contents, learning outcomes, etc.

The verification commissions started to work with a formal description of its work but with an important lack of definitions (as explained before) and fundamental and logistic problems. Among the last ones an important difficulty was the lack of a good management system of the proposals. Due to the lack a good definition of its task, commission members used their better knowledge to the proposals analyses.

Two points were taken especially into account:

- The name of the title should represent the delivered contents.
- The title description should not induce into error the future students reading the document with the intention of following these studies.

However, as classical engineering studies had associated professional capabilities supported by the corresponding professional associations, it soon appeared the need of defining the objectives and competencies of these studies. To solve this problem the MEC published in February 2009 these characteristics for all classical engineering studies making the equivalence of the *Grado* with the 3-years engineers and their capabilities and the Master with the 5-years engineers and their capabilities. However the definitions objectives and competencies of these studies were not an example of well doing because:

- The objectives were defined in terms of competencies.
- The competencies were defined in terms of teaching contents.

Also, this decision was against the previous definition in which the *Grado* gave the professional capabilities and the Master gave the specialization. With this decision the *Grado* gave the professional capabilities of the 3-years engineers in its concrete specialties and after obtaining the Master they got all the professional capabilities of 5-years engineers. This approach has the inconvenience (detected by the CODDI with respect the previous Informatics studies) of passing from a specialized knowledge to a general one.

In the case of Informatics Engineering and some other newly created they had not professional capabilities, this fact represented to place them in a level lower than the classical engineers and the CODDI fight to have at least a definition of its studies similar to the other engineering studies even if they had not professional capabilities. This was obtained in August 2009 when the MEC published the definition of objectives and competencies for the *Grado* and Master in Informatics Engineering [24] with a better conception avoiding the definition of objectives in terms of competencies and the competencies in terms of teaching contents. This definition included the five specific technologies defined in the ACM/IEEE-CS Computing Curricula [1] in a similar way to the other classical engineers that all of them had several specialties:

- Computer Engineering
- Software Engineering
- Computing
- Information Systems
- Information Technology

These specific technologies are different in its competencies but have the same objectives. The competencies structure is the following:

- Module of basic knowledge: 60 ECTS
- Module common to the informatics branch: 60 ECTS
- Specific technology module: 48 ECTS, different for each specific technology
- End of *Grado* project: 12 ECTS

The rest until 240 ECTS is at disposal of the University for strengthening the above mentioned topics or others, for stages in companies and for collateral activities.

With the existing degree of freedom for defining the title of the *Grado*, two alternatives were presented to the Universities:

- To propose a unique name with several technological specialties (or professions with professional capabilities, if any)
- To propose one or several names related to the technological specialties (or professions with professional capabilities) they want to develop.

In favour to independent titles for each specific technology or profession with recognized capabilities there are to be aligned with these professions and to use socially recognized names. Instead, for a unique title with technological specialities there are the limitations imposed by the local governments concerning the number of careers they were ready to fund, to be aligned with the White Book recommendations and to find the social recognition.

In order to avoid misunderstandings of the future students the criteria followed by the verification commission was to accept a specific name if it was adapted to a specific technology (e.g. Software Engineer) and a generic name (e.g. Informatics Engineer) in the case of including several specific technologies.

Criteria: The degree of freedom in the creation of new university curricula was maintained or increased. The names of the diplomas were fixed by the universities and these diplomas were also delivered by the universities who have the responsibility on the quality of the delivered diploma. Each university curriculum could be different.

5.2   Results of the Adaptation to the EHES

New computer careers are currently in their first years of implementation considering that the starting academic year was between 2008-09 and 2010-11. There is some uniformity after the definition of objectives and competencies of the *Grado en Ingeniería Informática*. The curricula verified previously to this definition have quite different structures. To access the details of these studies, one can access the *Registro de Universidades, Centros y Títulos*, RUCT, (Register of Universities, Centres and Degrees, RUCT) [25].

At present we find:

- 57 studies of *Grado en Ingeniería Informática*, of which 8 were verified before the definition of the objectives and competencies; those verified based in this definition should have, at least, two specific technologies but most of them have the five defined specific technologies, although, maybe for economic restrictions, they are not running all of them.

- 7 curricula of computer engineering, according with the corresponding specific technology.
- 8 curricula of information systems, according with the corresponding specific technology.
- 7 curricula of software engineering, according with the corresponding specific technology.
- 7 curricula of information technology, according with the corresponding specific technology.
- 1 curriculum of systems engineering, that is not in accordance with the defined specific technologies.

However, the adaptation of informatics studies (and most of the university curricula has been done without the adequate preparation for teachers to assume changes involving the adaptation to the EHES: the change from a paradigm based on the teaching effort of professors to another based on the learning effort of students with the modifications involved both at teaching infrastructure (decrease in large amphitheaters and increase in small rooms for seminars, spaces for study and group work of the students, increased laboratories, etc.) as well as the teachers task and dedication to follow the students learning process and to coordinating with other teachers of the same course to achieve a reasonably uniform weekly workload. Also some universities have proposed curricula that we can consider in the informatics domain but with different orientations and contents and without professional capabilities. Among them we can find:

- 6 curricula of *Grado en Ingeniería Multimedia* (Multimedia engineering), habitually composed by a third of informatics, a third of telecommunications and a final third of content generation.
- 8 curricula of *Grado en Ingeniera Biomédica* (Biomedical Engineering)
- 1 curriculum of *Grado en Informática y Servicios* (Informatics and Services)
- 1 curriculum of *Grado en Fotografía y Creación Digital* (Photography and Digital Creation)
- 1 curriculum of *Grado en Ingeniería en Organización de las Tecnologías de la Información y de la Comunicación* (Information and Communication Organization Engineering)
- 1 curriculum of *Grado en Ingeniería de Sistemas TIC* (ICT Systems Engineering)
- 1 curriculum of *Grado en Matemática Computacional* (Computational Mathematics)
- 1 curriculum of *Grado en Matemáticas e Informática* (Mathematics and Informatics)
- 1 curriculum of *Grado en Ingeniería en Desarrollo de Contenidos Digitales* (Digital Contents Development Engineering)
- 1 curriculum of *Grado en Diseñoo y Desarrollo de Videojuegos* (Videogames Design and Development)

5.3   Coming Steps

Follow Up Process

To prevent that the accreditation process discover that the implementation of curricula have not been made in accordance with the proposal made by the university, ANECA has proposed a monitoring process two years after the implementation of some curriculum and to be repeat every two years. The objective of this exercise is to analyze how the curriculum implementation has been carried out and inform universities about missing or not correctly implemented aspects, especially with regard to the procedures to ensure the quality of the educational process. These procedures are generally new to the universities and should ensure the new orientation of the teaching given by the Bologna agreement. The follow up process has been structured in the following way:

- Universities should not submit any documentation; they should only give access to the responsible people for monitoring the information university system so that they can see how the points proposed in the verification report have been implemented.
- From these observations a report is issued that allows the university to have an external and impartial view of its performance.

Accreditation Process

The accreditation process has been scheduled to be performed six years after the implementation of any new curriculum. However, there is still nothing defined: Neither by whom, nor how it will be done.

6   Conclusion

We have presented a short overview of the different criteria used in the university environment for setting up the computer education in Spain. To sum up:

- The story began by 1969, with the creation of the Informatics Institute, we have described a period of centralism. All centers which teaching informatics followed the same curriculum, at least formally. The idea of giving a professional diploma each year avoided the possibility of a good theoretical basis before giving the application knowledge.
- Next step, by 1976, three universities began to develop a Computer Science curricula. It was still an age of centralism as long as curricula have to be approved in Madrid by MEC, but for the first time in Spain each University centre could follow a different curriculum proposed without any guidelines and MEC delivered the same diploma. These curricula were proposed, according the university interests and the possibilities of their teaching staff.
- By the late 1980s the MEC started a general reorganization of all university studies. In the case of computer science it implied a reduction in the degree of creation freedom of new university curricula. The names of the diplomas, fixed

by MEC, passed from the old *Licenciado* (Licensed), a term associated to base sciences (like Mathematics, Chemistry or Physics) to the new *Ingeniero* (Engineer) a term associated to applied sciences. However, there was no such change in the curricula and the balance among computer science and computer engineering matters remained almost the same.

- Eventually, by 2000, the European Union decided to reorganize the member states' university systems in such a way that a convergence was reached around 2010. It was the so-called European Higher Education Space (EHES). Convergence had two folds. On the one hand, University studies should be organized in three levels: bachelor, master and doctorate. On the other hand, University studies should define for each course the effort required to the student, the European Credit Transfer System (ECTS), equivalent, approximately to 25 to 30 hours of work for the student including all his/her activities (theoretical courses, practical courses, seminars, personal study, exam preparation, etc.). Once again, we want to evaluate the implementation criteria. In this case, the degree of freedom in the creation of new university curricula was maintained or increased. The names of the diplomas were fixed by the universities and these diplomas were also delivered by the universities who have the responsibility on the quality of the delivered diploma. Each university curriculum could be different.

How will the future be? We think it will be necessary to wait ten years until we will be able to have an opinion about the success of this reform, mainly to evaluate how professors and students have changed their teaching and learning habits. This is, may be, the strongest challenge of this reform.

Acknowledgements. This work has been partially funded by the Spanish Ministry of Science and Innovation and the European Union FEDER funds, both in the framework of the project TIN2011-23889, *Eficiencia Energética, Virtualización y Rendimiento de Servidores.*

References

1. ACM/IEEE-CS: Computer science curriculum. Tech. rep., Report from the Interim ReviewTask Force (2008), http://www.acm.org/education/curricula/ComputerScience2008. pdf
2. Casanovas, J., et al.: Libro Blanco sobre las titulaciones universitarias de informática en el nuevo espacio europeo de educación superior. ANECA (2004)
3. Arroyo, L.: 200 años de informática. Espasa Calpe, Madrid (1991)
4. Aspray, W.: Was early entry a competitive advantage? US universities that entered computing in the 1940s. IEEE Annals of the History of Computing 22(3), 42–87 (2000)
5. Atchison, W.F., Conte, S.D., Hamblen, J.W., Hull, T.E., Keenan, T.A., Kehl, W.B., McCluskey, E.J., Navarro, S.O., Rheinboldt, W.C., Schweppe, E.J., Viavant, W., Young Jr., D.M.: Curriculum 68: Recommendations for academic programs in computer science: A report of the ACM curriculum committee on computer science. Commun. ACM 11(3), 151–197 (1968), http://doi.acm.org/10.1145/362929.362976

6. Clark, M.: State support for the expansion of UK University computing in the 1950s. IEEE Annals of the History of Computing 32(1), 23–33 (2010)
7. De Diego García, E.: Historia de la industria en España: la electrónica y la informática. Escuela de Organización Industrial, Madrid (1995)
8. Ensmenger, N.L.: The Computer Boys Take Over: Computers, Programmers, and the Politics of Technical Expertise. MIT Press, Cambridge (2010)
9. Fornes, J.: Los físicos en la facultad de informática de Barcelona, 1976-1992. Actesd'Història de la Ciència i de la Tècnica 5, 71–82 (2012)
10. Fornes, J., Herran, N.: Computing in transition: the origins of Barcelona's school of informatics, 1976-1984. IEEE Annals of theHistory of Computing 36(1), 18–29 (2014)
11. Galán, L.: 100 años de informática y telecomunicaciones: España siglo XX. Cuadernos de Historia de las Telecomunicaciones, Fundación Rogelio Segovia para el Desarrollo de las Telecomunicaciones (2005),
    http://books.google.es/books?id=P3i1AAAACAAJ
12. Campos, J.C., et al.: Informe sobre la adaptación de los estudios de TIC a la declaración de Bolonia. Tech. rep., unpublished document (For getting it, contact R. Puigjaner) (2002)
13. López García, A.: Introducció a la història de la informàtica en Espanya. Projecte Final de Carrera-UPC, dirigit per Miquel Barceló (2002)
14. López García, S.: El doble tañido del hierro: El tecnólogo José García Santesmases. In: Actes de les I Trobades d'Història de la Ciència i de la Tècnica, pp. 255–262. Societat Catalana d'Història de la Ciència i la Tècnica, Barcelona (1994)
15. López Garcóa, S.: Los precedentes de la informática y la automática en España (1925-1971). In: Tècnica i societat en el món contemporani, pp. 255–262. Museu d'Història de Sabadell, Sabadell (1994)
16. M.E.C.: Decreto 554/1969. BOE de 14/04/1969 - Sección I (March 1969), de 29 de marzo (Educación y Ciencia), por el que se crea un Instituto de Informática, dependiente del Ministerio de Educación y Ciencia, con sede en Madrid, y se regulan las enseõanzas del mismo
17. M.E.C.: Orden de 24 de junio de 1971. BOE de3/07/1971 (June 1971), por la que se aprueba el Plan de Estudios del curso de Programador de aplicaciones, Programador de Sistemas, Analista de Aplicaciones, Analista de Sistemas y Técnico de Sistemas
18. M.E.C.: Decreto 593/1976. BOE de 26/03/1976 - Sección I (March 1976), de 4 de marzo, por el que se crean Facultades de Informática en Barcelona, Madrid y San Sebastián
19. M.E.C.: Orden de 7 de junio de 1977. BOE de 27/07/1977 - Sección I (June 1977), por la que se aprueba el plan de estudios de la Facultad de Informática de Barcelona
20. M.E.C.: Real decreto 1459/1990. BOE de 20/11/1990 - Sección I (October 1990), de 26 de octubre, por el que se establece el título universitario oficial de Ingeniero en Informática y las directrices generales propias de los planes de estudios conducentes a la obtención de aquél
21. M.E.C.: Real decreto 1459/1990. BOE de 20/11/1990 - Sección I (October 1990), de 26 de octubre, por el que se establece eltítulo universitario oficial de Ingeniero Técnico en Informática de Sistemas y las directrices generales propias de los planes de estudios conducentes a la obtención de aquél
22. M.E.C.: Real decreto 1459/1990. BOE de 20/11/1990 - Sección I (October 1990), de 26 de octubre, por el que se establece el título universitario oficial de Ingeniero Técnico en Informática de Gestión y las directrices generales propias de los planes de estudios conducentes a la obtención de aquél
23. M.E.C.: Real decreto 1393/2007. BOE de 30/10/2007 - Sección I (October 2007), de 29 de octubre, por el que se establece la ordenación de las enseñanzas universitarias oficiales

24. M.E.C.: Resolución de 8 de junio de 2009. BOE de 4/08/2009 - Sección III (June 2009), de la Secretaría General de Universidades, por la que se da publicidad al Acuerdo del Consejo de Universidades, por el que se establecen recomendaciones para la propuesta por las universidades de memorias de solicitud de títulos oficiales en los ámbitos de la Ingeniería Informática, Ingeniería Técnica Informática e Ingeniería Química

25. M.E.C.D.: Registro de universidades, centros y títulos (RUCT), Registro de Universidades, Centros y Títulos (RUCT) (accessed on June 18, 2013)

26. Mounier-Kuhn, P.: L'Informatique en France de la seconde guerre mondiale au Plan Calcul. L'Émergence d'une science (Informatics in France from World War II to Plan Calcul: The Emergence of a Science). Presses de l'Université Paris-Sorbonne (2010)

27. Mounier-Kuhn, P.: Computer science in French universities: Early entrants and late comers. Information and Culture 47, 414–456 (2012)

28. Nonell, R. (ed.): 25 anys de la Facultatd'Informàtica de Barcelona. UPC, Barcelona (2002), http://www.fib.upc.edu/25e/llibres.htm

29. Presidencia del Gobierno: La informática en España 1976. Servicio central de informática, servicio central de publicaciones, Madrid (1977)

30. Puigjaner, R., Vergés, M.: Bases para un plan de estudios. NOVATICA (5) (1975)

31. Randell, B.: From analytical engine to electronic digital computer: The contributions of Ludgate, Torres, and Bush. Annals of the History of Computing 4(4), 327–341 (1982)

32. Sales, T.: La informática comercial española en la primera década (1960-1970): Apuntes para una historia de la informática en España. Novatica (34), 53 (1980)

33. Samet, P.A.: The evolution of computer science teaching and research in the UK. In: Computers in Europe. Past, Present and Future, Kyiv, October 5-9 (1998), http://www.icfcst.kiev.ua/SYMPOSIUM/Proceedings/Samet.pdf

34. Yuste, A., Palma, M.: Scanning our past from Madrid: Leonardo Torres Quevedo. Proceedings of the IEEE 93(7), 1379–1382 (2005)

Reasoning vs. Orthodoxy, or, The Lesson from the Fate of Russian "Reasoning Machine"

Valery V. Shilov and Sergey A. Silantiev

MATI – Russian State Technological University, Moscow, Russia
{shilov,intdep}@mati.ru

Abstract. This paper devoted to Russian scientist Alexander Schukarev and his work on logical machine. Historically, this work may be divided on two periods – before and after Russian October revolution. We try to understand and explain why Schukarev's activity in this field was ceased and his logical machine was forgotten for the long time.

Keywords: Stanley Jevons, Pavel Khrushchev, Alexander Schukarev, logical machine, reasoning, ideology.

1   Introduction

On 25 May 1865 the great English logician Stanley Jevons wrote to his brother Gerbert: "My newest job on hand is a reasoning machine, or logical abacus, adapted to show the working of Boole's Logic in a half mechanical manner. I got a rough model to work excellently the other night, and I think I can easily get it finished during the summer" [1, p. 205]. This "reasoning machine" was in fact the first version of the first in history mechanical engine which really may be called reasoning (or logical) machine – Jevons' famous "logical piano". At the beginning of XX century famous American philosopher and psychologist James Mark Baldwin in his Dictionary gave such definition: "Logical Machine: Ger. *logische Machina;* Fr. *machine logique;* Ital. *macchine logistiche.* An instrument devised to facilitate by mechanical means the handling of logical symbols or diagrams" [2, p. 28]. Baldwin added that "There are three such instruments which merit attention" [ibid.]; these "instruments" were constructed by Jevons (1869), John Venn (1881) and Allan Marquand (1881, 1883).

Martin Gardner gave remarkable review of the history of logical machines in his classic work [3]. However, he did not describe some of them because of various reasons. In particular, he did not know very interesting Jevons type logical machines invented in Russia by professor Pavel Khrushchev (1849-1909) and then improved by professor Alexander Schukarev (1864-1936) (Fig. 1).

Professor Khrushchev was prominent chemist. Circa 1900 he built his machine – but this is the only established fact. The further fate of machine is related with the name of Schukarev. That is why this paper devoted to this scientist and his work on logical machine. Historically, this work may be divided on two periods – before and

K.K. Kimppa et al. (Eds.): HCC11 2014, IFIP AICT 431, pp. 191–202, 2014.
© IFIP International Federation for Information Processing 2014

after Russian October revolution. We try to understand the reasons why Schukarev's activity in the field of logic and theory of cognition was ceased and his logical machine was forgotten for a long time. Exactly these reasons explain why until recently only few and rather brief publications about this machine are known [4-6].

Fig. 1. Pavel Khrushchev and Alexander Schukarev

2   Professor Alexander Schukarev: His Way in the Science

Alexander Schukarev was born on 2 November 1864 in Moscow in the family of petty officer. In 1889 he graduated from Moscow University, Faculty of Physics and Mathematics. Then he was a lecturer in several colleges. His scientific interests were formed under the influence of joint work with outstanding Russian thermo-chemist Vladimir Louginine. In 1890 Louginine established the first Russian thermo-chemical laboratory in Moscow University and Schukarev worked there as a laboratory assistant. In 1906 Schukarev received M. Sc. degree and in 1909 Doctor of Science degree. Then he was elected as a professor of general chemistry of Ekaterinoslav High Mining School. After two years of work there he became the professor of Kharkov Technological University. Almost all his further scientific activity spent in this University.

Significant part of Schukarev scientific publications was devoted to his main specialty – physical chemistry but he also was interested in the problems of logic, methodology of science and philosophy. From the beginning of 1900's Schukarev regularly published articles with philosophical analysis of natural science. In 1913 he published monograph under the title "Problems of theory of cognition and its applications to the natural science" [7].

3   First Acquaintance with Logical Machine

During his work in Kharkov University, Alexander Schukarev saw Khrushchev logical machine in one of physical-chemical laboratory storerooms. It was very interesting for Schukarev who investigated the problems of logic and theory of cognition. He recalled that he in fact had "inherited" the logic machine from Khrushchev. Probably it means that this machine was simply handed to the scientist.

Khrushchev machine as it prototype – Jevons logical piano – was constructed as a high drawer with keyboard on which separate messages were set. It had also indicator board with the openings where the possible term combinations were formed (Fig. 2). Unfortunately, the description of Khrushchev machine made by Schukarev contains a brief statement that its construction and principles of work are the same as Jevons one.

Fig. 2. Khrushchev logical machine (Source: [7, p. 52, 53])

Circa 1913 Schukarev made the improved variant of Jevons logic machine and described it (unfortunately also very laconically) in the article "Mechanization of thinking (Jevons logical machine)" published in 1925:

"I simply gave the instrument the smaller dimensions, made it from metal and eliminated some constructional defects. The further step forward was the connecting the special illuminated screen to the instrument. The work of machine is transmitted to this screen and results of "thinking" appear not in symbolic form as on Jevons machine but in ordinary verbal form [8]".

Schukarev so ended his description:

"In my device, the rear rods connect electrically with special screen consisting of 16 horizontal racks, each bearing two ordinary electrical lamps.

List of transparent paper with ordinary words written by drawing ink is hanged before these racks. These words coordinate with the combinations on rods. For example, let A designates "silver", B – "metal", C – "current conductor", O – "possess free electrons". Than the words "Silver – metal, current conductor, possess free electrons" will be written on the first upper line of illuminated screen against the first rack with the lamps.

In null machine position, all screen lamps are lit and all combinations could be seen very clear by audience. After installing definite sentences, some rods are lifted up and appropriate racks are deactivated. Only those combinations of concepts which compatible with given settings remain illuminated" [8].

4   New Life of Logical Machine

Logical machine regained the new life due to Schukarev. In 1912 he demonstrated it on the conference of Society of physical-chemical science at Kharkov University. This demonstration was repeated "almost 10 times" (apparently before various audiences) by "public insistence".

Undoubtedly, the character of modifications made by Schukarev (though he specified that they "were not of principle character") allows us to conclude that he built just new machine. It was not simple improvement of Khrushchev machine (Fig. 3). He wrote that machine "at present time [in 1912-1913 – *Auth*.] is the property of Kharkov University" [7, p. 49]. That is why we may suppose that after building of his own machine the inventor returned its prototype back to the University. Unfortunately, the fate of original Khrushchev machine is unknown.

During his public lectures Schukarev used the logic machine for supporting his opinions and theoretical statements. It is worth to mention that unlike Stanley Jevons who considered his machine useful only for the purposes of learning, Schukarev thought that "it may be used not only for that":

"In 1916 after several demonstrations of my device, which now is well known on the South Russia, I received the following letter from one of my students:

…"Local magistrate acquittal one of the accused person, which was motivated by the following justification: during the investigation there were no information excluded the absence of ill-will from the accused. Local jurists stated that this formula did not correspond to the acquittal verdict and they asked me to write you in order to check it with the help of logic machine".

I executed this request and set on machine:

A – "case", B – "contain information excluded the absence of ill-will", C – "charge". In result, I got the following combinations:

AbC   Abc   aBC   abC   abc

Thus, the given case A as it doesn't contain information excluding the absence of ill-will b allows the charge C and discharge c as well.

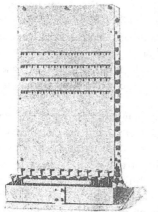 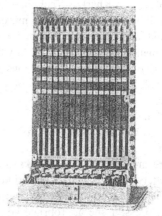

Общій видъ мыслительной машины.   Внутреннее устройство мыслительной машины.

Fig. 3. Schukarev logical machine (Source: [9])

Any other case a which contains information excluding the absence of ill-will B demands indisputable charge C.

Any other case a which also doesn't contain information excluding the absence of ill-will b allows the charge C and discharge c as well.

Thus, magistrate from Rostov was absolutely right in his acquittal verdict (because discharge is preferred to charge)" [8].

"It is possible that in other same lawsuits logical machine could find practical application" – so Schukarev completed his article. In Appendix to his monograph [7] and in the article [8] he also gave the example from the field of chemistry when logic machine helped to get "absolutely true" conclusions.

Until 1917 Schukarev demonstrated his machine not only in Kharkov but in other cities of South Russia. In April 1914 he gave some lectures in Moscow. It is known several newspaper advertisements about these lectures. For example, in the newspaper "Russkie Vedomosti" from 16 April 1914 we may read:

Thinking Machine

Public lecture of Professor A. N. Schukarev "Cognition and thinking" will be presented on Saturday, 19 April, in large auditorium of Polytechnic museum. Thinking machine will be demonstrated during the lecture. This apparatus allows to reconstruct mechanically the process of human thinking – to draw conclusions from determined statements. Initially, machine was built by mathematician Jevons and improved by the author of the lecture. Results of it operations display on the screen in verbal form.

One of spectators of this lecture gives additional information about Schukarev logic machine:

"Professor of Kharkov Technological Institute A. N. Schukarev presented in large auditorium of Polytechnic museum the lecture under the title "Cognition and thinking". He demonstrated "logic thinking machine", invented by Englishman Jevons and improved by the author.

<...> A. N. Schukarev reconstructed and modified it. This machine performed mechanical process of thinking more perfectly without human mistakes.

Machine consists of vertical box of 40 sm height, 25 sm width and 25 sm length. It has keyboard: its rear row designates subjects and front row designates verbs.

There are lines of rods (sticks) inside the box moving by keys pressing. Four letters A, B, C and D are printed on each rod. There are 16 rods at all. They can present all possible combinations of letters <...>

After pressing the appropriate keys the combinations of terms inconsistent with given premises are eliminated. Thus, only combinations consistent with premises are remained – that is logical conclusion <...>.

Machine mechanically and without mistakes draws the conclusion and works more perfectly than human brain.

<...> Professor A. N. Schukarev has long worked on the improvement of Jevons machine. He made the special modification – every rod connects with electrical contact. This contact closes the chain of lamps on illuminated screen with some sentences written on it. Every sentence corresponds to one of letter combinations. Some contacts are broken when the rods are moving and sentences incompatible with given premise become invisible.

Thinking machine draws the conclusions better than the man does because all the conclusions are derived from our experience. In this sense machines are more useful than human brain.

We have arithmometers which can add, subtract and multiple great numbers by simple turn of the handle. It is obvious that time demands to have logic machine capable for unmistakable conclusions when you only press the appropriate keys. It will keep for a man a lot of time for creative work, hypothesis, fantasy and inspiration" [9].

5   Scientist and Ideology: The Fate of the Doomed

Schukarev was continuing public presentations and further improvement of his machine until the 1925. It is known that besides regular demonstrations of logic machine in Kharkov, Schukarev showed it in Moscow and Leningrad. Logic machine caused the great interest of spectators as was earlier. However, after 1917 the situation in Russia was changing. To the mid of 1920's part of leading philosophers were expatriated and many others were prohibited to work and publish. All editions propagated "idealism and clericalism" were suppressed. Marxist monopoly was established in philosophy. Many traditional philosophical doctrines including formal logic were radically revised. In 1925 Soviet philosopher Ivan Orlov published the article "About the rationalization of brainwork" [10] in ideological journal "Pod znamenem marksizma (Under the banner of Marxism)". He criticized the scientific activity of Schukarev from the standpoint of Marxist dialectics.

The main Orlov thesis was – "he [Schukarev – *Auth.*] wants to convince us in the formal character of thinking and possibility of its mechanization by logical machine". Orlov declared that conception of formal character of thinking "drastically contradicts to the dialectic materialism". Orlov ascribes to Schukarev the statement that "machine will think instead of man". But Schukarev says only about possible mechanization of some thinking functions! First part of Orlov's article is completely based on falsifications of Schukarev ideas.

However, in post-revolutionary Russia not only Schukarev ideas were unclaimed but he himself was non grata person. If we get to know Schukarev better not only as a scientist but also as a man it would be more clear the fate of his logic machine. Unfortunately almost all known publications do not describe him particular as a man. That is why the unique document discovered by authors – memories of his Kharkov's colleague professor A. Filippov published in 1950 in Paris [11] – obtains specific value.

Memoirist describes Schukarev as a typical Russian pre-revolutionary professor who lived only for science and who "did not note surrounding reality". Schukarev of course saw and understood Soviet reality but it seems he principally ignored it. According to Filippov, Alexander Schukarev lived well enough as many other academicians worked in field of natural and technical science. Meantime many humanitarians "lived in poor hovels, languished from enforced idleness and wandered ragged along the streets". For example, professor of philosophy Vladimir Karinsky "did not differ in appearance from the ordinary beggar". However, Schukarev continued to live in the flat he occupied from Tsar Times. He dressed "decently and even smartly" and "came always dressed in frock-coat" on his public lectures.

But it is obvious that life position and behavior of such men as Alexander Schukarev were determined not only by the degree of material wellbeing. That is why his administrative superiors were in constant strain that Schukarev "will do some politically unacceptable thing". For example, memoirist writes that the so called "Circle ("Kruzhok") for studying of dialectic materialism" was organized in Kharkov soon after withdrawal of White Army at the end of 1919. Attendance of the Circle meetings was obligatory for all professors. On the very first meeting Schukarev made serious scientific report and at the end "he scratched forehead and said: oh yes, I forgot that the goal of our Kruzhok is the study of dialectic materialism. Well, what may I said about the learning of dialectic materialism? One can do everything, it doesn't matter, for example you may collect the white mice". Professor calmly went out but scandal erupted was hardly extinguished. Memoirist also provides interesting information about Alexander Schukarev logic machine:

"Especially famous was A. N. with his logic machine. In fact, it was machine of English logic Jevons and he only attached the large screen to it. All machine operations immediately displayed on the screen. On this screen, he demonstrated the specific examples of abstract character combinations. In whole, A. N. was wonderful constructor. For example, according to the opinion of specialists, the "calorimetric bomb" constructed by him was much better than that of famous French chemist Berthelot. Even before the revolution well-known journalist Alexander Yablonsky described in jocular form the misadventures of logic machine. Once during it demonstration one of the spectators (young girl student) was indignant – "this machine as any other machine is the instrument of people exploitation". Next time on the question: "do we have Constitution" machine answered: "not we, not have, not Constitution". Finally, police superintendent stopped the political dispute. These misadventures continued in Soviet period but now not as a joke. One time a year A. N. dressed in frock-coat visited "House of Scientists" (Club of scientists) and demonstrated operation of his logic machine. He illustrated its work by such very "suitable" for Bolshevik examples as "the evidence of God existence". Needless to say, how violently the Marxists presented on the lecture attacked A. N. and his machine. However, these attacks did not produce any effect on A. N. He only laughed merrily and good-naturedly as a child" [11].

One more episode described by memoirist shows how much logic machine impressed spectators. Once after the usual antireligious lecture the propagandist who just "had proved the nonexistence of God" suggested the listeners to say their opinion. "To his surprise one of elderly University janitors stood up and began to speak. "You say – started this janitor – that God does not exist". Lecturer compassionately nodded. "But machine of professor Schukarev, – continued janitor, – had proved clearly that God exists". Surprised lecturer did not find what to answer (all Bolsheviks deeply believed in power of technology). Lecturer had just considered and disproved all known proofs of God's existence but overlooked the "machine proof". Probably, Alexander Schukarev himself would be surprised by such effect of his demonstrations!

The range of Schukarev scientific interests was always very wide. It was mentioned above that he did not limit himself by investigations in the field of special problems of physical chemistry. Beside the theory of cognition, he examined the problems of social life, human talent etc. He always sought the possibility to use mathematical methods in his researches. For example, he derived some empirical relations and then gathered statistical data with the help of volunteers. Professor Filippov recalled that "his *a priori* graphical curve was generally confirmed on practice".

Alexander Schukarev wrote: "regarding the politics, I never before the revolution nor after it wanted to participate in this kind of activity because I early admitted the thesis – "where the struggle begins there the creative work ends". I mainly was interested in the latter". To the end of 1920's such accentuated political indifference was interpreted as especially hostile to the Soviet power. Punishment must be expected earlier or later. Moreover, the scientist who "did not notice ... Soviet reality" obviously gave reasons for repressions.

When in 1929 Bolsheviks decided to establish Ukraine Academy of Science they really did this with great pompousness. Meetings and sessions were organized, articles in newspapers were published, pompous speeches were delivered etc.

Professor Schukarev was also invited at one of such ceremonial meetings. He came and said that it was no need absolutely to establish Ukraine Academy of Science because there were no worthy candidates to the members of this Academy. After the speech, he gathered his papers and went out not hear abuses to his address [11].

Immediately after this statement, the communist press began campaign of harassment. Newspapers wrote that though Schukarev was eminent scientist it is impossible to elect him to the members of Academy. Professor replied by sending the letter to the newspaper "Kharkov Proletarian" (of course it was not published). With old-fashioned courtesy ("Dear editor! Please do not refuse to take in consideration…") he fully agreed with the opinion not to be elected to the Academy. Firstly, there was no need in this Academy at all. Secondly, if there is a need to elect somebody, he must be devoted Marxist obligatorily, – "than we might finally find out what Marxism is."

All in all, "cup of patience" was overfilled. In the middle of 1920′s the "Explorating Chair of European Culture History" was founded in Kharkov. Its members were mainly non-Marxists humanitarians who were prohibited to teach at the universities. Alexander Schukarev was a member of this Chair as well. In 1929 Chair issued the volume of Works which very angered the Bolshevik ideologists. The newspaper "Communist" wrote: "Hostile elements oppose their own culture to the growth of socialist culture … Spongers got rich on the Soviet bread begin propagate bourgeois ideology and philosophy to the youth". Accusations were dreadful – denial of Party character of science, "clear idealism, clericalism, … reactionary, double-faced philosophy" etc. Schukarev article under the defiant to that period of time title "Alchemist-gnostic philosophy of play cards" caused especially violent attacks. Schukarev and his colleagues were named "the open agents of bourgeois philosophy, who … spit on our reality". Communists demanded to summon the Worker-Peasant Inspection and CheKa ("punishing sword of Revolution") for the struggle with "the demonstration of ideology which is alien to the proletariat". In result, the Chair was closed in 1930.

At first Schukarev did not suffer but situation around him became more and more threatening. Just that time the forty-year jubilee of Schukarev′s scientific activity was approaching. A. Filippov recalls:

> "Surely, I began thinking how to organize the celebration. Main specialty of A. N. was chemistry. That is why I decided to ask physicochemical society to arrange this celebration. The secretary of the society professor Mukhin agreed enthusiastically. After that, I several times met Mukhin but he did nothing. When I directly asked him – why? – the answer was – "I am afraid that A. N. could say something politically dangerous". <…> Finally, the celebration of A. N. science activity was not arranged at all" [11].

In result, Schukarev was forced to retire in 1931, but as far as we know he stopped the public demonstrations of his logical machine several years before. Soviet historians did not connect these two events. They did not even explain the reasons of Schukarev retirement. They also wrote that the only reason for canceling logical machine demonstrations was the sharply rejection of the idea of thinking mechanization by orthodox Marxist philosophers. They considered the logical machine as "fruitless and absurd venture" [5]. However, this point of view seems too simple. It is also doubtful that the single publication of his violent critic Ivan Orlov (by the way, the only one we know by name) could impress Schukarev so strong. We think that the reason not in this. Not only Schukarev's scientific and philosophical views but he as an individual was not acceptable for the Soviet power. The ideological campaign against him described above is evidently proved it.

Many of his colleagues were arrested or dismissed. But Schukarev was permitted to consult several research institutions. In particular, he cooperated with the Institute of Experimental Medicine studying living cell thermodynamics. He also continued to work on the large paper in the field of logic and philosophy entitled "Experience of substantiation of structural realism system". In 1934 scientist sent his manuscript to Moscow to the Lenin Library and to Leningrad to the Academy of Science Library. Shukarev was in poor health in last years and died in spring 1938. A. Filippov recalls:

> "Funeral was ceremonial. His colleagues and pupils pronounced heartfelt speeches. The only communist who delivered a speech was director of Institute of Experimental Medicine <...>. However, even he did not say anything about the "Party and Government" and "building the socialism in our country". All orators remembered Schukarev as a wonderful man and scientist" [11].

After the Schukarev's death his logical machine was forgotten as well as the Khrushchev's one. They were remembered in the USSR only at the beginning of 1960's. It was time of common enthusiasm by cybernetic ideas and active discussion of the problem – "Could machine think?" In 1963 academician Axel Berg who was the chairman of the Council on cybernetics saw by chance the half-century old advertisement about the demonstration of "thinking machine" in Polytechnic Museum. Berg was very interested and asked the staff of Polytechnic Museum to give him more detailed information.

23 March 1964 well-known Soviet historian of technology A. Yarotsky sent a letter to Axel Berg with the results of his search. Photocopy of the chapter about the logic machine from Schukarev book and English article about Jevons machine were attached to the letter. Yarotsky wrote: "Instinct did not deceive you – the problem is really interesting. I will be glad to continue my search and present you more information". At the same time, he hinted at ideological ambiguity of Schukarev person. ("Philosophical aspect of the problem is of acute interest", – Yarotsky wrote to Berg whom he notified that "Jevons was founder of so-called school of vulgar political economy" criticized by Marx [12]). Probably, particular for the reason of political ambiguity it took more than seven years when the first publication [4] about Khrushchev and Schukarev machines got published. For example, these machines just were not mentioned in detailed article "Logic machines" containing the historical review of logical machines from Lull till Marquand [13]. In general, the works [4-6] in fact are the only ones which describe the logical machines constructed by Khrushchev and Schukarev.

Only in last years several papers were published where an attempt was made to evaluate newly the life and works of Alexander Schukarev [14-17]. Today, A. N.

Schukarev and P. D. Khrushchev finally gained deserved recognition and got the worthy place in the pantheon of Russian science. Schukarev memorial plaque was erected on the wall of Kharkov Polytechnic Institute on 21 October 2011 since of 75 years of his death (Fig. 4).

Fig. 4. Schukarev memorial plaque (Source: [16, p. 186])

6   Conclusion

Authors of this paper hope that it is clear now why the logical ("reasoning") machine of Alexander Schukarev was so rarely mentioned in Soviet scientific literature. Never in conditions of totalitarian political regimes talented but dissent persons can create and live in full mere. Creative scientific work and life of professor Alexander Nikolaevich Schukarev was uneasy beginning from 1917. He could not did what he wanted to do in the field of philosophy and logic. But he never agreed to make ideological compromises and keep a virtue of the real Scientist and Man.

References

1. Letters & Journal of W. Stanley Jevons. Edited by his wife. Macmillan and Co., London (1886)
2. Baldwin, J.M.: Logical Machine. In: Dictionary of Philosophy and Psychology, vol. II, pp. 28–30. MacMillan and Co., New-York (1902)
3. Gardner, M.: Logic Machines and Diagrams. McGraw Hill Book Co., New York (1958)
4. Veligzhanin, V.A., Povarov, G.N.: K istorii sozdaniya logicheskikh mashin v Rossii (К истории создания логических машин в России). Voprosy Filosofii, 3, 156–158 (1971)

5. Povarov, G.N., Petrov, A.E.: Russkie logicheskie mashiny (Русские логические машины). In: Kibernetika i logika, pp. 137–152. Nauka, Moskva (1978)
6. Povarov, G.N.: The First Russian Logic Machines. In: Trogemann, G., Nitussov, A.Y., Ernst, W. (eds.) Computing in Russia. The History of Computer Devices and Information Technology, pp. 51–62. VIEWEG, Wiesbaden (2001)
7. Schukarev, A.N.: Problemy teorii poznaniya: v ikh prilozhenii k voprosam estestvoznaniya i v razrabotke ego metodami (Проблемы теории познания: в их приложении к вопросам естествознания и в разработке его методами). Mathesis, Odessa (1913)
8. Schukarev, A.N.: Mekhanizatsiya myshleniya: Logicheskaya mashina Dzhivonsa. (Механизация мышления: Логическая машина Дживонса). Vestnik znaniya, 12, pp. 825–830 (1925)
9. Sokov, A.N.: Myslitel(naya mashina (Мыслительная машина). Vokrug Sveta 18, 287 (1914)
10. Orlov, I.E.: O ratsionalizatsii umstvennogo truda (О рационализации умственного труда). Pod Znamenem Marksizma 12, 72–93 (1926)
11. Filippov, A.: Dva sovetskikh professora: Dva portreta. I. A. N. Schukarev (Два советских профессора: Два портрета. I. А. Н. Щукарев). Vozrozhdenie, 7, 101–104 (1950)
12. Fet, Ya.I.: Kibernetika v Politekhnicheskom muzee (Кибернетика в Политехническом музее). In: Rasskazy o kibernetike, pp. 154–159. Novosibirsk (2007)
13. Biryukov, B.V., Shestakov, V.I., Kaluzhnin, L.A.: Logicheskie mashiny (Логические машины). In: Filosofskaya entciklopediya, T. 3, pp. 232–234. Sovetskaya entsiklopediya, Moskva (1964)
14. Shilov, V.V.: Logicheskie mashiny P. D. Khruscheva i A. N. Schukareva (Логические машины П. Д. Хрущова и А. Н. Щукарёва). Kibertoniya, 1, 17–27 (2012)
15. Shilov, V.V.: K istorii russkikh logicheskikh mashin (К истории русских логических машин). Informatsionnye tekhnologii (Prilozhenie) 8, 20–21 (2012)
16. Shilov, V.V.: Istoriya logicheskikh mashin (История логических машин). LIBROKOM, Moskva (2014)
17. Koshkin, V.M., Dulfan, A.Y.: Professor Aleksandr Nikolaevich Schukarev. Trudno byt' geniem (Профессор Александр Николаевич Щукарев. Трудно быть гением). Fakt, Kharkov (2011)

The Personal Documentary Funds of the Computer Technology Founders at the Polytechnic Museum

Marina Smolevitskaya

Scientific Researcher, Computer Collection Curator
Polytechnic Museum, Moscow, Russia
smol@polymus.ru, msmolevitskaya@yandex.ru

Abstract. The Polytechnic Museum has the Fund Collection "Electronic Digital Computing Machines". This Fund Collection is the only one of such variety and size in Russia. There are more eight hundred objects and over two thousands documentary, printed, graphic items today. All four generations of electronic digital computing machines are presented in the Museum. The main part of the Fund Collection is the developments of domestic scientist. The Museum created thirteen personal funds of Russian scientists who devoted their activity to computer science. There are biographical and official documents, scientific manuscripts and publications, descriptions of inventions and certificates of authorship for them, pictures at work and pictures from the family albums in these personal funds.

Keywords: Polytechnic Museum, collection, electronic digital computing machines, documents, pictures, papers, personal funds (unit-linked collections of documents), computer technology founders, Russian scientists.

1   Introduction

During the long years of its existence the Polytechnic Museum tries to limelight events and people which many generations are obliged. One of the most important areas of the museum activity is the restoration in memory of the wider community the contribution of Russian engineers and scientists. The museum has implemented the project "History of Russian engineering thought", including research, exposition, collection and educational activities. One of the goals of this project is to create a database about the heritage of outstanding Russian scientists. Research results are reflected in a series of publications "Problems of cultural heritage in the field of engineering." In accordance with this project, the museum hosts exhibitions and events devoted to outstanding creators of science and technology that helps maintain a high level of public recognition of our scientists and engineers.

In the Polytechnic Museum more than 20 years the scientific exposition Information Technology Department collected exhibits related to the biography, scientific and professional activities creators of computer technology in the Soviet Union and Russia. We opened 13 personal documentary funds on "Domestic science and

K.K. Kimppa et al. (Eds.): HCC11 2014, IFIP AICT 431, pp. 203–213, 2014.
© IFIP International Federation for Information Processing 2014

engineering schools in the field of Computing and Informatics," which includes more than 800 authentic merchandise, documentaries, printed and graphic materials. The Polytechnic museum holds documentary funds academician S.A. Lebedev, academician V.M. Glushkov, corresponding member of the USSR Academy of Sciences I.S. Brook, his disciples – M.A. Kartsev and N.Ya. Matyuhin, talented creators B.I. Rameev and Yu.Ya. Bazilevskiyi, the developer of the only ternary computer in the world N.P. Brusentsov, mathematician S.N. Mergelyan, Director of the Moscow factory accounting machines V.S. Petrov, founders of the national school of cybernetics A.A. Lyapunov and V.A. Kitov, academician V.S.Burtsev. All of them have made an invaluable contribution to the domestic computers park and the further development of the domestic computing.

The personal documentary funds stored in the Polytechnic Museum are presented amply in the collection of articles "Problems of cultural heritage in the field of engineering". This article describes only the four personal documentary funds: S.A. Lebedev, V.S. Burtsev I.S. Brook and M.A. Kartsev. In the future, the author expects to perform a description of all personal funds of the founders of the domestic computing.

Sergey Lebedev (1902 - 1974)

Academician Sergey Lebedev - an outstanding scientist in electrical and power engineering and founder of the domestic computing [1].

The name of Lebedev related major events in the history of national computing:

- creation of the first national computers with stored program – Small Electronic Calculating Machine (SECM, in Russian - MESM) in 1951 and in 1953 - Large and in the future High-speed Electronic Calculating Machine (HsECM, in Russian – BESM);
- development of serial first-generation computer M -20 and then the second-generation computers, software-compatible with the M-20 (1958 , 1968);
- creation of high-performance general-purpose computer BESM-6 with a capacity of 1 million operations per second, a record in the second half of the 60s to the computer park of the USSR and Europe (1966);
- issue powerful computer systems for the missile defense system (since 1956);
- organization of the engineering development school of universal high-performance machines – supercomputers.

Lebedev's personal fund № 44 was created and updated through the cooperation of the museum with his daughter Natalia Lebedeva. Currently the fund has 44 storage units. These are Lebedev's manuscripts, rough drafts in notebooks and notepads, inventors' certificates, scientific works in electrical engineering, electric power and computer technology, photos of this scientist alongside his computers, photos from family albums.

The Polytechnic Museum has a number of documents related to the biography of Sergei Lebedev and his professional activities. There are handwritten memories of his sister famous artist Tatyana Mavrina, a decision to impose Lebedev Director of The Institute of Precision Mechanics and Computer Technology (IPM CT) of USSR

Academia of Science and the ruling on his election as a academician in 1953, business cards, letters with colleagues. The museum store personal items belonging to Lebedev, and even has a bookshelf made him.

The name of Lebedev was awarded The Institute of Precision Mechanics and Computer Technology, which has a small museum.

Since 1994 Department of Informatics, Computer Science and Automation of Russian Academy of Sciences annually awards a prize named after Lebedev for the best work in the development of computing systems.

The international scientific community in the face of IEEE Computer Society recognized the merits Lebedev in 1996, giving him the title «Computer Pioneer».

In the same year Victor Glushkov and Alexei Lyapunov have got this title too.

Lebedev followers created their own scientific schools and groups.

Vsevolod Burtsev (1927 - 2005)

Academician Vsevolod Burcev was one of the Lebedev's disciples. Before graduating from the Moscow Energy Institute Bourtsev began his scientific and engineering activity under the guidance of S. Lebedev in IPM and CT [2]. Already at the stage of graduate design V.Burtsev became one of the leading developers of domestic electronic computing machines.

In 1952-1955 the result of joint work with the staff of Radio Research Institute was the creation of two specialized computer "Diana- 1" and "Diana- 2" for the automatic removal of data from radar and automatic tracking of air targets. Being responsible executor, V.Burtsev proposed the principle of selection and digitization of the radar signal. Based on this principle removal of target data from radar and putting them into the computer were done, an experiment for simultaneous tracking of multiple targets computing machine was successfully conducted. Further development of this work was the creation of a series of computers designed for ballistic missile defense (BMD).

The creators of the first missile defense system G.Kisunko, S.Lebedev and V.Burtsev received the Lenin Prize. The Notice of the Committee on Lenin Prizes in science and technology, which is also stored in the museum, evidenced.

Multicomputer complex of MDS (the eight machines 5E92b with automatic backup) has been tested in a real work in 1967. Later serial machines 5E92b became the basis of the country's missile defense system, ensured parity with the U.S. in the "cold war" and played an important political role in the conclusion of agreement to limit missile defense in 1972.

Thru selfless work V.Burtsev got the full confidence of academician Lebedev and became his assistant in creation of a reliable high-performance control and information systems for anti-missile and space monitoring centers.

In 1969-1972 V.Burtsev, as chief designer, created the first onboard computer of the third generation for ammunition combat anti-missile system C-300. Now these computers are on alert and are sold to other countries.

When S.Lebedev died, V.Burtsev was appointed director IPMCT. Continuing the work of his teacher, Bourtsev put a lot of effort to create a family of super-computers "Elbrus" and further development works in the field of missile defense.

In 1973-1985 Vsevolod Bourtsev led the development of multiprocessor computing systems "Elbrus-1", "Elbrus-2", as the chief designer. The fundamental construction questions of universal processors with marginal productivity were resolved when creating complex "Elbrus".

In 1986-1993 the architecture of supercomputers based on the new, not the von Neumann principle, providing parallelized computational process at the hardware level was developed under the leadership V.Burtsev. This architecture uses the principles of optical data processing, has highly regular structure and achieves performance 10^{10}-10^{12} op/s. The principal feature of the proposed architecture is automatic dynamic allocation of computing resources between the individual processes.

In 1992 V.S. Bourtsev was elected a member of the RAS in the Department of Informatics, Computing and Automation (specialty "Computing and Electronic Components").

Until his death (14.06.2005) academician V.Burtsev was the supervisor of fundamental research on the development of various unconventional architectural solutions HPC machines using new physical principles, as well as the system software to create data-processing systems at peak performance 10^{12}-10^{14} op/s.

The fund of academician Vsevolod Burcev was formed by his wife Tamara Burtseva. This fund № 42 is one of the most rewarding interesting evidence of scientific thought and evidence of the practical implementation of his ideas in the domestic computers, which function reliably now.

Burtsev's documentary fund has over 70 storage units. There are manuscripts (rough notes in notebooks and notepads) diploma project dedicated random access memory of the famous BESM, inventors' certificates, the photos of scientist at work, the publishing of his scientific works.

The Polytechnic Museum has a number of documents related to the Burcev's biography and his professional activities. There are a brief autobiography, characterization of production and social activities, dated November 17, 1976, schedule debugging MVK "Elbrus-2", documents related to the preparation of receiving the title of academician of the Russian Academy of Sciences, correspondence and personal items belonging to V.Burtsev.

Bourtsev, like some of the other students of Moscow Energy Institute, participated in the preparation of preliminary design documentation of BESM. This material formed the basis of his diploma project, also stored in the documentary fund.

The materials associated with the creation of two specialized computer "Diana- 1" and "Diana- 2" and a series of computers designed for ballistic missile defense (BMD) are an extremely important part of the personal documentary fund of V.Burtsev in the Polytechnic Museum.

«With our sites Rockets go flying start» - so Chief Designer missile defense system (MDS) Georgiyi Kisunko wrote in the book of his poems, donated Burtsev and now also stored in the documentary fund. This book complements the pencil drawing of a polygon with a launcher made G.Kisunko.

Many of the documents of his personal fund are evidenced by the creation of the family of super-computers "Elbrus".

The works of V.Burtsev dedicated parallelism of computational processes and the development of supercomputer architecture, including multiprocessor computing system "Elbrus" were included in section of fund publications.

Vsevolod Sergeevich Bourtsev awarded the Lenin and State prizes, awarded many orders and medals. He was awarded the Lebedev's prize of the Russian Science Academy for his series of works "Theory and practice of high-performance multiprocessor computers".

Isaak Bruk (1902 - 1974)

Biography of I.Brook is known from the memoirs of his sister, Mira Brook, the reports and the papers of his colleagues and disciples (Yu.Rogachev, N.Prohorov, A.Zalkind), thier manuscripts and typescripts are stored in the museum.

The museum fund № 213 of corresponding member of the USSR Academy of Sciences I.S. Brook is not the most extensive and there are 45 items of documentary and pictorial materials. Besides the documents related to the creation of electronic computers in our country, it contains not less interesting materials Brook's work in the field of electricity and mechanical devices for the solution of differential and integral equations.

The very interesting photo of Brook on the background of his mechanical integrator, which he had built in 1939, is in his personal fund besides his wonderful portraits and others pictures. Integrator allowed to solve differential equations of order 6.

The articles of I.Brook "The mechanical device for the approximate solution of differential equations of Laplace-Poisson" (1946), "The unexcited turbo generator asynchronously" (1947) and others, stored in the museum fund, demonstrate his works in the field of electrical engineering and the development of new computing devices.

Prior to digital technology I.Brook engaged in the development of analog computers [3]. In August 1948, together with a young engineer B.Rameev, he presented a project of automatic electronic computer. A little later, the State Committee of the USSR Council of Ministers on the implementation of advanced technology in the national economy gave I.Brook and B.Rameev Copyright Certificate for number 10475 for the invention of the digital computer with a priority date of December 4, 1948, which is also stored in the Polytechnic Museum.

This is the first official document concerning the development of computer technology in the USSR. Professionals in the field of computing technology were not in our country, and I.Brook hired graduates and undergraduates N.Matyuhin, T.Aleksandridi, M.Kartsev. All of them became prominent scientists, computing designers. Isaak Brook photographed surrounded by his colleagues and students on one of the photos stored in his museum fund.

In April 1950 the decree of the Presidium of the USSR Academy of Sciences was issued on the development of electronic digital computing machine M-1 in Electrical laboratory, headed I.Brook, of Energy Institute of the USSR Academy in Moscow. December 15, 1951 Director of the Energy Institute of the USSR Academy

G.Krzhizhanovskiyi puts his signature on the statement of completion of the establishment of the automatic computer M-1.

Automatic computer M-1 was the first in Russia small digital electronic computer with stored program. The script report for work "Automatic digital computer [M-1]" is stored in personal Brook's fund.

In April 1952 Brook launches new project: designing computer M-2. Nuclear research calculations for Atomic Energy Institute, calculations on the strength of dams constructing Kuibyshev's and Volga's hydroelectric power plants, calculations of thermodynamic and gas dynamic parameters of air for problems related to the launch of missiles were done on this machine.

Almost simultaneously with the construction of the M-2 I.Brook began development of the machine M-3. Based on it, the computer was started in Armenia, Belarus, Hungary and China. The books and the articles on these machines are presented in the Brook's fund.

I.Brook formulated possibilities and principles of controlling machines; their differences from mainframes and put immediate tasks of their application in automatic control in his articles of 1955-1957's.

In 1956 I.Brook made the presentation, which outlined the main directions of industrial applications of computers, at the session of the USSR Academy of Sciences. Two years later the note "Development of the theory, principles of construction and use of specialized and control machines" was prepared under his guidance. These documents were the impetus for the formation a number of research organizations and design offices to control machines and systems in the Soviet Union. In particular, the Institute of Electronic Control Machines of the USSR Academy of Sciences was created. The first director was appointed I.Brook .

The several major events in the history of domestic computer technology related to the name I.Brook:

development the first national automatic digital computer with a stored program M1 in 1951;

conception of small computers for massive engineering and scientific calculations in research institutes and design offices, alternative to the concept of high-performance super-computers;

formulation of a scientific problem "Development of the theory, principles of construction and use of specialized and control machines";

creation of the Engineering School of development and application control machines.

Pioneering works of I.Brook had the strongest influence on the development of computer technology in our country in the 40-60s of the last century.

I.Brook published more than 100 scientific papers. Scientist I.Brook had the talent of the inventor and the experimenter. He received more than 50 invention certificates, 16 of them in the last 5 years of life, when he was already at an advanced age.

The followers and the colleagues I.Brook (B.Rameev, N.Matyuhin, M.Kartsev, G.Lopato, B.Naumov), continuing the tradition of his school, have created themselves teams and scientific schools, played a significant role in the development of domestic computing. Also the Institute of Electronic Control Machines continues the tradition of the school I.Brook. Since 2008 it bears his name.

Mikhail Kartsev (1923 - 1983)

Michael Kartsev, one of the disciples of I.Brook, was born on May 10, 1923 in teachers' family in Kiev [3, 4]. All the Great Patriotic War he fought on the tank and participated in the liberation of Romania, Hungary, Czechoslovakia and Austria. This is evidenced by photos of M.Kartsev in those years, Diploma "Participant of fights for liberation from Nazi invaders ..." and the other fund documents.

After demobilization in 1947 M.Kartsev began to study on the radio department of the Moscow Power Engineering Institute. Being a fifth year student, he began to work in Energy Institute of the USSR Academia of Sciences in the laboratory of electrical systems headed I.Bruk. In this laboratory one of the first Soviet computers - M-1 was created. I.Bruk entrusted development of machine control device - the main program sensor to M.Kartsev.

In 1952, already qualified engineer Kartsev headed the design team of the computer M-2. Works on its creation were conducted as soon as possible from April to December 1952. The photos of the young engineer Mikhail Kartsev are stored in the personal fund of this scientist.

In 1957 M.Kartsev began to work in creating of the computer equipment, focused on the use of early warning systems and missile attack space surveillance. At that time it was the most difficult tasks of the amount of information to be processed, according to the requirements of computing speed, memory and hardware reliability.

In 1958, the special laboratory under the guidance of M.Kartsev was established in the Institute of Electronic Control Machines. It was intended to create the computer M-4 for control and data processing radar space surveillance. M-4 marked a new milestone in the activities M.Kartsev as the chief designer.

M-4 was one of the first computers built by transistors. The RAM cube of M-4 is stored in the museum's collection, photographs of racks with power supply and control panel of the M-4, link rack of Computer M-4 with radar are presented in the personal fund of M.Kartsev. Peripheral processors for parallel computing and eliminate contradictions between the CPU and external devices have been introduced in the M-4 for the first time.

In 1962 the M-4 passed state tests as part of the experimental complex radar and was proposed for serial production.

Original handwriting of Kartsev as the original computer architect clearly manifested in this development. The arithmetic unit was conveying. Operation of results obtain with high (double) precision ensured that extends the use of the computer at various levels of the computer system.

Modified with advanced transistors, this machine was produced serially and called M4-2M. It has performed 220,000 operations per second with high reliability (its mean time to failure was 800-1,000 hours) and was mainly used for the system of missile warning.

M4-2M computer in many of their characteristics was at the world's best computer technology of the time. Designed in 1965-1966 on the same elements of external devices and external computer M4-3M allowed to combine together dozens of computers M4-2M in a single computer network. The photos of M4-2M, its block diagram are stored in personal fund of Kartsev.

The computing complexes built on the base of M4-2M, provided round the clock operation mode of combat duty. They performed radar information processing securely at all levels of prevention, to ensure the military and political leadership of the country with reliable information about the situation in space.Manufacture of computers M4-2M lasted until 1985, and use - to mid-1990s. Several examples of these computers are in operation at the present moment.

The results of research conducted during the creation of this series formed the basis of M.Kartsev's doctoral dissertation, which he defended in 1965. The USSR State Prize was awarded to him in 1967 for the introduction of M4-2M computers and computer systems in the missile attack warning.

1967 turned out to be significant for Kartsev. Research Institute for Computing Systems was founded on the basis of the development team headed by him of this computer system, and he was appointed director of this institute.

Since 1965 M.Kartsev focused his creative work on the theoretical studies have been aimed at the search for opportunities to improve performance computing facilities. A multiprocessor computer system structure, which can provide simultaneous (parallel) solution of problems of the parts, has a real opportunity to get higher performance at the same level components.

Kartsev showed four kinds of parallelism and defined for each type of possible hardware implementation. Especially large tasks, that usually require high performance computing facilities, have generally a greater or lesser extent all kinds of parallelism. Therefore, multiprocessor computer systems are the most versatile way to create computer systems with the best possible performance. Kartsev's manuscripts and publications of his works kept in the museum indicate to this.

In March 1967 M.Kartsev made the presentation at the symposium in the Siberian Branch of the Academy of Sciences in Novosibirsk, which recounted not only ideas but also many technical solutions for creating a computer system with a capacity of one billion operations per second. It was a bold statement for the time: computers with a capacity of one million operations have not created but here the application sounded a billion! But the depth of study, specific schemes and their interaction convinced of the reality of this complex.

The final stage of Kartsev research questions of multiprocessor computer systems building has been a functional study of the structure of multicomputer complex M-9, submitted to the expert committee in the summer of 1967. Low level of integration of electronic circuits mastered the electronics industry at the time, did not allow realizing this project to life.

Only in 1969, the institute under the leadership of Kartsev could begin to develop one part of the M-9 - vector multiprocessor computer M-10 on the basis of emerging chip (Series 217), and an experimental model was made in August 1971. Such rates of development have influenced on the health of chief designer - a massive heart attack put him to bed a few months. But, fortunately, everything ended well.

In September 1973, the first industrial prototype passed a comprehensive review successfully, and production began in December of the same year and continued until the end of the 80s.

M-10 is a synchronous multiprocessor system with an average capacity of 5 million operations per second and an internal memory of 5 MB. It had the ability to carry out parallel processing of data in various formats, to dynamically change the clustering of processors to match the data format.

In 1977 the USSR State Prize was awarded to the team of developers of M-10 and Kartsev was awarded the Order of Lenin.

In 1976-1977, when the domestic electronics industry had mastered the production of integrated circuits, new, more compact memory devices for M-10 have been developed. This allowed more than halve the amount of equipment, size and power consumption of the computer, while maintaining all of its specifications. Machine with the new memory devices called M-10M. Both machines were completely interchangeable and compatible software.

The several units of the M-10 and M-10M components are in museum collection: standard logic block, RAM on ferrite cores, permanent memory unit condenser type on metal punch cards, permanent memory unit of the M-10M on magnetic core with diametric holes and others. The photos of computing complex from 3 M-10 computers, the pictures of the several units of the M-10 are stored in the Kartsev personal fund.

Parallel architecture contribution in productivity was so significant that before 80s the computer M-10 was the most powerful computer in the USSR. In terms of performance it exceeded domestic machines (BESM-6 - 4.2 times, the older models of UCS - 5.6 times). Information on the use of M-10, as well as on the previous machine M4-2M was closed to 90s. Only 10 years after the start of development M.Kartsev managed to get permission to publish materials on the M-10 in one of the collections of articles of the Academy of Sciences of the USSR.

In the computer systems of the M-10 computers M.Kartsev proposed and implemented the concept of a fully parallel computing system - with parallelization at all four levels (programs, commands, data and words).

New generation radars required a significant increase in performance computing facilities. In 1979, the institute under the leadership of Kartsev began developing computer fourth generation of the M-13. This supercomputer designed for wide use in processing large amounts of information in real time.

The exposition of the Museum shows the layout of the M-13, which is complemented by the layout of the radar "Darial U-4", also the cell fiber-optic communication line of the M-13 for transmission over fiber optic cable (transmitter-to-board, board-receiver and splitter) is exhibited. The several photos multiprocessor computer M-13 are stored in the Kartsev personal fund.

The heritage of Kartsev is significant and weighty. It created a whole range of them unique computers and systems: M-2, M-4, M4-2M, M-5, M-10, M-13, made significant contributions to computer science. Their practical significance for our country is very high. The museum has been carefully preserved inventors' certificates obtained Kartsev on separate devices of his computers and multiprocessor systems.

In 1995 the museum collection of computers was replenished the some blocks of high-performance computers M-series, created under the direct supervision of Mikhail Kartsev, one of the most prominent developers of computers and systems in our country.

In subsequent years, the staff of the Research Institute of computer systems and son Vladimir Kartsev transferred to the museum documentary materials, allowed to form the museum's personal fund № 215 of this outstanding creator.

Now the museum collection of computers and the personal documentary fund constantly replenished with new exhibits thanks to the collaboration with the institute and family of M.Kartsev.

Currently 9 original blocks and units of computers and 1 layout, developed by the ideas of M.Kartsev in the Research Institute of computer systems, are stored and exhibited in the museum. Personal documentary fund of this scientist is 30 items of documentary materials related to his creative and professional activities.

Kartsev's son found his military poems in the family archives. Red Army newspaper "Stalin Banner" with printed Kartsev poem "It is so! ..." and a handwritten version of this poem Vladimir Kartsev gave the Polytechnic Museum.

The series of books written by him was the table as the developers of computers and students of technical universities in related disciplines: "Arithmetic Units of Electronic Digital Computing Machines" (1958), "The Arithmetic of Digital Machines (1969)," Architecture of Digital Computing Machines"(1978), "Computing Systems and Synchronous Arithmetic" (1978).

Kartsev mission was computer science and technology. This brought him happiness and creativity and grief. He devoted all his spare time - at work, at home, on vacation.

M.Kartsev belongs to the category of scientists, whose enormous scientific achievements in life have not been evaluated and officially recognized academic elite.

In 1993 the leadership of the Research Institute of Computing Systems has made the institution name M.Kartsev assignment.

2   Conclusion

In 2013 the main building of the Polytechnic Museum was closed for reconstruction. But the museum continues to conduct research on cultural heritage of the peoples of Russia in the field of science and technology. Work in the framework of "Outstanding engineering projects of Russia" and "Engineering Heritage XIX-XX centuries" continues, adding even more personal funds of Russian scientists, inventors and designers.

The updated exposition of the Museum is planned to open in 2018. Most of the materials from personal funds of scientists - founders of the national computer technology will be on display in the exhibition hall of computers, making it the more interesting and meaningfully for visitors.

References

1. Lebedev, S.A.: To the 100 anniversary from the birthday of the founder of the national computer technology / Burtsev V. (Responsible Editor), FIZMATLIT, Moscow (2002) СергейАлексеевичЛебедев. К 100-летию со дня рождения основоположника отечественной электронной вычислительной техники / В.С.Бурцев (отв. ред.). М.: ФИЗМАТЛИТ, 2002. 440с.: ил

2. Burtsev, V.: Parallelism of Computational Processes and Development of Supercomputing Architecture. In: Torchigin, V., Nikolskaya, Y., Nikitin, Y. (eds.) TORUSPRESS, Moscow (2006) БурцевВ.С. ПараллелизмвычислительныхпроцессовиразвитиеархитектурысуперЭВМ: Сборникстатей / В.П.Торчигин, Ю.Н.Никольская, Ю.В.Никитин (сост.). М.: ТОРУС ПРЕСС, 416 с.: ил (2006)

3. Malinovskiy, B.: History of Computing in Persons. Kiev, (1994) Малиновский Б.Н. История вычислительной техники в лицах. Киев: фирма «КИТ», ПТОО «А.С.К.», 1995. С. 174-197

4. Kartsev, M.A.: Creators of domestic electronics. Issue 3 / Zenin, V., (Author-Composer), Malashevich, B., (Editor), TECHNOSFERA, Moscow (2013) МихаилАлександровичКарцев. Созидатели отечественной электроники. Вып. 3. / В.Н. Зенин (сост.), Б.М.Малашевич (ред.). – М.: ГК Синерджента: Техносфера, 464 с.: ил (2013)

History of the Use of Computers and Information Technology in Education in Universities and Schools in Victoria

Arthur Tatnall[1] and Bill Davey[2]

[1] Victoria University, Melbourne, Australia
[2] RMIT University, Melbourne, Australia
Athur.Tatnall@vu.edu.au, Bill.Davey@rmit.edu.au

Abstract. This paper investigates the development of courses in computing and use of computers in education in universities (from the 1930s) and schools (from the 1970s) in Victoria, Australia. The paper describes the significant events of the era and investigates the relationship between the development of courses in the universities and the more vocationally oriented Colleges of Advanced Education (CAE): did one follow from the other? It also investigates the extent of the influence of the universities and CAEs on school computing.

Keywords: History, Computers in Education, History of University Computing, History of School Computing, Victoria.

1   Introduction: Early Use of Computers in Australia

In this paper we investigate the history of computers and education in both universities and schools in Victoria, Australia over the period from the 1930s to the 1990s. Primary and High School use of computers did not commence until the 1970s but prior to this there is a considerable and interesting history associated with the development of higher education courses relating to computing.

All of Australia's early computers were based in the universities with CSIRAC, Australia's first computer[1] that was operational in 1949, in general use at the University of Sydney from 1951-1956 and later at the University of Melbourne until 1964, and SILLIAC in Sydney from 1954 [1]. From the mid-1950s a number of these computers were opened to general use and practical training in programming was introduced at the Universities of Melbourne, Sydney, and New South Wales (NSW). Early training courses, each of a few weeks duration, were offered in the programming techniques appropriate to each machine [2]. This was the beginning of the use of computers in education in Australia.

---

[1] CSIRAC (or CSIR Mk1 as it was then called) was arguably the world's fourth of fifth digital electronic stored-program computer.

K.K. Kimppa et al. (Eds.): HCC11 2014, IFIP AICT 431, pp. 214–225, 2014.
© IFIP International Federation for Information Processing 2014

Prior to the late 1980s Australia had a two-tiered system of higher education: 'Universities' and 'Colleges of Advanced Education' (CAE). After 1990, a series of mergers saw the end of the CAEs and the creation of a number of new universities. Naming of these institutions is, however, a little more complex as in the 1950s and 1960s many of the future CAEs were called 'Technical Colleges', and in the 1970s and 1980s some became 'Institutes of Technology'. It should be noted that in this paper Technical College, Institute of Technology and College of Advanced Education can all be taken to apply to institutions of essentially the same nature. This paper will investigate the relationship between the development of courses in the universities and the CAEs: did one type follow from the other?

Significant educational computing in primary schools and high schools dates from the 1970s and came in two forms: teaching about computing and the use of computers to enhance learning in other subject areas. The paper will investigate the effect that the universities and CAEs had, or did not have, on each form of school computing, and how these forms of school computing related to each other.

The research described in this paper was qualitative in nature with data collected from published sources, interviews and personal observation.

2   Computers in Education – Universities and Schools

In Australia a number of distinct periods can be identified in the evolution of higher education and school courses in computing towards those we see today [3].

- 1930s-1950
  - From 1935: Courses in Technical Colleges on the use of punched-card Accounting/Tabulating Machines
- 1950-1959
  - From the early 1950s: University first generation computing using mainframes with punched-cards.
  - Computing courses were typically offered in Departments of Mathematics and had a considerable mathematical influence.
- 1960-1969
  - 1965: The Commonwealth Government Programmers-in-Training scheme. Beginnings of mini-computer based computing courses in the CAEs.
- 1970-1979
  - Growth of CAE courses, typically using mini-computers and punched-cards.
  - Beginnings of school computing using mark-sense cards on mini-computers located at local universities.
- 1980-1989
  - 1980-1990: Introduction of the micro-computer.
  - Courses at universities and CAEs move increasingly to the use of micro-computers.
  - Rapid increase in the use of micro-computers in schools.
- 1990 to the present

Each of these periods will now be described in detail.

2.1   The Period from 1930s-1950

From about 1935, several courses began to be offered in Victorian Technical Colleges in the use of punched-card operated *accounting/tabulating machines*. These courses were very much business-oriented in outlook and whilst not what we would now call *computing* courses, did lay some ground work for future courses in business computing [4].

The first courses in *Theory of Computation, Computing Practices and Theory of Programming*, what we might now call aspects of Computer Science, were introduced in 1947 by Trevor Pearcey (the principal designer of CSIRAC) in the Department of Mathematics at the University of Sydney. At this point, computing was very much a mathematical study. At that time, of course, to use a computer at all required knowledge of programming, and it was several years before computing was seen anywhere other than Statistics and Mathematics Departments [5, 6].

Although Australia at that time, along with the UK and USA, was in the forefront, the situation in other countries was similar and much has been written on this [7-12].

2.2   The Period from 1950-1959

In 1956 CSIRAC moved from Sydney and was re-located at the University of Melbourne. Programming courses were given regularly in Melbourne from 1956, and in 1959 a subject in *Numerical Methods and Computing* was developed (delivered by Pearcey) in the BA course in Pure Mathematics. During this period several university computer systems were opened to general use and courses involving practical training in programming and the application of computers were introduced in the universities of Melbourne, Sydney and NSW. In 1959 the first post-graduate diploma in *Numerical Analysis and Automatic Computing* was offered by the University of Sydney [13].

2.3   The Period from 1960-1969

In the early 1960s most educational institutions, and particularly the Technical Colleges, were still teaching about punched-card operated accounting machines. During this period, however, a great deal happened in relation to computing in higher education, perhaps the most important being the decision (taken in the late 1950s) by the Australian Commonwealth Government to computerise the operation of the Department of Defence and the Post Master General's Department (PMG), so creating a massive requirement for trained computing personnel [14].

At this time the universities were only just starting to come to grips with the issue of whether computing was a part of mathematics or should be considered as a new discipline [3]. With courses which were quite theoretical in nature, relatively few staff and sparse facilities, the universities were largely unprepared for the demands of the Commonwealth which needed courses with a substantial component that was vocational in nature. The universities had little interest in providing such courses [4] so in 1960 the Australian Government's Commonwealth Public Service Board set up the *Programmers in Training* (PIT) scheme initially of twelve weeks duration as a temporary measure to alleviate the severe shortage of programmers and other computer professionals in Commonwealth Government departments. The PIT courses were oriented towards training staff for the establishment and running of commercial and administrative computing applications.

Although regarding this training as successful in providing a 'crash computing course' the Public Service Board recognised a need to set up longer courses and began designing a full-year long *Programmer-in-Training* (PIT) course. The first of these PIT courses ran in 1965 and initially drew upon the Defence and PMG staff experience with both computerised, and existing non-computerised administrative systems. Maynard, who was then an O&M[2] Inspector with the PMG, (1990) describes this course as a "*double-decker sandwich course of one year duration combining periods of formal classroom education with on-the-job training*" [4]. The PIT courses took over 20 hours/week of formal class time for a year and operated initially in Canberra and Melbourne (Maynard, 1990; Pearcey, 1988). The 46 week course covered the topics: *introduction to the course and the service; computer equipment and techniques, computer mathematics (statistics), programming, systems analysis and design.*

One of the first educational institutions in Australia to adopt business computing as a priority was Caulfield Technical College[3] offering, in 1961, a *Certificate of Accounting (DP)* course and by 1967 a *Diploma of Business Studies (Data Processing).* Maynard, now a lecturer at PIT, [14] suggests that these courses were the forerunner of many of today's courses in Information Systems [3]. From this period on, university and other higher education computing courses were seen to become 'respectable' and were soon widely available. In 1962 Royal Melbourne Institute of Technology (RMIT) got its first computer – an Elliot 803, and in 1963 short evening post-diploma courses were offered at Caulfield Institute of Technology (formerly Caulfield Technical College) on *Punched-Card Systems, Accounting Machine Applications, Commercial Electronic Data Processing and Principles of Analogue Computing.* Surprisingly, in that same year, a survey suggested that businesses in Victoria believed that they would need only ten programmers in the next ten years [5] – perhaps there would be no need for all these new computer professionals!

Other courses were introduced at this time at Caulfield Institute of Technology, Bendigo Institute of Technology and Footscray Institute of Technology. These courses had titles like: *Diploma of Information Processing, Post Diploma of Electronic Computing and Associate Diploma in Accountancy (Data Processing), Certificate in Electronic Data Processing (Operating and Coding), Diploma of Business Studies (Data Processing), Information Processing Diploma* and an *Electronic Computing Post Diploma* [15, 16].

In the university sector, the University of Melbourne established a Department of Information Science [5] and offered courses in the *Theory of Computation*, and Monash University set up a Department of Information Science in the Science Faculty and offered *Computer Science* in its science degree. Monash's first computer was a

---

[2] Organisation and Methods.
[3] After a series of amalgamations Caulfield Technical College became Caulfield Institute of Technology and then went on to become a part of Monash University.

7,000 word Sirius *with two sets of Ferranti/Creed model 75 tape editing equipment [17-19]*. Changes in technology then meant that such courses typically moved from delivery on an institution's mainframe to one of its new mini-computers producing a fundamental change in the content and availability of computing courses.

2.4   The Period from 1970-1979

In 1970 the Commonwealth Public Service Board decided to hand over the running of PIT courses to Caulfield Institute, Bendigo Institute, Canberra CAE and NSW Institute of Technology (Maynard 1990). According to Greig & Levin [20]:

> *"The Public Service Board believed that the increasing use of sophisticated computer equipment at the colleges and their need for increasing numbers of trained 'computer personnel' made such a development desirable."* [20 :7]

The 'new' PIT scheme commenced operation at the CAEs in 1971. This was very important as it could be seen as the beginning of higher education courses of business computing and information systems.

2.4.1   University and CAE Computing Courses

From the early 1970s computing courses began to proliferate in Universities and CAEs, but at this time Chisholm Institute of Technology (the former Caulfield Technical College), like most other universities and CAEs, was still using punched-cards for students to enter their programs. It was not until the end of this decade that micro-computers began to enter higher education institutions [14].

In 1971 the 'new' Programmer-in-Training programme supported 235 trainees Australia-wide [21]. This new scheme had the wider objective of providing trained computer personnel to industry as well as the Commonwealth and State Public Service [5] and comprised both full-time classes and on-the-job training.

Although teaching in Computer Science began in Australia's universities of the 1950s, CAEs courses in Business Computing only commenced in the 1960s. The growth in CAE courses owed a great deal to the Commonwealth *Programmer-in-Training (PIT)* scheme which became the model for many future courses in Business Computing. The reluctance of the universities to become involved in what they saw as little more than vocational training opened the way for the CAEs to develop this curriculum area. Juliff, an academic at Caulfield Institute of Technology and later Victoria College, [15] suggests that university Computer Science was, at this time, taught mostly by people whose primary love was mathematics and that was the flavour they gave to their courses. They saw no need for courses to be relevant to the real world. The PIT scheme, on the other hand, was very business-oriented in design. It is thus clear that courses in Business Computing in the CAEs did not diverge from university Computer Science courses, but developed from those of the PIT scheme.

2.4.2 Computing in Schools

It was in the early 1970s that school computing began when a small number of computers started to appear in Australian schools, typically resulting from the exposure of particular teachers to computing during their university studies. In 1972, for example, Burwood High School was loaned a PDP-8 computer by Digital Equipment [22] and the following year McKinnon High School received an Innovations Grant to enable the purchase of an 8k Wang computer also used by Teletype terminal access by Box Hill High School. These early computers were used by mathematics departments almost exclusively for the teaching of programming [22].

The biggest impact on schools at this time was introduction of the Monash Educational Computer System (MONECS). Before the advent of the PC it was impossible for an average school to have hands-on access to a computer. In 1974 a group at Monash University produced a system using mark-sense cards that allowed a class of 30 students to each get two program runs in a one-hour period [23]. The MONECS system was used to teach programming in FORTRAN or BASIC. At this stage schools saw computing as a branch of mathematics concerned with algorithm design.

Another development at this time was experimentation by the Victorian Technical Schools with use of Control Data's 'PLATO System' [24] for computer-assisted instruction, mainly for the training of apprentices. The system was, however, very expensive and its use did not proceed.

The arrival of the Apple II in 1977 saw the end of this period and the beginning of real advances in the use of computers in schools. Watsonia High School (where we were both teaching at the time) was one of the first high schools in Australia to obtain an Apple II computer [25]. At around $2,000 for a 16k Apple II that used a tape drive (not supplied – you simply used your own cassette recorder) and a television (also not supplied) as a monitor the Apple II was (almost) affordable for schools. This was before the days of the ascendancy of the IBM PC, MS-DOS and the Apple Macintosh and schools made use of the Apple II and a variety of other micro-computers.

In 1978-1979 the Victorian Education Ministry [22, 26] produced a plan for the introduction of computers to schools and it was not long before several different streams of computer education emerged:

- Computers across the curriculum – computer use in different subject areas
- Computer Science
- Programming in mathematics
- Use of word processors by secretarial studies students
- Logo
- Computer industry/business training in Technical Schools [27].

In the late 1970s the Education Department's Secondary Mathematics Committee recognised the potential of computers in mathematics and other aspects of education and set up a Computer Travelling Road Show consisting of teachers with some knowledge of computing who travelled around the state in groups of two or three, normally bringing a 16k Apple II with tape drive. Visits to schools around the State were used to promote the use of computers all subject areas. Each demonstration by the 'Road Show' was typically to an entire teaching staff, with students being sent home for the day. Another important school curriculum support mechanism used by the Victorian Ministry of Education in the late 1970s and early 1980s was the Regional Subject Consultants who were practicing school teachers seconded from their schools, usually on a part-time basis [28]. They rarely had any interaction with school students, working instead to support the work of teachers and school principals in using computers.

2.5   The Period from 1980-1989

In 1980 Chisholm Institute (like most other tertiary institutions) was still using a mini-computer, with terminals for students to enter their programs. Around this time, however, traditional *Business Computing* (later *Information Systems*) curricula were beginning to develop in the CAEs and most courses had a core of similar topics which were typically based around subjects related to systems analysis and design, database design, business programming (which was typically done using third generation such as BASIC, COBOL or Pascal) and systems implementation. Many of these courses also had an introductory computer networking unit which was probably the most technical and close to the discipline of Computer Science. Subjects handling computer architecture probably delved well into the realm of Computer Science and were often electives. By 1985 micro-computer adoption in tertiary institutions was widespread [29].

2.5.1 Computer Awareness Courses in Schools

In 1980 the Secondary Computer Education Curriculum Committee was formed with a brief for the production of *Computer Awareness* course guidelines, the investigation of *Computer Science* as a discipline, the publication of computer education articles, the collection, propagation of public domain software and the provision of in-service education [6].

Although in developed countries around the world today secondary school students are very 'aware' of information technology and its many use, this was not the case in the early to mid-1980s and *Computer Awareness* courses sought to address the twin problems of poorly prepared teachers and a mystical understanding of the nature of computers. Such a course would typically cover the following topics:

- How a computer works, computer programming, history of computing
- Business and commercial uses of information technology
- The social implications of increased use of computers.

Interestingly, although teachers of Mathematics were the prime movers in these early days, mathematics classes did not embrace computers into the later 1980s. What appears to have happened is that programmable calculators were seen as more relevant to teaching mathematics. In many cases the Mathematics teachers interested in school computing moved over to the teaching of computing: *Computer Awareness* or *Computer Science*, and gave up any attempt to use computers in mathematics, which today would be one of the subject areas making least use of computers.

The role of mathematics in the adoption of computers in schools appears to be a common phenomenon around the world as one article from The Netherlands notes:

In addition in the participating schools mainly math teachers appeared to be the early adopters of the new subject, because of their knowledge, experience and interest in information technology [30].

Authors from many countries including UK [31-33], Ireland [34], Israel [35], The Netherlands [30, 36], USA [37], Finland [38] and Poland [39] make similar comments. This is just a small sample of many articles by authors that remark on the role and future of mathematics and mathematics teachers in the early adoption of computers in schools in their own countries.

2.5.2 Computer Science Courses

In 1981, as a result of several years of effort by a group of CAE and university academics, *Computer Science* was first offered as a Year-12 Higher School Certificate (HSC) subject in Victoria, although personnel from the Education Department had little involvement in determining the nature and content of this subject [40].

It is interesting to look at reactions to this new subject from tertiary institutions, schools and the general public. Melbourne and Monash universities, which saw themselves as guardians of academic standards, rejected the subject, not allowing its inclusion in admission scores for their courses. Their stated reason for this was that the component of assessment allotted to formal examination was only 35% (rather than the more typical 50%). When pressed, some academics from these institutions admitted that they considered the subject of little serious academic worth, and 'not an appropriate subject to study at a secondary school level'. The newer universities (Deakin and La Trobe) and the CAEs did accept it as a valid study. Parents, students and employers also readily accepted the value of HSC Computer Science [40].

Teachers, however, were not universally in favour of the new subject with some claiming it to be an elitist academic subject, too difficult for some students. Others noted that the ratio of girls to boys taking *Computer Science* was low and suggested that it was becoming a *boys' subject*. Perhaps the most damaging criticism though came from those teachers who claimed that the presence of a specialist subject detracted from the use of computers across the curriculum as it put too great a strain on school computing facilities.

2.5.3 Support for School Computing from the Commonwealth Government

In April 1983, the Federal Minister for Education and Youth Affairs announced that the Government would set up a National Advisory Committee on Computers in Schools. In its report *Teaching Learning and Computers in Schools* [41] the Committee made comprehensive recommendations covering curriculum development, professional development, support services, software/courseware, hardware and organisation. The Commonwealth also provided $18.7m in funds to support these activities.

In the early 1980s the Victorian Education Department created the State Computer Education Centre (SCEC) to support and control school computing. Financed through the Commonwealth and State Computer Education Programs, SCEC was set up in

1985 with twenty-seven full-time professional positions. SCEC played a significant role in setting the direction of educational computing in Victoria for the next three years: it developed policy, produced curriculum documents, evaluated and distributed educational software, evaluated computer hardware and produced the 'recommended list' of computer systems for use in schools, facilitated interstate contacts and the sharing of resources, conducted professional development activities and generally co-ordinated computer education in the state [26].

2.6   The Period from 1990 to the Present

In relation to senior secondary school curriculum, a review in the early 1990s replaced the Higher School Certificate by the Victorian Certificate of Education (VCE) that extended over Years 11 and 12. This also saw the demise of Year 12 *Computer Science* and its replacement by three new subjects: *Information Processing and Management*, *Information Systems* and *Information Technology in Society*. An additional new subject: *Information Technology* was offered only at Year 11.

In the 1990s computing curriculum continued to grow in the universities and at the start of this period 1,400 students were studying computing related subjects in Victorian universities. What happened in universities and schools after this time with the advent of the Internet, Web, on-line learning, laptops and smart phones is beyond the scope of this paper.

3   Conclusion

In this paper the three strata of the Victorian education system have been traced in the decades from 1930 to the early 1990s. It can be readily seen from this analysis that universities were the original users of electronic computers but that they had little influence on the vocationally based CAE sector. It can also be seen that the forces shaping school computing were again largely divorced from the influence of the tertiary sector. Schools in Victoria embraced the freedom afforded by the relatively low cost micro-computers and early work of pioneers within schools and the Ministry of Education had the effect of broadening the use of computers in schools beyond the rather restricted initial uses in universities.

Of course this is a little simplistic. Teachers mostly became enthused due to initial contact with computers in their university pre-service education and we have not mentioned the significant in-service education provided by Faculties of Education in the 1980s. Within these limitations it can be said that the decentralisation of school based curriculum development in the 1970s and 1980s in Victoria had a marked effect on the direction of school computing. It can also be concluded that the divergent origins of computing in CAEs and Universities lead to a distinct divergence between *Computer Science* at Universities and *Information Systems* in CAEs.

References

1. McCann, D., Thorne, P.: The Last of the First - CSIRAC: Australia's First Computer. The University of Melbourne, Melbourne (2000)
2. Bennett, J.M., Broomham, R., Murton, P.M., Pearcey, T., Rutledge, R.W. (eds.): Computing in Australia. The Development of a Profession. Hale & Iremonger (in conjunction with the Australian Computer Society), Sydney (1994)
3. Tatnall, A.: Curriculum Cycles in the History of Information Systems in Australia. Heidelberg Press, Melbourne (2006)
4. Tatnall, A.: A Curriculum History of Business Computing in Victorian Tertiary Institutions from 1960 - 1985. In: Education. Deakin University, Geelong (1993)
5. Pearcey, T.: A History of Australian Computing. Chisholm Institute of Technology, Melbourne (1988)
6. Tatnall, A.: The Growth of Educational Computing in Australia, in History, Context, and Qualitative Methods in the Study of Education. In: Goodson, I.F., Mangan, J.M. (eds.), pp. 207–248. University of Western Ontario, Canada (1992)
7. Bonfanti, C.: Information Technology in Italy: The Origins and the Early Years (1954 - 1965). In: Tatnall, A. (ed.) Reflections on the History of Computing. IFIP AICT, vol. 387, pp. 320–347. Springer, Heidelberg (2012)
8. Kovács, G.: Hungarian Scientists in Information Technology. In: Tatnall, A. (ed.) Reflections on the History of Computing. IFIP AICT, vol. 387, pp. 289–319. Springer, Heidelberg (2012)
9. Fet, Y.: From the History of Russian Computer Science. In: Tatnall, A. (ed.) Reflections on the History of Computing. IFIP AICT, vol. 387, pp. 265–288. Springer, Heidelberg (2012)
10. Sanders, N.: A possible first use of CAM/CAD. In: Tatnall, A. (ed.) Reflections on the History of Computing. IFIP AICT, vol. 387, pp. 43–56. Springer, Heidelberg (2012)
11. Deane, J.: Australia's WREDAC – it was Rocket Science. In: Tatnall, A. (ed.) Reflections on the History of Computing. IFIP AICT, vol. 387, pp. 1–21. Springer, Heidelberg (2012)
12. Lawson, H.: Experiences and reflections. In: Tatnall, A. (ed.) Reflections on the History of Computing. IFIP AICT, vol. 387, pp. 69–88. Springer, Heidelberg (2012)
13. Pearcey, T.: The Origins of Modern Computers, in Computing in Australia. In: Bennett, J.M., Broomham, R., Murton, P.M., Pearcey, T., Rutledge, R.W. (eds.) The Development of a Profession, pp. 1–9. Hale & Iremonger (in conjunction with the Australian Computer Society), Sydney (1994)
14. Maynard, G.: Interview on the History of Business Computing, Melbourne (1990)
15. Juliff, P.: Interview on Business Computing Curriculum, Melbourne (1990)
16. Juliff, P.: Interview on Business Computing Curriculum, Melbourne (1992)
17. Davey, B., Parker, K.R.: Turning Points in Computer Education. In: Tatnall, A. (ed.) HC 2010. IFIP AICT, vol. 325, pp. 159–168. Springer, Heidelberg (2010)
18. Lukaitis, A., Lukaitis, S., Davey, B.: The Birth of Information Systems. In: Tatnall, A. (ed.) HC 2010. IFIP AICT, vol. 325, pp. 206–215. Springer, Heidelberg (2010)
19. Ainsworth, A.B.: Monash University's First Computer (January 2009),
   http://www.infotech.monash.edu.au/about/projects/museum/
   papers/first-computer-at-monashuniversityv7.pdf
20. Greig, J., Levin, P.: Computing at Chisholm: The First Twenty Five Years, 1965-1989. Chisholm Institute of Technology, Melbourne (1989)

224   A. Tatnall and B. Davey

21. Philcox, R.: The Commonwealth Public Service Board and the Introduction of Computer Technology, Early Australian Computer Systems, pp. 208–224. University of Melbourne, Melbourne (1978)
22. Salvas, A.D.: Personal communication, Melbourne (1985)
23. Monash Computing Museum. MONECS Deamon Educational Computer system (2003, February 2004), http://www.csse.monash.edu.au/museum/
24. Plato Learning. History of Plato Learning (February 2004), http://www.plato.com/aboutus/company_history.asp
25. Tatnall, A., Davey, B.: Making History relevant Through the Provision of Education, Stories and Interactive Experiences. In: Tatnall, A., Blyth, T., Johnson, R. (eds.) HC 2013. IFIP AICT, vol. 416, pp. 35–44. Springer, Heidelberg (2013)
26. Tatnall, A.: The Role of the State Computer Education Centre of Victoria, in MA (preliminary) thesis, Education, Editor. Deakin University, Geelong (1985)
27. Tatnall, A., Davey, W.: Streams in the History of Computer Education in Australia. In: Impagliazzo, J., Lee, J.A.N. (eds.) History of Computing in Education. IFIP, vol. 145, pp. 83–90. Kluwer Academic Publishers, Massachusetts (2004)
28. Tatnall, A.: Schools, Students and Curriculum in Victoria in the 1970s and 1980s. In: Tatnall, A., Davey, B. (eds.) History of Computers in Education. IFIP AICT, vol. 424, pp. 246–265. Springer, Heidelberg (2014)
29. Tatnall, A.: Innovation and Change in the Information Systems Curriculum of an Australian University: a Socio-Technical Perspective. Central Queensland University, Rockhampton (2000)
30. Voogt, J., ten Brummelhuis, A.: Information Literacy in the Netherlands: Rise, Fall and Revival. In: Tatnall, A., Davey, B. (eds.) History of Computers in Education. IFIP AICT, vol. 424, pp. 83–93. Springer, Heidelberg (2014)
31. Demant, D.: Whatever You Do . . . . Don't Put the Computer Room near the Maths Department! or, I was an Early Adopter, an Enthusiastic Disseminator, but Now. In: Tatnall, A., Davey, B. (eds.) History of Computers in Education. IFIP AICT, vol. 424, pp. 110–120. Springer, Heidelberg (2014)
32. Millwood, R.: From Mathematics Teacher to Computer Assisted Learning Researcher. In: Tatnall, A., Davey, B. (eds.) History of Computers in Education. IFIP AICT, vol. 424, pp. 302–309. Springer, Heidelberg (2014)
33. Passey, D.: Early Uses of Computers in Schools in the United Kingdom: Shaping Factors and Influencing Directions. In: Tatnall, A., Davey, B. (eds.) History of Computers in Education. IFIP AICT, vol. 424, pp. 131–149. Springer, Heidelberg (2014)
34. Leahy, D., Dolan, D.: The Introduction of Computers in Irish Schools. In: Tatnall, A., Davey, B. (eds.) History of Computers in Education. IFIP AICT, vol. 424, pp. 164–173. Springer, Heidelberg (2014)
35. Barta, B.-Z., Shapiro, L., Millin, D., Engel, E.: The Rise of Information and Communication Technology Era in the Israeli Educational System. In: Tatnall, A., Davey, B. (eds.) History of Computers in Education. IFIP AICT, vol. 424, pp. 174–196. Springer, Heidelberg (2014)
36. Zwaneveld, B., Schmidt, V.: The Dutch Situation: An Ever Continuing Story. In: Tatnall, A., Davey, B. (eds.) History of Computers in Education. IFIP AICT, vol. 424, pp. 212–238. Springer, Heidelberg (2014)
37. Parker, K.R., Davey, B.: Computers in Schools in the USA: a Social History. In: Tatnall, A., Davey, B. (eds.) History of Computers in Education. IFIP AICT, vol. 424, pp. 203–211. Springer, Heidelberg (2014)

38. Koivisto, J.: Computers in education in finland. In: Tatnall, A., Davey, B. (eds.) History of Computers in Education. IFIP AICT, vol. 424, pp. 239–245. Springer, Heidelberg (2014)

39. Sysło, M.M.: The First 25 Years of Computers in Education in Poland: 1965 – 1990. In: Tatnall, A., Davey, B. (eds.) History of Computers in Education. IFIP AICT, vol. 424, pp. 266–290. Springer, Heidelberg (2014)

40. Tatnall, A., Davey, B.: The Life and Growth of Year 12 Computing in Victoria: An Ecological Model. In: Tatnall, A. (ed.) HC 2010. IFIP AICT, vol. 325, pp. 124–133. Springer, Heidelberg (2010)

41. Commonwealth Schools Commission, Teaching, Learning and Computers. Report of the National Advisory Committee on Computers in Schools. Commonwealth Schools Commission, Canberra (1983)

A Privacy Preserving Design Framework in Relation to an Environmental Scanning System for Fighting Organized Crime

Anne Gerdes

Department of Design and Communication,
University of Southern Denmark, Kolding, Denmark
gerdes@sdu.dk

Abstract. This paper represents preliminary recommendations regarding the development of a privacy preserving system design framework related to the EU project, ePOOLICE, which aims at developing an environmental scanning system for fighting organized crime by providing law enforcement agencies opportunities for strategic proactive planning in response to emerging organized crime threats. The environmental scanning is carried out on a variety of sources, focusing on early warning and the disclosure of crime trends, not on individuals. Consequently, personal data are not relevant in the information context of ePOOLICE, and therefore the system will not make use of any kind of sensitive information. Particular attention are paid to the environmental scanning of data streams from social networking sites; based on the assumption that ethical and privacy issues with regard to social media scanning represent a significant challenging scenario to meet in developing a privacy preserving framework for ePOOLICE.

Keywords: Privacy preserving design, engineering ethics, environmental scanning, open source intelligence, organized crime fighting.

1   Introduction

The ePOOLICE project[1] aims at developing an efficient and effective environmental scanning system as part of an early warning system for the detection of emerging organized crime threats and changes in modus operandi, focusing on e.g., illegal immigration, cocaine trafficking, human trafficking and cybercrime. In the ePOOLICE system the environmental scanning is carried out on data streams from a variety of sources, counting both open sources (e.g.; Web resources, news, statistics, libraries, research reports, and social media) and restricted sources (e.g.; hospital statistics,

---

[1] Project full title: "early Pursuit against Organized crime using envirOnmental scanning, the Law and IntelligenCE systems". Grant agreement no: 312651, THEME [SEC-2012.6.3-1]:[Developing an efficient and effective environmental scanning system as part of the early warning system for the detection of emerging organised crime threats - Capability Project].

K.K. Kimppa et al. (Eds.): HCC11 2014, IFIP AICT 431, pp. 226–238, 2014.

border traffic statistics, financial transaction statistics, narratives from police districts). Consequently, different kinds of public online data streams, including social media data streams, feeds into the system's knowledge repository that provides a rich taxonomy of domain knowledge. Moreover, data processing is facilitated by means of data analysis techniques, enabling the extraction of descriptive and predicative meanings used for inferring hidden states, i.e.; weak signals or indicators of organized crime activities. For example, one type of indicator may be an indicator of another type of organized crime; hence organized cannabis growing also indicates human trafficking (manpower for cannabis farming).

ePOOLICE operates at the strategic level of open source intelligence and takes into account modus operandi and crime trends. Consequently, personal data are not relevant in the information context of ePOOLICE, and therefore the system will not intend to make use of or aggregate personal data or maintain a database for storing or managing personal data or other kinds of sensitive information.

The environmental scanning in ePOOLICE is conducted via a broad-spectrum scan of open sources; the system functions as a tool for tactical planning focusing on modus operandi, hotspot locations, crime patterns and (mega-) trends. Hence, the use context of ePOOLICE is situated at the strategic level, implying that the system does not support the operational level at all, but serves a pure preventive purpose in scaffolding sense-making activities carried out by law enforcement agents and analysts engaged in countering threats and acting proactively in dealing with upcoming trends in organized crime.

In this paper, particular focus is on threats to privacy occurring through the use of open source material from social networks; followed by an outline of preconditions for a privacy preserving design framework to be implemented in dealing with privacy issues raised by system functionalities. The reason for paying special attention to social media scanning is motivated by the fact that social networking platforms contain a vast amount of personal and or sensitive information and are typically conceived of as trusted personal networks among friends. As such, social media scanning represents a particular challenging topic to deal with in developing a privacy preserving framework for ePOOLICE. Hence, it is assumed that the type of potential ethical and privacy issues that may occur in relation to social media scanning are likely to occur in a weaker version in the scanning of other sources (e.g.; news, statistics, university research reports, demographic data). It is important to stress that all though the focus of this report is on social media scanning, this position does not entail the negligence of potential different types of privacy issues related to the scanning of other types of sources, which may require different means or techniques to solve.[2]

1.1 Purpose and Scope

With the above mentioned in mind, the purpose of this paper is to clarify and outline:

---

[2] For example, privacy preserving methods suitable for social networking data streams would not be suitable for trajectory data.

- ethical and privacy issues in relation to environmental scanning of open source data streams in the shape of social networking sites.
- an overview of privacy preserving data mining techniques, which may be applied in ePOOLICE in order to deal proactively with privacy protection in the context of environmental scanning of open source documents from social networking platforms.
- a preliminary privacy preserving system development design framework, which meets the threats of privacy infringements or violations without hindering the knowledge discovery opportunities of the system and the end user.

1.2   Paper Structure

Section 2 represents an overview of ethical and privacy issues related to the environmental scanning of open source data streams, specifically emphasizing data streams from social networking sites. Section 3 presents an overview of the Privacy by Design paradigm and privacy enhancing methods of relevance for the development of a preliminary privacy preserving design framework. As the project progresses, this framework will be refined continuously in order to be able to balance data privacy and data utility by carrying out privacy impact assessments of tools, processes and methodologies developed. Section 4 summarizes the current findings.

2   Ethical and Privacy Issues in Relation to Environmental Scanning of Data Streams from Social Networking Sites

Advancements in data mining techniques used on social networking platforms have exacerbated privacy concerns. Gradually, individual citizens have become more and more transparent to a variety of actors and at the same time they have experienced a reduction in transparency with right to knowledge of what is being known about them, where and by whom. On top of this, as Web users, we contribute to our own potential de-privatization by spreading information about ourselves on the Web, i.e., by being present at social networking platforms, or by enjoying the convenience of seamless internet transactions based on personalized services in exchange for personal data. Needless to say, that this might raise privacy concerns associated with the lack of autonomy in controlling the flow of information about oneself across different contexts, as well as lack of confidentiality and trust in relying on that intended or unintended information-based harm will not occur.

From a legal point of view, personal information in social networking platforms is protected by the EU Data Protection Directive (Directive 95/46/EC). The requirements of this directive with right to the anonymity of the data subject is meet in the design intentions behind ePOOLICE, since the environmental scanning of social networking sites provides a systematic approach for exploring and mapping patterns of communication and relationships among networks at a general level without singling out actors, i.e. unique data subjects. Consequently, within the overall framework of the ePOOLICE project no data subject is identified or under surveillance, and no personal and intimate information *per se* is involved in the identification of relevant data and interpretation of relevant patterns of information and knowledge. But since personal (and often also sensitive) information is highly accessible online, the inherent risk of unintentionally identifying data-subjects during the raw data scanning process of social media is fairly high. Here, we have to bear in mind, that personal data includes information, which may identify an individual indirectly by means of different fragments of sources. Furthermore, the environmental scanning may come up with patterns of information and point to indicators that hold the potential to sort groups by race, belief, gender or sexual orientation, etc. Still, when based on objective statistical analysis, the use of criminal profiling by law enforcement agencies is legal. Nevertheless, following the precautionary principle, we need to stress the importance of avoiding potential discrimination, which affords categorization of people into damaging stereotypes.

Even though environmental scanning may slip under the radar of legal privacy restrictions, social media scanning may still imply privacy discomfort among people, due to privacy concerns regarding information traffic across contexts representing distinctive spheres in life. Users on social networking platforms are typically aware that data shared on social media (such as Facebook and Twitter) resides in a public or semi-public sphere. Applying privacy settings may well decrease the group of people with access to your data, but still not hinder that data are spread to others. But we cannot per default presume that people, when engaging in producing and sharing online content on social media platforms (Facebook, Twitter or blogs) do not have any expectations of privacy. All though users are aware that data are to some extent public it is reasonable to assume that they probably do not expect their online content to be made available as raw data set for environmental scanning. Consequently we may refer to *informational privacy* as individuals' ability to control the flow of personal information, including how information is exchanged and transferred [14].

A justificatory conceptual framework, for the systematic exploration of people's reactions to technology can be found in Nissenbaum [9], who has coined the term "contextual integrity" in order to explain for and tie adequate protection against informational moral wrongdoing. According to Nissenbaum, information flows always have to be seen in relation to context-sensitive norms, representing a function of: (1) the types of information in case, (2) the respectively roles of communicators, and (3) principles for information distribution between the parties. Consequently, contextual integrity is defined, not as a right to control over information, but as a right to appropriate flows of personal information in contexts with right to two norms [9: 127 ff]: Norms of "appropriateness" and norms of "distribution", i.e., the moment of transfer of information from part X to $Y_{1...n}$. Violations of one of these norms represent a privacy infringement [9].

In the case of ePOOLICE, new flows of information are established and may cause a potential violation of contextual integrity, since information gathering via environmental scanning of communication streams on social networking sites may possibly be judged inappropriate to that context and violate the ordinary governing norms of distribution within it. Likewise, the width spread scope of the scanning may raise concern among citizens. Here, we have to strike a balance, which can ensure that the infringement of privacy is minimally invasive for human rights without obstructing the opportunities for the intended aim of open source intelligence.

In ePOOLICE, social media data streams feed into the system's knowledge repository that provides a rich taxonomy of domain knowledge and facilitates data processing through fusion techniques[3], which enable the extraction of descriptive and predicative meanings used for inferring hidden states, i.e.; weak signals or indicators of organized crime activities. All though a human analyst evaluates all system output, a risk still exist that the knowledge discovery techniques to disclose emergent trends in social network data streams may deduce patterns that could be sensitive. Also, the aggregation power and scope of ePOOLICE facilitates analysts' reasoning, but at the same time requires that the analyst is particular careful in the evaluation of possible emergent patterns and predictive meanings in order not to get "carried away" by the knowledge discovery power of the system.

To summarize, in the development phase of ePOOLICE, the privacy preserving framework of ePOOLICE must balance data privacy and data utility in addressing:

1. the risk of unintended identification of individuals (data subjects) during the social media scanning.
2. the risk of disclosure of sensitive patterns due to the data analysis techniques applied.
3. citizens' surveillance concerns raised by social media scanning.

Points 1 and 2 are situated at the level of technical system development, whereas point 3 resides at the societal level. Also, but beyond the scope of this paper, the institutional and organizational level have to be dealt with in order to address ethical and privacy issues, which may arise in the use context of ePOOLICE. The abovementioned list will be extended during the project life time with the aim of systematically identifying and meeting future challenges as the development of ePOOLICE progresses (see www.ePOOLICE.eu).

3   Overview of the Privacy by Design Paradigm and Privacy Preserving Methods

The concept *Privacy by design* (PbD) was coined by the Canadian information and privacy commissioner Ann Cavoukian [2]. The philosophy behind PbD stresses the importance of pro-actively building privacy into the design, operation and management of information processing technologies and systems. To accomplish this, the following 7 fundamental principles are listed [2]:

- "Proactive not Reactive; Preventative not Remedial
- Privacy as the Default

---

[3] Fusion techniques use converted data from diverse sources, such as multi-source and multi-lingual information, which includes credibility assessment, with the purpose of disclosing patterns or correlations.

- Privacy Embedded into Design
- Full Functionality – Positive-Sum, not Zero-Sum
- End-to-End Security – Lifecycle Protection
- Visibility / Transparency
  Respect for Users."

These principles, taken together with the legal requirements, will form the basis of the privacy preserving framework of ePOOLICE.

As such, ePOOLICE has to be developed in legal compliance with EU member states privacy legislation. At the international level, the European Convention for the Protection of Human Rights and Fundamental Freedom (ECHR), which the European charter of Human Rights is based on, feeds into the local laws of EU member states and stresses the importance of the citizens' right to privacy and protection of personal data. Likewise, the Code of Fair Information Practices (which dates back to the 1973 report from the *US Secretary's Advisory Committee on Automated Personal Data Systems*, the U.S. Department of Health, Education and Welfare) expresses five fundamental principles of data management and record keeping, which still encapsulate the core of subsequent privacy guidelines. Hence, the Convention for the Protection of Individuals with right to Automatic processing of Personal Data (Council of Europe, 1981) positions data protection as a fundamental right, subsequently backed up by the Data Protection Directive (Directive 95/46/EC), to which member states national legislations are aligned. This directive is currently undergoing transformation and the status of the new directive is not yet settled. Also, the non-binding OECD Guidelines of Protection of Privacy and Transborder Flows of Personal Data (1980, revised in 1999) codifies eight internationally agreed upon principles related to fair information practices. Main elements in these FIPs guidelines and regulations are:

- The principle of fair and lawfulness – the processing must be legitimate and pursue specified purposes; data must be adequate, relevant, not excessive; accurate and up to date, and not stored for longer than necessary
- The principle of processing legitimacy: stresses the necessity to obtain the data subject's consent – some exceptions do exist (exhaustively listed)
- The principle of prohibition to process sensitive data (unless exceptions exhaustively listed: explicit consent of the data subject, if the data have been made public by the data subject)
- The principle of the rights of the data subject: including rights of access, rectification, erasure; to opt out, to not be subject to a decision based on some automatic processing)
- The principle of confidentiality and security of the data processed
- The principle of obligation to notify the supervisory authority (declaration or authorization)
- The principle of accountability of the data controller
- The principle of adequate level of protection in case of data transfer to third countries

In combination with legislation of member states, Principles of fair information practices (FIPs) and the PbD principles provide a useful guide for the development of a privacy preserving framework, which may be achieved by building the FIPs and the PbD-principles into all relevant phases of the ePOOLICE system's life cycle.

3.1   Preliminary Outline of a Privacy Preserving Framework and Privacy Preserving Methods

A privacy preserving framework must be set up for in order to inscribe privacy in all design and developmental phases of of ePOOLICE. In what follows, I intend to elaborate on how to meet privacy challenges relevant in the context of social media scanning by addressing the above mentioned 3 points summarising privacy risks (section 2) and by briefly pointing to the PIA methodology.

3.1.1   Addressing the Risk of Unintended Identification of Data Subjects during the Raw Social Media Scanning

The environmental scanning system moves across and filters all potentially relevant information sources and maintains and "learns" which patterns to look for, where to look and how reliable the source is, and mark the credibility of the information. In order to focus the scanning process, the environmental knowledge repository (EKR) represents a dynamic ontology of domain knowledge. Hence, in the EKR, domain knowledge is going to be stored temporary with the risk that data fragments might facilitate identification of data subjects. Therefore, use of filter techniques for hiding data or knowledge patterns, which disclose data subjects must be in place. The scanning is further facilitated by fusion techniques (a fusion tool box) used for knowledge discovery with the purpose of forming hypotheses about patterns of weak signals suggesting emergent trends in organized crime.

ePOOLICE does not collect intelligence to be used at an operational level for finding or monitoring individual suspects. Still, issues of potential misuse have to be dealt with, especially in the case of social media scanning, since it is unavoidable that the raw data streams from social media scanning will include personal data about both direct (i.e. name, address) and indirectly identifiable individuals (i.e. photos). Here an attack model representing a scenario of the aim of a malicious individual or party may inform system design with the aim of protecting data from any kind of misuse - such as "mission creep", implying that data are used for other purposes than the purpose for which they were collected, or privacy breaches violating individuals' privacy. Therefore, the system developers must define categories of disproportionate analytical queries, from which alert-systems may be designed such as to automatically block processing in case of attempt of illegal processing. Also, system functionalities must be in place in order to permit management of different user-levels of authorization. Consequently, logging of system access and processes applied may ensure tracking of possible unauthorized use of data and further support control procedures by internal data controllers as well as by independent authorities.

Anonymization techniques have to be brought to play to ensure that no personal or sensitive data are available in the data material from social media scanning [3].

According to the EU data directive 1995/46/EC, all means likely reasonable to be used either by the data controller or by any other person to identify a said person should be taken into account in order to determine if a person is identifiable. Hence, to minimize the risk of identifying a person, anonymization techniques may be applied to obtain individual privacy, but this is not a trivial task. As such, simply removing direct identifiers is not sufficient to yield anonymity. For instance *k-anonymity* hides a unique individual among k-1 others, thereby disclosing the real data by transforming them in a way which makes impossible the re-identification under a fixed anonymity threshold. But this technique does not provide privacy in cases where sensitive values in an equivalence-class lack diversity [8] – for instance data regarding age, health and zipcode may for a given class be equivalent and thereby unintentionally support re-identification. Hence, examples of re-identification from seemingly anonymous data have been described. As an example, Sweeney managed to re-identify the medical record of the governor of Massachusetts [13]. Also, the AOL search record of a user linked to a photo re-identified the person [1].

Obviously, anonymization in the context of ePOOLICE is challenging. However, to safeguard the system against misuse, which may reveal the identity of individuals, ePOOLICE must take steps to apply a privacy preserving framework, which allows for the anonymization of data and the build in of alert and blocking systems, which restrain potential misuse of data.

3.1.2   Addressing the Risk of Disclosure of Sensitive Patterns due to the Data Analysis Techniques Applied

Fusion techniques in ePOOLICE are used for inferring hidden states with the purpose of predicting emerging trends in organized crime (OC). Hence, in applying the knowledge discovery technique referred to as formal concept analyses, the aim is to discover as many signals of indicators as possible for new OC treats. Also, the idea of primary and secondary indicators will be qualified by the notion of temporal proximity, i.e. by paying attention to primary indicators as those associated with emerging or ongoing OC, considered short range radar detection, which equals detection monitoring. On the other hand, secondary indicators are associated with the opportunity for OC before it occurs, i.e. facilitators for new OC threats and part of a long radar detection system, which equals situation monitoring.

In order to enhance the recognition of weak signals and predictive meanings, the fusion tool box in ePOOLICE employs "soft fusion" techniques, which combine automated fusion and human fusion processes, thereby enabling utilization of experts abilities to interpret signals and identify complex patterns. Furthermore, decentralized fusion is introduced to support modular solutions, whereby complex fusion systems can be build and distributed over multiple devices. Environmental scanning, facilitated by such fusion products, provides the system with the kind of knowledge discovery power, which enables it to spot emergent patterns and weak signals of OC. As such, the system extracts predictive meanings, which exceed the scope of the original data set. These findings are subsequently presented to and evaluated by the analyst in order to scaffold further analysis and the forming of hypotheses.

Issues related to the use of fusion to infer hidden states raise serious concerns regarding surveillance since the linking of different forms of data from the scanning of social network interactions may possible be invasive to the privacy of individuals or groups. Moreover, social networking data are semantically rich, which makes anonymization a demanding task in the first place, since the extra semantics facilitates linking such data to background knowledge with the risk of disclosing sensitive data. Hence, knowledge discovery tools, i.e.; fusion techniques for linking data, infringe upon individuals and groups control of how information relating to them, their interactions and their networks are represented, and subsequently what patterns of predictive meanings can be inferred from such fused information.

With the development of advanced fusion techniques in ePOOLCE, the inference problem increases, i.e., the problem known from challenges in securing databases from having users to pose queries and deduce unauthorized information from the legitimate responses they get from the database [15]. Taking into account the concept of contextual integrity, we may find parallels between the inference problem and the possible treats to privacy from social media scanning and applied fusion techniques in ePOOLICE. For example, analysts may infer sensitive hypotheses, implying the potential identification of an individual. Consequently, to ensure that sensitive hypotheses cannot be deduced from social media scanning, methods of inference control must be taken into consideration.

To sum up, the development of the system must take proper steps to ensure that every phase in the data processing – all way through from the handling of raw social media data to the final extraction of predictive patterns - avoid identification of data subjects. Likewise, the challenge that reverse engineering techniques could disclose data subjects must be addressed in a way that balance privacy and traceability, since, in some situations, tracking is necessary in order to evaluate the credibility of system output. Hence, to a restricted group of users (data controllers) this option must be available even at the risk of disclosing fragmented data, which may identify data subjects.

3.1.3   Addressing Citizens' Surveillance Concerns Raised by Social Media Scanning

Privacy issues in ePOOLICE may be adequately dealt with from a legal perspective and still yield privacy concerns due to the fact that alterations in flows of information may lead to violation of contextual integrity (see above, section 2). As mentioned above, users on social network sites may feel intimidated from learning that their online interactions serve as raw material for social media scanning. Hence, the overall judgment of ethical implications related to ePOOLICE goes beyond the scope of a standalone privacy evaluation of the system, implying that the context-sensitive tradeoff between privacy and security and citizens' right has to be taken into consideration as well.

From a public point of view, an example of European citizens' opinion on privacy and security issues can be found in a participatory technology assessment, which concludes that citizens are open to legitimate security measures for crime prevention, whereas reference to terror treats does not justify privacy limitations for most citizens

[12: 26 ff]. Consequently, it seems to be the case that people are prepared to value security over legitimate restrictions of informational privacy in specific contexts reflecting individual dimensions of security. To elaborate on this from a legal point of view, any limitation to fundamental rights of privacy and personal data protection has to respect some basic principles in order to be legitimate and ensure that privacy is not violated. As such, limitations have to rest on a legal basis and must be formulated with such a degree of precision that it enables citizens to understand how their navigation and conduct in society are affected by the given limitation. Moreover, a restriction must pursue a legitimate aim, i.e., be in accordance with listed legitimate aims, formulated within each article of rights in the ECHR, as aims that justify interference. Furthermore, any limitation must correspond to a real need of society and must be seen as an efficient instrument (for instance in relation to crime reduction and security). Finally, the principle of proportionality seeks to guarantee that the limitation is balanced to the aim pursued. In order to minimize the infringement of privacy rights and to assess the proportionality of a restriction, the main issues to settle are whether the overall effect of the constraint is reasonable and whether it is the least intrusive mean available. Here, to ensure that privacy is not violated, the ePOOLICE project must see to that the requirement of proportionality of the privacy restriction is satisfied. Given these circumstances, the ePOOLICE project strives to enhance both privacy and security by introducing pro-active privacy preserving design principles throughout all stages of the development process. In this way, the project seeks to develop technological solutions that support privacy compliant use.

Yet, a problem still resides in the fact that an assessment of proportionality is not easy to deal with in a precise manner. Judging whether the privacy interference caused by ePOOLICE is a suitable, necessary and adequate mean for fighting organized crime on a strategic level, implies, among other things, a measurement of security gains. But, security advantages are not easy to calculate – neither ahead nor ex-post. Hence, from the fact that security technologies have proved to be effective, we cannot presuppose this outcome for ePOOLICE in advance. Also, if it turns out to be the case, ex-post, that we observe a decline in organized crime after the implementation of ePOOLICE, we still need to carry out a thorough evaluation to justify if and how ePOOLICE contributed to this outcome.

Nevertheless, in the case of ePOOLICE, and taking into consideration the recent focus on intelligence surveillance (the NSA surveillance case), we need to emphasis the importance of transparency. In general, when dealing with intelligence, citizens express concerns about the fact that they do not have insight in how information about them is used and for what purpose. During the system development phase, it is of outmost importance to find ways to enter into dialogue with European citizens in order to disseminate awareness about the ePOOLICE project.

3.2   General Recommendations for Setting Up a Privacy Preserving Framework

In order to fully integrate privacy by design per default into the design process, the ePOOLICE project has established an ETHIC-TECH team consisting of consortium members (system developers and members with legal and ethical expertise)[4]. Accordingly, it is of outmost importance to make room for dialogue between engineers and experts in law and ethics in order to enact ethics during the system development process. Understanding the ethical impact of systems in context implies engaging in what Nissenbaum - who together with Friedman [5], is one of the leading figures in the field of value sensitive design (see for instance: [4], [10]) - coins "engineering activism" [11], and Van Hoven addresses as "front-loading ethics" [16] in proposing a proactive approach to bring ethics to design. This ideal of activating ethical expertise in order to improve system development is encapsulated in the below mentioned quotation by Nissenbaum [11]:

"Humanists and social scientists can no longer bracket technical details - leaving them to someone else - as they focus on the social effects of technology. Fastidious attention to the before-and-after picture, however richly painted, is not enough. Sometimes a fine-grained understanding of systems - even down to gritty details of architecture, algorithm, code, and possibly the underlying physical characteristics - plays an essential part in describing and explaining the social, ethical, and political dimensions of new information technologies."

Consequently, the overall objective of the ETHIC-TECH team is to scaffold activities within the privacy preserving design framework of ePOOLICE, with the purpose of striking a balance between data utility and data privacy. Hence, the privacy preserving framework is implemented in the scientific and technical coordination of the project to ensure that the project work flow of ePOOLICE incorporates a robust practice, which integrates ethical evaluation of tools, processes and techniques developed and or applied during the system development process. This is done with the aim of identifying and countering privacy threats without diminishing the knowledge discovery opportunities, which are essential to the project. Moreover, regular privacy assessments (PIAs) of potential privacy risks must be carried out in order to minimize negative privacy impacts in deliberation with relevant stakeholders [6]. In ePOOLICE we will make use of the data protection impact assessment (DPIA), which has been defined by the European Commission as a tool for evaluating potential privacy risks in relation to data processing[5]. For the time being, there is no standard to carry out PIA or DPIA since different methodologies coexists. Hence, in order to build in specific methodologies for ePOOLICE, in addition to risk methodologies, we will take inspiration from PIA-methodologies, as well as the methods used in the security technology project VIRTOUSO [7].

4   Concluding Remarks

In this paper, special attention has been paid to ethical and privacy issues related to social media scanning due to the fact that this type of environmental scanning is taken

---

[4] Also, an external ethical advisory board with European experts on legal and ethical issues is in place.

[5] Commision recommendation, March, 9th, 2012, regarding preparations for the roll-out of smart meterings systems (2012/148/EU), §I, 3 (c.), See: http://eur-lex.europa.eu/ LexUriServ/LexUriServ.do?uri=OJ:L:2012:073:0009:0022:EN:PDF

to be particular demanding in connection to the ePOOLICE project. All though personal data are not relevant and no database are maintained for storing or mining personal and or sensitive data, privacy issues still arise. Hence, the risk of misuse, the risk of unintended identification of individuals and the risk of disclosure of sensitive patterns of information must be dealt with adequately by inscribing privacy preserving techniques into the design of ePOOLICE. Furthermore, due to citizens' general surveillance concerns related to intelligence, it is imperative to promote transparency about the ePOOLICE project.

The implementation of privacy protection in the design is not a trivial task. Therefore, a privacy preserving framework shall incorporate ethical evaluation of tools, processes and techniques developed all through the system development process. In accordance with the Privacy by Design philosophy, it is important to balance data utility and data privacy in order to meet privacy threats without obstructing the knowledge discovery opportunities in ePOOLICE.

Acknowledgments. The author would like to thank Estelle De Marco, Inthemis Managing Director, for fruitful collaboration on the ePOOLICE project as well as for valuable comments, which helped shape this article.

Research leading to these results has received funding from the European Union's Seventh Framework Programme (FP7/2007-2013) under grant agreement n° 312651.

References

1. Barboro, M., Zeller, T.: A Face Is Exposed for AOL Searcher NO. 4417749, The New YorkTimes, http://www.nytimes.com/2006/08/09/technology/ 09aol.html?pagewanted=all (accessed January 6, 2014)
2. Cavoukian, A.: Privacy by Design – The 7 Foundational Principles, http://privacybydesign.ca (accessed January 6, 2014)
3. Di Vimercati, D.C., Foresti, S., Livraga, S., Samarati, G., Data Privacy, P.: Definitions and Techniques. International Journal of Uncertainty, Fuzziness and Knowledge-Based Systems 20(6), 793–817 (2012)
4. Flanagan, Howe, Nissenbaum: Enbodying Values in Technology: Theory and Practice. In: Hoven, J.V., Weckert, J. (eds.) Information Technology and moral Philosophy, pp. 322–354. Cambridge University Press (2012)
5. Friedman, B., Kahn, P.: Human Values, Ethics and Design. In: The Human-Computer Interaction Handbook, pp. 1177–1201. L. Erlbaum Assoc. Inc., Hillsdale (2003)
6. Hert, P.D., Kloza, D., Wright, D., et al.: Recommendations for a privacy impact assessment framework for the European Union, PIAF (Privacy Impact Assessment Framework) project, Grant agreement JUST/2010/FRAC/AG/1137– 30– - CE– - 0377117/00– - 70, Deliverable D3, p. 5 (November 2012), http://www.piafproject.eu/ Deliverables.html (accessed January 6, 2014)
7. Koops, B., Cuijpers, C.: D 3.2 Analysis of the legal and Ethical Framework in Open Source Intelligence. Versatile Information Toolkit for End-users Oriented Open Source Exploitation. Project number: FP7 – SEC – GA – 2009 – 242352 (2012)
8. Machanavajjhala, A., Gehrke, J., Kifer, D.: ℓ-Diversity: Privacy Beyond k-Anonymity. ACM Transactions on Knowledge Discovery from Data 1(1), Article 3, 1–52 (2007)

 9. Nissenbaum, H.: Privacy in Context – Technology, Policy and the Integrity of Social Life. Stanford Law Books, Stanford (2010)
10. Nissenbaum, H.: Values in technical design. In: Mitcham, C. (ed.) Encyclopedia of Science Technology and Ethics, pp. 66–70. MacMillam, New York (2005)
11. Nissenbaum, H.: How computer systems embody values. Computer – innovative technology for professions, pp. 117–119 (March 2001, 2003)
12. Raguse, M., Meints, M., Langfeldt, O., Peissl, W.: Prepatory Action on the enhancement of the European industrial potential in the field of Security research. Tech. report, PRISE (2008), http://www.prise.oeaw.ac.at/publications.htm (accessed January 6, 2014)
13. Sweeney, L.: K-anonymity: a model for protecting privacy. International Journal of Uncertainty Fuzziness Knowledge Based Systems 10(5), 557–570 (2002)
14. Tavani, H.: Informational privacy, data mining, and the internet. Ethics and Information Technology 1, 137–145 (1999)
15. Thuraisingham, B.: ACM SIGKDD Explorations Newsletter 4(2), 1–5 (2002)
16. Van Den Hoven, J.: ICT and Value Sensitive Design. In: Goujon, P., Lavelle, S., Duquenoy, P., Kimppa, K., Laurent, V. (eds.) The Information Society: Innovations, Legitimacy, Ethics and Democracy. IFIP, vol. 233, pp. 67–72. Springer, Boston (2007)

On the Probability of Predicting and Mapping Traditional Warfare Measurements to the Cyber Warfare Domain

Marthie Grobler[1,2] and Ignus Swart[1]

[1] Council for Scientific and Industrial Research, Pretoria, South Africa
[2] University of Johannesburg, Johannesburg, South Africa
{mgrobler1,iswart}@csir.co.za

Abstract. Cyber warfare is a contentious topic, with no agreement on whether this is a real possibility or an unrealistic extension of the physical battlefield. This article will not debate the validity and legality of the concept of cyber warfare, but will assume its existence based on prior research. To that end the article will examine research available on traditional warfare causes, elements and measurement techniques. This is done to examine the possibility of mapping traditional warfare measurements to cyber warfare. This article aims to provide evidence towards the probability of predicting and mapping traditional warfare measurements to the cyber warfare domain. Currently the only way of cyber warfare measurement is located in traditional information security techniques, but these measurements often do not adequately describe the extent of the cyber domain. Therefore, this paper aims to identify a set of criteria to aid in the prediction of cyber warfare probability.

Keywords: cyber warfare, metrics, prediction, probability, traditional warfare.

1   Introduction

This article will not debate the validity and legality of the concept of cyber warfare, but will assume its existence based on prior research performed by Heickerö [10] and Liles, Rogers, Dietz and Larson [14]. To that end this article will examine the history of research available on traditional warfare pre-requisites and measurement techniques. This is done to examine the possibility of mapping traditional warfare measurements to cyber warfare.

Currently the only way of measurement is located in traditional information security techniques. While applicable, the measurements do not adequately describe loss, posture or any of the pre-requisites found in traditional warfare. This article aims to provide evidence towards the probability of predicting and mapping traditional warfare measurements to the cyber warfare domain.

K.K. Kimppa et al. (Eds.): HCC11 2014, IFIP AICT 431, pp. 239–254, 2014.
© IFIP International Federation for Information Processing 2014

2   Predicting Traditional Warfare

There have been many attempts to predict and prevent traditional warfare. Unfortunately, many of the causes identified as precursors for warfare cannot be manipulated towards predicting warfare [23]. This section looks at the accepted causes of traditional warfare and builds on these causes as metrics for traditional warfare.

2.1   Causes of Traditional Warfare

Research by Van Evera [23] and Schelling (in [23]) focus on the causes of war that relates to the character and distribution of national power. The hypotheses of these works are that warfare is more likely when:

1. **Nation states fall prey to false optimism about the outcome of war.** This occurs when nation states exaggerate their own chances of winning crises and wars, or when they underestimate the cost of war. For example, when nation states are so sure that their military force is stronger than an opponent, they may be less risk averse and take bigger risks.
2. **The advantage lies with the first side to mobilise the attack.** This occurs when nation states launch pre-emptive attacks to prevent their opponents from attacking first. This has a negative impact on diplomacy, since nation states tend to conceal their capabilities and grievances for fear that open displays of strength or grievance could trigger another nation states' pre-emptive attack. For example, Hitler's 1940 attack on Norway was purely a move to advance the Germans' position in the war.
3. **The power of nation states fluctuates sharply, with large windows of opportunity and vulnerability.** Fluctuations in power tempt nation states to launch preventive attacks and rush into war sooner if they predict their own vulnerability to grow in the future. In some cases diplomacy becomes hurried in an attempt to resolve disputes before power wanes, often resulting in less valuable diplomatic agreements or a complete loss of diplomacy. For example, in the 16th century the weaker Dutch nation revolted against the Spanish due to their imminent subjugation to Spanish rule.
4. **Resources are cumulative.** This occurs when the control of resources enables a nation state to protect or acquire other resources that can be readily used to seize more resources. It is found that cumulative resources often predict further gains or losses. Therefore, the greater the cumulativity of conquerable resources, the greater the risk of war. This was illustrated as far back as the Roman wars that forced tax collection from conquered nations to continue the war effort.
5. **Conquest is easy.** Easy conquest is a master cause of other potent causes of war, raising all the risks they pose. This was clearly demonstrated when China and the League of Nations did nothing to stop the invasion of Manchuria by Japan in 1932.

These causes of war will form the foundation of this research study, and will serve as the main metrics to measure damage and potential loss due to warfare.

2.2   Traditional Warfare Elements

For the purpose of this paper, war can be defined as a state of armed conflict between different countries or different groups within an environment. There are a number of theories about the elements that comprise traditional warfare. For the purpose of this research study, the thinking of Clausewitz will be followed. Although not exhaustive, the authors felt that Clausewitz's thinking is most representative and applicable to the cyber domain. Clausewitz (in [19]) believed that an offensive act has to meet certain criteria in order to qualify as an act of war:

- **It has to have the potential to be lethal.** If an act cannot be considered as potentially violent, it is not an act of war. A real act of war is always lethal, for at least some participants on at least one side. Although none of the hypotheses listed in Section 1.1 mentions violence, this element links to all the causes of warfare in that the offending nation state aims to gain control over the defending nation state, thereby debilitating the defending nation states. This debilitation can take the form of death of soldiers or the destruction of the defending nation state's resources.
- **It has to be instrumental.** The act of war has to have a means and an end. Generally, physical violence or the threat of force is the means. The end is to force the enemy to accept the offender's will, or to render one opponent defenceless. In terms of the hypotheses listed in Section 1.1, causes 2, 3 and 4 addresses the means of war, whilst cause 1 and 5 addresses the end of war.
- **It has to be political.** While the motivation for war might include a variety of factors, ultimately it has to be government sanctioned and can thus be considered as political. Therefore, war's larger purpose is always political in nature. It transcends the use of force and is never an isolated act. Therefore, a political entity or a representative of political entity has to have an articulated intention that has to be transmitted to the adversary at some point during the confrontation. In terms of the hypotheses listed as causes for traditional warfare, cause 3 relates to politics.

2.3   Metrics for Traditional Warfare

The hypotheses in Section 1.1 and the supporting elements in Section 1.2 can be concatenated into five factors, considered as metrics for predicting traditional warfare. These five factors are presented as the following formula for predicting the possibility of traditional warfare:

Possibility of traditional warfare =	Nation state political power fluctuations
	AND Potential for lethality
	AND ((False optimism
	AND Offending nation state advantage)
	OR Easy conquest)

In order to predict the possibility of traditional warfare, three conditions need to be met. These conditions are:

- **Condition 1:** The offending nation state needs to have political power fluctuations present, including a political purpose and non-isolated events.
- **Condition 2:** The potential for lethality needs to be present.
- **Condition 3:** This condition is complex with three sub conditions (either the first two sub conditions need to be true, or the third sub condition needs to be true):

- **Sub condition 1:** The offending nation state needs to have false optimism regarding its own capability.
- **Sub condition 2:** The offending nation state needs to believe that their actions will lead to an advantageous position, often due to cumulative resources.
- **Sub condition 3:** The offending nation state needs to believe that the war will be an easy conquest, referring to the target's capability.

The next section aims to apply the formula for predicting the possibility of traditional warfare to cyber warfare, in an attempt to identify a set of criteria specific to the cyber domain to aid in the prediction of cyber warfare probability.

3   Defining Cyber Warfare

Cyber warfare is a contentious topic, with no agreement on whether this is a real possibility or an unrealistic extension of the physical battlefield. Regardless of this ongoing debate, however, the cyber domain is playing a definite role in warfare. Whether it is a full blown Denial of Service attack, hacking attempt or the use of secured online communication to discuss strategy and tactics, technology has a definite place in the warfare domain. Accordingly, cyber warfare can be seen as both offensive and defensive operations against information resources, conducted because of the potential value that information resources have to people [24]. This section will look at the definition of cyber warfare, before mapping the formula for predicting the possibility of traditional warfare to cyber warfare.

Legally, there is no concept such as cyber war. The United Nations Charter specifies when a nation state can use force in self-defence against an act of aggression, but this refers only to armed conflict [4], see Condition 1. To complicate this further, there is no such thing as a digital only war. It is therefore not accurate to assume that cyber war is a war fought only in the cyber domain, only between cyber elements [8]. *"Although cyberspace is a man-made domain, it has become just as critical to military operations as land, sea, air and space"* [19]. Therefore, it is understandable that some entities claim that cyber war is the fifth domain of warfare (after land, sea, air and space) [22]. For the purpose of this paper, the Oxford Dictionaries [17] definition of cyber war is adopted:

The use of computer technology to disrupt the activities of a state or organisation, especially the deliberate attacking of communication systems by another state or organisation.

The impact that cyber warfare has, however, is indisputable. Already in 1995 the following statement were made by Chinese Major General Wang Pufeng: *"In the near future, information warfare will control the form and future of war. We recognize this developmental trend of information warfare and see it as a driving force in the modernization of China's military and combat readiness. This trend will be highly critical to achieving victory in future wars."* [13].

3.1   Acts of Cyber Aggression

As in traditional warfare, each war consists of several battles, i.e. no attack is isolated (refer to Condition 1). In the cyber domain, these battles are referred to as acts of cyber aggression. Currently, there is no international treaty in place that establishes a legal definition for an act of cyber aggression. However, research by Carr [4] reasons that these acts include:

- Cyber attacks against government or critical civilian websites or network without accompanying military force.
- Cyber attacks against government or critical civilian websites or network with accompanying military force.
- Cyber attacks against internal political opponents.
- Cyber intrusions intro critical infrastructure and networks.
- Acts of cyber espionage.

While a variety of factors can be added to the list, it can be argued that the categories listed by Carr is fairly comprehensive. For example, the global worker is irrelevant since any action from the worker would fall into the categories defined by Carr.

According to research done by Filiol [8], acts of cyber aggression have five definite characteristics. Although these characteristics are generic enough to be applicable to any cyber related act, these characteristics form the foundation of the discussion of cyber aggression..

- **Dematerialisation.** Anonymity is a key factor in cyber war since true anonymity is a sought after skill in itself. By achieving anonymity, the attackers actually showcase how easily they can perform an action without detection. Therefore, the true origin of the attack must remain hidden, and it must be possible to wrongly frame an innocent party as the perpetrator of the attack. Although the potential level of anonymity may give attacking nations the courage to take appropriate risk in an attack, the anonymity will not get the message of superior cyber-warfare capability across. Therefore, from a military perspective, the main interest is to avoid or delay the target reaction by misleading it (refer to Sub conditions 2 and 3).
- **Cancelling time and space limits.** By extending the war domain, this serves as a strong barrier for the attacker. All traditional restrictions are removed from the planned attack, making the potential scope for attack much bigger. Network connections will make it possible to have immediate access from anywhere and at any time (refer to Sub condition 2).
- **Gaining control over time and space, over physical resources.** The aim of war is to gain such control over the physical world in order to use these resources to the maximum benefit of the cyber war's intended outcome (refer to Condition 2 and Sub condition 2).

- **Exploit the complexity, interdependencies of modern systems.** The attacking nation does not have to directly attack the target, but rather attack unsecured targets which have some kind of interdependencies on the actual target. E.g. by attacking transportation facilities, critical infrastructure, etc. not only the government but also the civilians are inconvenienced. The affected civilians will, in turn, put increasing pressure on the originally intended target, the government (refer to Sub condition 3).
- **Exploit generalised intelligence.** The aim is to openly collect a large amount of possible useless or common data and compile in order to have significant and deep knowledge of a given target (refer to Condition 1 and Sub condition 3).

4   The Status of Current Information Security Metrics

To measure information security a holistic approach needs to be followed. In an attempt to organise and structure information security measurements, the MITRE Corporation has defined several key areas that are affected by any measurement in cyber security readiness. Therefore, all the categories in Fig. 1 need to be taken into account due to the complexity of information interaction points. As such, it becomes

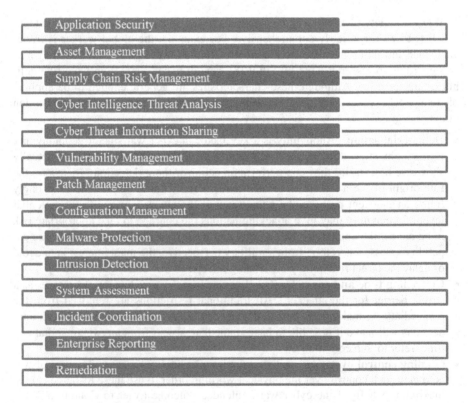

Fig. 1. Categories affecting information security [16]

a complicated process to measure all these categories accurately. This often results in false optimism (Sub condition 1) about the status of information security management within a nation state, and the ability of a nation state to protect against potential cyber attacks. In addition, this false optimism can also lead to an easy conquest (Sub condition 3), if a nation state overestimates its own cyber abilities (refer to Section 1.3).

Metrics for information security currently fall into two areas: high level metrics that assess what a nation is investing in via policy and response teams, and on a more technical side, measurements for the vulnerability of software/devices/services. Both types of metrics can be measured: the high level metrics through research such as the Cyber Readiness Index (CRI) and technical metrics through applying standards such as Common Vulnerability and Exposures (CVEs) to applications/devices/services. Technical difficulties in the measurement of either exist that does not just affect individual nations but is a global area of concern. It is therefore important to distinguish between the two areas of measurement and factor in both, since taking either into account in isolation can lead to incorrect assumptions regarding the state of a nation state's information security posture.

4.1   Cyber Readiness Index

The CRI examined 35 countries that have embraced ICT and the Internet to evaluate each country's maturity and commitment to cyber security across five essential elements. These elements were identified based on where cyber security can be used to protect the value and integrity of previous ICT investments and enable the Internet economy [9]. The five essential elements are:

- **Articulation and publication of a National Cyber Security Strategy.** The country has to have articulated and published a National Cyber Security Strategy that describes the threats to the country and outlines the necessary steps, programmes and initiatives that must be undertaken to address the threat. In fulfilling this element, the country has to address the percentage of Gross Domestic Product (GDP) embraced by the plan, identify commercial-sector entities affected by and responsible for implementation of the plan as well as critical services, and establish continuity of service agreements for each critical service [9]. This element links to Sub conditions 1 and 2.
- **Operational Computer Emergency Response Team (CERT) or Computer Security Incident Response Team (CSIRT).** To facilitate national incident response in the event of natural disasters or man-made disasters that affect critical services and information infrastructures, a CERT/CSIRT should be in place. In fulfilling this element, the country has to publish an incident response plan for emergencies and crises, put in place incident management, resiliency and recovery capabilities for critical services and information infrastructures, and have a network of national contact points for governmental and regulatory bodies [9]. This element links to Sub condition 2.

- **Demonstrate commitment to protect against cyber crime.** The country's involvement with international treaty agreements is assessed by means of treaty ratification. By ratifying a treaty, a country has an obligation and right under international law to uphold its political commitment. In fulfilling this element, the country needs to determine what percentage of GDP is affected by cyber crime, prepare an annual threat assessment to government and critical infrastructure networks, establish criminal offenses under its domestic law for cyber actions against computer systems, networks and computer data, and review existing laws and regulatory governance mechanisms applicable to cyber crime [9]. This element links to Condition 1 and Sub condition 2.
- **Information sharing mechanism.** An information sharing mechanism needs to be in place to enable the exchange of actionable intelligence/information between government and industry. In fulfilling this element, the country needs to have mechanisms in place for cross-sector incident-information sharing, have a rapid assistance mechanism and have the ability to declassify intelligence information and share it with rest of government and critical industries [9]. This element links to Condition 1.
- **Investment in cyber security research and funding of cyber security initiatives.** The country needs to invest in cyber security basic and applied research (innovation) and be funding cyber security initiatives broadly. In fulfilling this element, the country needs to dedicate a specified percentage of GDP (or government budget) to cyber security research and development, determine the research/production conversion and commercial adoption rate of research programmes, have universities offer a degree program in cyber security, have a commitment to interoperable and secure technical standards, determined by internationally recognized standards bodies, as well as a commitment to protect intellectual property, including commercial trade secrets, from theft [9]. This element links to Sub condition 1.

While the CRI provides guidelines on how to assess the state of a nation's cyber security readiness, it remains a complex and daunting task. Defining a single metric to quantify the impact that people, software and systems have on cyber security is also highly improbable due to the number of factors involved in the process [3]. As a result of the mentioned uncertain nature and the varying fields affected by cyber security, a proliferation of adopted measurements has emerged (refer to Fig. 1). It is thus clear that some form of formalised structure is emerging in the information security community to standardise the way information security is measured and represented. This is a crucial step towards effectively measuring the security posture of an organisation and even on a larger scale a country.

4.2   Common Vulnerability and Exposures

One of the most frequently used metrics is the CVE metric as depicted in Fig. 2. CVEs are used to assess the security of software on a computer/device by disclosing specific vulnerabilities discovered in a structured format. While the metric is useful in describing a potential vulnerability that exists for a given software system, several shortcomings exist. While CVEs have a clearly defined structure making it useful to communicate to various individuals, the data entered into the respective fields are still very subjective and controlled by the creator of the specific CVE [1]. This opens up the potential for wrongful classification of a severity that could indicate that a device has a critical vulnerability when in fact the device is safe. This links to Sub condition 1.

```
- <entry id="CVE-2010-0311">
  - <vuln:vulnerable-configuration id="http://nvd.nist.gov">
    - <cpe-lang:logical-test negate="false" operator="AND">
      - <cpe-lang:logical-test negate="false" operator="OR">
          <cpe-lang:fact-ref name="cpe:/a:sun:java_system_identity_server:8.1.0.5" />
          <cpe-lang:fact-ref name="cpe:/a:sun:java_system_identity_server:8.1.0.6" />
        </cpe-lang:logical-test>
      - <cpe-lang:logical-test negate="false" operator="OR">
          <cpe-lang:fact-ref name="cpe:/a:sun:java_system_access_manager" />
          <cpe-lang:fact-ref name="cpe:/a:sun:opensso_enterprise:8.0" />
          <cpe-lang:fact-ref name="cpe:/a:ibm:tivoli_access_manager_for_e-business" />
        </cpe-lang:logical-test>
      </cpe-lang:logical-test>
    </vuln:vulnerable-configuration>
  - <vuln:vulnerable-software-list>
      <vuln:product>cpe:/a:ibm:tivoli_access_manager_for_e-business</vuln:product>
      <vuln:product>cpe:/a:sun:java_system_access_manager</vuln:product>
      <vuln:product>cpe:/a:sun:java_system_identity_server:8.1.0.6</vuln:product>
      <vuln:product>cpe:/a:sun:java_system_identity_server:8.1.0.5</vuln:product>
      <vuln:product>cpe:/a:sun:opensso_enterprise:8.0</vuln:product>
    </vuln:vulnerable-software-list>
```

Fig. 2. CVE example

The uncertainty regarding the CVE critical score is but one of the problems with current measurements available. Several other factors such as the vulnerability recorded might simply be the by-product of an even bigger vulnerability that the researcher have missed. A further factor is that no single organisation controls the complete set of all available CVEs [5] and more importantly, the individual CVEs are contributed by the security community. This leads to duplication, differences in measurements and the possibility of software with severe vulnerabilities being completely missed. This links to Condition 1.

Even if all of the inconsistencies and inaccuracies are ignored and trust is placed in a reputable vendor, further technical challenges await. Work conducted by Espinahara and Eduardo [7] highlight just how inaccurate even the most sophisticated current information security assessment software can be. While the software works fine when the language is set to English, a simple change of system language can render the vulnerability scanner nearly useless. In essence this means that any measurement currently performed on non English computer systems has the potential to be grossly inaccurate. Furthermore, vulnerability scanners can mostly only identify vulnerabilities related to software while previously it was made clear that information security spans a whole range of categories that need to be taken into account.

While the use of CVEs proves to be useful in measuring some information security aspects, this method does not guarantee complete information security protection. There are many factors that can result in negative or skewed metric results. As a result, CVEs is not a fool proof method of measurement.

5   Mapping Traditional Warfare Metrics to Cyber Warfare

This section maps the traditional warfare factors identified in Section 1.3 to the cyber domain. This mapping is done in aid of developing a cyber military doctrine and establishing metrics to measure information security damage and potentially measure of loss due to cyber warfare. The aim is to prove the validity of the formula presented in Section 1.3 within the cyber domain. In proving this validity, each of the traditional warfare conditions needs to be discussed in terms of the cyber (information security) domain. It should be noted that this mapping process is not straightforward since the Internet and cyber domain is largely intangible and therefore difficult to map to the real world traditional warfare domain.

5.1   Condition 1: Political Power Fluctuations

The offending nation state needs to have political power fluctuations present. For this condition to be true, the cyber actions should contribute to the nation state's political power fluctuations to some degree.

Especially since 2010's start of the Arab Spring, digital tools such as YouTube, Twitter and Facebook have defined many social movements by giving rise to a new generation of activism. In many of these uprisings, the Internet, mobile phones and social media played a pivotal role in the organising of protests by activists. Public information supplied by social networking websites has played an important role during modern-day activism, especially since it is employed as a key tool in expressing thoughts concerning unjust acts committed by the government [12]. In addition, *"digital media has been used by many protestors to exercise freedom of speech and as a space for civic engagement"* [18]. In this sense, freedom of speech can be classified as the political right to communicate one's opinions and ideas using one's body and property to anyone who is willing to receive them.

In addition, work done by Collier and Hoeffler, Collier et al. and Arnson (in [2]) have identified a link between civil wars and grievances such as inequality or a lack of political rights. It is believed that, although resources are central to the duration and intensity of war, the roots and objectives of war are often founded in politics. In the cyber domain, the high availability of Internet-based, low-cost cyber-weapons that can target civilian information assets has become a growing threat to the economic and political stability of modern societies that depend on today's information infrastructures [13]. In the cyber domain, political power fluctuations are extremely prevalent since the Internet is an artificial environment that can be shaped in part according to national security and political requirements. In addition, cyber attacks are flexible enough to be effective for information warfare and propaganda, espionage, and the destruction of critical infrastructure [20].

5.2   Condition 2: Potential for Lethality

For this condition to be true, the cyber actions should have the potential for lethality for at least one of the acts of cyber aggression. By extension of the definition for aggression (feelings of anger or antipathy resulting in hostile or violent behaviour, readiness to attack or confront), any act of cyber aggression can be regarded as having the potential for lethality. The acts of cyber aggression as identified by Carr [4], can be explained in the cyber domain as follows:

- **Cyber attacks against government or critical civilian websites or network without accompanying military force.** The recent breach of the South African Police's (SAPS) whistle-blowers' web portal is an example of a major cyber attack against a government. The dumped data contained numerous personally identifiable records that could lead to the identification of people who have provided information to the SAPS in confidence.
- **Cyber attacks against government or critical civilian websites or network with accompanying military force**. Many high-profile cyber-attacks initially targeted the military. For example, the 1986 Cuckoo's Egg incident had Clifford Stoll tracking German hackers who were scouring American military systems. In 1994, hackers infiltrated Griffis Air Force Base computers to launch attacks at other military, civilian and government organisations [13].
- **Cyber attacks against internal political opponents**. If technology is utilised in internal political agendas, it is a real possibility that digital acts can result in physical violence. For example, the Tunisian part of Arab Spring saw Internet censorship, data harvesting by the government, laws restricting online freedom of expression and hactivism (as performed by Anonymous' *Operation Tunisia*). These online actions had a very tangible violent outset.
- **Cyber intrusions into critical infrastructure and networks**. Critical infrastructure protection is a crucial part of cyber protection, as was illustrated by the Stuxnet attack. If a nation state's national critical infrastructure is attacked, it can have a devastating impact on most aspects of civilians' lives, including transport, communication, water and sanitation, etc. For example, if the transport sector is affected, it would have an impact on all emergency services, since no fire brigade or ambulance would be able to perform their duties. If the communication sector is affected, it could potentially lead to large scale hysterics, since people will be unable to contact their friends and families. These scenarios have the potential for lethality.
- **Acts of cyber espionage.** Few nations can claim to not have been affected by some form of cyber espionage, either by participation or by victimisation [25]. Documents that were released by whistle-blower Edward Snowden have revealed just how prevalent cyber espionage is. These documents claim that the United States' PRISM program is capable of indiscriminately intercepting and analysing information received from email, phone and video. Similarly, the United Kingdom has admitted to spying on delegates for the G20 international summit in London 2009 [21]. In the APT1 report, the Mandiant group documents their search for a Chinese hacker group that has launched a massive espionage network affecting nations on all continents [15]. Figures from the report reveal that as much as four Terabytes of data has been exfiltrated from a single company; this is reckoned as the longest active backdoor found: four years and three months.

5.3   Condition 3: Needs of the Offending Nation State

For this condition to be true, either both the first two sub conditions, or the third sub condition needs to be true.

Sub Condition 1: False Optimism

The offending nation state needs to have false optimism regarding the outcome of the war. This condition is two-fold. Many cyber incidents receive little or no public acknowledgment [13]. As such, people are often not informed about the actual extent and implications of cyber attacks. For example, at the time of writing, very little statistics are available for cyber crime in South Africa. This is largely due to the fact that no legislation is in place that obliges victims to report the crimes. There are a number of initiatives that allows for the reporting of crime in South Africa, but few of these cater for the reporting of cyber related crimes. As such, many crimes go unreported and the resultant available statistics are often skewed.

In addition, the enormous proliferation of technology and hacker tools makes it impossible to be familiar with all of the technology advances. Software updates and network reconfigurations also increase the unpredictability of the battlespace of cyber conflict with little or no warning [20]. As such, it becomes easy to have false confidence in one's cyber abilities, and accordingly, the outcome of a cyber war (refer to Section 3).

Sub Condition 2: Actions Lead to an Advantageous Position

The offending nation state needs to believe that their actions will lead to an advantageous position. Towards this end, the Internet has a number of salient characteristics that makes it a powerful tool in achieving this perceived advantage [6]. These are:

- **Reach.** The Internet has a global reach, with 2,405,518,376 Internet users in more than 233 countries worldwide [11]. This greatly enhances the potential for cumulative resources.
- **Ease.** Anyone with an Internet connection can become a cyber warrior or unwittingly allow their computer to be used as part of a zombie network.
- **Anonymity.** The Internet allows users to be completely anonymous, often giving people more confidence to say or do what they want online.

Sub Condition 3: Easy Conquest

In order for an offending nation state to believe that the war will be an easy conquest, the CRI can be used as measurement tool of cyber power on a governance level (refer to Section 3). Not only can the CRI be used to assess a nation state's own cyber capability to perform a cyber attack, but the target nation state's CRI can be assessed to predict the ease with which such a cyber attack will be performed and the technical skills with which the target will receive the attack and retaliate. In contrast with the process for traditional warfare, the proximity of adversaries is determined by connectivity and bandwidth, not terrestrial geography [20]

6   Testing the Formula for Predicting Cyber Warfare

In order to test the applicability of the formula for predicting warfare in the cyber domain, the validity of the conditions will be tested for the Israeli-Palestinian cyber conflict that took place between July 1999 and April 2002. A similar test was done to test the formula on the Estonia cyber conflict. However, due to limited space, the rationale was not included in the article.

6.1   Condition 1: Political Power Fluctuations

In September 2000, Israeli teenage hackers created a website to jam Hezbollah and Hamas websites in Lebanon. The teenagers launched a sustained Distributed Denial of Service attack that effectively jammed six websites of the Hezbollah and Hamas organisations and the Palestinian National Authority. In response, Palestinian and other supporting Islamic organisations called for a cyber Holy War. Hackers struck three high-profile Israeli websites belonging to the Israeli Parliament, the Ministry of Foreign Affairs, and the Israeli Defence Force information site. They also targeted the Israeli Prime Minister's Office, the Bank of Israel and the Tel Aviv Stock Exchange [20]. By targeting political entities and by calling this war a cyber Holy War, the first condition of political power fluctuations can be considered as true, since there is a political undertone and a number of non-isolated acts occurred.

6.2   Condition 2: Potential for Lethality

As illustrated in Section 4.2, any attack on critical infrastructure has the potential for lethality. During the Israeli-Palestinian cyber conflict, attacks were made against companies providing telecommunications infrastructure [20]. Therefore, the condition of lethality potential can be considered as true.

6.3   Condition 3: Needs of the Offending Nation State

For this condition to be true, either both the first two sub conditions, or the third sub condition needs to be true.

Sub Condition 1: False Optimism

By January 2001, the Israeli-Palestinian cyber conflict had struck more than 160 Israeli and 35 Palestinian websites; 548 Israeli domain websites were defaced [20]. These conquests could potentially give both sides false optimism in terms of their chances of victory, rendering the first sub condition true.

Sub Condition 2: Actions Lead to an Advantageous Position

Palestinian hackers defaced an Internet Service Provider and left a message claiming that they could shut down the Israeli ISP NetVision, which hosts almost 70 percent of all the country's Internet traffic [20]. By disabling the opponent's Internet access, the Palestine side rendered the sub condition of performing actions to lead to an advantageous position true.

Sub Condition 3: Easy Conquest

In 2013, Israel's networked readiness index is ranked 15th up from rank 20 in 2012, whilst Palestine does not feature on the index. This year's index coverage includes a 144 economies, accounting for over 98 percent of global GDP. This presents an interesting point to consider that it could be possible for countries to not participate in such rankings and effectively allow potential aggressor nation states to believe that they are easy prey, whilst obfuscating their offensive cyber capabilities until it was too late.

6.4   Formula for Predicting Cyber Warfare

Based on the discussions above, the following conditions for predicting the possibility of cyber warfare are met:

$$
\begin{aligned}
\text{Possibility of cyber warfare} = \quad & \text{Nation state political power fluctuations} \\
& \text{AND Potential for lethality} \\
& \text{AND ((False optimism} \\
& \text{AND Offending nation state advantage)} \\
& \text{OR Easy conquest)} \\
= \quad & \text{True} \\
& \text{AND True} \\
& \text{AND ((True} \\
& \text{AND True)} \\
& \text{OR True)}
\end{aligned}
$$

From this case study, it can be argued that the Israeli-Palestinian cyber conflict adheres to all the requirements to enable the early prediction of this cyber war.

7   Conclusion

Currently the only concrete way of measuring the status of the cyber domain is located in traditional information security techniques whether it be on a technical or policy level. While applicable, the measurements do not adequately describe loss, posture or any of the pre-requisites found in traditional warfare. Although it is possible to perform an analysis of characteristics of the ICT society with regard to domination threats, economic sustainability, etc., these measurements have not yet been employed according to the literature survey performed by the authors. Accordingly, this article aimed to provide evidence towards the probability of predicting and mapping traditional warfare measurements to the cyber warfare domain. As such, this article worked to find an alternative way of predicting the possibility of cyber warfare, since traditional information security measurements are not adequate.

The article looked at current information security metrics, the CRI and CVEs, and provided an alternative method of predicting the probability of cyber warfare. A formula predicting the possibility of traditional warfare was articulated based on existing literature. The conditions for this formula were mapped to cyber warfare theory to prove the validity of this formula in the cyber domain. In addition, this formula was tested by applying it to the Israeli-Palestinian cyber conflict. This conflict is generally accepted as a cyber warfare incident. As such, the conditions are met by the acts of cyber aggression to affirm that cyber warfare took place. This article showed that the formula can be applied to the cyber domain. The value of this formula lies in the potential for pre-emptively identifying potential cyber war incidents. By pro-actively analysing global news and especially citizen journal journalism through social media platforms for indicators of the elements of the formula for predicting the possibility of cyber warfare, it may be possible to predict to occurrence of potential cyber war incidents, and as such, limit the potential damage caused, if the incidents cannot be prevented in totality. This extraction of collective intelligence falls beyond the scope of this article, but can be considered for future work in extending the formulate for predicting the possibility of cyber warfare.

References

1. Allodi, L., Massacci, F.: How CVSS is DOSsingyour patching policy and wasting your money (2013), http://media.blackhat.com/us-13/US-13-Allodi-HOW-CVSS-is-DOSsing-Your-Patching-Policy-Slides.pdf (accessed November 20, 2013)
2. Baten, J., Mumme, C.: Does inequality lead to civil wars? A global long-term study using anthropometrics indicators (1816-1999). European Journal of Political Economy 32, 56–79 (2013)
3. Boehme, R., Freiling, F.: On metrics and measurements in Dependability metrics: Advanced lectures. In: Eusgled, I., Freiling, F., Reussner, R. (eds.), pp. 7–13. Springer, Heidelberg (2008), doi:http://dx.doi.org/10.1007/978-3-540-68947-8_2
4. Carr, J.: Inside Cyber Warfare. O'Reilly Media, Sebastopol (2011)
5. Christey, S., Martin, B.: Buying into the bias: Why vulnerability statistics suck (2013), http://attrition.org/security/conferences/2013-07-BlackHat-Vuln_Stats-draft_22-Published.pptx (accessed November 18, 2013)
6. Delany, C.: Online Politics: The Tools and Tactics of Digital Political Advocacy (2011), http://www.epolitics.com (accessed October 8, 2013)
7. Espinahara, J., Eduardo, L.: Lost in translation (2013), http://conference.hitb.org/hitbsecconf2013kul/materials/D2T3%20-%20Luiz%20Eduardo%20and%20Joaquim%20Espinhara%20-%20Lost%20in%20Translation.pdf (accessed November 20, 2013)
8. Filiol, E.: Operational aspects of cyberwarfare or cyberterrorist attacks: What a truly devastating attack could do. In: Ryan, J. (ed.) Leading Issues in Information Warfare & Security Research, vol. 1, pp. 35–53. Academic Publishing, Reading (2011)

9. Hathaway, M.: Cyber readiness index 1.0 (2013),
   `http://belfercenter.hks.harvard.edu/files/`
   `cri-methodology-1-point-0-final.pdf` (accessed November 21, 2013)
10. Heickerö, R.: Some aspects on cyber war faring in information arena and cognitive domain
   (2007), `http://www.dodccrp.org/events/11th_ICCRTS/html/`
   `presentations/157.pdf` (accessed November 25, 2013)
11. Internet World Stats. 2013. Internet usage statistics - The internet big picture (2013),
   `http://www.internetworldstats.com/stats.htm` (accessed October 29,
   2013)
12. Kassim, S.: Twitter revolution: How the Arab Spring was helped by social media (2012),
   `http://www.policymic.com/articles/10642/twitter-revolution-`
   `how-the-arab-spring-was-helped-by-social-media` (accessed October 9,
   2013)
13. Knapp, K., Boulton, W.: Cyber-Warfare Threatens Corporations: Expansion into Commercial Environments. Information Systems Management 23(2), 76–87 (2006)
14. Liles, S., Rogers, M., Dietz, J., Larson, D.: Applying traditional military principles to
   cyber warfare (2012), `http://www.ccdcoe.org/publications/`
   `2012proceedings/3_2_Liles&Dietz&Rogers&Larson_ApplyingTradit`
   `ionalMilitaryPrinciplesToCyberWarfare.pdf` (accessed November 25,
   2013)
15. Mandiant. Exposing One of China's Cyber Espionage Units (2013),
   `http://intelreport.mandiant.com/Mandiant_APT1_Report.pdf`
   (accessed November 19, 2013)
16. MITRE. By Cyber Security Area (2012),
   `http://measurablesecurity.mitre.org/directory/areas/`
   `index.html` (accessed November 29, 2013)
17. Oxford Dictionaries. Cyberwar, `http://www.oxforddictionaries.com/`
   `definition/english/cyberwar` (accessed November 22, 2013)
18. Pew Research. The role of social media in the Arab uprisings (2012),
   `http://www.journalism.org/2012/11/28/role-social-media-`
   `arab-uprisings/` (accessed October 9, 2013)
19. Rid, T.: Cyber war will not take place. Journal of Strategic Studies 35(1), 5–32 (2012)
20. Schreier, F.: ND. On cyberwarfare. DCAF Horizon 2015 Working Paper No. 7
21. Symantec. Internet Security Threat Report (ISTR), vol. 18, `http://www.symantec.com/`
   `content/en/us/enterprise/other_resources/b-istr_main_report_`
   `v18_2012_21291018.en-us.pdf` (accessed November 30, 2013)
22. UNICRI. ND. Cyberwarfare, `http://www.unicri.it/special_topics/`
   `cyber_threats/cyber_crime/explanations/cyberwarfare/`
   (accessed November 22, 2013)
23. Van Evera, S.: Causes of war: Power and the roots of conflict. Cornell University Press,
   New York (1999)
24. Van Niekerk, B., Maharaj, M.: The Information Warfare Life Cycle Model. SA Journal of
   Information Management 13(1), Art. 476 (2011)
25. Verizon. The 2013 Data Breach Investigations Report (2013),
   `http://www.verizonenterprise.com/resources/reports/rp_data-`
   `breach-investigations-report-2013_en_xg.pdf` (accessed November 18,
   2013)

Security and Privacy as Hygiene Factors of Developer Behavior in Small and Agile Teams

Kai-Uwe Loser and Martin Degeling

Institute of Work Science, Ruhr-University Bochum, Germany
{kai-uwe.loser,martin.degeling}@rub.de

Abstract. User motivations are often considered in human computer relations. The analysis of developer behavior often lacks this perspective. Herzberg's distinction of motivators and hygiene factors adds a level for the analyses of those sociotechnical phenomena that lead to skipping of security and privacy requirements especially in agile development projects. Requirements of security and privacy are not considered nice-to-have, but as necessary hygiene factors of systems attractiveness, motivation for extra effort is low with respect to those requirements. The motivators for developers – functionality that makes a system special and which is valued by customers and users are dominant for the decisions about priorities of development – hygiene factors like many security requirements get a lower priority. In this paper we introduce this theory with relation to known problems of (agile) development projects with respect to implementing security and privacy. We present this with a case study of mobile app development in a research project that we analyzed by security and privacy aspects.

Keywords: security and privacy, agile development, Herzberg's theory, motivation.

1 Introduction

Agile development aims to quick results to fulfill requirements and user needs for early prototypes and feedback. But with the speed of development security and privacy requirements tend to be overseen. This is especially relevant for IT landscapes like those of mobile apps which is shaped by high innovation pressure and a large number of similar applications developed by very small teams or individuals. At first security awareness approaches focusing on development teams seem appropriate to improve this situation, but in many cases they are found to be not sufficient. Analyzing this situation with a background on work motivation can help to find solutions to this problem. This paper aims to show the relevance of this background with an analysis in relation to the motivator-hygiene-theory of Herzberg. To contextualize the theory we report on a study of an agile development project where we analyzed the security and privacy awareness in comparison to the implementation details of the developed systems. Results are similar to assumptions that others as we argue to increase

K.K. Kimppa et al. (Eds.): HCC11 2014, IFIP AICT 431, pp. 255–265, 2014.

intrinsic motivation of software developers. Our study was part of a large research project on technology enhanced learning, where a strong relevance of privacy and security was recognized early due to the application domains (e.g. healthcare). The research and development project was split up in several small development teams, each developing (mobile) applications for different kinds of for learning in work situations. The overall project had a strong commitment on security and privacy issues and several steps were taken to actively support and foster those topics in the developed applications. Nevertheless only a few of them in the end incorporated them in their basic design and early versions. In the final phase of the project we found various requirements being open issues, we then took a closer look at the list of requirements and from our personal involvement contextualized their history.

The next two sections will give an overview of Herzberg's original theory and related work. The following three sections will present the case study, which we will analyze in relation to Herzberg's theory. We will conclude with some ideas on solutions to the problem situation that becomes obvious by the analysis.

2   The Herzberg Two-Factor Theory

As a psychologist and work scientist Frederick Herzberg conducted several studies about satisfaction at work in various countries [1, 2]. He found that one set of needs of employees is closely linked to work satisfaction another to work-dissatisfaction. The hypothesis was that satisfaction is a key to work motivation and work performance.

The first group of needs and factors is called *motivators*. Motivators for work are for example challenging work, recognition of the work by others or self-determination at work. Improving motivators, Herzberg suggested, can lead to higher job satisfaction.

The second group of factors is called *hygiene factors*. Examples for hygiene factors are salary, workspace qualities and conditions or work-life balance. Hygiene factors are supposed to create dissatisfaction if they are not reaching a certain level. Raising those factors beyond that level will not lead to improved satisfaction.

Within the field of organizational psychology the theory was developed further and integrated into more elaborate theories of motivation. Miner [3] refers to various critics to the empirical methods. Especially the assumed link between satisfaction and work motivation and therefore work performance has been critiqued to be too simplistic and studies show that some results are no longer tenable [3]. But there are still several researchers referring to the theory e.g. Bassett & Jones [4]. Especially the simplicity leads to an easy analysis of phenomena with relation to motivation and can help to find ways to improve it. Herzberg himself proposed "Job Enrichment". Therefore the theory was adopted in several domains. In general it is used as an analogy e.g. for user experience design [5] or behavior analysis [6].

This distinction between motivators and hygiene factors can also be transferred to requirements in software engineering. Hygiene requirements may include usability aspects or functionality that is expected, like a user interface that includes known elements and forms with buttons and menus and basic features to work without errors.

Some other requirements may become features that seem to be the motivating aspects for a buy or use decision like innovative features other applications do not offer or a user interface that stands out from others. This complements a "nice-to-have" vs. "mandatory" distinction. At first this seems similar, but in detail it regularly leads to different clusters and to a higher priority to "Nice-To-Haves". Many hygiene aspects would be considered as mandatory on the general level. Nevertheless importance of an effort in fulfilling the detailed requirements and motivation of developers to implement these may be low. Usability and security requirements are examples of this: protection for example by encrypted data transfer is – although simple and should be mandatory - often omitted because the implementing developer will not get positive feedback when fulfilling such a requirement. Developers realize that certain functionality is motivating for customers or users to use an application (Motivators), whereas others are not provoking positive feedback once (Hygiene). So customers' views are often closely linked to the developer perspective. We therefore use the distinction of Herzberg's work motivational aspects as an analogy to separate different kinds of requirements. We think that differentiating requirements into the two categories will help tackle especially the hygiene requirements because those will need extra effort to become appropriate attention. Having the distinction of hygiene factors and motivators in mind, we will go on with the problems of security and privacy engineering and then describe a case study to illustrate the application of Herzberg's distinction especially for security and privacy requirements.

3   Security Engineering

Security Engineering aims at structured and controllable processes to implement reliable systems and applications. Common goals of security engineering are confidentiality, integrity and availability of data. These goals focus on the infrastructure and the organization as a whole. From a privacy engineering perspective new approaches [7, 8] argue to integrate unlinkability, transparency, intervenability in a similar way as privacy protection goals into software engineering.

Several researchers ([9–11]) have identified that secure software not only requires secure algorithms but that their usage has to be fostered in software engineering processes. To be able to do this it is crucial that software developers are aware of security and privacy issues as well as of possible solutions. Although they are trained to do so it is necessary that relevant topics are regularly practiced.

There are publications (e.g. [10]) offering a comprehensive list of possible solutions, best-practices and approaches to develop secure information systems. They mainly include the strategy to do proper system engineering, make an extensive risk analysis and threat assessment, improve an application to avoid the problems identified and to introduce various steps to control the process. Most approaches suggest adding additional process steps in the waterfall software engineering process and propose to introduce security assessments and threat analysis. These work for a lot of situations but fail for those projects that do not have a strict outcome oriented management. Especially in agile projects where requirements change over time, are re-evaluated and re-prioritized or user stories are developed continuously require more flexible approaches. Siponen et al. [12] for example propose to introduce security aspects into feature driven development by identifying and classifying security relevant actors and objects for each requirement. Boström et al. [13] developed a method to include security assessment practices in XP programming and Besznosov et al. [14] propose to stick with those common agile methods and artifacts that allow security reviews without extending documentations and use semi-automated testing to assure security in software.

In contrast to these rather formal techniques that are integrated with agile software development models we want to focus on the behavior of software developers. Firstly because they have to translate user requirements for security and privacy into the technical domain. And secondly because in agile development approaches and small teams where development models are not followed strictly developers have to make decisions about how the requirements are implemented and are often responsible for assessing the trade-offs between for example security and usability [15]. In addition their knowledge of the domain and technologies and presumptions about the importance of a specific requirement is crucial for the decisions about implementing privacy and security. As decisions made by developers in agile projects are much more related to individual knowledge and perception of a problem motivational factors become more relevant as they decide on whether or not and in which depth a security and privacy aspects are addressed.

4   Case Study Description

Our work is based on the experience in a research project on technology enhanced learning in workplace situations. It included several smaller agile software development projects building apps for various domains. About 20 applications (apps) were developed to support employees in learning about their work practice by capturing data from day to day practice. The apps were based on multiple platforms from desktop to web-based systems and mobile apps for tablets and smartphones. Development teams consisted of 1-3 people that developed around 20 apps in three years. From the beginning security and privacy were important issues for the development since capturing work performance data to allow employees to learn from it, implies that this data has to be persistently stored and evaluated. The apps were developed in domains ranging from employees in hospitals, care homes or sales agents in an IT company. They included automated to manual tracking of work e.g. with a tracking application on personal computers that records how long which application with which file was used; recording who meets whom during a work day with proximity sensors people were wearing; allowing users to frequently capture their mood during meetings by clicking mood maps or asking them to write down their personal views and self-assessments after talking to clients or patients. To elaborate on the idea of the project and the awareness and presence of security and privacy issues we will present one app as examples where the security shortcomings are also visible in the next section.

Right from the beginning severe privacy and security implications were identified. The threat model includes that a specific user and practice can be identified and analyzed by abusers from outside a company or organization, which are interested in work practices of a competitor. An internal threat is that employees fear the misuse of their data by their employers and supervisors trying to control their work and assessing their efficiency which is especially important due to the nature of the project were users were free to participate or not. This leads to a number of higher level requirements and discussions about privacy and security problems and possible solutions for individual apps as well as for an overall framework connecting all developed apps.

4.1   Approach to Raise Security Awareness

In the beginning of the project, we found security awareness to be an important part of approaching the goal of secure systems. One basic idea was that, if all developers were aware of issues, the apps' quality with respect to those requirements will meet the standards. The following list gives an overview of the actions taken:

1. Organizational support to target security and privacy issue
   (a) In the original work plan a work package was dedicated to privacy, security and system integration testing as an activity all development partners have to participate in.
   (b) Project management fostered discussion about this topic by proposing workshops at every project meeting covering privacy and security issues.
1. Raise developers awareness
   (a) Again workshops within the groups of developers where the topics were discussed in detail.
   (b) A "developers' cheat sheet" for privacy and security measurements was developed including condensed information about when and how to encrypt data and what data (not) to collect.
1. Make security and privacy assessments
   (a) Later on we did some example privacy and security assessments for a sample of the apps and published the results to the developers. Additional requirements were discussed and developed from the results. This led to a continuous presence of the topics.
   (b) We made a user survey to generate more requirements from the user level that were mostly about personal control and transparency [16]. The evaluation focused on revealing details about the difference of assumed privacy awareness of users and actual behavior. The results have shown that most users are very critical about privacy and security in general and especially have a limited trust in their employers to be honest in how they use their data.

4.2   Application Example

Apps where developed for different work contexts. Some of the domains were less critical from a security point of view than others. One app for example was used to aggregate information from public sources like twitter to allow members of emergency teams of large mass events to support reflection about the current situation to better coordinate the helpers involved. Since we want to focus on the requirements for privacy and security and due to the lack of space we focus on an app that had higher security needs.

Requirements engineering took place in workshops that were held with users and other stakeholders that focused on the applicability and usability of the app. As we followed an agile development approach the first ideas were based on storyboards produced in workshops with application partners. Based on those storyboards user stories were written and adapted after prototypes realizing those stories were tested.

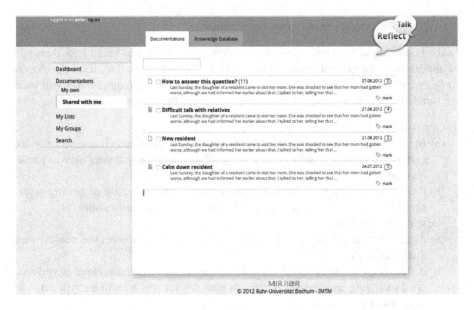

Fig. 1. Screenshot of the TalkReflection App showing a list of documented conversations

The TalkReflection app (s. figure 1) is used by staff in a hospital and homes for dementia care to document conversations they have with patients and relatives, especially to document discussions with them and record rationale of care decisions. They document the conversation by stating, what it was about, who was involved and what the decisions were. In addition users are asked to document their own perception of the conversation, how they felt, how the conversation partner reacted on an emotional level and what hypothesis about reasons for their own mistakes they have. Afterwards the users are able to share their documentation and comment on others'. In more detail the idea behind the app is that there is on the one hand a demand to document those conversations and rationale for reasons of liability. If, for example, some sort of accident happens after a decision a physician made with a relative about a patient who cannot be asked themselves, it would be positive if details about the decision and the context of the decision are documented. In addition the app can be used by staff members to reflect on how they behaved and felt during a conversation. This was found to be useful as for most physicians it is not part of their training to learn how to cope with difficult conversations and how to improve their reactions towards relatives that are often stressed by the situations and diseases of their relatives.

The app, similar to others developed, has serious implications with regard to security and privacy that were categorized on two levels. From **an organizational perspective** there were high requirements for the security goals integrity and confidentiality. In the first place the organizations wanted to protect their company data; in the second, and especially for companies working in the healthcare sector, they also wanted to protect third party data like information about clients or patients..

From **the users' perspectives** a separate group of questions about privacy and the security of the applications arose as employees thought they might be used by their employers to control their work practice and may sanction certain kinds of behavior. Therefore features had to be included addressing this kind of problems by access control and prevention of unauthorized access and usage of the data.

After the overall concerns and contexts were evaluated several workshops were held with experts and stakeholders from the hospital itself including participants like the data protection official, the director of IT-security and the works council. In addition external IT-security experts were consulted as the rather small development teams of 2 to 3 persons were not considered as experts in the field.

To the time of writing only few of the security requirements are currently implemented and those that were considered, were supposed blocking the field experiments. The IT department required encrypted connections for the apps since they only opened up those ports in the firewall.

After a large number of prototypes the apps are evaluated and used by the application partners on a regular basis now. Nevertheless they are still considered "beta" and the following sentences are cited from a statement of a developer on the current status of privacy and security: "The privacy aspect has been considered within the planning of the application. Although there is no detailed plan for privacy safeguarding at the moment, we considered multiple approaches within the applications architecture. Thus we are primed for different kinds of privacy safeguarding." The developers' excuse is that still everything is possible – but the requirements are not met currently. The following section will present various examples from the case study to illustrate and motivate the distinction of requirements into the hygiene and motivator categories.

5   Discussion

To come back to Herzberg's theory of motivators and hygiene factors we consider security and privacy requirements in general similar to hygiene factors and have to compare them with motivators. Potential users will not use a system just because it has well implemented privacy and security mechanisms, but it will inhibit them if it is not assured or will result in discontinuity of use if disclosed. We assume that security and privacy requirements are usually seen as a necessary presupposition in a world where not everybody is able to test if all the requirements are met. Since they regularly are not visible to end users, they are always assumed to be implemented. From a developers' perspective in a world where users are free to choose to use or not to use an application the product acceptance (e.g. number of installations from mobile app stores) has become one of the main motivators. In this logic privacy and security should be implemented but are at the same time not resulting in positive feedback since they are often not visible at all. Therefore they can be considered hygienic factors.

We want to discuss this hypothesis in context of some observations of decisions made during the development of the described web application.

5.1   Motivator Type Requirements: A Personal Link

Motivators in our case are bound to those requirements which are related to the innovative ideas, aspects that make the prototypes new, interesting and exciting. While these are motivators especially for users that use an application because of its novelty this, in the same term, motivates developers to implement them. The observations showed that this especially holds true if a requirement is linked to a personal promoters. If a feature is requested by a (possible) user within a workshop with developers, this specific technical implementation gets linked to a personal relationship; a personal motivation for implementing grows.

5.2   Hygiene Type Requirements: Implemented When Easy

Also risking negative feedback several security and privacy related requirements were not implemented in the prototypes. Although implementation is simple using the right tools only those requirements were implemented that were easy to achieve e.g. encrypted data transfer through https and certificates for xmpp servers. Other, like data storage encryption, were not implemented although it might, in the long term, hindering wide spread application.

One explanation for this behavior is that security and privacy requirements are develop top down. Security and privacy and related requirements are derived after the functional requirements are clarified. The functional requirements especially in agile development processes are always bound to people and their problem situation. Security and privacy on the other hand are difficult to link specific situations but related to overall needs, which leads to a lack of focus on these requirements.

5.3   Not Implemented Requirements: Organizational Solutions

Especially agile development leads to regular priority decisions. Therefore more complex security requirements or requirements which need a higher effort were skipped with various excuses and strategies to defer the task. An example is the ability for users to (easily) delete their personal content, which was identified as a privacy requirement. Since databases were regularly reset after a prototype test was conducted, some apps are still missing the possibility to delete content by users. And they are not only missing a delete button but also the routines that handle deletions and keep data structures and for example threaded discussions intact.

Other requirements were moved from technical to organizational solutions. For example one proposal was to build modules that automatically scan written documentations for real names of patients and relatives to change them to an unlinkable pseudonym. Since that was never implemented, the requirement was omitted and replaced by additional rules for the handbooks saying users are not allowed to use real names and instead should use codes generated from room numbers and initials. Another common pattern for questions of how much data may be collected was to answer them with additional consent forms having the idea in mind that any data collection is legally allowed and almost every data processing is possible if the users decided to allow it in the first place. Those examples are instances of strategies leading to a transfer of effort (and responsibility) to others. If a requirement is important enough, somebody else can implement that.

5.4   Ideas for Approaching the Avoidance of Hygienic Requirements

Theoretically, requirements bound to motivators naturally become a higher priority while for the implementation of hygiene factors processes need to be actively redesigned. While for some basic features like encrypted storage technical solutions might be feasible that just make implementation easier. The general problem that a sophisticated implementation is not visible to any user, cannot be solved that way.

Instead requirements should be linked to motivators that foster *intrinsic motivations* of developers. One motivator is the personal link to a user in the process: are there promoters of a specific requirement? Somebody that you offend, if you do not fulfill a specific requirement? A better motivation would be if you would feel to help somebody personally. The positive motivations (promotion) are better motivators than negative outcomes (prevention) [17]. The question a developer should answer is: "Is there anybody giving positive feedback if security requirements are met?"

Another idea can be borrowed from motivational approaches in other domains like User Experience Design, to improve hedonic aspects: with the idea of "Funology" [16] in mind another approach would be to make it a game. Two groups of app-developers could reciprocally attack the others' system, leading to improvements based on competition.

These arguments on motivational considerations can also be discussed in relation to proposed approaches in the literature. Instead of adding security considerations to feature cards as proposed by [12] which are already the formalized perspective of involved people and features, it might be better to start earlier on the level of user stories and including security aspects in interviews for requirements engineering. Discussing implications of specific security flaws with data subjects may give security requirements a face and a personal background to add other levels of motivation and a motivator background.

6   Conclusions

The discussion of the motivational aspects is trying to focus on the motivational aspects coming from the distinction between motivators and hygiene factors. As mentioned earlier the theory was attacked to be too simplistic and also in this case some forces of development are not considered in detail, and some problems might have been avoided by more strict development processes for example. On the other hand the case study described regularly visible real world phenomena and points to other approaches to overcome the problems.

Our experience from the case study is that security awareness and external analysis is not sufficient to ensure that especially agile development projects adequately consider security and privacy aspects although developers need guidance in developing secure and privacy aware systems. We tried to explain the problems recognized with motivational aspects. In development processes developer motivations are not sufficiently reflected. From this point of view security requirements have to be considered as hygienic factors: users and customers do expect their fulfillment but do not actively promote them. Our experience shows that with limited resources of time this kind of requirements will be deferred and easily skipped. Even though developers are highly aware of the security and privacy needs this is regularly the case.

We presented an example and discussed motivational aspects as one part of socio-technical topics of development of privacy and security. That awareness for security and privacy issues in software development is not enough when developing apps in small teams became obvious. The results point to improvements in development processes including the categorization of motivators and hygiene factor requirements, where different kinds of process controls should be followed. Knowing that Herzberg's Distinction is a too simplistic view on motivation for work one may state that especially the simplicity seems to make it useful, like other abstractions. Further research in relating theories about motivation to security processes and development processes seems to be an important extension of this work.

References

1. Herzberg, F., Mausner, B., Snyderman, B.B.: Motivation to work. Transaction Publishers (1959)
2. Herzberg, F.: The motivation-hygiene concept and problems of manpower. Pers. Adm. (1964)
3. Miner, J.B.: Organizational Behavior 2: Essential Theories of Process and Structure. M.E. Sharpe (2005)
4. Bassett-Jones, N., Lloyd, G.C.: Does Herzberg's motivation theory have staying power? J. Manag. Dev. 24, 929–943 (2005)
5. Hassenzahl, M.: Experience Design. Technology for All the Right Reasons. Morgan and Claypool, Penn State University (2010)
6. Crompton, J.L.: Adapting Herzberg: A conceptualization of the effects of hygiene and motivator attributes on perceptions of event quality. J. Travel Res. 41, 305–310 (2003)
7. Hansen, M.: Top 10 Mistakes in System Design from a Privacy Perspective and Privacy Protection Goals. In: Camenisch, J., Crispo, B., Fischer-Hübner, S., Leenes, R., Russello, G. (eds.) Privacy and Identity Management for Life. IFIP AICT, vol. 375, pp. 14–31. Springer, Heidelberg (2012)
8. Rost, M., Pfitzmann, A.: Datenschutz-Schutzziele—revisited. Datenschutz Datensicherheit 33, 353–358 (2009)

9. Sodiya, A.S., Onashoga, S.A., Ajayi, O.B.: Towards building secure software systems. Issues Informing Sci. Inf. Technol. 3 (2006)
10. McGraw, G.: From the ground up: The DIMACS software security workshop. Secur. Priv. IEEE 1, 59–66 (2003)
11. Anderson, R.: Security engineering: a guide to building dependable distributed systems. Wiley, Indianapolis (2008)
12. Siponen, M., Baskerville, R., Kuivalainen, T.: Integrating Security into Agile Development Methods. In: Proceedings of the 38th Annual Hawaii International Conference on System Sciences, HICSS 2005, p. 185a (2005)
13. Boström, G., Wäyrynen, J., Bodén, M., Beznosov, K., Kruchten, P.: Extending XP practices to support security requirements engineering. Presented at the (2006)
14. Beznosov, K., Kruchten, P.: Towards agile security assurance. In: Proceedings of the 2004 Workshop on New Security Paradigms, pp. 47–54 (2004)
15. Spiekermann, S., Cranor, L.F.: Engineering Privacy. IEEE Trans. Softw. Eng. 35, 67–82 (2009)
16. Degeling, M., Ackema, R.: D9.1 User studies on privacy needs, privacy model and privacy guidelines (2011)
17. Higgins, T.: Promotion and Prevention: Regulatory Focus as a Motivational Principle. Advances in Experimental Social Psychology. Academic Press (1998)

Towards an Ontological Model Defining
the Social Engineering Domain

Francois Mouton[1], Louise Leenen[1], Mercia M. Malan[2], and H.S. Venter[3]

[1] Defence Peace Safety & Security, Council for Industrial and Scientific Research,
Pretoria, South Africa
moutonf@gmail.com, lleenen@csir.co.za
[2] University of Pretoria, Information and Computer Security Architecture Research Group,
Pretoria, South Africa
malan747@gmail.com
[3] University of Pretoria, Computer Science Department, Pretoria, South Africa
hventer@cs.up.ac.za

Abstract. The human is often the weak link in the attainment of Information Security due to their susceptibility to deception and manipulation. Social Engineering refers to the exploitation of humans in order to gain unauthorised access to sensitive information. Although Social Engineering is an important branch of Information Security, the discipline is not well defined; a number of different definitions appear in the literature. Several concepts in the domain of Social Engineering are defined in this paper. This paper also presents an ontological model for Social Engineering attack based on the analysis of existing definitions and taxonomies. An ontology enables the explicit, formal representation of the entities and their inter-relationships within a domain. The aim is both to contribute towards commonly accepted domain definitions, and to develop a representative model for a Social Engineering attack. In summary, this paper provides concrete definitions for *Social Engineering*, *Social Engineering attack* and *social engineer*.

Keywords: Bidirectional Communication, Compliance Principles, Indirect Communication, Ontology, Social Engineering Attack, Social Engineering Attack Ontology, Social Engineering Definitions, Social Engineering History, Taxonomy, Unidirectional Communication.

1   Introduction

Social Engineering (SE) is focused on the exploitation of a human in order to gain unauthorised access to information and falls under the umbrella of the Information Security spectrum. Humans are the focal point of most organisations but they also pose a risk to their organisations. An organisation's sensitive information places them at risk if it falls in the wrong hands. Examples of sensitive information are the secret recipe that gives the Kentucky Fried Chicken meals their distinctive flavour or the personal banking information of clients.

K.K. Kimppa et al. (Eds.): HCC11 2014, IFIP AICT 431, pp. 266–279, 2014.
© IFIP International Federation for Information Processing 2014

Although organisations usually employ advanced technical security measures to minimise opportunities for unauthorised individuals to gain access to that information, it is vital that they consider the risk of their staff members falling victim to SE attacks. Humans often react emotionally and thus may be more vulnerable than machines at times. An organisation with sensitive information's biggest threat is not the technical protection, but the people who form the core of the organisation. Attackers have realised that it is easier to gain unauthorised access to the information and communications technology infrastructure of an organisation through an individual, rather than trying to penetrate a security system.

In a 1995 publication, the authors Winkler and Dealy posit that the hacker community has started to define SE as "the process of using social interactions to obtain information about a victim's computer system." [1]. The most popular definition of SE is the one by Kevin Mitnick who defines it as "using influence and persuasion to deceive people and take advantage of their misplaced trust in order to obtain insider information" [2].

An individual may be at the risk of exposing his or her own personal information to a social engineer. It is also the case that more and more individuals are exposed to electronic computing devices as the costs of these devices are decreasing drastically. Electronic computing devices have become significantly more affordable during the past few years and due to this nearly everyone has access to these devices. This provides the social engineer with more victims to target using skillfully crafted SE attacks.

Social engineers use a variety of techniques to manipulate their victims with the goal of extracting sensitive information from them. The title of Kevin Mitnick's book, *The art of deception: controlling the human element of security*, suggests that SE can be seen as an art of deception [2].

Various articles define SE and give descriptions of an SE attack. The definitions are diverse and often reflect one aspect of an approach relevant to a particular research project. Commonly agreed upon definitions that include all the different entities in SE are required. The purpose of this paper is to craft definitions and develop an ontological model for SE. Several papers, each with a different view on SE, have been studied and analysed to develop this model.

An ontology is a technology that allows for a formal encoded description of a domain and allows for the representation of semantic information: all the entities and their inter-relationships can be defined and represented. It also has powerful reasoning capabilities [3]. The ontological model presented in this paper will be implemented in future to provide an SE ontology.

The rest of this paper is structured as follows. Section 2 provides a background on different existing SE definitions and proposes more structured definitions for terms within the domain of SE. Section 3 discusses some existing taxonomies for the SE domain. Section 4 expands on the definitions provided in section 2 by providing an SE attack classification model as well as an ontological model for SE attacks. Section 5 concludes the paper by providing a summary of the contributions.

2   Defining Social Engineering

The earliest literature that the authors found on SE is an article by Quann and Belford (1987) [4]. According to these authors SE, whilst still in its infancy, is seen as "an attempt to exploit the help desks and other related support services normally associated with computer systems" [4]. SE was later described as "trickery and deceit, also known as Social Engineering", according to Kluepfel (1989) [5, 6]. Even in one of the most prominent hacker magazines, the 2600: The Hacker Quarterly[1], the term *Social Engineering* was not widely used. One of the articles entitled, "Janitor Privileges", explains in great detail how to perform an SE attack, however the term *Social Engineering* is never mentioned in the article [8].

The following definitions of SE illustrate that there exists no single, widely accepted definition:

- "a social/psychological process by which an individual can gain information from an individual about a targeted organization." [9]
- "a type of attack against the human element during which the assailant induces the victim to release information or perform actions they should not." [10]
- "the use of social disguises, cultural ploys, and psychological tricks to get computer users to assist hackers in their illegal intrusion or use of computer systems and networks." [11, 12]
- "the art of gaining access to secure objects by exploiting human psychology, rather than using hacking techniques." [13, 14]
- "an attack in which an attacker uses human interaction to obtain or compromise information about an organization or its computer system." [15, 16, 17, 18]
- "a process in which an attacker attempts to acquire information about your network and system by social means." [19, 20]
- "a deception technique utilized by hackers to derive information or data about a particular system or operation." [21, 22, 23]
- "a non-technical kind of intrusion that relies heavily on human interaction and often involves tricking other people to break normal security procedures." [24]
- "a hacker's manipulation of the human tendency to trust other people in order to obtain information that will allow unauthorized access to systems." [25, 26]
- "the science of skilfully manoeuvring human beings to take action in some aspect of their lives." [27, 28]
- "Social Engineering, in the context of information security, is understood to mean the art of manipulating people into performing actions or divulging confidential information." [29]
- "the act of manipulating a person or persons into performing some action." [30, 31]

---

[1] A magazine which was established by Emmanuel Goldstein in mid January 1984 and contains articles regarding the undergound world of hacking. The individuals publishing in this magazine are mostly individuals who are already facing several charges regarding computer related crimes. [7]

- "using subversive tactics to elicit information from end users for ulterior motives." [32]
- "using influence and persuasion to deceive people and take advantage of their misplaced trust in order to obtain insider information." [2, 33, 34, 35, 36]
- "the use of social disguises, cultural ploys, and psychological tricks to get computer users to assist hackers in their illegal intrusion or use of computer systems and networks." [37]

These definitions specify different ideas as to what SE involves. Two of these definitions specifically focus on gaining information from an organisation [9, 15, 16, 17, 18]. Several of the definitions define SE as the manipulation and persuasion of people in order to get information or to persuade someone to perform some action. Furthermore, some of the definitions are formed around gaining access to computer systems and networks. The only element that all of these definitions have in common is that a human is exploited in order to gain some unauthorised information or perform some action.

The authors of this paper propose the following definitions:

- *Social Engineering*: The science of using social interaction as a means to persuade an individual or an organisation to comply with a specific request from an attacker where either the social interaction, the persuasion or the request involves a computer-related entity.
- *Social engineer* (noun): An individual or group who performs an act of Social Engineering.
- *Social engineer* (verb): To perform an act of Social Engineering. When the verb is used in the Past Perfect form, it means a successful Social Engineering attack has occurred. For example, "The target may not know that he or she has been social engineered."
- *Social Engineering attack*: A Social Engineering attack employs either direct communication or indirect communication, and has a social engineer, a target, a medium, a goal, one or more compliance principles and one or more techniques.

Section 4.2 elaborates more on these definitions. Apart from the several definitions available for SE, there are also various taxonomies which try to encapsulate SE and the structure of an SE attack. In existing literature, a few taxonomies were proposed to provide some structure to the domain of SE. All of these taxonomies have inherent flaws in them and these flaws are discussed in the following section.

3   Existing Taxonomies

Several taxonomies are studied and discussed in this section: Harley [38], Laribee [39], Ivaturi & Janczewski [40], Mohd et al. [41] and Tetri & Vuorinen [42].

3.1   Harley

Harley [38] is one of the first articles to present a taxonomy for the SE domain, and in fact proposes two different taxonomies. The first one defines the following SE techniques and related attacks: Masquerading, Password stealing, Dumpster diving, Leftover, Hoax Virus Alerts and other Chain Letters, Spam and Direct Psychological Manipulation. This taxonomy mixes social compliance principles with techniques.

The second taxonomy defines seven user vulnerabilities: Gullibility, Curiosity, Courtesy, Greed, Diffidence, Thoughtlessness and Apathy. Even though these vulnerabilities are mostly the reasons why individuals are susceptible to SE attacks, they do not specify an SE attack as such. The same SE attack can be performed using more than one of the mentioned vulnerabilities, which clarifies that these vulnerabilities are not the unique establishment of what an SE attack entails. Vulnerabilities of a human, not limited by the seven mentioned above, lead to the susceptibility of an attack.

3.2   Laribee

Laribee [39] identifies two different models, namely a trust model and an attack model. According to Laribee, SE is complex and typically requires multiple communications and targets. The two models are meant to be applied, individually or together, at various times to attain each individual attack goal [39]. The trust model describes how the social engineer establishes a trustworthy relationship with the target, whilst the attack model describes how a social engineer performs an information gathering attack. The attack model is limited to four techniques: deception, manipulation, persuasion and influence. In the attack model the social engineer is only able to use one of these techniques. Furthermore, after the technique has been performed, the attack model feeds into the trust model where the aim is to build a trustworthy relationship.

These models are problematic because not all SE attacks require a continuous relationship since there is not always the need to build a trustworthy relationship with the target. A social engineer generally uses a combination of compliance principles and techniques to perform a single SE attack.

3.3   Ivaturi and Janczewski

Ivaturi & Janczewski [40] classify an SE attack to be either *person-person* or to be *person-person via media*. *Person-person* is when there is direct communication involving a human, whereas *person-person via media* involves some medium used to communicate. The medium can be text, voice or video. Person-person attacks involve impersonation. Different techniques are described.

This taxonomy contains a well-defined structure for different SE techniques, as well as the types of attacks in which they are used. It is very similar to the structure of the direct communication part of our model, as further on proposed in section 4.1. Their study only focuses on direct communication and does not further elaborate on a scenario where indirect communication can be used for an SE attack.

3.4   Mohd et al.

Mohd et al. [41] classify an SE attack as being either human-based or technical-based. Human-based attacks apply some techniques that are combined to form an attack, such as "in person" and "simple persuasion". The one technique cannot be used without the other. The items they regard as types of attacks are techniques that form a single attack, rather than being used separately as individual attacks.

Their technical-based attacks are mediums used within an SE attack such as "Email, Software, Web sites". Another example is "Denial of Service" which is not an SE attack; it is an attack on a service and brings down a system instead of extracting information from it. The latter effect is the aim of an SE attack.

In summary, the Modh et al. model describes techniques used in SE attacks instead of depicting an SE attack as a whole.

3.5   Tetri and Vuorinen

Tetri & Vuorinen [42] studied several papers on SE and critically analysed them in order to present an overview of SE. They defined three main dimensions of SE: persuasion, fabrication and data gathering.

Persuasion involves getting someone to comply with an inappropriate request. The paper identifies two features of persuasion: *Direct interaction* and *active engagement between the intruder and the target* [42]. Fabrication involves techniques such as impersonation and using a false identification document to deceive victims into thinking the attacker is someone else. Data gathering is the process of gaining information from the target.

The authors of this paper agree with Tetri & Vuorinen's description of persuasion although it can be seen as a compliance principle from a psychological perspective. The definitions of fabrication and data gathering on the other hand, are techniques aimed at aiding an SE attack rather than being a phase of an SE attack.

The authors take these taxonomies into account and attempt to improve on these ideas by identifying three different subcategories of an SE attack, as well as, to develop a structured SE attack ontological model. The next section firstly proposes the Social Engineering Attack Classification and then proposes an ontological model for an SE attack.

4   Ontological Model

In this section the authors motivate and present an ontological model for SE. Subsection 4.1 discusses a classification of an SE attack based on the type of communication that is employed. In subsection 4.2 a broader view is provided which defines the different parts of an SE attack.

4.1   Social Engineering Attack Classification

An SE attack, as depicted in Figure1, can be divided into two main categories: An indirect attack and a direct attack.

An indirect attack refers to an incident where a third party medium is used as a way of communicating. Third party mediums typically include physical mediums such as flash drives, pamphlets or other mediums, such as web pages. Communication occurs through third party mediums when a medium is accessed by a target, without direct interaction with the social engineer.

A direct attack is an incident where two or more people are involved in a direct conversation. This conversation can either be one-sided or two-sided. Due to this, this type of attack is further classified into two ways of communicating: Bidirectional or unidirectional communication.

Bidirectional communication is when two or more parties take part in the conversation, in other words, a two-way conversation occurs. Each party consists of an individual, a group of individuals or an organisation. A popular example of an attack in this category is an impersonation attack, where the social engineer impersonates the target in order to gain access to something which the target has access to.

Unidirectional communication is a one-sided conversation where the social engineer communicates with the target, but the target has no means to communicate back with the social engineer. This is normally done through some communication medium such as bulk e-mails or short message service (SMS). An example of a popular attack in this category is an e-mail phishing attack sent from the attacker to the target.

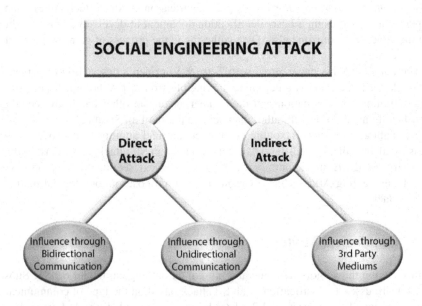

Fig. 1. Social Engineering Attack Classification

The rest of this subsection explains the different categories, bidirectional communication, unidirectional communication and indirect communication, in more detail with an example of each. Each example discusses the various parts of an SE attack, as defined in section 2: a social engineer, a target, a medium, a goal, one or more compliance principles and one or more techniques. Compliance principles are principles used by the attacker, aided by different techniques, in order to persuade the target, through some medium, to comply with a request.

Bidirectional communication (Figure 2) is defined as a two-way conversation between two people. In the bidirectional communication category, the social engineer can either be an individual or a group of individuals. The target of the attack can be an individual or an organisation. The mediums that are frequently used for bidirectional communication are e-mail messages, face-to-face conversations or telephone conversations. Any compliance principle, technique and goal can be used in combination with a bidirectional communication medium.

An example of an SE attack that uses *bidirectional communication* is one where a social engineer attempts to influence a call centre agent into divulging sensitive information regarding a specific client. In this example, both the attacker and the target are *individuals*. *Pretexting* is used as the technique for this attack because the social engineer impersonates the client whose information the social engineer wishes to obtain. The compliance principle used in this example is *authority*, because the client impersonated by the social engineer acts as if he or she has authorised access to the information. The goal of the attack is to gain *unauthorised access* to the client's sensitive information.

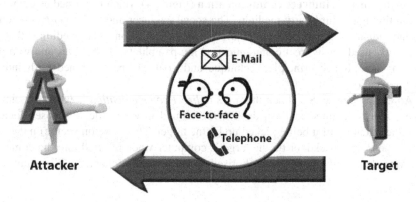

Fig. 2. Bidirectional Communication

Unidirectional communication (Figure 3) is very similar to bidirectional communication, except that the conversation only occurs in one direction: From the social engineer to the target. The social engineer and the target can either be an individual, a group of individuals or an organisation. The mediums that are frequently used for unidirectional communication are one-way text messages, e-mails or paper mail messages. Any compliance principle, technique and goal can be used in combination with unidirectional communication.

An example of an SE attack that uses *unidirectional communication* is an e-mail phishing attack where the target places an online order at some online store and waits for delivery of the item. The phishing e-mail is masked as an e-mail from the online store informing the target that a limited offer is available relating to the order. The target recognises the link between the e-mail and his order and clicks on the infected link. The target is specifically chosen. *Phishing* is the SE technique used for this attack and *scarcity* is the compliance principle. Since the e-mail states that it is a limited offer, the target feels that he or she has to explore this limited opportunity before it becomes unavailable. The infected link gives the social engineer *unauthorised access* to the target's computer.

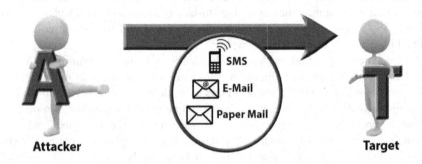

Fig. 3. Unidirectional Communication

Finally, there is **indirect communication** (Figure 4) which is defined as communication through a third party medium. The social engineer and the target can be either an individual, a group of individuals or an organisation. The mediums that are frequently used for indirect communication are pamphlets, flash drives and web pages. Any compliance principle, technique and goal can be combined with indirect communication.

An example of an SE attack that uses *indirect communication* is when a social engineer leaves an infected flash drive lying around in a specifically chosen location with the intention of it being picked up by the target. The infection vector on the flash drive opens up a backdoor on the target's computer when inserted into the computer, allowing the social engineer unauthorised access to the computer. In this example the

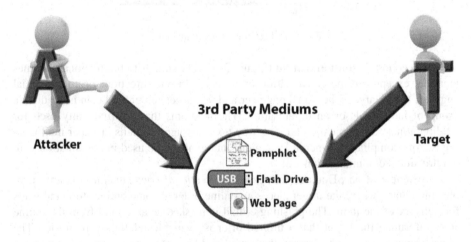

Fig. 4. Indirect Communication via 3rd Party Medium

social engineer, as well as the target, are *individuals*. The technique used for this attack is known as *baiting* because a physical object is left in visible view of a target. The success of the attack relies on the curiosity level of the target. The compliance principle used is *social validation*, which states that someone is more willing to comply if they are performing some action they believe to conform to a social norm. The target may feel socially obliged to attempt to find the owner of the lost flash drive. This leads to the target plugging the flash drive into his or her computer which then activates the backdoor and unknowingly grants access to the social engineer. The goal of the attack is *unauthorised access* to the target's computer.

4.2   Social Engineering Attack Ontological Model

The model that is presented in this section has been compiled from various other taxonomies and the authors' classification of SE attacks. The purpose of this ontological model is not just to define the domain but also to form the foundation for an ontology for SE attacks. Our argument is that a taxonomy is too limited to define SE and SE attacks sufficiently. An ontological model provides additional structure to fully define this domain. According to Van Rees (2003), a taxonomy is a hierarchical structure to aid the process of classifying information, while an ontology is a well-defined set of definitions that create a taxonomy of classes and the relationships between them. Van Rees also states that "an ontology resembles both a kind of taxonomy-plus-definitions and a kind of knowledge representation language." [43].

It is clear from the other taxonomies discussed previously, that their authors tend to mix techniques, compliance principles, mediums and phases of an attack. Our ontological model represents each entity of an attack as well as the relationships between entities.

An ontology allows a formal, encoded description of a domain: All the relevant entities, their attributes and their inter-relationships can be defined and represented in a machine-readable model. Gruber (1993) defines an ontology as "formal, explicit specification of a shared conceptualisation." [44]. Noy and McGuinness define an ontology as: "...a common vocabulary for researchers who need to share information in a domain ...includes machine-interpretable definitions of basic concepts in the domain and relations among them." [45]. Ontologies have automated reasoning facilities that enable the derivation of new information from the facts contained in an ontology.

The model is based on our definition of an SE attack as depicted in Figure 5. We defined a *Social Engineering attack* (Section 2) to have:

- one Social Engineer;
- one Target;
- one or more Compliance Principles;
- one or more Techniques;
- one Medium; and
- one Goal.

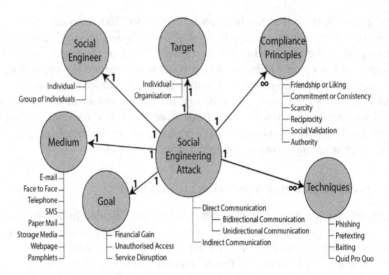

Fig. 5. An Ontological Model of a Social Engineering attack

Each of the six entities is represented as a different class in the model. The subclasses of each class are shown in Figure 5. For example, the *Social Engineering Attack* class has two subclasses: *Direct Communication* and *Indirect Communication*. In turn *Direct Communication* has two subclasses: *Bidirectional Communication* and *Unidirectional Communication*.

The model, in its current state, provides the building blocks to further expand the model into a full ontology. As a future task, when the ontology is built from this model, additional relationships between these classes can be developed and described in detail. One example of a relationship between two classes is *performsAttack* between the *Social Engineer* class and the *Target* class. Our model partially represents our definition of *Social Engineer* (Section 2): *An individual or group who performs an act of Social Engineering.* The latter part of the definition requires representation of the verb *social engineer* and will be presented in the ontology as the relation *performsAttack*.

Further development of the ontology will be performed as future research.

5   Conclusion

Organisations usually employ advanced technical security measures to minimise opportunities for unauthorised individuals, however, every organisation has employees who are likely to be susceptible to SE attacks. As electronic computing devices becomes more prevalent, the group of individuals who can be targeted by Social Engineering is increasingly significantly. These reasons motivate why SE is such an important field of research. Although SE is a discipline that enjoys increasing attention, it is still not well defined. This paper provides an overview of several definitions from the literature and shows that many researchers define SE to suit their specific topic of research.

In order for the field of Social Engineering to mature, it is required to have commonly accepted domain definitions. Based on all of the definitions and existing taxonomies that have been examined, this paper proposes both a Social Engineering Attack Classification as well as a Social Engineering Attack Ontological Model.

The Social Engineering Attack Classification divides an SE attack into two classes: a direct attack and an indirect attack. The direct attack is further subdivided into an attack utilising bidirectional communication and an attack utilising unidirectional communication. The indirect attack class is further defined as an attack utilising third party mediums as a communication platform.

The Social Engineering Attack Ontological Model expands on the Social Engineering Attack Classification by providing six entities of an attack as well as the relationships between these entities. This model currently represents the definition of an SE attack and partially represents the definition of a social engineer.

In summary, this paper is able to provide definitions for several terms within the domain of Social Engineering. The most important of these terms are Social Engineering and Social Engineering attack. The first one is defined as: *The science of using social interaction as a means to persuade an individual or an organisation to comply with a specific request from an attacker where either the social interaction, the persuasion or the request involves a computer-related entity.* The latter term is defined as: *A Social Engineering attack employs either direct communication or indirect communication, and has a social engineer, a target, a medium, a goal, one or more compliance principles and one or more techniques.*

Additional work is required to fully develop the ontological model. This includes the expansion of classes as well as the relationships between classes. In future work it is also required to represent the different phases of an SE attack.

References

1. Winkler, I.S., Dealy, B.: Information security technology?.don't rely on it: A case study in social engineering. In: Proceedings of the 5th Conference on USENIX UNIX Security Symposium, SSYM 1995, Berkeley, CA, USA, vol. 5, p. 1. USENIX Association (1995)
2. Mitnick, K.D., Simon, W.L.: The art of deception: controlling the human element of security. Wiley Publishing, Indianapolis (2002)
3. Uschold, M., Gruninger, M.: Ontologies and semantics for seamless connectivity. ACM Special Interest Group on Management of Data 33(4), 58–64 (2004)
4. Quann, J., Belford, P.: The hack attack - increasing computer system awareness of vulnerability threats. In: 3rd Applying Technology to Systems; Aerospace Computer Security Conference, United States, American Institute of Aeronautics and Astronautics, pp. 155–157 (December 1987)
5. Kluepfel, H.: Foiling the wiley hacker: more than analysis and containment. In: Proceedings of the 1989 International Carnahan Conference on Security Technology, pp. 15–21 (1989)

6. Kluepfel, H.: In search of the cuckoo's nest [computer security]. In: Proceedings of the 25th Annual 1991 IEEE International Carnahan Conference on Security Technology, pp. 181–191 (1991)

7. Goldstein, E.: The Best of 2600, Collector's Edition: A Hacker Odyssey. Wiley Publishing, Inc., Indianapolis (2009)

8. Voyager: Janitor privileges. 2600: The Hacker Quarterly 11(4), 36–36 (Winter 1994)

9. Thornburgh, T.: Social engineering: the "dark art". In: Proceedings of the 1st Annual Conference on Information Security Curriculum Development, InfoSecCD 2004, pp. 133–135. ACM, New York (2004)

10. Nohlberg, M.: Securing Information Assets: Understanding, Measuring and Protecting against Social Engineering Attacks. PhD thesis, Stockholm University (2008)

11. Abraham, S., Chengalur-Smith, I.: An overview of social engineering malware: Trends, tactics, and implications. Technology in Society 32(3), 183–196 (2010)

12. Erbschloe, M.: Trojans, worms, and spyware: a computer security professional's guide to malicious code. Butterworth-Heinemann (2004)

13. Boshmaf, Y., Muslukhov, I., Beznosov, K., Ripeanu, M.: The socialbot network: when bots socialize for fame and money. In: Proceedings of the 27th Annual Computer Security Applications Conference, ACSAC 2011, pp. 93–102. ACM, New York (2011)

14. Boshmaf, Y., Muslukhov, I., Beznosov, K., Ripeanu, M.: Design and analysis of a social botnet. Computer Networks 57(2), 556–578 (2013), Botnet Activity: Analysis, Detection and Shutdown

15. Kvedar, D., Nettis, M., Fulton, S.P.: The use of formal social engineering techniques to identify weaknesses during a computer vulnerability competition. Journal of Computing Sciences in Colleges 26(2), 80–87 (2010)

16. McDowell, M.: Cyber security tip st04-0141, avoiding social engineering and phishing attacks. Technical report, United States Computer Emergency Readiness Team (February 2013)

17. Cruz, J.A.A.: Social engineering and awareness training. Technical report, Walsh College (2010)

18. Culpepper, A.M.: Effectiveness of using red teams to identify maritime security vulnerabilities to terrorist attack. Master's thesis, Naval Postgraduate School, Monterey, California (September 2004)

19. Mills, D.: Analysis of a social engineering threat to information security exacerbated by vulnerabilities exposed through the inherent nature of social networking websites. In: 2009 Information Security Curriculum Development Conference, InfoSecCD 2009, pp. 139–141. ACM, New York (2009)

20. Doctor, Q., Dulaney, E., Skandier, T.: CompTIA A+ Complete Study Guide. Wiley Publishing, Indianappolis (2007)

21. Hamill, J., Deckro, R.F., Kloeber Jr., J.M.: Evaluating information assurance strategies. Decision Support Systems 39(3), 463–484 (2005)

22. Joint Chiefs of Staff: Information assurance: Legal, regulatory, policy and organizational legal, regulatory, policy and organizational considerations. Technical Report Fourth Edition, Department of Defense, Pentagon, Washington (August 1999)

23. Hamill, J.T.: Modeling information assurance: A value focused thinking approach. Master's thesis, Air Force Institute of Technology, Wright-Patterson Air Force Base, Ohio (March 2000)

24. Braverman, M.: Behavioural modelling of social engineering-based malicious software. In: Virus Bulletin Conf. (2006)

25. Åhlfeldt, R.M., Backlund, P., Wangler, B., Söderström, E.: Security issues in health care process integration? a research-in-progress report. In: EMOI-INTEROP (2005)
26. Granger, S.: Social engineering fundamentals, part i: Hacker tactics (December 2001)
27. Schoeman, A., Irwin, B., Richter, J.: Social recruiting: a next generation social engineering attack. In: Uses in Warfare and the Safeguarding of Peace (2012)
28. Hadnagy, C.: Social Engineering: The Art of Human Hacking. Wiley Publishing, Inc. (2010)
29. Espinhara, J., Albuquerque, U.: Using online activity as digital fingerprints to create a better spear phisher. Technical report, Trustwave SpiderLabs (2013)
30. Nemati, H.: Pervasive Information Security and Privacy Developments: Trends and Advancements, 1st edn. Information Science Reference (July 2010)
31. McQuade III, S.C.: Understanding and managing cybercrime. Prentice Hall, Boston (2006)
32. Spinapolice, M.: Mitigating the risk of social engineering attacks. Master's thesis, Rochester Institute of Technology B. Thomas Golisano College (2011)
33. Lenkart, J.J.: The vulnerability of social networking media and the insider threat new eyes for bad guys. Master's thesis, Naval Postgraduate School, Monterey, California (2011)
34. Bezuidenhout, M., Mouton, F., Venter, H.: Social engineering attack detection model: Seadm. In: Information Security for South Africa, pp. 1–8 (2010)
35. Mouton, F., Malan, M., Venter, H.: Development of cognitive functioning psychological measures for the seadm. In: Human Aspects of Information Security & Assurance (2012)
36. Mouton, F., Malan, M.M., Venter, H.S.: Social engineering from a normative ethics perspective. In: Information Security for South Africa, pp. 1–8 (2013)
37. Kingsley Ezechi, A.: Detecting and combating malware. Master's thesis, University of Debrecen, Hungary (June 2011)
38. Harley, D.: Re-floating the titanic: Dealing with social engineering attacks. In: European Institute for Computer Antivirus Research (1998)
39. Laribee, L.: Development of methodical social engineering taxonomy project. Msc, Naval Postgraduate School, Monterey, California (June 2006)
40. Ivaturi, K., Janczewski, L.: A taxonomy for social engineering attacks. In: Grant, G. (ed.) International Conference on Information Resources Management, Centre for Information Technology, Organizations, and People (June 2011)
41. Mohd Foozy, F., Ahmad, R., Abdollah, M., Yusof, R., Mas'ud, M.: Generic taxonomy of social engineering attack. In: Malaysian Technical Universities International Conference on Engineering & Technology, Batu Pahat, Johor (November 2011)
42. Tetri, P., Vuorinen, J.: Dissecting social engineering. Behaviour & Information Technology 32(10), 1014–1023 (2013)
43. Van Rees, R.: Clarity in the usage of the terms ontology, taxonomy and classification. CIB REPORT 284(432), 1–8 (2003)
44. Gruber, T.R.: A translation approach to portable ontology specifications. Knowledge Acquisition - Special Issue: Current Issues in Knowledge Modeling 5(2), 199–220 (1993)
45. Noy, N.F., McGuinness, D.L.: Ontology development 101: A guide to creating your first ontology. Technical report ksl-01-05, Stanford Knowledge Systems Laboratory (March 2001)

Human Perception of the Measurement of a Network Attack Taxonomy in Near Real-Time

Renier van Heerden[1], Mercia M. Malan[2], Francois Mouton[1], and Barry Irwin[3]

[1] Defence Peace Safety & Security, Council for Industrial and Scientific Research,
Pretoria, South Africa
rvheerden@csir.co.za, moutonf@gmail.com
[2] University of Pretoria, Information and Computer Security Architecture Research Group,
Pretoria, South Africa
malan747@gmail.com
[3] University of Rhodes, Computer Science Department, Grahamstown, South Africa
b.irwin@ru.ac.za

Abstract. This paper investigates how the measurement of a network attack taxonomy can be related to human perception. Network attacks do not have a time limitation, but the earlier its detected, the more damage can be prevented and the more preventative actions can be taken. This paper evaluate how elements of network attacks can be measured in near real-time(60 seconds). The taxonomy we use was developed by van Heerden et al (2012) with over 100 classes. These classes present the attack and defenders point of view. The degree to which each class can be quantified or measured is determined by investigating the accuracy of various assessment methods. We classify each class as either defined, high, low or not quantifiable. For example, it may not be possible to determine the instigator of an attack (Aggressor), but only that the attack has been launched by a Hacker (Actor). Some classes can only be quantified with a low confidence or not at all in a sort (near real-time) time. The IP address of an attack can easily be faked thus reducing the confidence in the information obtained from it, and thus determining the origin of an attack with a low confidence. This determination itself is subjective. All the evaluations of the classes in this paper is subjective, but due to the very basic grouping (High, Low or Not Quantifiable) a subjective value can be used. The complexity of the taxonomy can be significantly reduced if classes with only a high perceptive accuracy is used.

Keywords: Network Attack, near real-time, Network Attack Taxonomy.

1 Introduction

Network attacks do not have a time limitation, but the earlier its detected, the more damage can be prevented and the more preventative actions can be taken.

This paper builds on a previous taxonomy, the taxonomy is used a base to measurement of a network attack taxonomy in near real-time. The taxonomy we use was

K.K. Kimppa et al. (Eds.): HCC11 2014, IFIP AICT 431, pp. 280–292, 2014.
© IFIP International Federation for Information Processing 2014

developed by van Heerden et al (2012) with over 100 classes. These classes present the attack and defenders point of view. The degree to which each class can be quantified or measured is determined by investigating the accuracy of various assessment methods.

We classify each class as either defined, high, low or not quantifiable. For example, it may not be possible to determine the instigator of an attack (Aggressor), but only that the attack has been launched by a Hacker (Actor). Some classes can only be quantified with a low confidence or not at all in a sort (near real-time) time. The IP address of an attack can easily be faked thus reducing the confidence in the information obtained from it, and thus determining the origin of an attack with a low confidence. This determination itself is subjective.

All the evaluations of the classes in this paper is subjective, but due to the very basic grouping (High, Low or Not Quantifiable) a subjective value can be used. The complexity of the taxonomy can be significantly reduced if classes with only a high perceptive accuracy is used. The taxonomy refers to both the view of the attacker and the defender with relation of network attacks, whereas other taxonomies concentrate on either attack or defend.

Table 1 is a recap the network attack taxonomy developed in van Heerden (2012) [1, 2].

Table 1. Taxonomy classes

Class	Description
Actor	The group or individual that is performing the action of an attack.This class points to the entity that physically performs the attack, not to the person instigating the attack.
Actor Location	The physical location, such as a country or a state, from where an attack was launched.
Aggressor	The mastermind behind the attack. This person, group or organisation can be the actor or can instruct the actor to attack a network. For example, Brenner suggested that France, Russia, Japan, China, Germany, Israel and South Korea are actively engaged in economic espionage by means of the Internet and computer network attacks [3, 4].
Asset	The non-personalised item that is under attack. This class distinguishes between different assets that can be attacked. Examples of assets are information stored as data, the system that uses computers or the network infrastructure itself.
Attack Goal	The goal that the Aggressor wants to achieve. The first four goals correspond with the traditional CIA$+$+ information security principles (Confidentiality, Availability, Integrity Authentication).
Attack Mechanism	The approach used in the attack. This approach refers to the methodology that was used in the attack. This class has over thirty sub-classes which describes some of the methodologies available.

Table 1. (*continued*)

Attack Scenario	The broad categories which attacks can belong to. Further explained below.
Automation Level	The degree that the attack can be programmed automatically beforehand compared to the amount of manual effort required during the attack.
Effects	The impact of an attack and are classified as four levels: Null, Minor, Major and Catastrophic. "Null" refers to no effect on the target, "Minor" to recoverable damage and "Major" to non-recoverable damage. "Catastrophic" refers to damage of such a nature that the target ceases to operate as an entity, for example the declaration of bankruptcy.
Motivation	The incentive for the attack.
Phase	The temporal stages of an attack. These temporal phases are developed by evaluating the most commonly used phases during an attack [5, 6].
Sabotage	The form of damage or loss that has been achieved by the attack and is classified as either physical, financial, virtual or reputational. *Physical* sabotage refers to physical damage to a device, *Financial* sabotage refers to monetary loss. *Virtual* sabotage occurs when computer resources are lost (such as processing, bandwidth or memory). *Reputational* loss is not a measurable, tangible loss but may result in other related problems for a company at a later stage.
Scope	The network type that is attacked and are further classified into three types: Corporate network, government network and private network. *Corporate networks* are networks controlled by private companies, *Government networks* are networks controlled by the government and *Private networks* are networks that serves one person in his/her private capacity.
Scope Size	The size of the network under attack. If the attack affects a large portion of the internet or multiple countries, the scope size is referred to as a *Global network*. A *Large network* represent large corporates or significant government networks such as state departments. There are no solid definitions that separate small, medium and large networks and thus the separation is a subjective judgement. *Single* size is used to present attacks on a single person or a single computer.
Target	The *Target* The physical devices targeted in the attack, such as a *Server, Personal computer, Network infrastructure* or *SCADA*.
Vulnerability	The methodology of the attack and denotes the weakness exploited in the attack.

The *Attack Scenario* class was originally developed by van Heerden (2012) [2, 1]. These scenarios are:

- Denial of Service,
- Industrial Espionage,
- Web Defacement,
- Unauthorised Data Access,
- Financial Theft,
- Industrial Sabotage,
- System Compromise,
- Cyber Warfare and
- Runaway Malware.

2   Taxonomy Quantification

Each of the classes and sub-classes can either be directly or indirectly quantified. They can also be defined by the system under attack's configuration. Some classes cannot be quantified in a near real-time environment. There are three levels of quantification. This paper describes in which of the three levels of quantification each class is classified when measured. Some classes are not measured but defined by the nature of the attack and thus an accuracy of the quantification is assigned to it. Four levels of accuracy are assigned: High, medium, low or not quantifiable.

Fenz et al states [7]:

"Since the threat probability or in influencing factors cannot be determined quantitatively, a qualitative rating is used in this approach. In contrast to a quantitative rating with which it is hardly possible to determine the occurrence of a certain threat with a 67% and not with a 68% chance, a qualitative rating (e.g.high, medium, and low)"

Since the accuracy of quantifying the classes are also defined, the researcher effectively uses three levels of qualitative ratings.

Each of the classes defined in Section 2 are investigated as to how they can be measured or quantified in near real-time. Some of the classes are quantified by definition, and do not require any sensors to determine their value and these classes are referred to as: Defined. For example, the target of an attack is not measured or quantified, but rather defined by the attack.

Some attacks are named after the target, such as the cases of the SCO and SpamHaus attacks. Some classes can not be measured in near real-time environment. These class's values only become apparent long after an attack and even then it is sometimes only speculation. For example, the *Aggressor* can not be determined in a near real-time environment and for some attacks the real power behind the attack is never determined or proven.

2.1   Actor Quantification

The *Group Actor* sub-class and its sub-classes, *Organised Criminal Group*, *Protest Group* and *Cyber Army*, can be quantified by their IP addresses. An IP address can be used to find the physical location of a *Group Actor*. Free and subscription geolocation databases exist which claim to be capable of identifying the physical location of any IP address worldwide and the lookup of IP addresses is thus considered a direct quantification. By utilising the gained IP location, the group that owns or rents the location can be determined. The *Group Actor* can be determined indirectly by using the IP address.

Shavitt studied the accuracy of geolocation databases and found that the results of most databases are similar, that the accuracy cannot be trusted [8]. Errors included wrongful estimation of distances and incorrect identification of the country. IP addresses can be spoofed, and intermediate computers located anywhere in the world can be used for attack.

For these reasons, using IP to locate the Group Actor is assigned a low accuracy. IP address location falls within the Network Layer.

The *Hacker* sub-class and its sub-classes *Script Kiddy* and *Skilled Hacker* can be quantified by looking at the pattern of an attack. Stoll [9] documented one of the first hacking attempts by a skilled hacker. It was determined that the hacker was extremely skilled by printing out all the keystrokes of the attack. Script Kiddies use standardised tools of which the characteristics (or fingerprint) are static and can be identified. For example, the pattern of standard Nmap scans can easily be identified [10]. By using an elaborate honeypot, the skill level of a *Hacker Actor* can also be determined [11]. Script Kiddies will attack the honeypot directly with standard tools such as Metasploit[1] with all the possible exploits, whereas skilled hackers will use more subtle techniques and only targeted exploits and also try to hide their origin [12].

The skill level of hackers can also be deduced by the consequences of their attacks. If the attack was successful in web defacement or a secure server was compromised, it can be assumed that a skilled hacker was involved. Tripwire[2] and other Host-based Intrusion Detection Systems (IDS's) can alert system administrators to compromises, although they can not prevent attacks. They notify administrators that some secure data has been accessed or modified.

For these reasons, the Hacker Actor can be measured indirectly, and the accuracy is low. Honeypot measurements fall within the Session Layer. Host-based IDS's work in the Application Layer.

Insider threats can be detected by internally-orientated honeypots or telescopes [13, 14]. These insider honeypots work according to the same principle as externally-orientated honeypots, but reside within a network and are not accessible from outside. Externally-orientated honeypots are connected to external networks and capture traffic from attackers from outside the scope of the defender's network. Insider honeypots can detect a *Normal User* but not an *Administrator*.

Administrators have access to most of the network. No network can be made safe against its own administrators, and thus administrators fall within the unmeasurable group whereas normal users can be measured directly. When such honeypots are triggered, the odds of it being an insider is low due to possible false positives or attackers

---

[1] http://www.metasploit.com/
[2] http://www.tripwire.org/

masquerading as insiders. As previously stated, Honeypot measurements fall within the Session Layer.

All the sub-classes for the *Actor* class have a low accuracy, thus is summary, the *Actor* class accuracy in defined as low.

2.2   Actor Location Quantification

The *Actor Location* class and its sub-classes can be measured similarly to the *Group Actor* sub-class by means of IP location. Only a single look-up in a geolocation database is required, thus it is considered to be directly measurable. The values from geolocation database are also considered unreliable, with Poese stating that these geolocation databases are accurate at a country level but not at a city level [15]. An alternative method to find the location of IP addresses is to use latency measurements [16]. Katz was able to achieve a medium error of 67 km in optimal circumstances. The same accuracy problems as stated for the *Group Actor* apply to the *Actor Location* sub-classes and thus the accuracy is considered to be low. As mentioned above, an IP address falls within the Network Layer.

2.3   Aggressor, Motivation, Effect and Sabotage Quantification

The *Aggressor* cannot be quantified in near real-time. In most cases the aggressor is only determined months after an attack. For example, it took a few months before the aggressor behind the Stuxnet attack was confirmed [17]. The aggressor and people behind most viruses is difficult if not impossible to obtain [18].

The *Aggressor* class and its sub-classes are considered as being not quantifiable. The same holds for the motivation of an aggressor, which can also not be determined in near real-time. The type of sabotage caused by an attack can only be calculated after the full impact of an attack is known, and thus can to be measured in real-time. The effects of an attack can only be quantified with a full investigation into the compromised systems and assessments of the damage done. This means that the *Aggressor*, *Effect*, *Motivation* and *Sabotage* class and its sub-classes cannot be measured in near real-time.

2.4   Asset Quantification

The *Access* and *System* sub-classes of the *Asset* class can be measured with automated testing scripts. These testing scripts simulate human requests at a very basic level, and can indicate when access to the system, or the system functionally have been altered. Stout stated that automated testing is critical to a quality website and his statement holds true for all servers [19]. The scripts directly measure access and the system's functionality, and the accuracy of these quantifications are regarded to be as high, on the Application layer.

The *Data* sub-class of *Asset* class can be quantified by host-based IDS. These sensors are capable of determining alterations to data. Typically, two main aspects of the data can be measured, namely unauthorised access or unauthorised manipulation of the data [20]. These quantification are direct and occur in the Application layer. Although there is a possibility for false alarms [21], these quantifications are considered to have a high accuracy.

The *Network* sub-class of the *Asset* class can be quantified indirectly by looking the networking performance of devices or testing whether systems in the network can communicate [22]. Communication errors, hardware breakdown or system misconfiguration can be possible reasons for disruption of communications. The accuracy of quantifying an attack on the network is regarded as high. Network communications are on the Network Layer.

All the sub-classes for *Asset* class have a high accuracy, and thus *Asset* class accuracy is defined as high.

2.5   Attack Goal Determination

The *Attack Goal* can be determined indirectly by finding the asset which is under attack. Similar to the *Data* sub-class of the *Asset* class, the *Destroy Data*, *Steal Data*, *Gain Control*, *Spread* and *Change Data* sub-classes can be determined by host-based IDS [20]. The *Disrupt* sub-class can be determined indirectly by looking at the type of attack that is launched on a honeypot or similarly to the *Network* sub-class of the *Asset* class, by monitoring network performance [20, 23].

The accuracy of determining the goal is considered to be high. These determinations occur in the Application layer, and on the Network layer if the disruption is with communication.

The *Gain Resources* sub-class of the *Attack Goal* class can be determined by intercepting communications that do not fit the normal profile. Strayer developed a system that identifies networks that support malicious traffic[3]. Thus malicious traffic bound for addresses listed in their system can be null-routed. The Finding Rogue Network project has since been discontinued, but similar work is done commercially by Lastline[4]. It can be determined if local systems are being used as a springboard for attacks on others. Since this determination depends on the accuracy of the identification of malicious networks, and the possibility of misconfigured networks looking like botnets, the determination of *Gain Control* are considered of low accuracy.

This determination uses IP addresses as references, thus it occurs in the Network Layer.

Since five out of the six sub-classes have a high accuracy, the *Attack Goal* class accuracy is defined as high.

2.6   Attack Mechanism Determination

The *Information Gathering* sub-class of the *Attack Mechanism* class can be indirectly measured by detecting scans. These scans can be detected by interpreting access logs or analysing network traffic [24]. Port scanning and vulnerability scan determination

---

[3] http://maliciousnetworks.org/
[4] http://www.lastline.com/

have a high accuracy rate. Port scanning is determined on the Network and Transport layers and have a high accuracy.

The *Brute Force, Escalation, Spoofing, Session Hijack* and *Buffer Overflow* sub-classes can be identified by network-based IDS and by looking at access logs. These are directly identified by matching known methods to observed events. These events are defined in the Application layer. The accuracy of identifying these attacks mechanisms are high.

The *Spear Phishing* and *Social Engineering* sub-classes can be identified by specially crafted traps that lure such attackers to a fake target [25, 26]. These traps operate in the Application layer. Due to the difficulty of detecting social engineering attacks, to determine that one of these attack mechanisms was used has a low confidence [27, 28, 29].

The *Network Based* sub-class can be identified indirectly by intercepting strange communications or by monitoring the amount of traffic on the system [30]. These strange communications can be occur in Data, Network or Session layers. Although it is difficult to distinguish between attacks and innocent network anomalies, it is simple to detect and thus the accuracy is high.

The *Malware* attack mechanism can be identified either on the OSI Application layer with Antivirus software, or in the OSI Network layer by IDS software [31]. Malware can be identified directly and the accuracy of the identification is high with a low false positive rate. False positive is when a classifier classifies some item as harmful incorrectly [32]. Malware that is not detectable is also a concern [31]. False negative refers to malware that is not detected. In Figure 1 the difference between False Negative and False Positive is shown. The detection of *Malware* has a high accuracy.

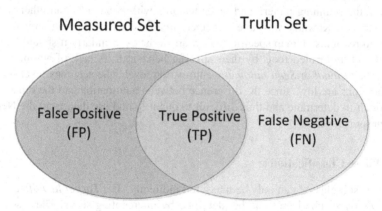

Fig. 1. The Difference between False Negative and False Positive

If a sub-system is abused, it can be measured simply by looking at at systems logs. The processing utilisation and disk usage can be measured on systems directly. Firewalls and some advanced routers can measure the network throughput, thus identifying bandwidth abuse. The detection of *System Abuse* has a high accuracy.

A *Web Application* such as a *SQL Injection* or a *Web Crawl* attack mechanism can be detected directly with specially crafted traps or logging of unusual web behaviour [33]. Error messages can also be used to detect *SQL Injection* attacks [34]. SQL queries can be used to identify safe request and then identity attacks by restricting the allowed queries [35]. Misuse of Web applications are detected in the Application layer and has a high accuracy level.

XSS Web Application attack mechanisms can be detected indirectly by comparing posted URL to black-listed sites [36], by identifying typical XSS coding patterns [37]. The detection and prevention of XSS attack are difficult because of incomplete implementations, inherent limitations, the complexity of development frameworks and the requirement for run-time compatibility [38]. The efficiency of this detection method is determined by the quality of the blacklist and accuracy level is low and is detected in the Presentation layer.

Denial-of-Service attack mechanisms can mostly be detected by filtering incoming network traffic [39]. Mirkovic presented a taxonomy in defences that can be used against DoS attacks, which includes: system security, protocol security, resource accounting, resource multiplication, pattern matching, anomaly detection, filtering, automated reconfiguring, rate limiting and agent identification [40]. The accuracy of detecting DoS attack mechanisms is high.

Since most of the sub-classes of the *Attack Mechanism* class have a high accuracy, the accuracy for the *Attack Mechanism* class is high.

2.7   Automation Level Quantification

The *Automatic* sub-class of the *Automation Level* class can be indirectly quantified by observing the scanning pattern and other features with honeypots and other scan detection sensors. Kuwatly was able to detect Nmap[5] scans by training their detection systems to recognise Nmap specific scan characteristics. Similarly it should be possible to detect automated tools by their specific behaviour. A lack of automation can point to the *Manual* or *Semi-automatic* automation level. The accuracy level for these quantifications are low, since the difference between automation and the other modes are difficult to determine and thus difficult to quantify and use data from the Network and Transport layers.

2.8   Phase Classification

The *Phase* sub-classed can only be measured indirectly. The *Target Identification* and *Reconnaissance* sub-classes can be identified by intercepting scans. These scans can be IP or Port based, or scans that crawl through web pages. The accuracy of determining that an attack is in the reconnaissance phase is high after a scan has been detected. These scans occur in the Network, Transport, or Session layers.

---

[5] http://nmap.org

The "Ramp-up" sub-class can be identified with honeypots or anomaly detectors that identify strange communications or attempts at obtaining unauthorised access. These measurements occur in the Application layer and have a medium accuracy.

The "Damage" sub-class is measured when the network, computers or systems stop working according to specifications. Host-based IDS can determine if the network is currently being damaged. It is difficult to determine if damage is being caused by an attack or by some other unrelated error, thus the accuracy is medium. Damage can be measured in the Network or Application Layers.

The "Residue" sub-class can be detected by communications similar to these in the Damage phase, but only on a limited scale. These measurements can also be influenced by other system errors and thus are considered to be of medium accuracy. Residue can be measured in the Network or Application Layers.

The "Post-Attack" sub-class can be measured by detecting unallocated communications after an attack. These are typically IP connections to and from unknown hosts at strange times. These measurements take place in the Network Layer. It is difficult to prove that the same attacker is snooping around again, thus these measurements are considered to be of low accuracy. Phase on average is of medium accuracy.

2.9   Scope and Scope Size Measurement

The target scope and the scope size are defined by the entity under attack. These classes represent physical attributes of the target, which can not be measured or quantified, but rather should be considered to be defined.

2.10   Target Monitoring

The *Target* class and its sub-classes can be monitored indirectly by observing which systems are not performing as expected.

The *Network Infrastructure* sub-class can be observed by monitoring network performance in the Network layer. Attacks that affect the *PC* sub-class can be observed with anti-virus software. Antivirus software monitor data in the Network, Session and Application layers. The *Server* sub-class can be monitored by heart-beat sensors or data integrity sensors [41]. These sensors monitor on the Application layer.

Industrial Equipment are monitored directly via their control software [42]. Industrial equipment can monitor communications in the Physical, Network and Application layers. Even though system problems or other errors can also lead to system failures, monitoring these classes are considered to be highly accurate.

2.11   Vulnerability Identification

The *Vulnerability* class and its sub-classes can be directly identified with a combination of IDS and honeypots [43]. Although IDS can have false positives (incorrectly identify attacks), their accuracy are considered to be high.

3 Conclusion

In Table 2, a summary of the required quantification is shown. This table lists all the classes with respect to quantification methodology and accuracy. Only five of the classes is considered quantified or measurable of high accuracy: *Asset, Target, Vulnerability, Attack Mechanism* and *Attack Goal*. Three classes are considered low: *Automation Level, Actor* and *Actor Location*. Four classed can not be measured or quantified in a near real-time environment: *Sabotage, Effect, Aggressor* and *Motivation*. The remaining two classes are defined: *Scope* and *Scope Size* and OSI layer within which the classes are quantified. The quantification are tabulated with respect to OSI layer and Accuracy level. By only considering which elements of the taxonomy can be measurement of a network attack taxonomy in near real-time. Thus by only this reduces elements are of use when looking at attacks in near-real time

Table 2. Summary of the Measurement Taxonomy

Class	Quantification	Accuracy
Actor	Indirect	Low
Actor Location	Direct	Low
Aggressor	Not Quantifiable	N/A
Asset	Direct	High
Attack Goal	Indirect	High
Attack Mechanism	Indirect	High
Automation Level	Indirect	Low
Effect	Not Quantifiable	N/A
Motivation	Not Quantifiable	N/A
Phase	Indirect	Medium
Sabotage	Not Quantifiable	N/A
Scope	Defined	N/A
Scope Size	Defined	N/A
Target	Indirect	High
Vulnerability	Direct	High

References

1. van Heerden, R., Pieterse, H., Irwin, B.: Mapping the most significant computer hacking events to a temporal computer attack model. In: Hercheui, M.D., Whitehouse, D., McIver Jr., W., Phahlamohlaka, J. (eds.) ICT Critical Infrastructures and Society. IFIP AICT, vol. 386, pp. 226–236. Springer, Heidelberg (2012)
2. van Heerden, R.P., Burke, I., Irwin, B.: Classifying network attack scenarios using an ontology. In: Proceedings of the 7th International Conference on Information-Warfare & Security (ICIW 2012), pp. 311–324. ACI (2012)
3. Joyal, P.: Industrial espionage today and information wars of tomorrow. In: 19th National Information Systems Security Conference, pp. 139–151 (1996)

4. Burstein, A.: Trade secrecy as an instrument of national security–rethinking the foundations of economic espionage. Arizona State Law Journal 41, 933–1167 (2009)
5. Grant, T., Venter, H., Eloff, J.: Simulating adversarial interactions between intruders and system administrators using ooda-rr. In: Proceedings of the 2007 Annual Research Conference of the South African Institute of Computer Scientists and Information Technologists on IT Research in Developing Countries, pp. 46–55. ACM (2007)
6. van Heerden, R., Leenen, L., Irwin, B., Burke, I.: A computer network attack taxonomy and ontology. International Journal of Cyber Warfare and Terrorism 3, 12–25 (2012)
7. Fenz, S., Neubauer, T.: How to determine threat probabilities using ontologies and bayesian networks. In: Proceedings of the 5th Annual Workshop on Cyber Security and Information Intelligence Research: Cyber Security and Information Intelligence Challenges and Strategies, p. 69. ACM (2009)
8. Shavitt, Y., Zilberman, N.: A geolocation databases study. IEEE Journal on Selected Areas in Communications 29(10), 2044–2056 (2011)
9. Stoll, C.: Tracking a spy through a maze of computer espionage, vol. 1. Doubleday (1989)
10. Ezzeldin, H.: Nmap detection and countermeasures. Online (March 2008) (accesed September 5, 2012)
11. Kibret, W.E.: Analyzing network security from a defense in depth perspective. Master's thesis, Department of Informatics University of Oslo (2011)
12. Yung, K.H.: Detecting long connection chains of interactive terminal sessions. In: Wespi, A., Vigna, G., Deri, L. (eds.) RAID 2002. LNCS, vol. 2516, pp. 1–16. Springer, Heidelberg (2002)
13. Spitzner, L.: Honeypots: Catching the insider threat. In: Proceedings of the 19th Annual Computer Security Applications Conference, pp. 170–179. IEEE (2003)
14. Myers, J., Grimaila, M., Mills, R.: Towards insider threat detection using web server logs. In: Proceedings of the 5th Annual Workshop on Cyber Security and Information Intelligence Research: Cyber Security and Information Intelligence Challenges and Strategies, pp. 54–58. ACM (2009)
15. Poese, I., Uhlig, S., Kaafar, M.A., Donnet, B., Gueye, B.: IP geolocation databases: unreliable? ACM SIGCOMM Computer Communication Review 41(2), 53–56 (2011)
16. Katz-Bassett, E., John, J.P., Krishnamurthy, A., Wetherall, D., Anderson, T., Chawathe, Y.: Towards ip geolocation using delay and topology measurements. In: Proceedings of the 6th ACM SIGCOMM Conference on Internet Measurement, pp. 71–84. ACM (2006)
17. Sanger, D.: Obama order sped up wave of cyberattacks against iran. Online (June 2012) (accessed August 24, 2012)
18. Shiffman, G., Gupta, R.: Crowdsourcing cyber security: a property rights view of exclusion and theft on the information commons. International Journal of the Commons 7(1), 93–112 (2013)
19. Stout, G.: Testing a website: Best practices. Technical report, Reveregroup (2001) (accessed January 2, 2013)
20. Lunt, T.F.: A survey of intrusion detection techniques. Computers & Security 12(4), 405–418 (1993)
21. Tjhai, G., Papadaki, M., Furnell, S., Clarke, N.: Investigating the problem of ids false alarms: An experimental study using snort. In: Jajodia, S., Samarati, P., Cimato, S. (eds.) Proceedings of the IFIP TC 11 23rd International Information Security Conference. IFIP, vol. 278, pp. 253–267. Springer, Boston (2008)
22. Hariri, S., Qu, G., Dharmagadda, T., Ramkishore, M., Raghavendra, C.S.: Impact analysis of faults and attacks in large-scale networks. IEEE Security & Privacy 1(5), 49–54 (2003)

23. Kuwatly, I., Sraj, M., Al Masri, Z., Artail, H.: A dynamic honeypot design for intrusion detection. In: IEEE International Conference on Pervasive Services (ICPS), pp. 95–104 (2004)
24. Bhuyan, M.H., Bhattacharyya, D., Kalita, J.: Surveying port scans and their detection methodologies. The Computer Journal 54(10), 1565–1581 (2011)
25. Merritt, D.: Spear phishing attack detection. Master's thesis, Air Force Institute of Technology (March 2011) (accessed January 1, 2013)
26. Mouton, F., Malan, M.M., Venter, H.S.: Social engineering from a normative ethics perspective. In: Information Security for South Africa, pp. 1–8 (2013)
27. Bezuidenhout, M., Mouton, F., Venter, H.: Social engineering attack detection model: Seadm. In: Information Security for South Africa, pp. 1–8 (2010)
28. Mouton, F., Malan, M., Venter, H.: Development of cognitive functioning psychological measures for the seadm. In: Human Aspects of Information Security & Assurance (2012)
29. Mouton, F., Leenen, L., Malan, M.M., Venter, H.S.: Towards an ontological model defining the social engineering domain. In: 11th Human Choice and Computers International Conference, Turku, Finland (July 2014)
30. Heberlein, L.T., Dias, G.V., Levitt, K.N., Mukherjee, B., Wood, J., Wolber, D.: A network security monitor. In: Proceedings of Computer Society Symposium on Research in Security and Privacy, pp. 296–304. IEEE (1990)
31. Christodorescu, M., Jha, S.: Testing malware detectors. ACM SIGSOFT Software Engineering Notes 29(4), 34–44 (2004)
32. Owen, D.: What is a false positive and why are false positives a problem? Online (May 2010) (accessed November 21, 2012)
33. Manmadhan, S., Manesh, T.: A method of detecting sql injection attack to secure web applications. International Journal of Distributed and Parallel Systems 3, 1–8 (2012)
34. Ciampa, A., Visaggio, C.A., Di Penta, M.: A heuristic-based approach for detecting sql-injection vulnerabilities in web applications. In: Proceedings of the 2010 ICSE Workshop on Software Engineering for Secure Systems, pp. 43–49. ACM (2010)
35. Win, W., Htun, H.H.: A simple and efficient framework for detection of sql injection attack. International Journal of Computer & Communication Engineering Research 1(2), 26–30 (2013)
36. Jim, T., Swamy, N., Hicks, M.: Defeating script injection attacks with browser-enforced embedded policies. In: Proceedings of the 16th International Conference on World Wide Web, pp. 601–610. ACM (2007)
37. Scholte, T., Robertson, W., Balzarotti, D., Kirda, E.: An empirical analysis of input validation mechanisms in web applications and languages. In: Proceedings of the 27th Annual ACM Symposium on Applied Computing, pp. 1419–1426. ACM (2012)
38. Rao, T.: Defending against web vulnerabilities and cross-site scripting. Journal of Global Research in Computer Science 3(5), 61–64 (2012)
39. Karig, D., Lee, R.: Remote denial of service attacks and countermeasures. Technical Report CE-L2001-002, Princeton University Department of Electrical Engineering (October 2001) (accessed January 1, 2013)
40. Mirkovic, J., Reiher, P.: A taxonomy of ddos attack and ddos defense mechanisms. ACM SIGCOMM Computer Communication Review 34(2), 39–53 (2004)
41. Bhide, A., Elnozahy, E.N., Morgan, S.P.: A highly available network file server. In: Proceedings of the 1991 USENIX Winter Conference, pp. 199–205. Citeseer (1991)
42. Yang, D., Usynin, A., Hines, J.W.: Anomaly-based intrusion detection for scada systems. In: 5th International Topical Meeting on Nuclear Plant Instrumentation, Control and Human Machine Interface Technologies (NPIC & HMIT 2005), pp. 12–16 (2006)
43. Gula, R.: Correlating ids alerts with vulnerability information. Technical Report Revision 4, Tenable Network Security (May 2011)

Proposed Model for a Cybersecurity Centre of Innovation for South Africa

Joey Jansen van Vuuren, Marthie Grobler, Louise Leenen, and Jackie Phahlamohlaka

DPSS, CSIR, Pretoria, South Africa
{jjvvuuren,mgrobler1,lleenen,jphahlamohlaka}@csir.co.za

Abstract. Most communications in the new era are dependent on Information and Communication Technology (ICT). In addition, infrastructure is becoming increasingly interconnected. This not only makes lives easier, but also leaves technology users more vulnerable. Cybercrime, digital espionage and other cyber disturbances dictate the news reports on a daily basis. In general, cyber-attacks are no longer confined to small-scale rogue hackers. Cyber-attacks are now a part of organised crime and the underground economy, posing a real threat to critical infrastructure; possibly with state actors driving these actions. The responsibility to protect ICT stretches beyond individual companies, sectors and even beyond nations. The authors of this paper propose a Cybersecurity Centre Of Innovation (CCOI) as a central point for the South African government, business and academia to create a secure cyber space for the country: a cyber space without crime that is resilient and resistant to disruptions; a cyber space that promotes innovation, helps the economy and enhances national security. The key driver of the proposed CCOI is collaboration; solutions to cyber risks require a combined approach. This paper describes the organisational structure, functions, activities and benefits of a CCOI.

Keywords: Cybersecurity, South Africa, Centre of Innovation, national security.

1 Introduction

The increase in African broadband access has had a significant impact on Internet access in South Africa. More rural communities are becoming integrated into the global village due to increased hardware and software corporate donations, the proliferation of mobile Internet devices and government programmes aimed at bridging the digital divide through major broadband expansion projects. These measures facilitate the rapid growth in the number of South African Internet citizens through desktop or laptop computers, iPads and mobile phones. South Africa currently has a greater exposure to cyber threats than before the significant increase in broadband availability in 2009 (Jansen van Vuuren et al. 2010); however, a large percentage of the population have not received adequate training in cybersecurity awareness, nor regular and sustained exposure to technological devices and broadband Internet access. An additional threat is that South Africa in many ways serves as the Internet entry point to the African continent and could therefore be used as a central point for launching cyber

K.K. Kimppa et al. (Eds.): HCC11 2014, IFIP AICT 431, pp. 293–306, 2014.

warfare type attacks on the rest of the world. Cybersecurity has therefore been identi-fied as a critical component contributing towards National Security in South Africa. (Jansen van Vuuren et al. 2009).

A particularly serious dimension of the cyber domain is that attacks and crimes may be orchestrated from anywhere in the world. Many countries do not have effective laws to deal with cyber crime, and there are not sufficient international col-laboration and standards in place yet to deal with the complexity of these crimes and attacks.

The next section provides a motivation for the establishment of a South African Cybersecurity Centre of Innovation.

2   Motivation

South Africa has largely kept up with the global ICT trends and usage. While overall Internet penetration is still fairly low, in most provinces less than 10% (StatsSA 2012), the use of Internet today is essential for government, business and organisa-tions. Further ICT development in South Africa, such as increased penetration of broad bandwidth Internet access, will lead to an exponential increase in risks as in-adequate user experience, awareness and sophistication lead to increased vulnerability to cyber threats, even when counter measures exist (this holds at individual, organisa-tion and government level).

While South Africa has not had a major cyber-attack similar to recent attacks on the United States, Estonia, Korea, the United Kingdom, Iran and Georgia, evidence points to the real possibility of an attack. Information from the South African Police Service and other sources indicate the existence of botnets (controllable malware clandestinely installed on a computer), as well as botnet control servers on South African networks. In general, these risks and threats cause a lack of confidentiality, integrity and availability of information and ICT systems belonging to government, business and citizens. Although technology is not the only defence, when threats spread within seconds they can no longer be dealt with through human intervention - technology is required to implement resilient network and service infrastructures that can mitigate against such threats. The nature of ICT systems makes it possible for a single incident to affect all systems that are connected in the same network. It is there-fore not sufficient for an individual firm or government to work in solo on resolving these incidents.

Currently, the majority of Internet users in South Africa have access to the Internet from their workplaces or via their mobile phones (Jansen van Vuuren et al. 2012). These developments indicate that South Africans are becoming more active online. In addition, an online environment has no border control such as employed in physical borders. There is no police force to guard against those entering the country online. This means that everyone who goes online is on his/her own regarding malicious and criminal activities. Users cannot protect themselves adequately from these incidents. The current situation in South Africa is that each role player in the ICT industry has their own response mechanism, of which most are not congruent with their clients, neighbours and competitors. While there is significant cyber security expertise in

South Africa, the country is at risk because there is neither a national understanding nor a coherent action plan in terms of addressing cybercrime in South Africa.

In this paper the authors argue that the establishment of a Cybersecurity Centre of Innovation (CCOI) should rectify this situation. The aim of CCOI is to offer a platform for collaboration of all entities that can contribute to a secure cyberspace for South Africa.

Section 3 gives an overview of similar initiatives on other countries. In Section 4 the authors give an outline of the structure, function activities, opportunities and benefits of a CCOI. The paper is concluded in Section 5.

3 Similar Initiatives

A number of international cyber security innovation initiatives have been launched. This section provides an overview of some of these initiatives which serve as input to the Cybersecurity Centre of Innovation.

3.1 Advanced Cyber Security Center (ACSC)

ASCS is a not-for-profit consortium that was launched and supported by Mass Insight Global Partnerships. From its offices at MITRE in Bedford, Massachusetts, the Advanced Cyber Security Center uses the advantage of New England's unparalleled academic, industrial and research resources to develop next-generation solutions and strategies for protecting the nation's public and private IT infrastructure. The centre focuses on sharing cyber threat information, the development of innovative ways to address the most advanced cyber threats in next-generation cybersecurity research and development, as well as creating education programmes that will address the shortfall in cyber talent (ASCS 2013). The centre also functions as a cybersecurity operations centre (MITRE Corporation n.d.).

The centre has three key initiatives:

- Information sharing between expert practitioners and researchers to conduct threat analysis; identification of new threat indicators and the sharing of best practices under a Non-Disclosure Agreement. A cyber portal is used to share sensitive real-time threat information, building on the trust established at the "in person" sessions.
- Research and development, and education where cybersecurity solutions are developed to address cybersecurity gaps. Provision of graduate education opportunities for new talent in the cybersecurity field.
- Development of policies for federal legislation and the establishment of ASCS as best practice laboratory.

3.2 NexGen Cyber Innovation and Technology Center

The NexGen Cyber Innovation and Technology Center is aimed at preserving and protecting Lockheed Martin customer missions and addresses the greater cybersecurity challenges worldwide. It is a world-class centre designed for cyber research and development, customer and partner collaboration and innovation. At the centre, Lockheed Martin and partner technologies are integrated to create rapid prototypes to speed the innovation of solution delivery and provide seamless security. Through this meshing of innovation, technology and talent, Lockheed Martin and its partners work to solve the most difficult cyber challenges and help customers to define their own solutions (Lockheed Martin 2013).

The centre is fully equipped for live cyber technology exercises and demonstrations to help customers integrate solutions and test them in environments that are representative of their missions. The centre is the anchor point for a new Global Cyber Innovation range, enabling safe testing in both simulated and real world environments for the development of integrated cyber solutions. Some of the centre's key features include:

- Seven collaboration areas.
- A Global Cyber range.
- Cloud computing platforms.
- A green IT data center (Lockheed Martin 2013).

3.3   Cyber Innovation Centre (CIC)

The CIC is a not-for-profit corporation located in Bossier City, Louisiana that has been established to meet growing cyber demands by promoting research, education, and technological innovation and transfer of knowledge with strategic alliances between governmental agencies, private industry and academic institutions. In order to achieve this they partner with the United States government (National Security Agency and Department of Homeland Security), industry, research and academia. The CIC uses their National Integrated Cyber Education Research Center (NICERC) to create a knowledge-based workforce and to do academic outreach.

The CIC goals are to:

- Stimulate innovation-based economic growth through strategic partnerships.
- Develop a knowledge-based workforce.
- Foster collaboration and serve as a conduit for governmental agencies, private industries and academic institutions to share ideas and advance research.
- Build the necessary critical infrastructure that will attract federal programs to the area (Cyber Innovation Centre 2013).

3.4   Centre for Cyber Security Sciences (CCySS)

The CCySS in the United Kingdom was created in early 2011. It is based on the work done by research groups within the City University of London's School of Engineering and Mathematical Sciences, the School of Informatics and the Cass Business School (City University London n.d.). The Centre is invaluable through its combination of expertise in reliability, safety and security in audit and risk management. CCySS focuses its work in three critical areas. These are:

- Impact of cybersecurity on business, including impact on information risk govern-ance, economics of security, information risk decisions.
- Security of the Internet, World Wide Web and cloud, and a deep analysis of related attacks.
- The evaluation and communication of the dependability and trustworthiness of complex socio-technical systems, using formal, rigorous and quantitative methods and associated evidence.

The centre's organisational structure is made up of nine core members and eight asso-ciate members. These members are active in contributing to the university's under-graduate and postgraduate programmes. The centre supports the doctoral students in research areas related to cybersecurity (City University London n.d.).

3.5   Academic Centre of Excellence for Cyber Security Research

The Academic Centre of Excellence for Cyber Security Research in the United King-dom was created in 2012. The Centre is home to leading researchers, covering a wide range of cybersecurity related areas, including cryptography, human factors in secu-rity, end-to-end systems security, language-based security, program verification and analysis, automated program analysis, verification of computer software, vulnerability discovery, malware analysis and classification of code and the improved defences and mitigations (EPSRC (Engineering and Physical Sciences Research Council) 2013).

The Centre is tasked to assist the United Kingdom government, businesses and consumers in being more resilient to cyber-attacks by extending knowledge and en-hancing skills in cybersecurity. In particular, the centre is tasked to:

- Enhance the United Kingdom's cyber knowledge base, skills and capability through original research.
- Provide top quality graduates in the field of cyber security.
- Support GCHQ's (the parent company) cybersecurity mission.
- Drive up the advancements and the level of innovation (Information Security Group, 2013).
- Address cybercrime and make the United Kingdom one of the most secure places in the world to do business in cyber space.
- Help to shape an open, vibrant and stable cyberspace which the United Kingdom public can use safely and that supports open societies (EPSRC (Engineering and Physical Sciences Research Council) 2012).

This research will allow leading United Kingdom academics in the field of cybersecu-rity to connect with industry security experts and international researchers to tackle some of the United Kingdom's toughest challenges in cybersecurity. This collabora-tive approach between academia, industry and government will ensure that research is relevant and inspired by real world, cutting edge, security issues (EPSRC (Engineering and Physical Sciences Research Council) 2013).

3.6   Research Institute in the Science of Cyber Security (RISCC)

RISCC was created in 2012 at the University College London in the United Kingdom. The institute will work alongside the University of Aberdeen, Imperial College, Queen Mary College, Royal Holloway, Newcastle University and Northumbria University (Kaelin 2012).

The institute is focused on giving organisations more evidence to allow them to make better decisions, aiding in the development of cybersecurity as a science. It collects evidence about what degree of risk mitigation can be achieved through a particular method, including the costs of its introduction and on-going costs such as the impact on productivity, to balance the total cost of ownership against the risk. The institute's main goal is to move security from common, established practice to an evidence base, the same way it happened in medicine (UCL 2013). The institute will focus on four research areas:

- Productive security by assistance to decision makers in the field of information security to make more optimal choices with respect to both the security and productivity of organisations.
- Choice architecture for information security by the establishment of rigorous mathematical approaches to include uncertainty about unknowns in cybersecurity analysis in an attempt to derive a theory about the value of rigour. Research is done in terms of consumerisation, or the use in the workplace of people's own technologies.
- Games and abstraction to make better decisions and the development of new approaches to decision support based on game theory.
- Cybersecurity cartographies explore the methods that security managers use to develop, maintain and the use of visibility of both social and technical asset compliance behaviours for the management of cybersecurity risks (UCL 2013).

3.7   Global Cyber Security Capacity Building Centre (GCSCBC)

The aim of the GCSCBC (also referred to as the United Kingdom Cybersecurity Hub) is to understand how to deliver effective cyber security both within the United Kingdom and internationally. Its aim is to make this knowledge available to governments, communities and organisations to underpin the increase of their capacity in ways appropriate to ensuring a cyberspace which can continue to grow and innovate in support of well-being, human rights and prosperity for all (University of Oxford n.d.-a)

The GCSCBC is focused on developing a framework for understanding what works and what does not work across all cybersecurity dimensions in order to identify and adopt policies which have the potential to significantly enhance our safety and security in cyberspace in ways that respect other core values and interests, such as in privacy and freedom of expression (University of Oxford n.d.-a).

The GCSCBC is focused on helping the international community increase the impact, scale and pace of cyber security capacity building by:

- Investigating the drivers for current capacity building activities and the conditions required to increase resources.
- Providing the scientific framework to enable individuals and institutions to measure and understand effective cybersecurity, providing an evidence base and model for supporting benchmarking, policy formation and measuring effectiveness.
- Pooling, evaluating and sharing information on best practice and experiences in capacity building activities.
- Creating and keeping up to date a critical guide to global expertise on cybersecurity.
- Setting out what needs to be done in order to analyse priorities, and identify and close gaps in the global response (University of Oxford n.d.-b).

3.8   The Hague Security Delta (HSD) Cybersecurity

The HSD Cybersecurity in the Netherlands is a security cluster where companies, governments and research institutions work together on innovations and knowledge in the field of cybersecurity, national and urban security, protection of critical infrastructure and forensics. It was initiated by a consortium of Netherlands Organisation for Applied Scientific Research (TNO), Twynstra Gudde, the Hague University of Applied Sciences, HCSS, the Chamber of Commerce, the Netherlands Forensic Institute and the West Holland Foreign Investment Agency (HSD, 2013).   The most important initiatives include:

- The Cyber Security Academy's main initiatives are a master's program in Cybersecurity and a cybersecurity traineeship that is done in close cooperation with both public and private partners. Their facilities also include a communal place or 'campus', where professionals, researchers and students meet for education, research and sharing expertise in the field of cybersecurity.
- The Cyber Incident Experience Lab is used as a gaming lab where professionals and (top) managers gain new experience, insights and knowledge with respect to cybersecurity in familiar, challenging and real environments.

4   Cybersecurity Centre of Innovation for South Africa

This section contains details on the functions, constituency, organisational structure and benefits of the proposed centre.

The authors' preferred model amongst the similar initiatives is the ACSC discussed in Section 3.1. ACSC has managed to establish efficient processes to share information amongst government agencies, industries and academic institutions, and they have strong academic support. ACSC is funded by government and industry.

4.1   Functions

A key aspect of the centre is collaboration, since no single organisation can respond effectively taking into account that:

- Attacks are increasing in sophistication.
- Current solutions are not adequate.
- Organisations want to increase the training and and sophistication of their employees and solutions (Jansen van Vuuren 2014).

The CCOI should aim to establish a partnership between businesses and industry, academia, government and research institutions and to provide these partners with a greater understanding of cybercrime and practical applications in terms of defending against these crimes. The diagram below describes the benefits of such collaboration.

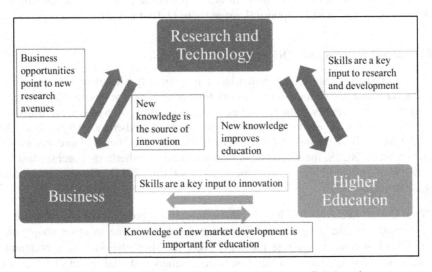

Fig. 1. Benefits of Business, Academia and Research Collaboration

This CCOI must be the central point of collaboration for cybersecurity activities in South Africa. It must serve the South African cyber community by focusing on:

- Cybersecurity related information sharing.
- Cybersecurity education and awareness.
- Cybersecurity research, development and innovation.

In addition, the CCOI must aim to be a world-class institution designed for cyber research and development, customer and partner collaboration and innovation, fully equipped for live cyber technology exercises and demonstrations required by industry and must be able to do safe testing in both simulated and real world environments for development of integrated cyber solutions.

Three key activities of the CCOI are discussed below.

The first key activity, cybersecurity information sharing, will be the coordination of collaboration to bring together expert practitioners and researchers in the field of cybersecurity.

This includes:

- Building cross sector networks and personal relations.
- Sharing best practices under a Non-Disclosure Agreement.
- Arrange technical exchange meetings for the exchange of technical information building of personal relationships among front-line cyber operations experts.
- Identify new threat indicators.
- Set-up and maintenance of a secure Cybersecurity Web Portal to enhance information sharing and access to key data.
- Collaboration with the South African Cybersecurity Hub (National Cyber Security Incident Response Team), the centre to be established by the Department of Communication with the objective to pool public and private sector threat information for the purposes of processing and disseminating such information to relevant stakeholders and to promote cybersecurity in South Africa.

The second key activity, cybersecurity education and awareness, will be to expand education opportunities for workforce and pipeline in the cyber security field.

This includes:

- Development of new cybersecurity qualifications and certifications.
- Expansion of education opportunities for pipeline and knowledge workers in the cybersecurity field.
- Availability of bursaries, internships and studentships.
- Hosting live cyber technology exercises and demonstrations required by industry.
- Cybersecurity awareness training for industry and citizen to gain an improvement of cybersecurity awareness for the workforce and citizens.

The third key activity, cybersecurity research, development and innovation, will be research with the focus to development innovation solutions to improve cybersecurity.

This includes:

- Cybersecurity research to improve cybersecurity and address cybersecurity gaps.
- Development of innovative cybersecurity solutions and patents.
- Appointing qualified research chairs.
- Conducting quantitative cybersecurity threat analysis and red teaming.
- Perform safe testing in both a simulated and real world environment for development of integrated cybersecurity solutions.
- Development of a scientific framework to enable individuals and institutions to measure and understand effective cybersecurity.
- Provide support for policy development and legislation.
- Protection and resilience of society, focusing on the government as a policy maker and regulator.

Cybersecurity research and development will mostly be funded by government and National Research Foundation where intellectual property (IP) will be open. Research support for industry will result in the propriety of IP.

4.2   Organisational Structure

The envisioned management and staffing requirements for the Cybersecurity Centre of Innovation is presented in Fig. 2.

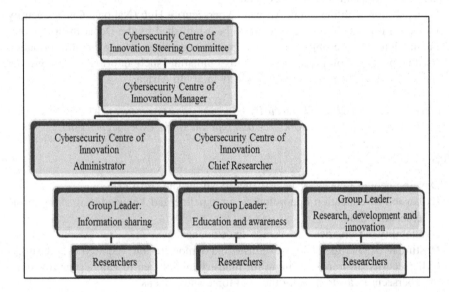

Fig. 2. Proposed Cybersecurity Centre of Innovation Management and Staffing

4.3   Constituency

Fig. 3 shows the relationships between the constituency partners of the CCOI. The CCOI will serve as a central point for the South African businesses and industry, the academia and higher education institutions, local and international research institutions and the South African government in terms of cybersecurity. In addition, the CCIO will have a direct relationship with the South African Cybersecurity Hub.

The role-players that have been identified include, but are not limited to, the following:

- South African businesses and industry consisting mainly of South African Banking Risk Information Centre (SABRIC), Security Operations Centres and Internet Service Providers.
- Academia and higher education institutions.
- Local and international research institutions.
- South African government departments.
- International Collaboration

- The International Multilateral Partnership Against Cyber Threats (IMPACT) is the cybersecurity executing arm of the United Nations' specialised agency - (ITU). As the world's first UN-backed comprehensive alliance against cyber threats, IMPACT brings together governments, academia and industry experts to enhance the global community's capabilities in dealing with cyber threats.
- International Centres of Cybersecurity Innovation.

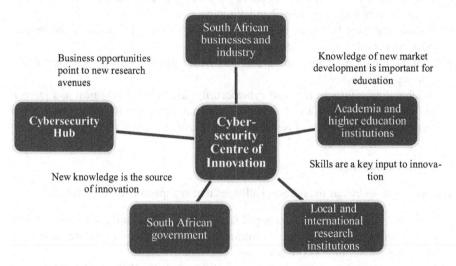

Fig. 3. Proposed Cybersecurity Centre of Innovation Relationships

4.4   Opportunities and Benefits

Some of the opportunities that the CCOI can pursue are:

- Collaborative development of technological competencies, as well as research, development and innovation leading to commercialisation or transfer of research, development and innovation industrialisation in the cybersecurity field.
- Establishing a recognisable hub for coordinated cybersecurity research, development and innovation.
- Contributing to building a new generation of cybersecurity specialists.
- Linking and strengthening cybersecurity pockets of excellence, both locally and internationally.
- Entrepreneurial activity through research-industry partnerships and the transfer of research results to the CCOI partners.
- Developing mechanisms for stakeholders to articulate needs and influence research and human capital development agendas.
- Enabling the community to utilise the implementation of South African ICT legislation and related standardisation.

Some of the identified benefits of establishing a CCOI include:

- National recognition regarding collaboration with the South African Cybersecurity Hub.
- Enabling cybersecurity-related early warning systems.
- A less vulnerable South Africa due to an increased and thorough understanding and operational response to cybersecurity threats.
- Protecting critical infrastructures based on a national information security strategy as well as local and international collaboration.
- Utilising the local ICT industry and expertise in a joint effort towards the investigation and combating of cybercrimes.
- Enabling the flow of innovation and knowledge from research to industrial and economic activities.
- Collaborating efforts in terms of cybersecurity research, development and innovation should result in a less fragmented national cybersecurity effort, with fewer overlaps and duplications of research, development and innovation efforts.

4.5   Key Challenges

The proposed centre has to address challenges that are specific to South Africa:

- Only the banking sector has managed to establish collaboration in terms of cybersecurity information exchange. Government and the rest of the private sector will have to establish similar collaborations.
- Academic institutions offer no formal qualifications in cybersecurity and no such curricula exist yet. This challenge can be addressed by establishing a group responsible for the curriculation of formal cybersecurity qualifications.

5   Conclusion

The establishment of the CCOI in South Africa is essential to combat the current cybersecurity threat. However, processes in South Africa make it difficult to establish collaboration. For example, although the establishment of the South African Cybersecurity Hub has started already in 2011, it is not yet operational and therefore the inherent value of collaborating with this entity cannot be fully understood. In addition, the National Cybersecurity Policy Framework and policies have not been published yet. As a result, many of the South African stakeholders are not comfortable to engage in any concrete action in terms of cybersecurity and cybersecurity collaboration. One of the reasons for the difficulty in establishing collaboration may be the lack of skills in cybersecurity. Another reason is that cybersecurity a rather vague and undefined concept. As such, there exist no concrete international agreement on the definition of cybersecurity or what exactly it is comprised of. In addition, the cyber domain tends to be volatile and fast changing, creating a competitive environment in which role players tend not to share information. This is partly because the domain is not clearly understood and roleplayers do not want to share their own personal information, but also because they do not want to give competitors an advantage in terms of work already done. Other countries experienced similar difficulties and this resulted in the development of cybersecurity innovation centres elsewhere.

An urgent need for international agreement on the definition of cybersecurity, as well as the definition of cybersecurity standards. Some efforts have been made by ISO/IEC 27032, but this standard is not commonly adopted by countries.

References

1. ASCS, Advanced Cyber Security Centre (2013), `http://www.acscenter.org/` (accessed November 6, 2013)
2. City University London (n.d.) Centre for Cyber Security Sciences (CCySS), `http://www.city.ac.uk/engineering-maths/research/cross-discipline-centres-and-groups/centre-for-cyber-security-sciences` (accessed October 30, 2013)
3. Cyber Innovation Centre. Welcome TO CYBER INNOVATION CENTER (2013) (accessed October 31, 2013)
4. EPSRC (Engineering and Physical Sciences Research Council). UK's first academic research institute to investigate the "science of cyber security" (2012), `http://www.epsrc.ac.uk/newsevents/news/2012/Pages/scienceofcybersecurity.aspx` (accessed November 6, 2013)
5. EPSRC (Engineering and Physical Sciences Research Council). UK's second cyber research institute launched (2013), `http://www.epsrc.ac.uk/newsevents/news/2013/Pages/secondcyberresearchinstitute.aspx` (accessed November 6, 2013)
6. Jansen van Vuuren, J., Grobler, M., Zaaiman, J.: Cyber Security Awareness as Critical Driver to National Security. International Journal of Cyber Warfare and Terrorism (IJCWT) 2(1), 27–38 (2012)
7. Jansen van Vuuren, J., Phahlamohlaka, J., Brazzoli, M.: The impact of the increase in broadband access on South African national security and the average citizen. Paper presented at the Information Warfare and Security. Airforce Institute of Technology (April 2009)
8. Jansen van Vuuren, J., Phahlamohlaka, J., Brazzoli, M.: The Impact of the Increase in Broadband Access on National Security and the Average citizen. Journal of Information Warfare 5, 171–181 (2010)
9. Jansen van Vuuren, J.C.: Cybersecurity Centre of Innovation. Cyber Shield, 5th edn. Wolf Pack, Johannesburg, South Africa (2014)
10. Kaelin: UK's GCHQ announces a new cyber security institute (2012) (accessed November 6, 2013), `http://www.techspot.com/news/50154-uks-gchq-announces-a-new-cyber-security-institute.html` (accessed October 30, 2013)
11. Martin, L.: NexGen Cyber Innovation & Technology Center (2013), `http://www.lockheedmartin.com/us/isgs/nexgen.html` (accessed October 30, 2013)
12. MITRE Corporation (n.d.) The Advanced Cyber Security Center (ACSC): A Cyber Threat Information Sharing Consortium, `https://www.ncsc.nl/binaries/en/conference/conference-2011/speakers/bruce-bakis/1/Bruce%252` (accessed October, 31 2013)

13. StatsSA. General household survey 2011, vol. PO318 (2012),
    https://www.statssa.gov.za/publications/P0318/
    P0318April2012.pdf (accessed April 10, 2013)
14. UCL. Research Institute In Science of Cybersecurity (2013),
    http://www.ucl.ac.uk/cybersecurity/about_us
    (accessed October 30, 2013)
15. University of Oxford (n.d.-a) Cyber Security – The Global Cyber Security Capacity Cen-
    tre, http://www.oxfordmartin.ox.ac.uk/institutes/cybersecurity
    (accessed November 6, 2013)
16. University of Oxford (n.d.-b) Global Cyber Security Capacity Centre,
    http://www.oxfordmartin.ox.ac.uk/downloads/cybersecurity/
    Global%20Cyber%20Security%20Capacity%20Centre.pdf
    (accessed November 6, 2013)

Performing Elderliness – Intra-actions with Digital Domestic Care Technologies

Sisse Finken[1] and Christina Mörtberg[2]

[1] Department of Informatics, University of Oslo, Oslo, Norway
finken@ifi.uio.no
[2] Department of Informatics, Linneaus University, Kalmar/Växjö, Sweden
christina.mortberg@lnu.se

Abstract. We discuss the process of meeting digital technology when entering a senior age, by taking a closer look at how different modes of independence and elderliness are (co-)constituted in relation to digital domestic care technologies. Specifically, we suggest reading independence and elderliness as shaped by both the discursive and the material. Our starting point is the notion of intra-action as introduced in Feminist Technoscience. Thinking through use and design of digital technology from a standpoint of Feminism prompts us to widen the perspective on living with such technologies and, thusly, to raise questions about the process of coming of age as an independent person with such care technologies.

Keywords: Performativity, intra-action, elderliness, digital care technology, smart house, participatory design.

1 Introduction

The upcoming change in demography, the so-called tidal-wave-of-elderly, is expected to bring about socio-economic challenges in Scandinavia as well as in other countries. In meeting such changes health care services have turned to digital technology and moved from public institutions to private homes. With such move senior citizens are provided an opportunity to live independently in their own homes, rather than living in public eldercare facilities or nursing homes. Such new technology-equipped homes bring about possibilities for senior citizens to continue their daily life with all the good that living and being at home can bring. In an effort to meet today's socio-economic challenges, the design and implementation of digital care technologies are increasing *and* becoming part of public welfare programs aiming to offer good care and services to societies' older population [1, 2]. Remmers [3], for example, argues that information and communication technology (ICT) is necessary to support older people in need of care, their relatives, and care workers.

In addition to an increased focus on ICT offered in support of aging and wellbeing, new understandings about prevailing norms and values relating to older people have emerged. In a co-design project (the Senior Interaction project [4]) concerning social

K.K. Kimppa et al. (Eds.): HCC11 2014, IFIP AICT 431, pp. 307–319, 2014.
© IFIP International Federation for Information Processing 2014

network and interaction among senior citizens, the researchers became aware that the seniors studied in the project did not identify as elderly but that they talked about other people as elderly and in need of digital technologies. In drawing on the experiences gained during that project Brandt et al. [4] suggest using the notion of *situated elderliness*. They propose this as a way of honoring seniors' experiences, in illustrating how elderliness is situated in a practice, and how it is something that comes into existence when people and technology meet.

Barad's [5] notion of intra-action forms a starting point for our discussion on independence, performativity, and care technology. We contribute new empirical material generated in Norway and Sweden, some of which derives from a study of lived experiences in a smart home care unit, the other of which derives from a workshop with seniors that elicited views about a possible future living with digital domestic care technologies. We have chosen to bring in these two different examples together in an effort to show how care technologies create realities through the inclusions and exclusions inherent in their designs, and how elderliness and independence evolve in unison with both discourses and materiality.

The paper is structured as follows. First we introduce the concepts of intra-action and performativity and explain how we have found them useful. We then situate digital domestic care technologies in relation to those concepts. Next we delineate the two empirical studies, their respective methods, and their respective analyses. We then enter the two empirical grounds. We conclude with specific findings from our research and some implications for design.

2   Intra-action and Performativity

We use the notion *intra-action* [5] as an entrance to discussing how elderliness and independence are constituted in performance when senior citizens meet digital domestic care technologies. As a concept intra-action raises methodological questions that are relevant both when studying practices and when designing for everyday use of technology, for it maintains that both subjects and objects should be taken into account and accounted for as bringing about agency. Karen Barad's notion of intra-action differs from the notion of 'interaction' that is more commonly used in design studies. Interaction implies a relation between pre-existing humans (subjects) and technologies (objects) in which agency is a human or a technological attribute [5, p. 139]. The notion of intra-action, in contrast, suggests that subjects and objects come into existence only when and as they encounter each other. Lucy Suchman [6] captures the distinction: "Whereas the construct of interaction suggests two entities, given in advance, that come together and engage in some kind of exchange, *intra-action* underscores the sense in which subjects and objects emerge through their encounters with each other." [6, p. 267, original italics]. Thus, with the notion of intra-action, "Nothing is delimited as a separate entity. Everything is always engaging something else, in specific ways designated by the concepts: intra-activity, i.e. matter and meaning, object and subject, nature and culture are all mutually articulated and mutually entangled." [7, p. 68].

Within the notion of intra-action we get an understanding of Barad's [5] grasp of 'performativity', which specifies by considering matter on par with discourse. This is captured by Heckman [8]: "Barad's goal here is to formulate a *materialist* theory of performativity that, while not denying the role of discourse that Butler emphasizes, also does not deny the role of the material. In contrast to Butler's concept, Barad's agential realist elaboration of performativity allows matter its due as an active participant in the world's becoming (2007:136)." [p. 76, original italic].

Integrating the concept of intra-action with a feminist methodology for studying design and use is helpful as we also seek to following Bardzell & Bardzell [9] who ask: "who are involved, and in what ways?" [p. 682]. Bringing into view an understanding of the becoming of objects and subjects, and how in orchestration they bring about particular re-configurations, also emphasizes the significance of who and what is included/excluded in the practices and activities [5] of design and use. There are no neutral positions [10], choices, involvements, or exclusions. That is, boundary making has "ontological implications" [8, p. 73].

Such insights are important for the analytical aim of this paper in terms of understanding how digital domestic care technologies blurs heterogeneity in a social group of people, who, with reference to [4], do not identify as elderly and in need of technologies.

In positioning ourselves at the crossroad of informatics and feminist science and technology studies we propose to understand interactions between humans and technology as material-discursive practices, in which materiality and meaning come into being when humans and technology intra-act [5]. We use intra-action as a starting point in our discussion of meetings between subjects and objects and the re-configurings that come into being through them (intra-actions). We hope to understand how 'elderliness' and 'independence' come about through such intra-actions (performativity); how the design of care technologies create realities through inclusion and exclusion; and how these realities are enacted and acted upon by mundane artifacts, senior citizens, care workers, researchers, and their research methods.

3   Digital Domestic Care Technologies

Due to asymmetrical power relations in society feminist scholars have generated knowledge about the gendering of (information) technology and the co-construction of gender and technology, e.g. [1]. In doing so feminist scholars have developed a pluralistic understanding of gender-technology relations [1]. Although we build on this knowledge in the present paper, we keep our main focus on performativity and intra-action.

In our previous work [11, 12] we have described how smart home technology is designed and implemented in homes of and for older people in Scandinavia. The implementation takes place in an effort to meet socio-economic challenges that follow from the so-called tidal-wave-of-elderly [13]. These challenges are met by way of re-organizing health care services, moving them from public institutions into homes [1], [14].   Besides meeting socio-economic challenges, smart homes bring about possibilities for living independently at home: "Smart homes offer the promise of increased independence and reduced need for caregiver support in the home." [2, p. 210]. In order to live at home for as long as possible, older people come to live with digital devices such as alarms, detectors, and sensors that monitor bodily movements and/or (unwanted) phenomena such as smoke, water, and/or heat. These digital technologies communicate via Internet or mobile connections, and give feedback on computer screens, mobile phones, or other mobile devices according to predefined actions and/or the very absence of them [15, 16, 17]. According to Lopez et al., "Caring depends on some form of security. [...]. It is a process of becoming, but one never quite gets there, as the safety provided by the home telecare service is always emerging, but never reached. That is to say, it depends on practices, technologies and bodies that follow different logics – security and care – at the same time, in a delicate balance." [18, p. 87].

In smart home seniors come to live independently with the aid of inbuilt care technologies. Simultaneously, these care technologies introduce an economy of normativity by which residents come to perform a specific caring self in order for the technology to remain a caring aid [12]. That is (in pointing to an example with bed alarms, which we previously have used [11, 12]): the act of leaving the bed during night and not returning within the programmed time frame prompts the triggering of an alarm. Such triggering is productive when the person needs help, but rather coun-ter-productive if the person just wants to sleep somewhere else in the house [19]. In this case, the person living at home materializes an object that can be measured by technology (see also [20]). In such measuring the heterogeneity of elderliness and independence is blurred. In other words, "Multiple positions exist at the same time, which means that identities are shaped in tensions between various positions; thereby, identities are neither uniform nor fixed but fragmented ([21]; [22])." [23, p. 163]. One such position comes about through intra-action with the care technology in the smart home. Thus, even though senior citizens use technology in their homes to support wellbeing and autonomy, it is also important to remember that they are not a uniform group; rather, they are a heterogeneous group with various wishes, demands, and expectations [24], who are situated in different spaces and time of different material-discursive entanglements [5].

In the next section we introduce our current fieldwork settings and our methods for generating and analyzing our material.

4   Empirical Settings - Generating Material

The workshop was held in December 2011 as part of the research project *Sustainable Ways of Living with Technologies – designing with and for senior citizens and care-givers*. The intention of the project was to design services with and for senior citizens in order to facilitate their day-to-day life and support wellbeing. The theme in the workshop was *A Good Day*, and included activities and technologies used during a good day. Three seniors, Alma, August, and Beathe, and two facilitators partici-pated in the workshop. At the time of the workshop, the seniors were between 68-79 years old. The seniors all lived in their own homes without help (neither manual nor digital domestic care services). The facilitators asked the participants to clarify some images (brought along by the researchers from magazines, newspapers, etc.) and their daily activities. The workshop was recorded after receiving permission to do so.

The participative methods used were cartographic mappings, which consist of sharing the created visual narratives by telling the other participants about mappings and future scenarios. The empirical material used in this paper is from the last activity – "imagining the future." However, the scenarios have to be considered in relation to the other activities and methods used during the entire process, that is, the doings and actions taking place in the workshop or in material-discursive practice [5].

Fig. 1. Cartographic mapping. Photo: Mörtberg.

The cartographic mapping method, developed by [25], see also [26], was the first activity held after the participants and the project were introduced. In the mappings the participants illustrated a Good Day from the morning to the evening, activities they participate in, who they meet, what kind of technologies they use to facilitate their daily lives, etc. The method is inspired by both ethnographic studies and participatory methods used and developed in Participatory Design, see Fig. 1.

The events from the smart house were generated as part of a larger research-project *Autonomy and Automation in an Information Society for All.* The smart house is a new build care unit consisting of 91 flats. It opened in the early fall of 2012, and is certified as a 'care plus' unit, which means that safety, security, wellbeing, quality of life, and independency are central issues. According to the local municipality, senior citizens aged 67+ having impairments (e.g. rheumatism) and/or disabilities (e.g. difficulties with seeing) can rent their own flat in care plus units. In this way, a care plus home is something halfway between a private home and a nursing home [27, 28].

Interviews, observations, and photography were carried out with and among residents, technologies, and employees of the smart house in different situations (e.g. at home, touring the house, during work) and at different events (e.g. bingo, craft work, literature circle, and exercising in the smart gym). With a particular interest in understanding negotiations, translations, and displacements that follow when care technologies move in and are to find their place among caregivers and residents.

When analyzing our material we have engaged in readings of meetings between subjects and objects and their re-configurings. In such meetings we have especially focused on how 'elderliness' and 'independence' come about in intra-actions and we have tried to understand how the design of care technologies creates realities in virtue of what they include and exclude. Within this, 'independence' and 'elderliness' are themselves instantiations of the present that are enacted and acted upon by us. In this way, we have been sensitized to specific readings of events and situations encountered in the field. Indeed, in line with [5], we could say that our mere presence (as ethnographer in the smart house and designer of a participative work shop) is part of the current focus on care politics, care work, and living, doing, care technology. As also noted by [29], "we want to emphasize that the "choice" of phenomenon and the "choice" of entities to be selected and foregrounded as enacted and enacting forces in the analysis (whether papers, architecture, technology, subjectivity, emotionally, socio-cultural categories, normativities, or something entirely different) depends on the researcher, on the research ambition, and ultimately on how the phenomenon in focus is demarcate and defined." [p. 351].

4.1   Smart House – Lived Experiences

In this section we offer three examples from our fieldwork in an attempt to demonstrate how the concept of intra-action informed our readings of events in the field.

(Example 1) When we first entered the smart house in the early fall of 2012 our attention was drawn to the entrance door of the house, Fig. 2.

Fig. 2. The door with Post-it notes and tinted foil.   Photos: Finken

When taking photos, 'interacting' with the door, thinking about displacements in design, talking with a care worker on a later occasion, and in analyzing our material from a standpoint of in- and exclusions, we learned about how new configurations of design and care work come about in encounters between subjects and objects.

On the large, glass, transparent entrance door, three Post-it notes were glued up. This entrance door opens automatically when one walks from outside and in; but when leaving the building, the door does not open automatically. One needs to push a button, placed to the right, at a lower position than can be reached by wheelchair. When pushing the button, the door slides open, and stays open until you are outside. Unfortunately, rather than stopping in front of the door and pushing the button, residents had been walking straight into the glass. Luckily nobody was hurt in such encounters with the too transparent and not visible glass door. To prevent accidents from occurring, the care workers had glued the Post-it notes up on the glass door (interview with care worker, October 2012). The door was later 're-designed' by adding tinted foil.

We read this as an example of how in-and exclusions in the design of technology have consequences for what *becomes*. The transparency of the door's can be said to be hindrance to enter into the free. The very design of the sensor/manually-controlled door, in this way, is displaced to the Post-it notes and the messages and drawings they carry. The Post-it notes, as such, come to work as markers of visibility (the door become visible), and as makers of an opening (push the button down there). In addition, the care workers come to partake in designing and re-configuring the house, while the Post-it notes come to partake in performing care work by way of sustaining a safe environment and independent living for the residents.

In a report by The Norwegian Directorate of Health we also find notions about independent living. It states that use of (health and care) welfare technologies within municipalities should regard the law of municipal health and care services as a baseline. This law, among other aims, seeks to: "[...] secure that the individual gets the possibility to live and reside independently and have an active and meaningful existence jointly with others" [30, p. 21. Translated from Norwegian].

(Example 2) Another example of in-and exclusion in design of technology concerns a light sensor in a flat. According to the resident, this sensor is too sensitive to movements and sounds, in that it automatically turns on the light in unwanted situations [31]. In order to avoid such experience of interference, the resident wraps silver foil around the sensor to block its workings "at inconvenient times." [31, p. 57]. See Fig. 3.

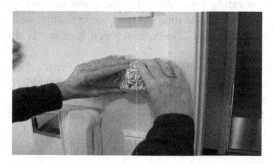

Fig. 3. A light sensor 'hacked' with foil. Photo: Finken

We read this situation as another example of how residents and employees of the house intervene in the design of technology to make it work. It matters what is in- and excluded for independence to be in place. Within we could further add that a heterogeneity of independence and elderliness surfaces through our reading of this situation as intra-actions, that came about in a flat on a winter day in 2013 between a resident, care technology, mundane kitchen artifacts, and two field workers (the first author and a master student) who were asking questions, observing, and taking photos (field dairy, February 2013).

(Example 3) Another example also illustrates how independence and elderliness are not fixed but rather vary according to the in- and exclusions in the design of the smart house with its digital care technologies, care workers, and residents. It was the spring of 2013 while introducing new master students to the house and its workings. Here we got to know that one of the residents spends most of the time in bed – only making a few visits to the bathroom and the kitchen (in the flat) – and cannot make the light turn on by moving the arms sufficiently enough to activate the sensor in the flat (field dairy, April 2013). Bringing in intra-action to analyze such situation also passes on understandings about independence and elderliness and how they come about in multiple relations between help from care workers, care technologies, and the residents him or her self. Thus, independency and elderliness are material-discursive phenomena enacted and acted on in different locations and times [5], [29].

With these examples from the smart house we want draw a parallel to design. Digital domestic care technologies feed on an idea of a homogenous group of citizens, through which the heterogeneity of older people also gets blurred. Callén et al. [32] make a similar point, stating that: "care technologies are generally used by people who have been considered to be vulnerable and in need of support." [p. 117]. Along these lines of thinking, there might as well be a blurring of the heterogeneity of users as described by Mort et al. [33] in their account of telecare. In the smart home, these users could be care personnel, residents, and relatives [12]. With respect to this we could say that the design of digital domestic care technologies, as many other technologies, builds on an ideal user, which, in practice, is a mere image [1]. A "user", or an old person or a care worker, in our case, is someone who becomes vis-à-vis technology – a someone who comes to perform as a specific "user" in order for the technology to do its caring job. With this we could say that independence is performed and intertwined with the discourses of society; thus, we find it fruitful to include performativity in design efforts, also when it concerns digital domestic care technologies.

Through the inclusion of normativity (e.g. what is expected of people of a certain age) and heterogeneity (e.g. various agencies) we learn that elderliness and independence is situated, coming into existence in various practices where discourses and materiality intra-act [2, 3]. In the following we meet three senior citizens who imagine living with digital domestic care technologies.

4.2   Imagining Digital Domestic Care Technologies

The participatory design workshop was held in December 2011 with three seniors and two facilitators. At the workshop everyone introduced themselves to each other and the facilitators presented the aim of the workshop. The seniors were then asked to illustrate what a good day is like, what they are doing, and what kind of technologies they use. Following this activity, the next concerned sharing their illustrations. After the seniors had shared their stories about a good day, Maria, one of the facilitators, continued the workshop saying, *"now, you have described your present day-to-day life, but can you imagine the future and how do you want life to be in the future and how do you expect things to work, then"*.

Here we listen to Alma, August, and Beathe's imaginations of their futures. August starts the creation of future scenarios, he says with a laugh, "a walker that moves easily". Timers are also discussed. Beathe highlights the difficulties of installing a timer to a modern kitchen stove with knobs. To this, Alma points out: "no one has thought of that one wants a modern kitchen stove". They conclude that there is a gap between the development of domestic digital technologies and the timers at disposal.

All three explain their desire to stay in their homes, if possible, but they were also aware that they probably would be dependent on some kind of help in the future. August says: "at some point, the time appears when you become dependent on others but you do not want to think so far but you are aware it will appear."

Digital domestic care technologies such as alarms and sensors are designed and implemented in smart homes to facilitate seniors' daily life and independent living and autonomy. Alma, August and Beathe discuss also these kinds of technologies when Beathe insists that it is not only elderly people that are in need of reminders; younger people also use mobiles to remember activities. But they also touch upon more intimate aspects of their daily life, Beathe says:

do I manage to keep time, to ensure that, to cook food, what kind of help do I need to facilitate this, and ... last but not least do I manage to go to the bathroom, and take a shower, do we have toilets that work so I can ... the most embarrassing, I think, is being dependent on someone else to help me in the bathroom. It is absolutely the worst thing I know or are you forced to use diapers depending on that care workers cannot help you frequently enough – the most basic need, I think this is really important, one should start here [on basic needs] –other issues will also appear. Certainly one can focus on other issues but just to start, what do you need, you need food for the day and you need to go to the bathroom and you need ... here I think it is the absolute first and most important [demands], because many [services/technologies] do not exist and they [designers] don't care enough.

The lively conversation continues around issues that are important for making their desire to stay in their homes as long as possible – alarms and timers, but also more intimate issues were in focus.

Seniors' expertise of their day-to-day life with all that it entails was in focus both in the narratives and also in the scenario building [4]. However, they located themselves in relation to today's situation but were also able to imagine a higher degree of dependence on various kinds of digital domestic care technologies. Alarms, timers and sensors were technologies the seniors had relationships to although they were not dependent on them at the time when the workshop was held. In the imaginations, the participants situate themselves differently in relation to digital domestic care technologies. With a reading of their performances or intra-actions we identified both in- and exclusion and how both independency and dependency unfolds [5]. Digital technologies' support and facilitation of remembering is not only a question of old or young. Both elderly and younger people are dependent on and use digital technologies. With the inclusion of mobiles and younger people remembering became not only a question for the workshop participants but also for other users. The participants – the users –became subjects by identifying themselves with younger people [8]. The body's presence, its lesser degree of mobility, and an increased dependence were also brought up in the participants' imaginations of their futures. When mobility, dependence, and embarrassment were included in the performances the importance of intimacy appeared. The necessity to design digital domestic care technologies to assist older people (bodies that lack both motor and cognitive abilities) in the bathroom, was important to them. Being sensitive to the more intimate aspects of everyday life is a question of in- or exclusion or where the boundaries are drawn in design of digital domestic care technologies [5], [11]. An awareness of elderliness (as heterogeneous), of expertise (that of the old people with respect to their own life), and of normativity (which is inherent in design choices), will help designers to better appreciate that and how elderliness and independence are situated. This might help contest the image of an ideal user and to draw boundaries in design that include all aspects of old people´s daily life.

5   Discussion

We have presented an alternative approach to understanding and examining 'interactions' between humans and technology [5]. We have been interested in understanding how 'elderliness' and 'independence' come about through intra-actions in which matter and discourse are accorded symmetrical analytical importance. In bringing [5] to serve as an analytical lens we have illustrated how the performance of independence is a process of *becoming with* digital care technology. Through such a reading there is no discrimination between subject/object. In other words, when performing elderliness in the smart home the person becomes an object to be sensed through its measureable presence or absence; independence becomes a specific, prescribed agency. Simultaneously, the technology becomes a subject with agency that acts (or not) on behalf of the object (the human). Subjects and objects, as such, are not prefixed from a standpoint of intra-action; rather, it is in their encounter with each other that they become and obtain their properties and boundaries [5]. The performativity of elderliness and independence is two-fold in the reading of the smart house and the workshop participants' imaginations, in that both subjects and objects are put to work in order for a more mutual relationship to unfold. The ideal user was also contested – elderliness is situated and unstable; it comes into existence in intra-actions dependent on what is included or excluded in design. For example, when mobile phones were included remembering emerged as a question of old and young. Dependency on other subjects and objects – humans or technologies – may also have implications for design, especially as a consequence of the human body's lack of abilities in particular contexts. Thus, it is a fruitful act to include more intimate aspects of day-to-day life when designing digital domestic care technologies. Older as well as younger people are subjects who become vis-à-vis digital technologies. Their being varies vary due to where they are located and what is included in the intra-actions.

In closing, we find it fruitful to recap the ways in which the concept of intra-action can serve as an active ingredient within the design of digital technologies or digital domestic care technologies. First of all, in moving the view of use and design from 'interaction' to 'intra-action' the awareness is steered towards an understanding of *being* as contingent and constituted through ongoing practices and activities, rather than as a prevailing attribute that is stable and located within a specific entity. Thus, we ask for 'changing the gender of design' [34] in line with a Feminist Technoscience methodology that does not separate the discursive from the material, and, which accounts for a heterogeneity of agencies [5]. Within this we want to re-emphasize that there are no innocent positions. This also goes for care technologies; they are situated in use practices and are themselves practices of design. Thus questions about the in-and exclusions inherent in designs have a bearing on the potentials for that which can or might *become*.

Acknowledgements. Special thanks goes to care workers and participating senior citizens – this research would not have been possible without you letting us in to your world. Finken thanks The Norwegian Research Council for funding *Autonomy and Automation in an IT society for All*, grant # 193172. Mörtberg thanks the Faculty of Technology, Linneaus University, for funding *Sustainable Ways of Living with Technologies – designing with and for senior citizens and caregivers*. Many thanks also to three anonymous HCC11 reviewers for constructive feedback and directions on how to sharpen our paper. We also owe thanks to Katie Vann for correcting our English. Preliminary results from the study in this paper have previously been presented orally at *The First Nordic STS Conference*, Norway, 2013; *EASST*, Denmark, 2012, and *CHI 2012*, USA.

References

1. Jansson, M., Mörtberg, C., Berg, E.: Old Dreams, New Means: an exploration of visionsand situated knowledge in information technology. Gender, Work and Organization 14, 371–387 (2007)
2. Genty, T.: Smart homes for people with neurological disability: State of the art. Neuro Rehabilitation 25, 209–217 (2009)
3. Remmers, H.: Environments for Ageing, Assistive Technology and Self-Determination: ethical perspectives. Informatics for Health & Social Care 35(3-4), 200–210 (2010)
4. Brandt, E., Binder, T., Malmborg, L., Sokoler, T.: Communities of everyday practiceand situated elderliness as an approach to co-design for senior interaction. In: Proc. of CHI Special Interest Group of Australia on CHI, pp. 400–403. ACM, New York (2010)
5. Barad, K.: Meeting the universe halfway: quantum physics and the entanglement of matter and meaning. Duke University Press, Durham (2007)
6. Suchman, L.: Human-Machine Reconfigurations. Plans and Situated Actions, 2nd edn. Cambridge University Press, New York (2007)
7. Højgaard, L., Juelskjær, M., Søndergaard, D.M.: The 'WHAT OF' and the 'WHAT IF' of Agential Realism. – In Search of the Gendered Subject. Kvinder, Køn & Forskning NR. 1-2, 67–78 (2012)
8. Hekman, S.: The Material of Knowledge. Feminist disclosures. Indiana University Press (2010)

9. Bardzell, S., Bardzell, J.: Towards a Feminist HCI Methodology: Social Science, Feminism, and HCI. In: CHI 2011, pp. 675–684 (2011)
10. Markussen, R.: Politics of Intervention in Design: Feminist Reflections on the Scandinavian Tradition. AI & Soc., 127–141 (1996)
11. Finken, S., Mörtberg, C.: The Thinking House: on configurings of an infrastructure of care. In: Proc. of the 3rd International Workshop on Infrastructures for Healthcare: Global Healthcare, June 23-24, pp. 44–47. The IT University of Copenhagen, Denmark (2011)
12. Finken, S.: HomeWork. Public care in private homes. In: Chandler, J., Barry, J., Berg, E. (eds.) Dilemmas for Human Services 2012, Papers from the 15th International Research Conference, London, September 1-2, pp. 32–39 (2011)
13. Thygesen, H.: Technology and good dementia care. A study of technology and ethics in everyday care practice. Ph.D. dissertation, Center for Technology, Innovation and Culture. Faculty of Social Sciences, University of Oslo, Norway (2009)
14. Roberts, C., Mort, M.: Reshaping what counts as care: Older people, work and newtechnologies. ALTER, European Journal of Disability Research 3, 138–158 (2009)
15. Aldrich, F.: Smart Homes: Past, Present and Future. In: Harper, R. (ed.) Inside the Smart Home, pp. 17–39. Springer (2003)
16. Bjørneby, S., Clatworthy, S., Thygesen, H.: Evaluering av BESTA-installasjon i Tønsberg. Report (1996)
17. Spingel, L.: Designing the Smart House: Posthuman Domesticity and Conspicuous Production. European Journal of Cultural Studies 8, 403–426 (2005)
18. Lopez, D., Callén, B., Tirado, F., Domènech, M.: How to become a guardian angel. Providing safety in a home telecare service. In: Mol, A., Moser, I., Pols, J. (eds.) Care in Practice. on Thinkering in Clinics, Homes and Farms. Transcript, pp. 73–91 (2010)
19. Fitzpatrick, G.: Keynote. In: 3rd International Workshop on Infrastructures for Healthcare: Global Healthcare, June 23-24. The IT University of Copenhagen, Denmark (2011)
20. Rapoport, M.: Being a body or having one: automated domestic technologies and corporeality. AI &Soc. 28, 209–218 (2013)
21. Hollway, W.: Subjectivity and Method. In Psychology Gender, Meaning and Science. Sage Publications, London (1989)
22. Lather, P.: Postmodernism and the Human Science. In: Kavle, S. (ed.) Psychology and Postmodernism, pp. 88–109. Sage Publications, London (1992)
23. Mörtberg, C.: Heterogeneous images of (mobile) technologies and services: a feminist contribution. NORA - Nordic Journal of Feminist and Gender Research 11(3), 158–169 (2003)
24. Gunnarsson, E.: I think I have had a good life" - The everyday lives of older women and men in a life course perspective. Ageing & Society 29, 33–48 (2009)
25. Elovaara, P., Mörtberg, C.: Cartographic Mappings: Participative Methods. In: Proc. of PDC, pp. 171–174. ACM (2010)
26. Elovaara, P., Igira, F.T., Mörtberg, C.: Whose Participation? Whose Knowledge? Exploring PD in Tanzania- Zanzibar and Sweden. In: Proc. of PDC, pp. 105–114. ACM (2006)
27. Field material collected from the local municipality concerning care plus
28. Finken, S.: Case Description – When Technologies Move to the Home. In: Bratteteig, T., Finken, S. (eds.) Book Based on the A3-Project "Autonomy and Automation in an ITSociety for All (to appear) (forthcoming)
29. Højgaard, L., Søndergaard, D.M.: Theorizing the complexities of discursive and material subjectivity: Agential realism and poststructural analyses. Theory & Psychology 21, 338–354 (2011)

30. Helsedirektoratet: Velferdsteknologi. Fagrapport om implementering av velferdsteknologi i de kommunale helse- ogomsorgstjenesterne 2012-2013 (2012), http://helsedirektoratet.no/publikasjoner/velferdsteknologi-fagrapport-om-implementering-av-velferdsteknologi-i-de-kommunale-helse-og-omsorgstjenestene-2013-2030/Sider/default.aspx (retrieved online January 04, 2014)
31. Jørmeland, C.: Displacement in Care Technology Design. Master thesis. University of Oslo, Dept. of Informatics (August 2013)
32. Callén, B., Domènech, M., López, D., Tirado, F.: Telecare research (Cosmo)politizing methodology. ALTER, European Journal of Disability Research 3, 110–122 (2009)
33. Mort, M., Finch, T., May, C.: Making and Unmaking Telepatients: Identity and Governance in New Health. Science, Technology & Human Values 34(9), 9–33 (2009)
34. Finken, S.: Changing the Gender of Design. In: Elovaara, P., Sefyrin, J., Öhman, M., Björkman, C. (eds.) Traveling Thoughtfulness – Feminist Technoscience Stories, pp. 85–93. Department of Informatics, Umeå University, Sweden (2010)

Electronic Patient Records and Benefits to Clinicians: An Actor-Network Study of a Technological Innovation in the NHS

Mhorag Goff

University of Salford, Salford, UK
m.goff@edu.salford.ac.uk

Abstract. This paper draws on findings from research in progress to discuss the ways in which EPRs are implicated in changing work practices for clinicians within the NHS in England. The study set out to question the apparent inevitability of this technology by investigating whether EPRs benefit their users. Recognising that they have been explicitly conceived to serve multiple purposes, the benefits to front line clinical users are dependent on the purposes for which EPRs are being used and the additional responsibilities and risks implied by the non-clinical interests inscribed.

The study uses Actor-Network Theory as a means to investigate the relationships that constitute the EPR, and in doing so to identify the entangled sets of interests brought to bear on the realisation of this technology. The findings suggest that sharing of patient data beyond the local largely privileges secondary uses while benefits to clinicians are concentrated on locally shared EPRs.

Keywords: electronic patient records, Actor-Network Theory, NHS.

1   Introduction

The National Programme for IT (NPfIT) was launched in 2002, as part of which a centrally defined programme of EPR development was set out for both primary and secondary care organisations across the NHS in England. Following the devolution of healthcare within the UK in 1999, England, Scotland, Wales and Northern Ireland have each taken a distinct approach to EPR development [1].

Electronic patient records (EPRs) are fundamental to visions of future health care delivery in the UK [2, 3]. They are expected to provide safer, quicker and better quality patient care as a key element of modernised information systems within the NHS [4, 5]. Discourses from government and IT suppliers about the promise of this technology hinge on notions of modernisation and 'seamless' care driven by pursuit of clinical and management information to evidence performance, reduce errors and achieve efficiencies [6]. This is to be realised through an 'information revolution', which involves improving the flow of information within the NHS [7].

K.K. Kimppa et al. (Eds.): HCC11 2014, IFIP AICT 431, pp. 320–332, 2014.
© IFIP International Federation for Information Processing 2014

The rationales for EPR development imply that in addition to its properties as a digital object its value derives from its networked-ness in terms of allowing wider sharing of patient information within and between organisations locally, regionally and nationally. The notion of improved information flows is based on the idea of abstracting clinical information captured at the point of care from the local context of production [8]. EPRs are therefore predicated on the 'networkedness' or scope of sharing of records and the patient information within them, apparent in the UK government's ambition to develop a nationally networked longitudinal electronic record. 'Networkedness' in this respect refers to the extent to which the EPR technology is being used to exchange information about patients and their care between NHS Trusts, which represent semi-autonomous organisational units under the direction of the government Department of Health.

In this respect the National Programme for IT embodies infrastructural ambitions for EPR systems, which can be seen as enablers of a range of benefits and transformative improvements to the ways in which healthcare is delivered including, for example, virtual consultations [9].

A key driver for the large scale development of electronic patient records is the opportunity for secondary uses of patient data to support care commissioning, administration and research [5], [2], [10] at Trust and national levels, including for example, analyses of patient 'casemix', which categorises patients on the basis of consumption of resources, and comparisons of patient outcomes between Trusts [11]. This relies on the development of standardised data formats and recording practices and the ability to (easily) extract and aggregate data from local EPRs for central use. However, the literature highlights the risks of prioritising a secondary uses agenda which places a burden of information provision on clinicians to capture patient data in the EPR when it adds little value to clinical work practices [8, 12].

The National Programme for IT has run over-budget, costing to date an estimated £9.8 billion [13]. It has been criticised for being some years behind schedule having been due to be completed in 2010 [14], against a backdrop of mixed success of EPR programmes globally [15], and a perception among some clinicians that EPRs are an administrative rather than a clinical tool [16].

The objectives of the National Programme for IT in relation to EPRs were only partially achieved before the NPfIT was dismantled in late 2011 [7], [14], notably in terms of the implementation of local EPR systems in hospitals, and the rollout of a nationally accessible Summary Care Record. The failure of the NPfIT to meet its original objectives, the significant costs and the scale of the ambitions with respect to EPR development justify questioning this technology. In particular it is recognised that a national EPR presents ethical issues, especially in relation to the uses of patient data [17], manifested in the ongoing controversy about the privacy of patient records. Therefore the potentially profound implications for healthcare professionals as users, for patients and for the nature of healthcare make it important to critically discuss this technology.

This paper focuses on exploring clinical users' experiences of EPRs, and the benefits and disadvantages to their work practices. In relation to their position at the forefront of healthcare provision, I start from the assumption that technologies such as the

EPR are intended to support the work practices of healthcare professionals and that this in turn will have ramifications for healthcare provision. I therefore aim to understand users' actor-networks for the EPR, as a means to discuss how the technology benefits them. Cresswell et al. [18] note that using Actor-Network Theory means being selective about what to include within scope and what to exclude, because of the impossibility of mapping the entire network. For this reason I explicitly include those involved with healthcare provision under the auspices of the NHS (whether within a Trust or in related bodies), while stakeholders such as patients, software providers and pharmaceutical companies, although they have an interest in EPRs, are out of scope.

In the context of a government vision of a nationally networked record the study sets out to find out what this means for the work practices of clinicians by investigating the reality of the technology as experienced in use. For this reason I have taken a meso level approach to investigating this technology using Actor-Network Theory, not within an individual organisational context, but in relation to multiple NHS organisations which will, if government strategy is realised, entail significantly interconnected EPR systems and extensive information flows.

2   Methodological and Theoretical Background

Data were collected through interviews with EPR users across 10 NHS Trusts in England in a number of roles in primary, secondary and ambulatory care as indicated in Figure 1 below. Participants include a number of non-clinical users, whose perspectives were originally sought as a means to better understand the secondary uses of EPRs, in addition to the use of documentary sources such as government reports. Through an iterative methodology of identifying actors and refining understanding of the actor-network, it was found that substantial investigation of non-clinical uses would be out of scope due to the explosion of complexity in the actor-networks, a challenge acknowledged in the literature [19].

Participant Trusts were selected for diversity of healthcare settings and on the basis of an existing EPR implementation. In addition to participant Trusts having a local EPR system Fig. 1 also shows the instances of inter-organisationally shared EPRs encountered in this study, including the Diabetes Record, the Summary Care Record and the Specialist Hospital EPR for which the scope of information sharing is indicated.

Among broadly socio-technical systems perspectives on information systems it has long been recognised that technological artefacts inscribe certain interests, values and ideals in relation to their domains of use, which tend to reflect and reproduce a particular view of organisational reality belonging to the dominant group or groups [20, 21]. This implies that a system does not necessarily support the work practices of all users [22, 23], and that power may be exercised through the use of a technology. This means that technologies cannot be considered neutral tools, rather they are political in nature, entangled with and emerging from a particular set of socio-material arrangements in a given implementation context [24].

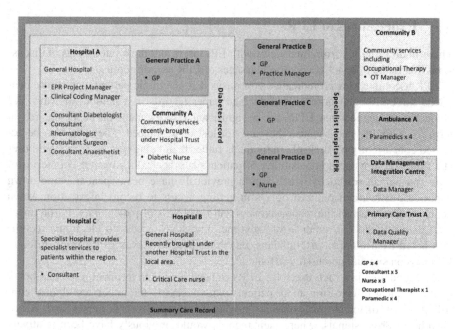

Fig 1. Participant Trusts and EPR users

Actor-Network Theory (ANT) holds that an entity exists as a product of a particular configuration of associations with a constellation of human (or social) and non-human (material) entities [25]. The hybrid nature of entities arises because the social is defined in relation to, and presupposes the material, and vice versa, such that they are inseparable [21]. Understanding the actor-network for a given phenomenon, such as the EPR, entails identifying the entities and relationships that constitute that actor-network, and in doing so appreciating the influences of various actors on the outcome. Any entity may have membership of multiple actor-networks [26] and that this also means a research object may be constituted by multiple actor-networks [27]. My focus will be on actor-networks for the EPR as defined by its users in their particular healthcare roles and settings.

The concept of inscription, central to Actor-Network Theory, is the translation of interests into material form [28] through the design, configuration and use of material artefacts. This concept is used to discuss the manifestation of interests within EPR systems in specific local settings, in doing so revealing the ways in which power and politics emerge from the actor-network. This paper therefore presents an Actor-Network Theory analysis of the implications of EPRs for clinicians' work practices through discussing their actor-networks for the technology. Through its agnosticism about scale [29] and its ability to trace connections between entities at micro, meso and macro level [30], ANT is able to support analysis of how this technology is manifested across multiple organisations, and therefore be sensitive to its networked aspects.

3   Experiences of EPRs

These findings derive from interviews with EPR users and draw out aspects of discussions that relate to benefits and disadvantages of EPR use, or non-use.

EPR users interviewed indicate a consensus that electronic patient records are beneficial through being more accessible than paper records in a number of ways. All clinical users agreed that EPRs are a significant improvement on paper records in terms of legibility and because they are not lost or misplaced. They can also be accessed concurrently by multiple individuals rather than being tied up by a single user at a time. The improved accessibility of patient records entails advantages in terms of time and human resources which would previously have been spent tracking down paper case notes, and reduced delays in getting access to record information which could otherwise affect the responsiveness and timeliness of patient care. Furthermore the flexibility and convenience of 'anytime, anywhere' access to electronic records was noted by a number of clinicians, enabling them to access EPRs from different locations on site and potentially off-site.

A second area in which users see EPRs as beneficial is in terms of more and better quality clinical information about patients, with access to the integrated clinical contributions of different professional groups, including doctors, nurses and Allied Healthcare Professionals, where their records would previously have been relatively inaccessible. Easier access to patient information also supports information sharing with healthcare professionals in other organisations as clinicians can respond more quickly and accurately to enquiries.

In this respect, a specialist hospital, which by definition treats patients usually treated by other healthcare providers, allows access to their EPR for local GPs and hospitals via web portal. Nevertheless access was found to be little used in practice, challenging the idea that EPRs might fulfil a knowledge management function.

Challenges are experienced in terms of the continued need for paper documents to bridge between Trusts. This reflects the distributed-ness of care pathways for patients, especially those with chronic conditions or multiple co-morbidities, so that Trusts need the means to communicate effectively with each other about their patients. The persistence of paper makes it necessary to scan forms and letters into electronic format, creating demand for additional human resource. Moreover users complain that scanned documents are inconvenient to use because of the time taken to open individual files and the difficulty of finding detail within them, although it was noted that thumbnails and bookmarking functionality help to mitigate this.

The continued reliance on paper also indicates that EPR systems remain largely local and are not integrated between Trusts, as originally envisioned by NPfIT. Certain types of information are shareable via EPR applications between Trusts, with local EPR systems of participant Trusts incorporating functionality allowing requests for tests and treatments, such as blood tests, X Rays and MRI scans, and communication of results to be done electronically through the EPR. The NHS healthcare model requires clinicians to request services from service provider facilities, often in other Trusts; therefore this functionality within EPR systems supports the model and is reported as being heavily used by clinicians.

Clinical specialisms are a significant shaper of EPRs and have a bearing on how well EPR systems fit with and support (or fail to support) work practices. In Critical Care and surgery EPRs are perceived as being of less value than in other specialisms. For chronic conditions such as asthma and diabetes that entail ongoing demand for healthcare services treatment cuts across multiple healthcare organisations, entailing a need for greater collaboration and information sharing. EPRs are seen as essential for effective management of chronic disease because of the need to track and monitor a range of physiological data from tests and readings over time, for example when monitoring of a patient's weight or blood sugar levels. This is impossible without structured records that facilitate filtering and organising of that information, and moreover EPRs provide the ability to manipulate and visualise that data.

"There's certain things that are very difficult to do without a computer, chronic disease management is one of them" (Business Change Manager, PCT A).

Diabetes is a specialism where the EPR is perceived as particularly beneficial, and for this reason a participant hospital Trust has developed a diabetes-specific area within their EPR which is shared with and contributed to by the community diabetes team and GPs in the local area. This presents a relatively rare instance of an inter-organisational EPR being used to provide 'seamless' care, and while still partial in content, is the closest to the vision of whole record sharing.

The patient empowerment and self-care agendas in the NHS aim to enable patients with chronic and lifestyle-related conditions to take greater responsibility for their own care [31], not least because such conditions are expensive to treat and potentially detrimental to long-term quality of life. A number of users reported that the ability to graph clinical data, such as blood pressure readings, for individual patients is particularly valuable in supporting effective consultations in relation to behaviour change, and the development of patients' own expertise.

Reduced duplication of recording is cited as an anticipated benefit of EPR systems [32] in relation to the integration of previously disparate records systems within Trusts. For example, clinical entries made in the EPR can be reused for hospital discharge letters to GPs by cutting and pasting content, thereby reducing rework. However, the efficiency and value of EPRs in terms of capture and sharing of (close to) real time patient data is predicated on the assumption of contemporaneous recording [33, 34], and where consultations are not office-based or clinicians are unable to enter data into the EPR at the bedside they rely on recording notes on paper or using a dictaphone for input later.

3.1   Materiality

The extent to which EPRs benefit users relates not only to content and scope of information sharing but also to material aspects of EPR use including interweaving of access and use with work practices. These considerations are closely tied to users' roles and healthcare settings, and represent one way in which non-human actors are significant within the actor-network.

Computing hardware presents physical considerations for EPR use in terms of whether there are enough devices and whether they are available in the locations they are needed, and the suitability of hardware, whether desktop or mobile devices, for particular settings and clinical functions. A nurse participant from a Critical Care ward complained of the lack of physical space for the Computers on Wheels, comprising a workstation attached to a trolley, provided for consultants to access EPRs at the bedside, and intended to be moved around the ward during ward rounds. There is also insufficient hardware for staff in other work spaces, such as the nurses' stations, as well as challenges with fitting EPR use around unpredictable work practices characteristic of urgent care settings.

Users are reliant on adequate broadband connection for network access, highlighted as an issue for community services where clinicians go out on home visits. In one Trust mobile broadband had been trialled with community Occupational Therapists, who reported problems with accessing and using EPRs in some geographic areas due to poor network coverage. A specialist consultant who regularly works outside his own Trust noted that network access permissions can be a barrier to EPR use when working away from his 'home' Trust site, highlighting that assumptions on which access is based do not fit all modes of working.

Material access issues highlight the localness of EPRs, in tension with the ambition for inter-organisational sharing which demands inter-connected access and recording-related processes. That material aspects of use may be a constraint reflects the largely autonomous nature of NHS Trusts and the need for robust information governance to manage the sharing of patient records in ways which protect patient privacy.

3.2 Distribution of Benefits

Benefits and disadvantages are not equally distributed, with hospital consultants acknowledging that junior doctors experience greater difficulties in gaining access to computers to view records, and that they do not have secretarial support to input clinical entries into EPRs on their behalf. In this respect secretaries shield consultants from having to alter their work practices too much and in this way consultants experience the benefits of the EPR without as many of the disadvantages.

Access to hardware also operates hierarchically so that if there is a shortage of computers there is an informal expectation that nurses, administrators, Allied Healthcare Professionals and junior doctors should give up a computer they are using for a consultant. Although not necessarily experienced as a burden or disadvantage by secretaries, the use of EPRs in hospital settings is reliant on their work, and it is acknowledged that anticipated efficiency gains from EPRs in terms of clinical activity must be offset against increased demands for secretarial time.

Users also reported that EPR use is associated with new information requirements and work responsibilities, reflected, for example, in an increase in recording compared with paper records. Furthermore in order to have an input into the ongoing development of EPRs users must invest time in keeping up to date with technical developments, and in training and familiarising themselves with the functionalities of the system.

3.3   Secondary Uses

An information-driven NHS entails increased demand for greater quantities of and more granular data. This is brought about in part by demand for internal and external accountability for use of resources and quality of care, and EPRs are envisaged as essential in supporting this strategy [35]. In this respect EPRs inscribe non-clinical purposes and agendas in addition to supporting clinical practice, and these include provision of data quantifying clinical activities and numbers and types of patients treated.

"Now you have to be able to not only *do* things to patients, you have to *prove* that you've done it. That's the only way you get paid." (GP, General Practice D).

This generates a requirement for diagnostic and treatment information to be captured in coded and structured form, for example, using Read codes, an alphanumeric coding scheme for representing diagnoses and treatments within electronic patient records, or drop down menus which provide a fixed set of options for documenting aspects of care. This places a demand on clinicians to record information in structured form, which they may not otherwise capture in this way for their own clinical purposes. One consultant expressed frustration that he could not order an ultrasound scan for a patient because the given body part was not available in the options for that field within the EPR. Restricting options for recording not only facilitates standardised clinical recording, it also constrains representation of reality and can therefore be used to present organisational activity in a better light [36].

The evidence-based medicine agenda is reflected in the use of EPRs as a mechanism to support the standardisation of clinical practice. In one participant hospital Trust, the EPR enables pre-configured sets of medications for anaesthetics and pain management use with certain categories of patient, which are provided in a drop down menu. This encourages the use of the standard prescribing protocols by making it easier to prescribe in this way and also therefore discourages clinicians from selecting more freely from available medications when prescribing. The protocols derive from National Institute of Health and Care Excellence[1] guidelines, thereby also making the EPR a tool to promote and legitimise the evidence-based medicine agenda.

This use of EPRs to encourage standardisation is linked with clinical audit and associated targets for care quality improvement, which acts as a form of performance management in relation to clinical practice. Recording in the EPR therefore reflects the accountability agenda, including that of medico-legal accountability.

"What is does is back up what you're doing so anything to do you can be held accountable for so if anything went to coroner's you've got proof that you've been doing your job." (Nurse, Hospital B).

For certain conditions explicitly targeted by the Department of Health the EPR is used as a checklist of activities to ensure not only that a minimum standard of care, but that there is recorded evidence to demonstrate that targets have been met. Care quality targets are also tied to payments for Trusts' services and additional financial incentives, for example, through the Quality Outcomes Framework for GPs and Payment by Results for hospitals. EPRs play a critical role in providing the evidence of

---

[1] http://www.nice.org.uk/

such activity and of the meeting of targets and other measures of performance against centrally defined criteria.

4   Discussion

Clinicians' experiences of EPR use are strongly mediated both by their material aspects and by the inscriptions that derive from non-clinical agendas, as outlined above. These inscriptions serve as mechanisms to enforce standards in clinical activity, not only through focussing attention on the achievement of targets and measurable indicators of good practice but also by selectively enabling and constraining particular recording practices which then feed into clinical behaviours.

Unsurprisingly users who have an interest in clinical research and management-related uses of data are more concerned about the availability of structured data than with narrative-style recording, with structured data more easily aggregated, while for clinical purposes narrative recording, for example in clinical notes, remains important. This highlights the tension between what is clinically useful and support for broader organisational objectives.

In general users are ambivalent but accepting of EPRs as a technology, creating a sense that use is inevitable and that there is no going back to paper records. This lack of criticality is recognised in other studies that investigate the implications of health information systems e.g. [37, 38], and arises, I suggest, because EPR use is entangled with the use of those inscriptions such that non-use is all but impossible and would disadvantage users. Moreover clinicians acknowledge the need to carry out some information activities for the wider benefit of the organisation.

In so far as non-clinical managerial and other agendas are inscribed within EPRs they are impossible to resist and as such power effects are played out through a variety of controls over clinical and non-clinical behaviours, mediated by the EPR. This pervasiveness therefore has implications for the ability of users to challenge or avoid non-clinical agendas. It is argued that the insinuation of an information system into the organisational context restructures users' entire social world, such that opposition becomes lost [39]. Their embeddedness within clinical activity means that EPR use tacitly acts to stabilise these inscriptions and legitimise the agendas of which they are a part. For example, their use to support performance measures such as those used in national league tables provides reciprocal legitimacy for both performance management mechanisms and for the EPR.

It is argued that an actor-network reshapes reality such that its existence becomes taken for granted [40]. In terms of users' limited criticality about EPRs it can also be argued from an Actor-Network perspective that the stabilisation of the EPR in any organisational context necessarily entails a reconfiguration of reality to accommodate the EPR such that it is hard to imagine the world without it. In this respect EPR use has become part and parcel of what clinicians do on a daily basis not only on a clinical level but also in terms of non-clinical activities around performance reporting and accountability. Once established such an entity may be taken for granted, hidden from view and closed to debate and scrutiny. This is particularly the case for infrastructures, which are by definition, intended to become 'part of the furniture' [26].

Nevertheless, it has been recognised within the Information Systems literature on power and information systems that users are not necessarily passive subjects in this respect, and may use EPRs to 'play the system' to their advantage e.g. [41], for example to produce more positive self-representations. Within this study users reported using data from EPRs as evidence to support their own performance appraisals and also to exploit the ways in which EPRs focus attention on particular measures to present their organisation in the best light in various 'figures'. One GP noted that performance targets imposed by the UK Department of Health had skewed clinical recording such that it had become a running joke among GPs that the Quality Outcomes Framework has "cured depression overnight", alluding to the observation that GPs are more reluctant to record diagnoses which entail setting in motion a set of clinical activities that are perceived as laborious.

Where benefits are experienced from inter-organisational sharing of patient information, this has been partial and related to particular sub-sets of patient information, such as the diabetes element of the EPR, and communication of tests and results.

5   Conclusion

Using Actor-Network Theory as a methodological approach reveals a range of interests and relationships implicated in the achievement of the EPR as a technological phenomenon, incorporating both clinical and non-clinical agendas. Reporting findings about clinicians' experiences of day to day EPR use grounds the envisioned aim of a nationally networked EPR within local realities. The ideal of a networked EPR as an infrastructure and enabler of wider uses of patient information has only been partially realised. Clinicians make use of certain aspects of inter-organisational sharing via EPRs, however low uptake and use of the national Summary Care Record, and low usage of the specialist hospital's EPR indicates that these instances have as yet failed to translate clinical interests in such a way that they can stabilise.

While the nationally networked EPR has not yet been realised, additional risks and responsibilities associated with EPR use are nevertheless related to the overall information strategy of which this is a part. While there are undoubtedly benefits to users, disadvantages also have to be absorbed in terms of additional responsibilities, such as increased recording, capturing information in coded form, and greater scrutiny of clinical practice which relate both to material aspects of use that mediate access within given use settings and inscriptions of non-clinical agendas.

EPRs bring benefits to clinicians in a number of fundamental ways, centred on more reliable access to patient information as compared with paper records, both for the records themselves and in terms of the availability of greater quantities and more sources of information about patients.

However, benefits and disadvantages are not experienced equally by all groups of users, such that EPRs may in some respects reinforce existing hierarchies and professional boundaries. This supports Vikkelso's [42] conceptualisation of technologically enabled organisational change in terms of shifts and redistributions rather than simply in terms of improvements. In this way the study reinforces findings from the literature that suggest that EPRs may be less transformative than expected because users try to minimise the impact on their work practices [29]. This also challenges the assumption that EPRs and health information systems will straightforwardly empower healthcare professionals by liberating them from certain activities and through increased and more democratic access to patient information, as acknowledged in the literature e.g. [42].

This study, by taking a meso level approach, offers an analysis of the EPR across a number of local instances, recognising it as a multiple research object. The research contributes to the literature on this topic by analysing benefits to clinical practice in relation to EPRs as local applications and as national infrastructure. It suggests that to date benefits have largely been experienced in relation to local organisational EPRs, restricted in networkedness to individual Trusts, challenging expectations behind the original objective of infrastructure-like nationally networked records. The benefits of the various types of EPR and the roles they play in supporting clinician's work practices will have implications for the successful achievement of EPRs as technological innovations, and will influence the feasibility of achieving the government's long-term vision for the information revolution in healthcare.

References

1. Greenhalgh, T., Morris, L., Wyatt, J.C., Thomas, G., Gunning, K.: Introducing a nationally shared electronic patient record: Case study comparison of Scotland, England, Wales and Northern Ireland. International Journal of Medical Informatics 82(5), 125–138 (2013)
2. Wanless, D.: Securing Good Health for the Whole Population: final report. HMSO, Norwich (2004)
3. Department of Health: Informatics Planning 2010/11, London (2009), http://www.dh.gov.uk/en/Publicationsandstatistics/Publications/PublicationsPolicyAndGuidance/DH_110335 (retrieved)
4. Burns, F.: Information for Health: An Information Strategy for the Modern NHS 1998-2005, NHS Executive (1998)
5. NHS Executive: Building the information core: implementing the NHS Plan (2001), http://www.dh.gov.uk/prod_consum_dh/groups/dh_digitalassets/dh/en/documents/digitalasset/dh_4066946.pdf (retrieved)
6. Department of Health: The power of information: Putting all of us in control of the health and care information we need. Department of Health. Department of Health, London (2012)
7. Takian, A., Cornford, T.: NHS information: Revolution or evolution? Health Policy and Technology 1(4), 193–198 (2012)
8. Berg, M., Goorman, E.: The contextual nature of medical information. International Journal of Medical Informatics 56(1), 51–60 (1999)
9. Nicolini, D.: The work to make telemedicine work: A social and articulative view. Social Science & Medicine 62(11), 2754–2767 (2006)
10. Thorp, J.: Secondary Uses Service Strategic Direction, NHS Connecting for Health (2007)
11. Care Record Development Board: Report of the Care Record Development Board Working Group on the Secondary Uses of Patient Information. Department of Health (2007)
12. Greenhalgh, T., Potts, H.W.W., Wong, G., Bark, P., Swinglehurst, D.: Tensions and Paradoxes in Electronic Patient Record Research: A Systematic Literature Review Using the Meta-narrative Method. Milbank Quarterly 87(4), 729–788 (2009)

13. House of Commons Committee of Public Accounts: The dismantled National Programme for IT in the NHS. The Stationery Office (2013),
    http://www.publications.parliament.uk/pa/cm201314/cmselect/cmpubacc/294/294.pdf
14. National Audit Office: The National Programme for IT in the NHS: an update on the delivery of detailed care records systems. The Stationery Office, London (2011)
15. Payton, F.C., Pare, G., LeRouge, C.M., Reddy, M.: Health Care IT: Process, People, Patients and Interdisciplinary Considerations. Journal of the Association for Information Systems 1(2), i–xiii (2011)
16. Jones, M.: Computers can land people on Mars, why can't they get them to work in a hospital. Methods of Information in Medicine 42, 410–415 (2003)
17. Anderson, R., Walport, M.: Do summary care records have the potential to do more harm than good? British Medical Journal 340, 1390–1391 (2010)
18. Cresswell, K., et al.: Actor-Network Theory and its role in understanding the implementation of information technology developments in healthcare. BMC Medical Informatics and Decision Making 10(1), 67 (2010)
19. Bonner, B., Chiasson, M., Gopal, A.: Restoring balance: How history tilts the scales against privacy. An Actor-Network Theory investigation. Information and Organization 19(2), 84–102 (2009)
20. Bloomfield, B.P., Coombs, R.: Information Technology, Control and Power: the Centralization and Decentralization Debate Revisited. Journal of Management Studies 33(2), 20–459 (1992)
21. Doolin, B.: Narratives of Change: Discourse, Technology and Organization. Organization 10(4), 751–770 (2003)
22. Berg, M., Langenberg, C., Kwakkernaat, J.: Considerations for sociotechnical design: experiences with an electronic patient record in a clinical context. International Journal of Medical Informatics 52(1), 243–251 (1998)
23. Hedström, K.: The Socio-Political Construction of CareSys. In: Damsgaard, J., Henriksen, H.Z. (eds.) Networked Information Technologies. IFIP AICT, vol. 138, pp. 1–18. Springer, Heidelberg (2004)
24. Law, J.: Notes on the theory of the actor-network: ordering, strategy, and heterogeneity. Systems Practice 5(4), 379–393 (1992)
25. Law, J.: Actor Network Theory and Material Semiotics, Centre for Science Studies and Department of Sociology, Lancaster University (version of April 25, 2007)
26. Star, S.L.: Power, technologies and the phenomenology of standards: On being allergic to onions. In: Law, J. (ed.) A Sociology of Monsters, pp. 27–57. Routledge, London (1991)
27. Law, J., Singleton, V.: Object lessons. Organization 12(3), 331–355 (2005)
28. Callon, M.: Techno-economic networks and irreversibility. In: Law, J. (ed.) A Sociology of Monsters: Essays on Power, Technology and Domination, pp. 132–161 (1991)
29. Latour, B.: On actor-network theory: a few clarifications. Soziale Welt 47, 369–381 (1996)
30. Nicolini, D.: Zooming In and Out: Studying Practices by Switching Theoretical Lenses and Trailing Connections. Organization Studies 30(12), 1391–1418 (2009)
31. Darzi, A.: NHS next stage review: interim report, Department of Health (2007)
32. Greenhalgh, T., Stramer, K., Bratan, T., Byrne, E., Russell, J., Hinder, S., Potts, H.: The devil's in the detail: final report of the independent evaluation of the Summary Care Record and Health Space programmes. UCL, London (2010)
33. Eason, K.: Local sociotechnical system development in the NHS National Programme for Information Technology. Journal of Information Technology 22(3), 257–264 (2007)

34. Sheikh, A., Cornford, T., Barber, N., Avery, A., Takian, A., Lichtner, V., Petrakaki, D., Crowe, S., Marsden, K., Robertson, A.: Implementation and adoption of nationwide electronic health records in secondary care in England: final qualitative results from prospective national evaluation in "early adopter" hospitals. British Medical Journal 343, 1–14 (2011)

35. The Information Centre: Health and Social Care Information Centre Strategic Plan 2012 - 2015 and Business Plan 2012 - 2013. NHS (2012)

36. Ramiller, N.C.: Constructing safety: System designs, system effects, and the play of heterogeneous interests in a behavioral health care setting. International Journal of Medical Informatics 76, S196–S204 (2007)

37. Mensink, W., Birrer, F.A.: The role of expectations in system innovation: the Electronic Health Record, immoderate goal or achievable necessity? Central European Journal of Public Policy 4(1), 36–59 (2010)

38. Checkland, K., McDonald, R., Harrison, S.: Ticking Boxes and Changing the Social World: Data Collection and the New UK General Practice Contract. Social Policy & Administration 41(7), 693–710 (2007)

39. Lowe, A.: Casemix accounting systems and medical coding: Organisational actors balanced on leaky black boxes. Journal of Organizational Change Management 14(1), 79–100 (2001)

40. Bowker, G.C., Star, S.L.: How things (actor-net) work: Classification, magic and the ubiquity of standards. Philosophia 25(3-4), 195–220 (1996)

41. Doolin, B.: Casemix Management in a New Zealand Hospital: Rationalisation and Resistance. Financial Accountability & Management 15(3-4), 397–417 (1999)

42. Vikkelso, S.: Subtle redistribution of work, attention and risks: Electronic patient records and organisational consequences. Scandinavian Journal of Information Systems 17(1), 3 (2005)

Information Technology – The Unredeemed Opportunity to Reduce Cultural and Social Capital Gaps between Citizens and Professionals in Healthcare

Jani S.S. Koskinen and Sari Knaapi-Junnila

Information System Science, Turku School of Economics, University of Turku, Finland
{jasiko,sari.knaapi-junnila}@utu.fi

Abstract. Patient empowerment and involvement are significant aims in long-term diseases, but short appointments give only little room for conversations. However, the patients need various information and support from healthcare professionals. So, there are pressures to develop new, effective ways for reciprocal communication in addition to the traditional ones.

Courses of action related in care, amongst other things, are unfamiliar to ordinary citizens, as professionals operate on their home ground having the power to control situations. Furthermore, healthcare jargon, often used in healthcare settings, is unintelligible for many laymen. This is problematic because it may inhibit the aimed empowerment and involvement from happening.

Key findings from Coper-pilot research project alongside the former research's findings indicate that cultural and social gap between citizens' and healthcare professionals' may hinder their communication and mutual understanding. Information technology and salutogenic approach together can act as means to reduce that gap by strengthening layman's position.

Keywords: information technology, cultural capital, social capital, professional-patient relationship, communication, health services, layman's terms.

1 Introduction

Patient involvement has become an important factor for healthcare and policy makers [1]. Research on patient centeredness and patient empowerment has shown the crucial meaning why people must have a possibility to participate to their own health care [2,3,4]. If people are treated in a paternalistic way, the outcome is not supporting patient commitment to their own care of health and wellbeing. At the same time there is a discussion in the society of how to support and encourage people to take better care of their health. The conflict is obvious but the reasons for this situation are complex and not easily solvable. In this paper, we are approaching this issue by presenting some common problems in healthcare and by reflecting those problems with research

K.K. Kimppa et al. (Eds.): HCC11 2014, IFIP AICT 431, pp. 333–346, 2014.
© IFIP International Federation for Information Processing 2014

which is conducted in the Coper-pilot project, a sub-project of the Pump-project[1]. Firstly, traditional behaviour in healthcare settings emphasizes the unbalanced interaction between patients and professionals. Secondly, in communication and language level occurs many problems that complicate interaction. Thirdly, also structural problems exists - the medical appointments are arranged mainly to meet professional's needs.

When thinking of the problems in healthcare, Bourdieu's work can be seen as a strong tool to help understanding the reasons behind faced problems. Bourdieu is one of the most known sociologist who has researched power and social relations in different organizations and different levels of social life [5,6,7,8]. The field of healthcare seems to be a field which has a strong own hierarchy, strict rules, dominant biomedical worldview and self-governing mechanism securing the field. Western healthcare is strictly regulated and healthcare professionals are required to have formal education and authorisation to act in their positions. This is essential for the safety of the patient, but it has also costs - it creates unequal relation between layman´s and professionals´ positions. When some field have very strong cultural and social capital, the field gains an extraordinary position in society. In this paper we claim that professional's cultural and social capital may leave patients outsiders or visitors in encounters within healthcare. The aforementioned forms of capitals are used as Bourdieu is using them in his own work [7].

Common language may miss in a patient-doctor interaction because of the differences of professionals´ and laymen´s cultural capital. If a doctor uses professional jargon when (s)he talks with patients, unintelligible language leaves the patients as an outsiders. This kind of behaviour can be seen as a symbolic violation. In addition to that, patient contacts with healthcare – like doctor's appointments – are still too often arranged in such a way that doesn't enable patient empowerment or cannot be described as patient centric. Current healthcare system seems to have such a strong biomedical worldview, which does not take the patients´ everyday life sufficiently into account.

The key area of this paper is in developing the worldview and the social and cultural characteristics of healthcare to better enable patients´ empowerment and participation. In addition, we argue that information technology can be used to reduce effects of the aforementioned problems of healthcare, even though technology itself is not in the focus of this paper. Patients´ cultural and social capital related their own health can be increased with proper technology, which is designed to meet the patients´ needs. That kind of systems can lower the needed effort for gaining such capital that establishes more equal relationship with healthcare professionals. So, information technology is seen as a tool which can be used to reduce the gap between patients and professionals, but the main aim of the paper is to raise awareness about the issue of problematic inequality of cultural and social capital in healthcare.

---

[1] The Pump project (2011–2014) is a project aiming to develop citizen-centric services to the field of health and well-being services in Finland. The project, funded by European Regional Development Fund (ERDF), is divided into five operational units. Each unit focuses on seamless service provisioning from a different perspective. In the Coper-pilot, the focus is on cardiac patients. http://workinformatics.utu.fi/coper/index.html

2   Cultural and Social Capital as a Source of Asymmetry between Citizens and Professionals in Healthcare

Cultural capital can exist in three forms: in an embodied state, in an objectified state and in an institutionalized state. The Embodied state is a form of capital, which is achieved by self-improvement or other personal investment, and thus has personal costs. One cannot get such capital by second hand; it is embodied to a person and in many cases in the person's body (e.g. gained capacity or embodied skill) [7]. Healthcare professionals have created this kind of capital by developing medical skills and knowledge. On the other hand, patients possess crucial understanding and information about their own life, health and potential consequences of their own actions, and that knowledge is not obtainable for others and thus is embodied state of their own. That kind of deep understanding differs from professional's capital and can be achieved only by living one's life. The objectified state is a kind of cultural capital which is objectified in its embodied form [7]. One form of this are writings which have cultural value in the society. In healthcare such cultural capital are e.g. papers and information systems (artefacts) which contains medical and other relevant information. Likewise, patient can have capital which is objectified: notes, diaries etc. but it seems that those are not recognised like the professionals' ones are. The institutionalized state is a form of capital which has granted a formal position (e.g. academic education, qualification for a physician´s job) and thus can be seen as the way to give recognition for some certain embodied skill or set of skills [7]. While embodied state of capital is implemented by personal self-improvement the institutionalized one is recognized by some institution or society, like doctors are usually licensed (institutionalization) to act. However, this institutionalization is not implemented for the capital possessed by patients, and thus it elevates the position of professionals by cost of the position of patients supporting asymmetricity in their relationship.

Bourdieu's social capital is such form of capital which is bounded to some social group. It can be seen as a network of relationships which produces benefits for its members. Usually the network members have some common goals and benefits. This social network (as healthcare is) is a product of investment strategies, individual or collective, and it establishes or reproduces the relations which are worthwhile for the network [7].

2.1   Status, Attitude and Organization Culture as Manifestations of Cultural and Social Capital

Healthcare professionals have gained certain cultural capital (education, knowledge and experience) during their education and practise of the profession. They need this kind of embodied capital to apply when practicing the care and treatments for patients. However, along with objectified and institutionalized capital (which are seen e.g. in courses of action and decision-making structures), it enables professionals to exercise power [1]. Doctors are highly respected professionals, who are often thought to be capable of even heroic actions. When healthcare professionals have such social capital, the inequality between professionals and patients is understandable but still not acceptable.

Buetow et al. have pointed out, that along with information societies, where increasingly many occupations have become professions, people´s behaviour have changed. These effects of modernisation has reduced social distances between doctors and evermore educated patients and revised healthcare´s traditional patterns to more modern ones. Many of these patients want to be active social actors and collaborate with their doctors. However, like less modern or non-modern patients, there are also non-modern doctors [9]. So, not everyone long for or welcome more active collaboration in doctor-patient interaction. Because of doctors´ medicine-based capital, their position in healthcare settings enable them to choose, what kind of course of action is used. As for patient, (s)he does not necessarily have sufficient authority for influencing them. Difficulties, that hinder the abandonment of traditional patterns[10,11] keeping patients more passive, involve both individual- and organization level in healthcare [10]. Still existing asymmetry of cultural and social capital in doctor-patient interaction may in part explain why these patterns are so hard to revise.

Patient-doctor interaction is significant when it comes to health outcomes [10,11,12,13,14] and patient satisfaction [10,11,15]. Successful communication strengthens the doctor-patient relationship, enhances their mutual agreement and improves patient´s self-care skills [11,16]. Moreover, it can increase the effect of medical treatment [14] and decrease costs through diminishing the need for diagnostic testing [17]. So, there are many reasons to put out for satisfactory patient-doctor interaction.

2.2   Unintelligible Language and Availability Restrictions of Information as Manifestations of Cultural and Social Capital

The relationship and interaction between patients and doctors have developed recently more equal in many countries [9,12]. By providing patients with more information, doctors can enhance communication as well as (care) outcomes [12]. Despite the progress, that has taken place, there are still issues, which need deeper inspection and advancement. Patient-centric care (or patient-driven approach), just like shared decision making, collaboration and partnership, is an issue, which has been discussed widely recent years, and its many advantages have been noticed [10,11]. If the common goal in healthcare is to improve patient-doctor interaction so that it would become a more equal partnership, common and mutually understandable language must exist.

Sometimes the obstacle to an effective communication can be for instance Latin terms and other uncommon words, that doctors use [12], when it comes to illness, operations and care. If healthcare professionals use difficult language - when also comprehensible terms could be used - it can be seen as using symbolic power. Symbolic power is a form of power, which is based on social and cultural capital of agents of some group (such as doctors), and is used to enforce the relations that constitute the structure of social space (in healthcare settings) [8]. When symbolic power is used, it emphasises a situation where professionals are hierarchically above patients. In such situations professionals have control over the information [12], situation and treatments instead of collaboration, even when the patient would wish the opposite action. Healthcare professional may have a noble goal to make right decisions and ensure the patients´ health and subsistence. However, if the patients are not trained to use that kind of healthcare jargon, it hinders their understanding of the facts related to their own condition and care. Obviously, this situation limits patients´ rights to consider their options and to be aware of potential consequences of their decisions. Furthermore it prevents their empowerment. Therefore, a severe effort to revise communication more effective and break down barriers of cultural differences between patients and healthcare professionals is essential.[12]

It appears that patients would be more eager to revise patient-doctor interaction style from biomedical style to more patient centric than doctors so far [17]. The modern-way, more equal, patient-doctor interaction seems also to create more benefits than costs to patients. These benefits, mostly related to communication and collaboration, would be worth providing to patients and also non-modern doctors, by assisting them if needed. [9]

2.3   Place, Course of Action and Operating Model as Manifestations of Cultural and Social Capital

There are many kinds of asymmetry when it comes to interaction between doctors and patients. These kinds of issues can link at the macro level with the operating model in healthcare organization whereas at the micro level they can relate to courses of action and structures of clinical visits. One micro level example is, who takes the initiative when a patient meets a doctor at clinical setting. Like ten Have has argued about doctor-patient interaction, usually there seems to be some level of consensus that it is the doctor´s right and responsibility to manage the agenda at appointment [18]. So, usually it is the doctor who is the initiator and the patient who responds to his/hers initiatives by asking questions. In this respect, the doctor has more power over talking points than the patient. When the interaction proceeds in such traditional way the doctor controls the situation, where disease-orientation in addition to biomedical issues are in the main part [10,11,17]. Because of this information about patients´ experiences, which could also be highly relevant to diagnosis and successful treatment, are inevitably taken to a back seat. For patients, gaining opportunities to ask questions from their doctors would be also important way to enhance understanding and satisfaction. [15]

Furthermore, Jones [19] has pointed out that after patients´ newsworthy answers in medical interviews, doctors do not usually offer to respond with an assessment although it would be a normal act in everyday talk and it would also be an excellent opportunity to give social support to their patients and to influence positively health outcomes. Instead, they do not respond at all, they just go on and stay strictly in the interview format. An action like this is surprising and troublesome for the patients and because of that there are gaps in the conversation when they think the doctor should answer with an assessment. Sometimes patients try again to get a response from their doctor. They can for example upgrade their answer, request an opinion or offer a lay diagnosis, but even then the doctors do not respond or when they do so, they use only a minimal acknowledgment token (for example "okay"). As Jones mentions, doctors pass up opportunities such as elaborating with their patients and showing empathy to them, when they direct attention away from patients´ answers. [19]

In Finland the citizens know quite a lot about illnesses because of good education. What is somewhat surprising, it seems that people tend to act in spite of that rather un-assertively with their doctor when the diagnosis is at issue. Peräkylä [20] has explored patients´ and doctors´ interaction in Finnish primary care with data which consisted of doctors´ diagnostic statements. He found that only in one thirds of the cases the patients responded by talking about diagnosis after their doctor had told the diagnosis to them. And, what is noteworthy, even then the patients responded with caution so that they displayed the doctor´s authority in medical reasoning. And further, he found that the way in which the doctor told about the diagnosis had a significant effect to the patient´s response. When the doctor explicated the diagnosis, it was more common that the patient responded by talking about diagnosis, otherwise not. [20] So it seems like the patients expect that their doctor puts across if it is appropriate for them to say something about that issue.

Patients are by no means passive members at these occurrences, they have also their ways to influence the conversations with the doctors, but it seems that they have to be careful. It is known that the patients can request a course of action, expand their answers to offer information which the doctor has not asked [19,21], request an opinion, or offer a lay diagnosis [19], which means a sort of explanation about the symptoms of illness that a person often makes himself/herself to make sense of his/her experiences, before (s)he decides to arrange an appointment to see a doctor [18]. However, when doing so, the patients are conscious of how sceptical the doctors might be if they tell about their lay diagnosis [21]. So, if they have enough courage, they try to tell their concerns in a delicate, respectful way and avoid to overtly challenge their doctor´s authority [18,21].

Visit length varies a lot between countries, but when longer visits exist, it enables the doctors to respect patients´ autonomy in clinical decision making [13]. A study conducted in six European countries (Belgium, Germany, Netherlands, Spain, Switzerland, United Kingdom) revealed that the mean length of consultations with general practitioner was only 10,7(SD 6,7) minutes. If the doctor perceived a psychosocial problem, consultation time increased significantly but this was not the case if the patient perceived the psychosocial problem (and the doctor not). So, the doctor has a remarkable impact on the duration of the consultation (and the issues at hand) although variables related to the doctor´s country and those related on patient have also an effect on the use of time. [22]

3   Coper-Pilot - Information Technology as a Possibility for Empowerment of Citizens

Salutogenic approach embeds with understanding of health as patients' experience of *home-likeness* in their own lives is used in Coper-pilot. This kind of viewpoint is needed if we are going to develop tools, like information systems, for patients [23]. The salutogenic approach focuses on wellbeing and life plan of people instead of sickness and other biomedical issues, which are the general points of view in healthcare. Hence, salutogenic approach foregrounds the patient´s role as a main actor.[24,25] The aspect, which is presented in this paper, is patients´ need to move from their current role into more active role as a professionals of their own life, and by implication of that, into equal partners with healthcare professionals. This is possible through proactive interventions in healthcare whilst developing information systems [23]. This approach - if put in practise - gives patients real possibilities to make informed consent about their care and treatments.

3.1   Coper-Pilot

Coper-pilot is a qualitative, citizen-driven research project, where University of Turku cooperates with Welfare Division of Turku and CGI Suomi Oy to develop and study a communal e-health-service. Defining what sort of requirements citizens have about e-health services has been a key issue in this pilot. Because we looked for patient-involving and empowering solutions, citizens with some kind of long-term disease were considered suitable for the target group. The decision about the target group was made together with the Welfare Division. Eventually, those citizens, who had some kind of heart related symptoms, and who were supposed to have an appointment at Internal Diseases Outpatient Clinic of Turku City Hospital because of those symptoms, were determined as the target group of the pilot. The study protocol was approved by University of Turku ethics committee and Welfare Division of Turku before the study began and the research team began to get in touch with citizens in May 2013.

Coper-pilot´s perspective to information systems can be defined as human scale. Our aim has been to find out ways in which e-services could assist and empower citizens in their everyday life and self-care to feel "home-like being-in-the-world" (see Svenaeus' definition of health [26]) even if there were some health issues on their hands. As for the term "Home-like", it could be figured as a state where one feels comfort in his/hers own life. So, the aim, amongst other things, was to gather understanding about our target group´s everyday life, their experiences about electronic services and their experiences about interactions between themselves and professionals in any kind of healthcare settings.

Citizens suitable for the above-mentioned target group were informed about the Coper-pilot by enclosing a letter of participation request in pursuance of the appointment notice to Internal Diseases Outpatient Clinic of Turku City Hospital. The research team provided the Internal Diseases Outpatient Clinic of Turku City Hospital with copies of the letters of participation requests, which were forwarded to the citizens by the departmental secretary (from May to December 2013). The citizens were asked to get in touch with research team if they were interested to hear more about this project or if they considered to get involved in it. After the citizens had been contacted the research team, they were given more information verbally and also on paper moreover they had an opportunity to ask further details before signing agreement of involvement in the research.

All in all 34 persons (13 women and 21 men) decided to participate in the Coper-pilot. Their average age was 68 and age range was 47 - 81 years. There were various data collection methods in Coper-pilot, and one of those was interviewing. In this context we are going to present only a few points that came out in the first round interviews. These thematic interviews (n=34) were held at places of interviewees´ choice, generally in a negotiation room at university or at their homes from June to December 2013. The interview themes dealt with health, well-being and being ill and also with experiences of healthcare and information technology in the interviewees´ everyday lives. In these individual and rather informal meetings two persons operated as interviewers at a time. The duration of each of the interviews was approximately two hours. All interviews were recorded digitally. The data collection and also lettering and analysis of its content were made by research team members (four persons).

Next we are going to present a few sections about aforementioned interviews. In some cases there seem to be problematic issues related to unequal cultural and social capital. At times the issues seem to be traditional behaviours or structural problems in healthcare settings that causes a friction between citizens and doctors. Also restrictions on availability of information and unintelligible language (language barrier and healthcare jargon) appear to separate the citizens from the professionals. Beside the problems, the citizens tell also about situations, where patient-doctor interaction has come true successfully and how this happened. All quotes are freely translated from Finnish to English for this paper. After the quote there is an identification letter and a number in square brackets.

3.2   Status, Attitude and Organization Culture as Manifestations of Cultural and Social Capital in Coper-Pilot

In Coper-pilot there were a wide variety of the citizens´ experiences, when it comes to doctors´ status and attitude in healthcare. Some of the citizens feel, that the organization culture enable the doctors to act nearly godlike, as for some of them have noticed positive progress, which has facilitated communication at least with some doctors. Like one citizen [A7] said, doctors attitude is quite important for a patient, it can be also a remarkable thing easing patient´s stress experience.

"It can be seen at hospitals even nowadays...their atmosphere has not changed a much, the doctor is the same as God, dictates everything...it is the hospital culture...it is such a wretched culture like Tutankhamun era, dominated by doctors..."[A8]

"He [the doctor] does not bother to listen and he has no time...and if he had [time], he has no interest...I can understand that...there are priests in a rut...doctors in a rut...they do not listen or tell nothing much..." [A12]

"The doctors have begun to treat people much better...I do not know if they know nothing, but it is nice to meet them...nicer than earlier, they treat people a bit better...Nowadays they ask, what kind of symptoms there are and what do I think that the problem is and things like that...In the olden days ...the patient was not allowed to know anything at all, he knew everything...even though not anywhere near...that much it has been changed..." *[A10]*

"It depends on the doctor, I must say. Yesterday there was a cardiologist whose attitude was positive. That is a very important point, I can see that now, how important it is... I nearly stopped to be stressed..." *[A7]*

The citizens admit readily, that beside doctors, it is also patients who have an influence to patient-doctor interaction and therefore also citizens have to be responsible for a good contact.

"The doctors will listen..., if you just tell them. But often there are such persons, who do not dare to ask anything....I have got all that I have asked. So, I could not ask anything more and I would not need either [anything more]. Therefore it has been very nice...It depends on a lot of the person, who happens to be on the opposing side, you have to take it into account. There are sometimes difficult ones on the opposing side...such [persons] might be also in healthcare..." [A14]

3.3   Unintelligible Language and Availability Restrictions of Information as Manifestations of Cultural and Social Capital in Coper-Pilot

In Coper-pilot it turned out that many citizens have difficulties getting information about their health, treatments and test results. Sometimes the citizens are not able to get information at all and sometimes the information they get is unintelligible for one reason or another (language barrier or professional jargon). These kind of situations make them angry and at the worst they can feel that the healthcare system have abandoned them.

"After heart operation I have been completely down and out. Information about myself is not obtainable hardy anywhere, because the only doctor appointments at the health centre are once a year. I have learned how hard it is to get information about myself.... It feels like dropping to nowhere, the operation... were handled correctly at the hospital but after that nobody...I have not been able to control..." [A3]

"There were 18 blood tests and the doctor told me nothing at all...I was angry at the night, why I was not allowed to know those...I realized that many issues, that I could had asked there right away, left once again without solving. Yet afterwards, I act up, why I did not ask those issues..." [A7]

Like the citizen cited beneath, many citizens were also interested, if there were some better than present-day ways to make an appointment (to a doctor or to an examination), to get results from examinations and to communicate with their doctor if needed during their care.

"It is one problem. I run, I have just been at the blood tests...Every time I have to call them. I think that it takes also the doctors´ time to no avail. If I could see that [blood test result] there [from computer]...it would be so much easier, the doctor would not have to, I would not have to bother every time the personnel at the health centre. Their time run out anyway..." [A3]

Even if the citizens manage to meet their doctor to get some information about their health, there can still remain some obstacles. Sometimes there seems not to be shared language between citizens and doctors: either the citizens find that some doctors´ have shortage of Finnish skills or their doctor speaks such professional language, jargon, that they are not able to understand. Lack of understanding causes uncertainty, because the citizen cannot be sure if (s)he has missed some important information. It is common that citizens just try to cope in spite of shortcomings in patient-doctor communication, many of them seek answers elsewhere (for example from Google) and only some of them continue asking until their doctor´s answer is understandable enough.

"All the medicines I use and I get from someone, I search for [from the computer], what it is, to which purpose it is used for and...It was just today, when I checked something about my blood test, what is the meaning of all those words...I have written them one by one to Google, that [an abbreviation of a blood test]and...One at a time it has turned out, what they are and what are those meanings..." [A10]

"It is that monks´ Latin in all those doctor´s accounts, even with Internet you do not manage to make out... what he is meaning...you can only guess...I could ask, if I and the doctor were just the two of us, but usually it is such a hurry that talking is out of question..." [A11]

"Generally speaking I have pretty good experiences about doctors....but when I had an Estonian... doctor...Finnish that she spoke was very weak...she said, she cannot understand...It causes to the patient such an uncertain feeling, that you doubt, if you can get all the information needed. But in other respect she was very kind and nice doctor..." [A20]

Fortunately sometimes a shared language between a citizen and a doctor is possible to find, but does the citizen have to understand medical jargon to make that happen? Is it not required, that the doctor would use such kind of terminology that the citizen can understand it?

"When I visited the cardiologist it was such kind of extremely good co-operation, although it was the first time I met him, we spoke immediately the same language...And he asked me, if I am a healthcare professional." [A27]

3.4   Place, Course of Action and Operating Model as Manifestations of Cultural and Social Capital in Coper-Pilot

The everyday difficulties, that the citizens told about healthcare´s practices, involved most often their doctors´ busyness, too brief appointments and missing possibilities to create a proper relationship in which they could collaborate with their doctor. Many citizens find it hard to settle their affairs with healthcare. Therefore, they are interested in seeking new courses of action to collaborate with their doctors, and they are also open to new operating models in healthcare organizations.

"Usually when you go to doctors´ practice, he is so busy that he has no time to even think. He is not listening." [A22]

"The situation is like that...the doctor´s...there is hurry and it can see...do not feel like bothering them..." [A1]

"Our healthcare is so foolish that these ...doctors change nearly every time when you go to doctors´ practice....There is no time to discuss, there is 15 minutes and

when there is a new patient, a new doctor relationship, it takes 13 minutes to get know each other, so the decisions should be made in 2 minutes." [A2]

"It is also such a nasty thing that you have to hop from one doctor to another doctor and every time you have to tell the same [story]..." [A28]

In those cases when the citizens are outstandingly pleased with their doctors and other health professionals, there seems to be typically a confidential, friendly and at best long relationship. The citizens have a high opinion on their doctor if they have positive, personal relationship with him/her, if they think (s)he is also competent and if they feel that the things move on smoothly.

"I have been in such a blissful situation, that I have had a personal doctor [at private sector], the familiar doctor... has helped me loads of, so I am in a better position than many other." [A21]

"There were a very good male nurse which was sometimes better than a doctor...In a small town, if the person have been there long time, he knows those people...and he is able to immediately..." [A23]

"He [the doctor] sent the referral immediately...so I will get there...Things like these, I feel that the things are taken care of...I do not have to ask everything separately..." [A24]

4   A Possibility to Increase Patients´ Cultural and Social Capital with Information Technology

People are not alike in their desire for autonomy in decisions related in health, in the matter of fact the differences are substantial although most of people want to engage in their health decisions. Although it is known that the desire for autonomy is higher among younger people, it is not clear if it relates to differences between generations or if the attitudes just change when the individual gets older. In any case, detection of patients´ wishes could simplify the patient-doctor interaction in both sides and moreover improve decision-making process.[27] By using information technology we can offer alternative solutions to log, watch and monitor personal health information so that both patients and healthcare professionals have an opportunity to take advantage of them. Furthermore, information technology enables many kinds of data capture, mediation and use. Accordingly, it is worthwhile for supporting self-care with individualized materials and communication between patients and healthcare professionals. [28,29] Moreover, the possibility to use web/video-appointments or communicate with safe web messages alongside with traditional appointments at health centre or by phone, gives long desired alternatives for individual needs. These kinds of new options may facilitate patients´ everyday lives and also the routines at health centres.

There are patients, who have difficulties to get involved in the decision-making process at the doctor´s practice when it comes to their illness, medical procedures and diagnosis. In our research some citizens consider that they have no ability or right to interfere in issues like that. Yet, it is known that patients commonly search information and talk with their family members about the symptoms of illness to search some kind of explanation to their experiences [18]. This kind on pre-clinical phase when a person is working with the lay diagnosis before (s)he makes an appointment to the doctor, could be one potential moment to take advantage of information technology with supports the needs of patients by offering different ways of communication, gaining and using the needed information even before the first meeting with a healthcare professional. Lee et al. [30], for example, have presented an interesting system, where patients´ (type 2 diabetes) clinical data was integrated into education material so that it enhanced learning and individual care also between the hospital appointments. They found the system easy, efficient and inexpensive in self-care. [30]

Adequate time is important when it comes to clinical visits, moreover it is important how the time is spent [13,31]. Because patients sympathize with pressures on their doctors, even a short visit does not bother if only the patient feels that the quality of time is good, and it is effectiveness of the communications and flexibility in time which influences on that [13]. It is interesting that even a small increase in actual time may have a notable impact to patient´s experience of the adequateness of time [13]. The possibility to communicate before the meeting could raise the quality of an appointment by giving the possibility for the patient to give more information or ask how to prepare for appointment. The technical limitations are not the problem, the needed technology is out there. Instead we need to focus on shifting the development from healthcare towards more patient or even citizen-centric direction [23].

At the fundamental level, ensuring that information system would be suitable for the patient needs, the aforementioned salutogenic approach of developing those systems is needed and should be used as guideline of development of healthcare [23,32]. The aim should be in finding such functions or solutions that support patient control of own life and well-being by enabling access to needed cultural and social capital with information technology. This also demands that the structure of healthcare and interactions between professionals and patients should be focused on patient's personal needs more than current system is doing.

5   Discussion

It seems that Bourdieu's conception of the cultural and social capital and salutogenic approach are strong tools when analysing the common problems in healthcare settings. The cultural and social capital, which is usually possessed by healthcare professionals, may leave patients in insecure positions. Likewise, the traditional biomedical worldview, which has not vanished yet, sets the patient to be an object with some medical problems and does not focus to the person behind the patient-role.

Based on the Coper-pilot´s preliminary findings, which support the former research, there exists a need to assist patients in narrowing still existing cultural and social capital gap in healthcare. We argue, that information technology offers countless opportunities, which are still unredeemed, to reduce cultural and social capital gaps between citizens and professionals in healthcare. The information system, which gives access to patient information and other medical information - that is easily understandable - would give the patients the capital they need: information about their own health and understanding about issue at hand. Then, translating the healthcare jargon to layman´s language, would give the needed common language for patient-doctor interaction. Information technology enables many alternatives for patient-doctor communication also between the traditional appointments so that interaction can meet both patients´ and professionals´ needs assisting their everyday lives.

For developing needed information systems we should have a new approach – the Salutogenic approach - which is designed to meet the people´s needs, not only the professionals´ and organizations´ needs, which is usually the case in healthcare. Salutogenic approach enables people to be more oriented towards their own health and wellbeing and thus makes possible to gain needed cultural and social capital so valuable in the field of healthcare. Future research, focusing healthcare interactions within different environments and methods, is needed for remeeding the available opportunities, that information technology has to offer.

Acknowledgements. Many thanks to the other members of the Coper-pilot team, Antti Tuomisto, Anna Korpela and Ronald Otim, for collaboration, support and significant comments - all that have been enormously helpful when we have written this paper.

References

1. Callaghan, G., Wistow, G.: Publics, patients, citizens, consumers? Power and decision making in primary healthcare. Public Administration 84(3), 583–601 (2006)
2. Mead, N., Bower, N.: Patient centredness: a conceptual framework and review of the empirical literature. Social Science & Medicine 51(7), 1087–1110 (2000)
3. Rappaport, J.: Terms of Empowerment/Exemplars of Prevention: Toward a Theory for Community Psychology. American Journal of Community Psychology 15(2), 121–148 (1987)
4. Holmström, I., Röing, M.: The relation between patient-centeredness and patient empowerment: A discussion on concepts. Patient Education and Counseling 79, 167–172 (2010)
5. Bourdieu, P.: Originally La Distinction translated by Nice R (1984) Distinction: A Social Critique of the Judgement of Taste. Harvard University Press, Cambridge (1984)
6. Bourdieu, P.: Homo Academicus. Translated by Collier P (1988). Polity Press, Oxford (1988)
7. Bourdieu, P.: The Forms of Capital. In: Richardson, J. (ed.) Handbook of Theory and Research for Sociology of Education, pp. 241–258. Greenwood, New York (1986)
8. Bourdieu, P.: Social Space and Symbolic Power. Sociological Theory 7(1), 14–25 (1989)
9. Buetow, S., Jutel, A., Hoare, K.: Shrinking social space in the doctor–modern patient relationship: A review of forces for, and implications of, homologisation. Patient Education and Counseling 74(1), 97–103 (2009)
10. Ponte, P.R., Conlin, G., Conway, J.B., Grant, S., Medeiros, C., Nies, J., Shulman, L., Branowicki, P., Conley, K.: Making Patient-centered Care Come Alive. Achieving Full Integration of the Patient's Perspective. Journal of Nursing Administration 33(2), 82–90 (2003)
11. Robinson, J.H., Callister, L.C., Berry, J.A., Dearing, K.: Patient-centered care and adherence: Definitions and applications to improve outcomes. Journal of the American Academy of Nurse Practitioners 20(12), 600–607 (2008)
12. Steinhart, B.: Patient autonomy: evolution of the doctor–patient relationship. Haemophilia 8(3), 441–446 (2002)

13. Braddock, C.H., Snyder, L.: The Doctor Will See You Shortly. The Ethical Significance of Time for the Patient-Physician Relationship. Journal of General Internal Medicine 20, 1057–1062 (2005)

14. Neumann, M., Edelhäuser, F., Kreps, G.L., Scheffer, C., Lutz, G., Tauschel, D., Visser, A.: Can patient–provider interaction increase the effectiveness of medical treatment or even substitute it?—An exploration on why and how to study the specific effect of the provider. Patient Education and Counseling 80, 307–314 (2010)

15. Robinson, J.D.: Asymmetry in action: Sequential resources in the negotiation of a prescription request. Text 21, 19–54 (2001)

16. Street Jr., R.L., Makoul, G., Arora, N.K., Epstein, R.M.: How does communication heal? Pathways linking clinician-patient communication to health outcomes. Patient Education and Counselling 74, 295–301 (2009)

17. Epstein, R.M., Franks, P., Shields, C.G., Meldrum, S.C., Miller, K.N., Campbell, T.L., Fiscella, K.: Patient-Centered Communication and Diagnostic Testing. Annals of Family Medicine 3(5), 415–421 (2005)

18. ten Have, P.: Lay diagnosis in interaction. Text 21, 251–260 (2001)

19. Jones, C.M.: Missing assessments: Lay and professional orientations in medical interviews. Text 21, 113–150 (2001)

20. Peräkylä, A.: Agency and Authority: Extended Responses to Diagnostic Statements in Primary Care Encounters. Research on Language and Social Interaction 35(2), 219–247 (2002), doi:10.1207/S15327973RLSI3502_5

21. Drew, P.: Spotlight on the patient. Text 21, 261–268 (2001)

22. Deveugele, M., Derese, A., van den Brink-Muinen, A., Bensing, J., De Maeseneer, J.: Consultation length in general practice: cross sectional study in six European countries. BMJ 2002; 325: 472.1 BMJ 2002; 325 (2002), doi: http://dx.doi.org/10.1136/bmj.325.7362.472

23. Lahtiranta, J., Koskinen, J.: Electronic health services for cardiac patients: a salutegenic approach. Finnish Journal of eHealth and eWelfare 5(2-3), 86–93 (2013)

24. Antonovsky, A.: Health, Stress and Coping. Jossey-Bass Publishers, San Francisco (1979)

25. Antonovsky, A.: Unraveling The Mystery of Health - How People Manage Stress and Stay Well. Jossey-Bass Publishers, San Francisco (1987)

26. Svenaeus, F.: The Hermeneutics of Medicine and Phenomenology of Health: Steps Towards Philosophy of Medical Practice. Kluwer Academic Publishers, Dordrecht (2001)

27. Cullati, S., Courvoisier, D.S., Charvet-Bérard, A.I., Perneger, T.V.: Desire for autonomy in healthcare decisions: A general population survey. Patient Education and Counseling 83, 134–138 (2011)

28. Steinberg, E.: Patient-Centric Communications Drive Quality, Fiscally Prudent Health Care Decisions. Employee Benefit Plan Review 60(8), 11–12 (2006)

29. Breen, G.-M., Wan, T.T.H., Zhang, N.J., Marathe, S.S., Seblega, B.K., Paek, S.C.: Improving Doctor–Patient Communication: Examining Innovative Modalities Vis-à-vis Effective Patient-Centric Care Management Technology. Journal of Medical Systems 33, 155–162 (2009)

30. Lee, T.-I., Yeh, Y.-T., Liu, C.-T., Chen, P.-L.: Development and evaluation of a patient-oriented education system for diabetes management. International Journal of Medical Informatics 76(9), 655–663 (2007)

31. Ogden, J., Bavalia, K., Bull, M., Frankum, S., Goldie, C., Gosslau, M., Jones, A., Kumar, S., Vasant, K.: "I want more time with my doctor": a quantitative study of time and the consultation. Family Practice 21, 479–483 (2004)

32. Knaapi-Junnila, S., Korpela, A., Koskinen, J., Otim, R.: Towards Citizens' Empowerment with the Coper-pilot. The 36th Information Systems Research Seminar in Scandinavia (2013)

PHR Revisioned – Navigating in the Personal Health Space

Janne Lahtiranta and Markku I. Nurminen

University of Turku, Turku School of Economics, Department of Management and
Entrepreneurship, Information Systems Science, Turku, Finland
{janne.lahtiranta@it.utu.fi, mnurmi@utu.fi}

Abstract. The field of health care and well-being services is changing due to
economic and societal reasons. One consequence of this ongoing change is that
individuals are encouraged to take an active role in their health and well-being
related endeavours. The objective of our conceptual work is to support this
change and identify mechanisms that can help individuals in their endeavours.
Our work is based on the findings of a project that are reassembled under the
metaphor of health navigator. The envisioned functions of the navigator are
analysed using activity theory as the underlying framework, and as a
consequence, human activity as the unit of analysis. The purpose of this
integrative work is to create a concept that draws together the complex aspects
that define one's position in the health space; the overarching state of health
related efforts.

Keywords: eHealth, Health Care Information Systems, Electronic Health
Records, Personal Health Information Management.

1   Introduction

In the changing health care landscape of today, navigating through series of health
related events (for example, in relation to diabetes) is a challenge to the patient.
Primary reasons for this include lack of integrative solutions and fragmentation of
health services. For example in Finland, the latter has led to a situation in which most
providers offer similar service but the overall volume for a single service is too small
[1]. Individual service providers are also disconnected from each other and from the
surrounding 'wired world' as the work of standardization organizations has not been
able to bring universally applicable solutions to the technical aspects of this dilemma.

On the level of an individual, the consequences of this kind of fragmentation are
rather evident, for example, if we look into the U.S. national health insurance program
Medicare. It is estimated that "average Medicare beneficiary sees two physicians and
five specialists a year, and that those with chronic illnesses see an average of thirteen
physicians a year", each focused on the particulars of their own specialty [2]. It
follows from this that it is practically impossible, or at least overtly encumbering, for
an individual to track one's position in the 'health space'; the overarching state of
health related affairs (cf. [3]).

K.K. Kimppa et al. (Eds.): HCC11 2014, IFIP AICT 431, pp. 347–361, 2014.
© IFIP International Federation for Information Processing 2014

In this paper we define a concept that will help individuals to understand a) where they are in terms of their illness or ailment, and b) what is their current position in relation to the health service providers. Our vision is that if these two goals can be achieved, it is possible to help the willing individuals to become active and cooperative actors in the matters of their health. The function of the concept is illustrated by comparing and contrasting the concept to an ordinary satellite navigation system (e.g. satnav).

Even though our approach is exploratory and conceptual, the underlying theoretical framework is activity theory. Our focus of investigation is on the end-user; how technology facilitates and affects attaining the user's health related aspirations, and what kind of notable transformations emerge with the employed technology. The discussed concept is also considered as a key element in avoiding and solving conflicts that may come up when personal preferences, formal processes of health care and norms of the surrounding society collide.

The findings of this project base on the national MyWellbeing project that ended in 2010. The purpose of the project was to look into the changing service landscape of the ICT-mediated health care services and define means for a citizen for coping with the services that are becoming more and more electronic by nature. In the project, a personal aid for managing individual's health related affairs called The Coper was conceptualized with industry partners on the basis of a state-of-the-art survey on solutions of personal health information management. The ideas presented in this paper are derived from the original concept of the artefact [4].

2   The Citizen as the Subject of Navigation

When using a satnav, the principal actor is the driver. There is a body of authorities (such as the government) that has created the required infrastructure (roads, bridges, etc.). They have also defined rules for using the infrastructure (traffic regulations). However, these authorities are rarely involved in planning and execution of a single trip; the driver eventually makes the decisions about the destination, route and most of the time schedule as well. The satnav is in place as a tool for supporting the decisions made by the principal actor.

Inspired by this, we suggest that even in the health space a willing patient (we prefer the term citizen) should be allowed to take this place instead of being subordinated to the health care delivery system of today. In this, our view to the relationship between the patient and the physician is close to the "informed model" presented by Scott and Lenert [5] in which the physician's role is support the patient and to ensure that he has "an adequate educational space" (ibid., p. 2).

Allowing the citizen to take the 'driver's seat' gives rise to two immediate interpretations. Firstly, regardless of the recent patient-driven developments in the field (cf. [6]), the health care delivery system of today is still primarily controlled by the authorities as is the relationship between the doctor and the patient. As such, the relationship can be regarded primarily as a paternalistic one [7]. In our interpretation, the mechanisms of the health care delivery are reversed (to a reasonable degree) and the role of the patient can be seen autonomous [8; 9].

This implies that even though the patient and the physician co-operate and work towards a common goal in the benefit of the patient, the latter one has the freedom to decide her goals and act accordingly to them (in other words, define how a single trip is carried out). It must be acknowledged that this view is not without its flaws, for example in terms of equality. People who have been more fortunate in terms of making a living are usually able to choose their route and means of travel more freely than the less-fortunate ones.

Secondly, considering the on-going discussion on the ownership and use of patient data (cf. [10; 11; 12]) we suggest that the ultimate owner of the health data is the citizen, not the health service provider or the EHR vendor. In order to successfully navigate to the chosen destination, and to the desired health outcome, the citizens should have up-to-date information on 'prevailing conditions' in a format and language they are able to utilize. In this, mechanisms that a) proof-read and correct health related documents such as patient narratives, and b) translate medical jargon into the language of the citizen are of the essence.

It is also in line with this viewpoint that the governmental data (such as quality information on patient safety issues) originating from the health sector should be opened up and made accessible in the spirit of an Open Declaration on European Public Services [13] as is already happening in the U.K. If the citizen is to act as a subject of navigation in the health space, all relevant information should be made available. Without it, the navigation occurs on the basis of intuition and anecdotal knowledge.

3   The Current Health Status: Where Am I?

One of the most essential functions of a satnav is the identification of the current position. Using the simplified diagnostic-therapeutic cycle (figure 1) as a basis for analysis, this feature corresponds in health care to observation and diagnosis (acquisition of the location data and visualization of the current location on the device).

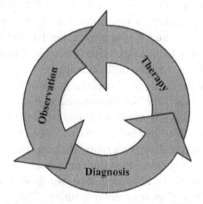

Fig. 1. Diagnostic-therapeutic cycle [14]

Whereas a satnav determines the current position on the basis of satellite signals, mobile network, etc., the closest corresponding positioning technology in the case of a health navigator comprises of health service provider's information systems (EHR, LIS, etc.), and in some cases technology acquired by the citizen (such as, blood pressure monitor). However, as it is in the nature of care, human element is an integral element in this positioning. In the health care of today, this means that the patients' preferences and actions are more and more in the crux of clinical decision making. They can be seen as key elements balancing the viewpoints of clinical state and circumstances, research evidence and clinical expertise [15].

On practical terms of navigating in the health space, we can imagine that the physician, or some other health care professional, receives on her screen one or more recommended (evidence-based) care pathways ('routes'). Taking citizen's preferences into consideration, one of them is chosen and personalized according to the situational and individual factors. The outcome of this process will be a personalized travel plan that consists of different transitions and different waypoints (such as, acquiring services from different providers). This travel plan of personalized health care is transferred to the citizen's health navigator to support her navigation through the space.

It should be kept in mind that these transitions mean changes in the state of the citizen, not moving from one physical location (or service provider) to another as is often the modus operandi, or dominant mode of operation, in the health care organizations of today. For example in the NHS (U.K.) there are approximately 37 million follow-up appointments per year and a significant portion of these visits are clinically unnecessary [16]. It is in our idealized view that data should 'move' and devices, such a medical imaging devices, arranged (when possible) within a health care organization according to the patient trajectories in the spirit of Patient Journey Modeling (cf. [17]).

The diagnosis is not always, so to speak, a 'one shot action'. Sometimes detailed investigations, such as laboratory tests are needed in order to arrive to a conclusion that leads to therapy (figure 1). In the context of the used metaphor, these investigations can be seen as a 'route' of its own. The target of such 'meta-navigation' is the correct diagnosis and the steps needed to reach this destination are taken in order to exclude inadequate alternatives. Similar investigations are needed when the progress of a therapy is evaluated. Using a metaphor has the advantage that unlike in the real life, the 'positioning technology' gives immediate analysis of the current state of affairs before, after and at the time of the therapy.

A generic feature of the concept of a route is the notion of *purposeful activity*. Purpose of a route is to reach the destination one step, or *transaction*, at a time. In terms of health care, the most obvious route is one from the state of illness or accident to the state of health the citizen had before. We call these kinds of routes *progressive*. Another type of route can be called *preserving*; the purpose of the route is not to reach a point in health space that is better than the current one. As certain illnesses are not curable and some injuries cannot be healed, it is sometimes realistic to maintain status quo, even if taking the 'route' seems counterintuitive. The progressive and preserving routes can be mixed with each other. For example, the therapy for diabetes (preserving) may have a subordinated route which aims at losing weight (progressive). It should be also noted that not all activities are active ones; they can be passive as well (for example, through avoiding certain behaviour, e.g. smoking). In this example, the activities can be interpreted of having pre-emptive characteristics as well.

The trigger for the first diagnosis can be dramatic, for example when the citizen comes to the hospital under emergency conditions. Sometimes small symptoms, or even changes in one's view on the world, can create a *fracture*, an identity disturbance affecting one's perceived mental image. In the basest form, fractures may originate from simple every day events, such as from an experienced pain or from a realization that climbing the stairs at work has become more exhausting than before and the clothes that used to fit are no longer comfortable.

We must be aware that not all citizens are able to take the responsibility of being principal actors in their health related endeavours. Children and many elderly people may need a *mediator*, a representative, for their activities. Similarly, some groups that behave destructively against other people or against themselves may need such a mediator. In these kinds of cases, the mediator may use the navigator on behalf of the actual beneficiary, providing that there are mechanisms in place that prevent misuse and identify potential health risks for the actual beneficiaries (cf. [18]).

Acknowledging personal preferences in the health care decision making, and in defining one's current position and route in the health space, borderlines a perspective described in the academic literature as empowerment [19]; giving power over one's health related decisions and actions primarily to the individuals themselves. This perspective can be seen as an extension to consumerism, a notion based on the "systematic creation and fostering of a desire to purchase goods and services in ever greater amounts" [20] as it encapsulates a notion of transformation from a passive patient to an active consumer who acquires products and services to according to one's personal preferences and needs. This notion reflects well with the individuals' instantaneous values and attitudes they express towards the (electronic) services of today.

However, in the health care context the notion encompasses some problems that stem from the knowledge base of the non-professionals. Especially when compared to health care professionals, Individuals do conscious and formal[1] health related decisions rather infrequently. When they do them, their decisions are often distorted with misconceptions and anecdotal knowledge [21]. This observation suggests that the citizen should be encouraged to externalize the diagnosis and allow the observation process to be led by a professional with a higher expertise than she has herself. There is a strong rationale and common sense behind this approach. However, it should be underlined that the overall project and the related information belong to the citizen.

A necessity to place the diagnosis to the hands of professional experts grows stronger whenever the decision leads to treatments with remarkable costs that will be, at least partly, supported by public subsidies. In this case, it is justified to require a

---

[1] We acknowledge that making a decision on what to eat is a health decision, if not necessarily a conscious or a formal one.

legitimation given by an authority for allowing a patient to consume subsidized services (medical imaging, etc.). One way to implement this kind of a control mechanism, that enables the function of universal health care, is to require that there is one responsible and authorized professional present throughout the personalized care plan. Not a professional who is replaced when the current provider organization or the field of medical specialty changes. This kind of an assigned professional, with a view to the overall situation from a clinical perspective, would be in a position to give the needed validation to subsidised treatments.

This kind of operation principle commonly known as case management is not new to the field of health care. For example, in the field of elderly care, case management is a common tool. It is commonly used for tailoring services in order to improve the quality of care of the elderly person [22]. To distinguish our view from the centralized coordination and leadership present in a professional setting, we acknowledge that the citizen has the overall authority and may act as a case manager even though there is a presence of a professional. With this notion, we want to acknowledge the shortcomings of a citizen in terms of health and medical expertise. The citizen is not a physician regardless of the amount and quality of personal decision support aids in her service (nor is a physician the citizen).

The role of a medical expertise is also highlighted during the journey; positioning can be seen as a feedback on the progress of the planned journey where possible deviations and delays are alerted. Since people rarely have medical devices that automatically detect and react to such deviations in the health space, this kind of feedback is often best performed by a health care professional. In this, the relationship between the citizen and the health care professional can be seen as an active partnership as described by Stevenson [23].

4   At the Intersection: Following the Route in the Health Space

Here the health navigator metaphor shows its strength. Equipped with the navigator, the citizen will see an overview of her projects. For each project, past and future transactions, and the current state are displayed. Ideally, this kind of overview will give the citizen a sense of purposefulness and meaningfulness in relation to the selected route. Some of the upcoming transactions (waypoints) may be self-services (such as taking prescribed medication), and transactions that base on professional services can be seen as ordered by the citizen who is the actual beneficiary.

As the citizen has access to the up-to-date location information (e.g. health data), she can decide the used intermediate stopping points (e.g. where health services are acquired). When health related decisions are made, open governmental data can be a valuable addition to other data sources, such as personal measurements or personal genetic data originating from biological repositories (or biobanks). For example, in the data.gov.uk project in the United Kingdoms, the open governmental data is already used in providing tools for the citizens to be used when making health related decisions. A practical example on this is the CareHomeMap application which can be used for tracking care home quality (figure 2).

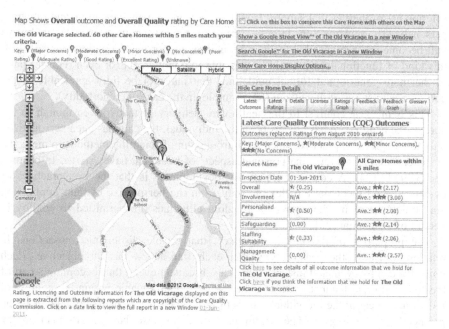

Fig. 2. The CareHomeMap application (http://carehomemap.com/ (accessed December 3rd, 2013)

One important consequence of the citizen-centric view on service acquisition and data ownership is that the citizen acts as a point of integration, supporting unification of different projects, service providers, etc. and related information sources into a single coherent collection regardless of the actual source or format of the information. And most importantly, the route is now controlled by the citizen herself rather than any single service provider (or unit).

As discussed, this approach also supports mediation such as case management [22], for example when one is unable to act due to health reasons (such as declined cognitive capabilities). In the light of the used metaphor, the individual acting in the role of a case manager can be compared to a travel agent. While the travel agency helps in planning the route (articulation), the agent acts as a tour leader taking care of practicalities (execution), such as schedule, co-travellers, etc. Naturally, in the field of health care the duties of a case manager are often more multifaceted than those of a travel agent. The role often encloses more than just coordinating services. Depending on the service provider, the role can be related to unemployment benefits, community resources and support groups (just to name few), covering a wide aspect of issues related to the health and well-being of the citizen.

According to our vision, the health navigator will structure the information according to the life cycles of the active projects, each of them having a route in the health space. On a practical level, the route may be displayed chronologically, for example, in a timeline. If wanted, the navigator can give a reminder of upcoming transactions, and advices for preparing to them. From this perspective, the envisioned solution has properties that support health literacy and patient education, and integrate personalized care instructions into the care pathways. As a consequence, the pathways will become inherently individualistic by nature, supporting the patient choice. With this kind of functionality, it could be possible to complement (or even replace) parts of the more generic and formal guidelines that may not be fully applicable to the current health status of the citizen (for example, in the case of comorbidity).

This is in *some* contrast to the health care delivery of today; even though in the core of the health care has always been the individual, the care has been personalized only to a degree. In practice, since the introduction of scientific methods to medicine at the end of 19th century, the personal aspects of treatment have "started to become endangered" [24]. A consequence of this development is that the best practices of evidence-based medicine are flexible only from the perspective of their application via clinical freedom; the degree of freedom clinicians are permitted to employ in benefit of the patient [25].

The properties of the health navigator, that enable displaying transactions in relation to each other, also imply that each transaction has an objective. Each objective can be evaluated instantly, or as a subsequent event, thus becoming a part of the follow-up and feedback record. The parts become a whole within the context of individual's health; the individual transactions can be seen as an assemblage from the perspective of a project. The health navigator can also be used to manage the contracts with service providers: for each intended transaction, an appropriate service provider must be found and selected. Scheduling, pricing (i.e. price and reimbursements) and finally actual payments must be performed.

The concept of a route in geographical navigation conforms well to that in the health space. More so when there is a pathway of care that aims at a positive change in the current health status of the citizen, such as in, in the case of an injury or sickness (cf. ibid; [26]). In terms of a route, the idea of a purposeful activity is a useful metaphor as it encloses the concepts of target, activities and motivation under an umbrella. More so, if the activity is by nature progressive and active. Regardless of the nature of the activity, they must be systematically analysed in terms of the goals of the project; otherwise they cannot be regarded as truly purposeful.

Continuing with the navigator metaphor, a satnav can be used with other forms of transport besides the obvious ones (by bicycle or on foot). For example, the navigator could be used in conjunction to collective transportation (train, ferry, flight, etc.). In our analysis, the driver operating in a 'self-service mode' becomes a consumer of external services offered by multiple providers; the citizen is expected to compose a route of feasible transactions that lead to the desired target. In order to reach the destination, the transactions must match with each other in terms of schedule, and there is a need for coordination for changing from one transaction to another.

Naturally, some transactions may require a reservation to be made in advance. Each transaction has a price and the chosen route should be economically feasible to the citizen. When applied to the health care setting, this metaphor means that when the citizen has formulated the purposeful project (i.e. set the destination), the health navigator should help in setting the 'milestones'; when one should be at the reception, how the 'tickets' are arranged (in other words, costs and reimbursement). In addition, the navigator should be able to 'reroute the trip' for example, if the citizen has missed an appointment.

Particularly in the health care setting, there should be a level of reflection present at all times. As discussed in the chapter 3, this implies to an involvement of a professional who supports the navigation efforts with one's professional expertise. While each purposeful project can be seen as singular trajectory from citizen's perspective, the projects may be linked within the level of a care pathway (such as, loss of weight, managing medication and taking care of skin problems can all be linked to the care pathway of diabetes) therefore having an impact on the actual service provisioning.

On the level of care pathways and service provisioning, two additional metaphors emerge, that further validate significance of supporting navigation in the health space; the map and the passengers. The map in an ordinary satnav is often a part of the business model of the device manufacturer. While the acquisition of the device is a singular transaction, the maps need to be updated constantly over the life cycle of the device. In terms of the health navigator, the map can be seen as a similar representation. The field of health care services changes rapidly and in order to acquire the services that meet the citizen's preferences in terms of price or quality (etc.), an up-to-date compilation, a map, of the services is needed whenever a route in the health space is planned.

While some of this information is available from the sources of open governmental data, the information often needs visualization and refinement. In this, new business opportunities for business emerge, for example in a form of Web 2.0 mashups (cf. [27]). Mashups are web application hybrids where different service and data sources are integrated in similar fashion to the CareHomeMap application (figure 2). Creating these kinds of solutions, and distributing them via application marketplaces, is already a tested and proven distribution mechanism for different mobile health and well-being applications, such as the online dermatology application, Skin of Mine[2]. In terms of the discussed concept, these kinds of solutions can be a way to actually realize the health navigator, or some of its functions.

The passenger metaphor broadens the discussion towards mediation and acting-on-behalf. While the number of electronic applications in the field of health and well-being increases, there will always be individuals who are not willing, or capable, of using them. In order to help these kinds of individuals to conduct their affairs online, supporting mechanisms are needed. From the perspective of navigation in the health space a passenger or in other words, a technology and health literate individual who helps in using the health navigator, can be of the essence. Especially in the today's 'wired world' where 'traditional' services are replaced with their electronic counterparts, mediation mechanisms, that help the individuals to conduct their affairs in the way they choose to, are more than welcome.

---

[2] https://www.skinofmine.com/ (accessed: November 19th, 2013).

5   Generalizations of the Concept

The notion of purposeful activity has proven to be a powerful generic concept. It lends itself to be applied according to the principles of S.L. Rubinstein's, L. Vygotsky's and A.N. Leontiev's activity theory, a framework explicitly formulated on the notion of human activity as a unit of analysis (cf. [28; 29]). The route can be seen as activity, whereas the transactions can be interpreted as actions through which the activity is realized. Activity also lends itself well for describing the preserving projects which need action without a visible change in order to avoid undesired changes.

Activity theory itself has been successfully used for interpreting and explaining work within the field of health care [30]. It is not, however, the only application area and the theory can be extended to many other (if not most) human activities. In the close vicinity of the health care are the social services, recreation and even everyday life. These areas that were examined in the context of the original MyWellbeing project as ones into which the generic concept of a purposeful project can be adapted.

There are other areas of life in which citizens can manage their activities with an application similar to the health navigator. One are in particular is highlighted in the context of health and well-being; supporting older people's independent living at home. While the overall objective (or goal) is to continue life at home, it can be realized in multiple concurrent projects. In order to meet the demands associate with the independent life of an elderly person, these projects can include acquiring specific living aids or renovating the house). In terms of services, the emphasis is (in all likelihood) on health care and home help services.

The needs of an elderly person are subject to change. Particularly in terms of services that help in coping with everyday life will probably change over time. The need of services is relative and subject to change; most of use perform daily tasks and maintenance of our homes independently during our working life. Someday our abilities to take care of these mundane tasks are reduced and the tasks become services provided by other parties. Most areas in which help is needed can be conceptualized as purposeful projects. These are operationalized as routes and managed with a solution that is domain-independent and more generic than the health navigator.

Regardless of the field of operation in which the concept is employed, the core functions of the health navigator are still in place. The contracts with the providers must be arranged (incl. financial aspects). The contracts include articulation and execution stages, similar to the diagnostic-therapeutic cycle in the figure 1. The cycle can be reduced to a more generic plan-do-check-act stages already present in the Shewhart Cycle originally defined as a tool for statistical analysis [31]. Even though the life situation of the citizen is an intangible whole, the contracts and the overall service portfolio should be analysed and operated as a coherent assemblage.

This kind of integration is often expressed as a need to manage the number of service providers, for example according to the principles of case management. This notion can also be seen as a function of trust. It is often easier to build the trust with a few than with a troop of miscellaneous service providers. In addition, creating a route with only few stop points is easier to create and usually more economical to travel (especially in terms of time and effort).

The navigator metaphor and the examples above, demonstrate the integrative power of the original Coper concept. The original concept, and its derivate the health navigator, integrate consistently all episodes of a care pathway, combining the both services and self-services to transactions of equal weight. The concept also integrates multiple parallel routes with each other, for example by making the laboratory results available to all relevant service providers. In this lies another viewpoint to the business logic of the concept; it uses the citizen as a point of integration, complementing the endeavours of the standardizing organizations. The concept also enables building protective privacy mechanisms on the level of the citizen who controls and owns the patient data.

If the needed mechanisms of trust are in place, this function has a potential of lowering the costs born from reorder of laboratory tests and other examinations. This saving can be significant since even though the situation has improved since the 1990's, it is estimated that in 2005 even 30% of tests were reordered in the United States because the result data could not be found [32]. Even though the amount of reorders is decreasing as integration capabilities of health care information systems is in general improving, there are still significant savings to be found [33]. The integrative capabilities have unique take on the partnerships as well since it is effectively a service provider neutral solution, integrating the public, private and the third sector service providers into a collage that is truly personalized health care.

6   Discussion

Similarly to the original concept of The Coper, the circumpunct of the health navigator is the citizen. This fundamental displacement of physician, or some other service provider from the focal point of health service industry, is of the essence when navigation in the health space is depicted. It supports individual's aspirations of becoming empowered in more concrete terms than just ideological assumption. Analysing the empowerment in the context of navigating in the health space, brings up the work by Aaron Antonovsky [34] on salutogenesis; an approach which challenges pathogenesis, taking the health rather than the illness (lack or reduced health) as a cornerstone to one's health and well-being.

Antonovsky also presented a concept of "Sense of Coherence" (SoC) in his works on the role of stress [35] which portrays the situation when one has certain clarity of life and believes that the world is under control. The three main components of the concept are:

- **Comprehensibility.** A belief that things happen in an orderly and predictable fashion, and a sense that one can understand events in life and reasonably predict what will happen in the future;

- **Manageability.** A belief that one has the skills or the ability, the support, the help, or the resources necessary to take care of things, and a sense that thing are manageable and within control;
- **Meaningfulness.** A belief that things in life are interesting and a source of satisfaction, and a sense that things are really worth the effort and there is a good reason or purpose to care about what happens.

The health navigator supports comprehensibility by having the citizen's health information available and providing access to general information, such as Current Care Guidelines (CCGs). The proposed chronological properties of arranging transactions in a relationship with each other can also be seen as a factor donating to this component. These properties also support manageability since it is possible to formulate a predefined route through the health space towards a desired destination. In addition, the proposed characteristics in terms of managing contracts with the providers (including the financial arrangements) potentially increase the sense of control. In terms of meaningfulness, the donating factor emerges from the purposefulness and meaningfulness of the selected route. As the health navigator supports systemic evaluation of the goals of the project, and as the citizen is the one formulating (possibly assisted) the goals from her individual(istic) perspective, it is possible to provide a comprehensive picture to the citizen on her current health status and on her current endeavours; to help her in determining her position in relation to the pre-set goal.

7   Conclusions

In today's changing health and well-being landscape, the citizen may face challenges that leave her powerless and lost. To support one's health related endeavours in the world that is becoming more and more 'wired' by nature, and in which the services providers are multiform and often disconnected, a truly personal aid that acts as a point of integration is needed. To depict properties of such a solution, and to highlight the role of the principal actor, the health navigator metaphor was described.

The metaphor was founded on a satnav, a mundane technological innovation that helped in defining what navigation in health space, an over-arching state of health related affairs could entail. The discussed issues included those of a route and a destination, concepts lending a hand to individual-centric data and service integration that is in the core of the health navigator concept. In the surrounding discussion, the role of the citizen as an active subject was touched upon in the context of purposeful activity; an individually driven endeavour, that encapsulates the individual's preferences, values and motivation under an umbrella.

The generic character of health navigator, and the navigation metaphor behind it, addresses some of the current challenges related to the fragmented health care landscape. It seems that the prevalent approach to addressing (technical) challenges associated with the fragmentation is to create centralized data repositories for limited use (such as, for a hospital district). A problem with this kind of monolith health repositories is that there is no connection to everyday life of the citizens; to the expanding sphere of well-being that overlaps with that of health care and is often associated to aspects such as prevention and proactivity. The citizen-centric view built on the navigator metaphor transcends this boundary and is open to everyday life, activities outside the trajectory set by a health care professional that principally bases on the clinical evidence and set guidelines. While this is, without doubt, a valid point of view, there is more to health than just medicine.

As a conclusion, it must be stated that a solution, even one that is close to the *idealized* model described here, is not on its own enough. There are already interesting solutions[3] in the market that give room to individual-centric management of health-related efforts, while leaving much to be desired in terms of privacy, trust and completeness; issues that are in the core of enabling navigation in the health space. In order to promote the citizen into the position of a subject in navigation, a systemic reform that would challenge the existing business models, service provisioning mechanisms and attitudes of individuals regardless of their role, is needed. With the conceptual work performed above, we hope to open up discussion that could lead to changes in the field that would really give the citizens a possibility of being the ones truly in charge of their health and well-being; to be truly empowered.

References

1. Teperi, J., Porter, M.E., Vuorenkoski, L., Baron, J.F.: The Finnish health care system: a value-based perspective. Sitra Reports 82 (2009)
2. Elhauge, E.: The Fragmentation of U.S. Health Care: Causes and Solutions. Oxford University Press, U.S (2010)
3. Pratt, W., Unruh, K., Civan, A., Skeels, M.: Personal Health Information Management. Communications of the ACM 49(1) (2006)
4. Lahtiranta, J., Nurminen, M.I.: Pärjäimen toiminnot ja ominaisuudet. In: Meristö, T., Muukkonen, P., Nurminen, M.I., Tuohimaa, H. (eds.) Pärjäin, Omahyvinvointi-hankkeen loppuraportti, Finnish (2010)
5. Scott, G.C., Lenert, L.A.: What is the next step in patient decision support. In: Proceedings of the AMIA Symposium 2000, pp. 784–788 (2000)
6. Swan, M.: Emerging patient-driven health care models: an examination of health social networks, consumer personalized medicine and quantified self-tracking. International Journal of Environmental Research and Public Health 6, 492–525 (2009)
7. Charles, C., Gafni, A., Whelan, T.: Decision-making in the physician-patient encounter: revisiting the shared treatment decision-making model. Social Science, Medicine 49, 651–661 (1999)
8. Hogg, C.: Patients, Power, Politics, From Patients to Citizens. Sage Publications, London (1999)
9. Torkkola, S.: Media sairastaa. Tiedepolitiikka 2001(3), 31–40 (2001)

---

[3] cf. http://thecarrot.com; https://www.healthvault.com; http://myphr.com/resources/choose.aspx (accessed: December 4th, 2013).

10. Rodwin, M.: The case for public ownership of patient data. Journal of the American Medical Association 302(1), 86–88 (2009)
11. Lee, L.M.: Ethical collection, storage, and use of public health data. Journal of the American Medical Association 302(1), 82–84 (2009)
12. Rodwin, M.: Patient data: property, privacy, the public interest. American Journal of Law, Medicine 36, 586–618 (2010)
13. Eups20: An Open Declaration on European Public Services (2010), http://eups20.wordpress.com/the-open-declaration/ (accessed: February 2, 2012)
14. Bemmel van, J.H.: Introduction and Overview. In: Bemmel van, J.H., Musen, M.A. (eds.) Handbook of Medical Informatics, pp. 3–17. Springer (1997)
15. Haynes, R.B., Deveraux, P.J., Guyatt, G.H.: Clinical expertise in the era of evidence-based medicine and patient choice. Evidence-Based Medicine 7(2), 28–36 (2002)
16. NHS: Outpatients: One Stop Models of Care (2013), http://www.improvement.nhs.uk/heart/sustainability/outpatients/one_stop.html (accessed: March 12, 2013)
17. Curry, J.M., McGregor, C., Tracy, S.: A Systems Development Life Cycle Approac to Patient Journey Modeling Projects. In: Kuhn, K.A., Warren, J.R., Leong, T. (eds.) MEDINFO 2007: Proceedings of the 12th World Congress on Health (Medical) Informatics: Building Sustainable Health Systems. IOS Press (2007)
18. Lahtiranta, J.: Changing Nature of Best Practices in eHealth. In: Salmela, H., Sell, A. (eds.) SCIS 2011. LNBIP, vol. 86, pp. 84–97. Springer, Heidelberg (2011)
19. Aujoulat, A., d'Hoore, W., Deccache, A.: Patient empowerment in theory and practice: polysemy or cacophony? Patient Education and Counseling 66, 13–20 (2007)
20. Davidko, N.: The concept of DEBT in collective consciousness (a socio-historical analysis of institutional discource. Studies About Languages 19, 78–88 (2011)
21. Ubel, P.A., Loewenstein, G., Jepson, C.: Whose quality of life? A commentary exploring discrepancies between health state evaluations of patients and the general public. Quality of Life Research 12, 599–607 (2003)
22. Banks, P.: Case management. In: Nies, H., Berman, P.C. (eds.) Integrating Services for Older People, A Resource Book for Managers, pp. 101–112. European Health Management Association (EHMA), Ireland (2004)
23. Stevenson, F.A.: General practitioners' views on shared decision making: a qualitative analysis. Patient Education and Conseling 50, 291–293 (2003)
24. Fierz, W.: Challenge of personalized health care: To what extent is medicine already individualized and what are the future trends? Medical Science Monitor 10(5), 111–123 (2004)
25. Middleton, S., Barnett, J., Reeves, D.: What is an integrated care pathway. What is..? Series, vol. 3(3). Hayward Group Plc., UK (2001)
26. Coiera, E.: Guide to Health Informatics, 2nd edn. Arnold, UK (2003)
27. Laudon, K.C., Traver, C.G.: E-Commerce: Business, Technology, Society, 5th edn. Prentice Hall, New Jersey (2009)
28. Sobkin, V.S., Leontiev, D.A.: The beginning of a new psychology: Vygotsky's psychology of art. In: Cupchik, G.C., László, J. (eds.) Emerging Visions of the Aesthetic Process: Psychology, Semiology and Philosophy, pp. 185–193. Cambridge University Press, Australia (1992)
29. Kaptelinin, V., Kuutti, K., Bannon, L.: Activity theory: Basic concepts and applications. In: Blumenthal, B., Gornostaev, J., Unger, C. (eds.) EWHCI 1995. LNCS, vol. 1015, pp. 189–201. Springer, Heidelberg (1995)

30. Engeström, Y.: Activity theory as a framework for analyzing and redesigning work. Ergonomics 43(7), 960–974 (2000)
31. Best, M., Neuhauser, D.: Walter A Shewhart, 1924 and the Hawthorne factory. Quality and Safety in Health Care 15, 142–143 (2006)
32. Gerntholtz, T., Heerden van, M.V., Vine, D.G.: Electronic medical records – why should you consider imlpementing an EMR. Continuing Medical Education 25(2), 24–28 (2007)
33. Hebel, E., Middleton, B., Shubina, M., Turchin, A.: Bridging the Chasm: Effect of Health Information Exchange on Volume of Laboratory Testing. Archives of Internal Medicine 172(6), 517–519 (2012)
34. Antonovsky, A.: Health, Stress and Coping. Jossey-Bass Publishers, San Francisco (1979)
35. Antonovsky, A.: Unraveling The Mystery of Health - How People Manage Stress and Stay Well. Jossey-Bass Publishers, San Francisco (1987)

Problem in Patient Information System Acquirement in Finland: Translation and Terminology

Minna Rantanen and Olli I. Heimo

University of Turku, Turku, Finland
{mimaran,olli.heimo}@utu.fi

Abstract. Healthcare information systems and their development has risen to be an issue discussed widely amongst Finnish media and public. The discussion varies from the many faults in design, functionality, usability and the enormous costs these systems produce to the citizens as well as how to best fix these problems. Yet it seems that common terminology with eHealth systems in the discussion is lacking rendering the quality of the discussion far from where it could be. Hence this paper will focus on the issue of terminology-based problems in Finnish public eHealth development discussion.

Keywords: Information Systems, Healthcare, eHealth, Terminology, Healthcare Information Systems.

> *"[I]t is probably unwise to try to define the EMR [Electronic Medical Records] in any form or way. It is more fruitful to observe that there are range of clinical activities that use and communicate information, and that some of these can be supported through the introduction of technology."*
> *– Enrico Coiera [1]*

1 Introduction

In this paper we discuss about the lack of clear definition both in Finnish and English research and teaching materials concerning *Healthcare Information Systems* (HIS). This lack of definition – which we will later demonstrate – creates rather curious and obviously unwanted situations to the society which may hinder the efficiency of the eHealth IS development process nationwide. First of all, the problem lies within the varied terminology in both English and Finnish.

In this context – due the lack of better term – we have translated the commonly used Finnish term *"Potilastietojärjestelmät"* as *Patient Information Systems* (lit., later PIS), whereas *electronic patient records* (EPR) and *electronic medical records* (EMR) are more commonly known terms used as the translation. Word "record" does not capture same amount of functionality that "information system" does. The term PIS is used in this paper as a one-time definition to clarify the Finnish-English

K.K. Kimppa et al. (Eds.): HCC11 2014, IFIP AICT 431, pp. 362–375, 2014.
© IFIP International Federation for Information Processing 2014

translation and the Finnish discussion and is not necessarily meant for common use – at least without careful consideration and discussion. The paper will focus on this problem in both translation and terminology in Finnish patient information system acquirement.

In next chapter the Finnish healthcare and eHealth areas are introduced. In third chapter the problems concerning the lack of common language are discussed. The reasons to focus for the aforementioned problems are briefly discussed in fourth chapter and fifth chapter introduces the current at-hand definitions and their contradictions with each other. The discussion about how these thing should be developed are analysed in sixth chapter.

2   Finland and eHealth

Finland differs as an area for eHealth solutions from many countries. As being a North European welfare state, Finland offers almost free medical services to its inhabitants (only minor fees) and participates on the payment of medicines prescribed by medical doctors. One of the key areas that limit the competition in Finnish eHealth market is the language support which is required in both Finland's official languages: Finnish and Swedish (which in larger scale are both minority languages not worth the trouble for many international eHealth software and hardware providers).

In Finland healthcare service is a basic right for every citizen and it is divided into two sectors: public and private. Public healthcare is funded by counties and the state of Finland. Funding is acquired in a form of public medical insurance and small clinical fees. Private healthcare is more expensive but citizens can apply for compensation from state when using these services. Finnish employers are required to pay for healthcare of their employees in private healthcare sector but the patients are often transferred to public healthcare to receive more complex treatment. Every citizen is part of healthcare system even before they are born. Therefore decisions in public healthcare information systems concern every citizen.

In healthcare information systems the scene is dominated by Tieto Oyj (former TietoEnator) c.a. 49% and CGI (former Logica) with c.a. 30% of public healthcare market share. While the eHealth scene in Finland has internationalized, new actors in the market have not been found but moreover the local business' have gone international, e.g. Tieto Oyj, or international companies have bought local ones, e.g. CGI. [2, 3, 4].

Patient information systems have been a subject of both public and professional discussion in Finland of late due to the government and its healthcare districts having procured numerous different PISs, latest of those being Helsinki and Uusimaa Healthcare district's Apotti program (see [5]and e.g. [6, 7, 8, 9, 10, 11]). Apotti's latest cost approximation is 162 300 000 euros and yearly costs 77 900 000 euros [12] which raised quite active discussion about the price and requirements of these systems. Yet it seems that a proper discussion is impossible due the differences in both translation and in terminology: we do not have a definition for PIS. Also *healthcare information system* is a commonly known term, but with its larger scale: all HISs are not PISs.

Thus in this paper the term *eHealth* is used as for all *electronic healthcare systems*; *Healthcare Information Systems* (HIS) as all information systems in healthcare sector (consisting everything from eHealth except the medical machines that are not exactly information systems for example Therac-25); EPR, EHR and EMRs as registries without proper functionalities and PIS as Patient Information System – a system that is a Healthcare Information System consisting on patient information and focusing on treating patients. In our definition HIS can be an EPR, EHR or EMR, PIS, or e.g. an online medical guide.

On international scale, Oh, Rizo, Enkin and Jadad [13] found similar problems concerning the definition of eHealth and similar problem has also been addressed by Häyrinen, Saranto and Nykänen [14] about Electronic Health Records (EHR). None the less they did not produce exact solutions to the research question we tackle in this paper – quite the contrary. We argue that the discussion around the subject of PIS in Finland seems to be more like Plato's Theory of Forms (see [15]), where the idea of a PIS should be in the mind of everyone.

3   The Problem

Yet the Theory of Forms is not a proper tool to discuss about something as complex as patient information systems. Whilst the idea of a horse or a chair might be common for most of us, the idea of a specialised information system is more dependent on who reflects it to the real world. Whilst an engineer can see the problem as a technical one, a sociologist or economist has quite a different view about the subject. Therefore whilst the reflected idea is subjective, we need something more clear to have a discussion upon.

The information system viewed in larger context consists of not only the technology nor the communications of the actors within the technology, but actually from any communication and delivery of information between the actors in real time or in stored format for their work tasks. Thus, the information system can consist of two persons just talking or from a nation-wide or international discussion boards, factory management systems etc. [16]

In this context the healthcare information systems are not only electronic patient records, electronic health records (EHR) nor computerised patient records (CPR), but much more. Therefore, according to Nurminen [16], a HIS is a combination of software, electronics, papers, doctors, nurses and patients, their stored data, knowledge and communication. Thus the topic, patient information systems, are not only technical problems nor solutions and they should not be viewed as such, but instead as a complex combination of workers and their tools flavoured and tied together with the communication between them. Yet, it sometimes seems that the technical and economical decisions seem to dominate both the discussion and the acquirement process (see e.g. [6, 7, 8, 9, 10, 11, 17, 18, 19, 20, 21, 22]).

Language problems seem to be a relevant factor in public discussions. While it seems that scientific discussion in English concerning different eHealth solutions is carried out with many different terms and in research these are used in contradiction with each other (see e.g. [13, 23]) the translation to Finnish makes it even worse. When the English terms are translated to Finnish, the translations themselves are in contradiction with each other (e.g. EPR can be translated a number of different ways). This contradiction in contradiction is obviously not a double negative.

Finnish Foundation of Nursing Education provides an online nursing dictionary *Hoidokki* which translates "potilastietojärjestelmät" as *"medical records systems"* (MRS) [24]. Other translation can be found from the *Apotti Program*, where the term is translated as *"patient data system"* [25] and Finnish researchers use terms such as *"electronic patient record"* (see e.g. [26]) in their English abstracts. Thus a common translation cannot be found. Problem with EMR's translation is that it represents only the database used to store medical information. Information systems are far more complicated than that.

Whereas the records are mere storages of data, information systems contain numerous functions. Records can be viewed as an archive, a set of papers, while the information system consists of both the papers and the people storing, reading and creating them. Even though Garets and Davies [23] describe EMR as application environment which consists of many different parts, EMR does not translate to Finnish as *'patient information system'*.

Yet the definition is not a dilemma only for Finns, but indeed part of a larger, international problem. The terms EMR and EHR are used as a representation of the same thing even though EMR includes data about how patient has been treated. In comparison, one EHR is a subset of EMR, which is derived from this information e.g. for healthcare decisions concerning whole healthcare system. [23]

Healthcare information systems seems to be the most comprehensive term covering all information systems used in healthcare. Thus all patient information systems are healthcare information systems but – as mentioned before – not all HISs are PISs. In this context though, the patient information system seems to be the most accurate translation for "potilastietojärjestelmät" and represents the context in which the term is used in.

PISs are rarely defined in any Finnish researches even if they are the subject of research. For example articles published in Finnish Medical Journal assume that the term is commonly known [27, 28]. When the term is discussed, definitions are often vague and superficial such as "PISs are information systems that save, store and transport patient information [29]. It might not be a problem that defining PIS is deliberately avoided because too many definitions can and are problems in health informatics as well.

Terms such as eHealth are defined in too many ways to understand what they really mean. [13] Making up definitions for the purpose of making up definitions does not solve the problem; quite the contrary, numerous different definitions make discussion harder because – yet again – the common language is missing. Since too many definitions for one term an easily identified problem, definition of PIS should be discussed carefully and not to be taken into use hastily – if at all. Any useful definition should be widely accepted and coherently used.

How people perceive PIS depends strongly on their role in healthcare. For the doctors and nurses PISs are daily used tools whereas economists view them from monetary perspectives. In Finnish media discussion about PISs has been especially focused on poor usability, information security and money (see e.g. [7, 8, 17, 18, 19, 20, 21, 22]). This shapes the conception of PISs in the minds of people that do not know much about topic. While the discussion is strongly focused on making better PISs and eHealth solutions in general, the public has limited ability to participate into the discussion partly due to lack of proper terminology. When this is enforced with the lacking of proper terminology from the professionals, the discussion turns limited towards not only the public but the whole society consisting of the professionals in different areas. Even if they would like to form a neutral concept or at least a form about PISs it is almost impossible since PISs are not defined in any easily findable sources. It can only be imagined how confusing this lack of information is for average patients since it is hard even for scientists researching the subject.

Since the definition of PIS depends strongly on a person it is impossible to have understandable public conversation about the subject that can include and empower everybody – or anybody – in Finnish society.

Koskinen, Heimo and Kimppa [30] argue that healthcare information systems (HIS) should be built not only to computer ethics, but especially to medical ethics to support the work process the information system is an inseparable part of. They extend the thought to the limit that medical ethics should be used as a common language of on what basis the information system should be built. The idea is more refined in an article by Heimo, Kimppa and Nurminen [31] to the extent that the information systems, work process and the ethical basis of both are inseparable from each other. In addition, we argue that the language, the used terminology, seems to be inseparable from the information systems and the work process they support.

Heimo, Koskinen and Kimppa [32] argue for a public (Habermasian) discourse to be used as a tool for developing information systems. Although this discourse could be – as the authors proclaim – important indeed, in the case of HIS procurement in Finland in its current state it is irrelevant. Without a common language the Habermasian discourse could not even start for its premises are not met. Thus if the Habermasian discourse or any other form of discussion is a part of the solution in procuring, the terminology should be standardised.

4   Healthcare Information Systems as a Critical Service

Due to the promotion of the health and wellbeing in the society, Healthcare Information Systems are a critical service to the patients. In countries like Finland (this case) where the basic medical care is arranged by the government, it can also be counted as a *Critical Governmental Information System*, and thus it has some similarities with other CGIS and thus while developing a CGIS, certain additional features to the development must be taken into account to minimize the amount of undesired consequences.

Heimo et. al. [32] define Critical Governmental Information Systems (CGIS) as following:

> "A critical governmental information system (CGIS), by definition, is an information system developed for governmental needs including data or functionality which is critical in nature to the security or wellbeing of individuals or the society as whole. It is a system where something invaluable can easily be compromised. These kinds of systems include eHealth, eDemocracy, police databases and some information security systems e.g. physical access right control."

Numerous case-studies show that due poor eGovernment solutions lives have been lost. The most classic example in the field is *the case London Ambulance Dispach System*, where due to the new information system ambulances were sent to wrong targets, causing several deaths and injuries [33, p. 292-293]. Other examples include the usage of THERAC-25 radiation treatment machines which caused at least six deaths [34] and numerous eVoting solutions, where elections have been compromised numerous times worldwide [35, p. 13-20, 36, 37].

Massive amounts of pre-allocated resources [38] are wasted while the systems are either inoperable or end up being discarded [30, 36, 39, 40, 41]. Thus, when countries have been developing CGISs, the room for errors has been exceeded.

In healthcare even the most valued thing – life itself – has its price. When the resources allocated are not limitless, some medical devices, some medications and some treatments cannot be paid – i.e. some people are not treated while others receive their treatment. When the aforementioned resources, that is money and work effort, are being used carelessly, people needlessly lose their access to their own health and wellbeing – as well as to their life. Therefore there should be no question should these things be taken with utmost importance. Moreover, if the acquirement of these information systems should be done virtuously (see Aristotle), that the system itself would be a virtuous one, it must be done with the best quality possible keeping the purpose of the system – health and wellbeing of the citizens – in the centre of the acquirement from the beginning [42][1].

Thus the government-acquired healthcare information systems are of great importance to the Finnish public. Whereas a citizen can choose whether or not to use the services of a certain private medical service provider, usually their only option with public healthcare is to use the services or to suffer. Thus the public discussion of how the citizens – the possible patients – should be treated is (and as it should be) a matter of clear importance to the whole society.

---

[1] NE 1096a10-1098b10.

5   Definitions and Their Contradictions

The field of healthcare is a field of specialization, divided to various different fields of the medicine all having their own special requirements for IS. That IS must support the work processes and procedures in a very fragmented healthcare system. Thus, many of the problems with eHealth systems, in addition to the other problems in IS development in general, mostly lie within this typical fragmentation of healthcare [30, 43]. Yet it seems that if the information system cannot be built on ethical basis supporting the healthcare [30] or if the terms and definitions are not common the system cannot fulfil its requirements.

While the field of healthcare is fragmented, so is the field of healthcare information systems. During the 1960s hospital information system developers in Finland were mainly doctors and amateurs that were interested in making healthcare more efficient. Hospitals developed their own individual systems and cooperation especially in the beginning was rare. Already in the early days the government was funding system development and soon noticed increasing costs of development. Cooperation was soon demanded and the power to direct the development was given to big hospitals. Biggest change in terms of hospital system development occurred in 1990s when counties were made responsible for funding majority of their costs. Counties started to purchase their own systems and information systems were evaluated by their potential efficiency and ability to save money. [44, p.11-30, 45, p. 63-85.]

This led to the current situation where both public and private sector have been fragmented information system wise. Many different PISs and versions of them are been used. PISs have been strongly customized to meet the needs of every healthcare units individually. Thus, it is challenging to define the basic body of PIS locally – and international community is yet to give the Finnish discussion much-needed aid due to the problems in defining terms like eHealth and EHR [13, 14].

It appears that PIS can include any subsystems that have something to do with patient information or taking care of patients. Because the main task of hospitals is taking care of patients, many of their systems are – or at least should be – supporting that process and be somewhat involved in handling the patient data. As mentioned not all PISs are HISs although it is hard to separate them. If information systems are viewed as social-technological systems instead of only technological system (see e.g. [16]), it could be argued that every person working with patients or handling their data is part of PIS.

In Finnish nursing literacy few attempts to define PIS have been made. According to Mäkelä [44, p. 63] PIS is "very wide and diverse software and database compilation that contains all information related to patients health and treatment" and "PIS connects patient information to another information in healthcare".

Mäkelä's definition is based on the idea that patient information makes PIS whereas Korpela and Saranto [46] aim to define PIS through the structure. They divide systems into core system and unit-based separate systems [46, p. 25]. According to them, the core systems are systems that handle patient information in comparison to the separate systems that are laboratory systems and such non-patient-information focused systems. This seems not to clarify the concept of PIS enough.

As another example of vague definitions, SITRA [A Finnish Innovation Fund] define the patient information systems as following:

> *"Patient information system is formed from one or more base system functional units which create functional unit healthcare services and together form a functional unit patient information registry (Arkkitehtuurimääräyssanasto 2007 [unavailable reference]). Patient information systems are e.g. EPR, communication system between hospital and laboratory, radiological image delivering and communication system, healthcare area's information system and image archive."*[2] [47].

The aforementioned quote is a good example of a definition concerning patient information systems. Not only is it in contradiction with other definitions, but it also lacks a proper definition: while the examples give the reader some image of what the writer has been trying to describe, the term 'functional unit' has as little meaning in Finnish as it has in English.

One part of this research was an e-mail survey for the people in close encounter with PISs such as governmental units, providers of PISs and healthcare districts etc. Surveys contained only one simple question: "How do you define patient information system?" but several of these queries turned out to be e-mail discussions. These original e-mails were sent to Ministry of Social Affairs and Health (STM), Minister of Social Affairs and Health, Finnish National Institute for Health and Welfare (THL), National Supervisory Authority for Welfare and Health Valvira, Accenture, CGI, Tieto Oyj and The Hospital District of Helsinki and Uusimaa and The Hospital District of Southwest Finland. On top of that survey was sent personally to politicians who are or have been discussing PISs within the last few years in Finnish media. The received information was combined with the literature review concerning eHealth solutions.

All the definitions gathered were in contradiction with other definitions. In addition, majority of people who answered the question acknowledged the lack of unanimous definition for Finnish. Only the representative of National Supervisory Authority for Welfare and Health Valvira was sure of the definition and that it has been made and clarified. The aforementioned representative believed strongly that the Finnish law defines PISs clearly enough. He also argued that definition can be found in certain Internet site, although this information was found to be incorrect. Valvira equates PISs with healthcare devices, such as blood pressure monitors and they claim they do not handle definitions but only legal requirements.

Also the preference in using term *electronic patient record* instead of PIS because of lacking definition came forth during the interviews. In this case tough, as

---

[2] "Potilastietojärjestelmä muodostuu yhdestä tai useammasta toimintayksikön perusjärjestelmästä, jotka tuottavat toimintayksikön terveydenhuoltopalveluja ja yhdessä muodostavat toimintayksikön potilasrekisterin (Arkkitehtuurimäärityssanasto 2007). Potilastietojärjestelmiä ovat esimerkiksi potilaskertomusjärjestelmä, laboratorion lähete- ja lausuntojärjestelmä, radiologisten kuvien lähete- ja lausuntojärjestelmä, terveydenhuollon aluetietojärjestelmä sekä kuva-arkisto."

mentioned before, using different term e.g. EPR does not answer the question or solve the problem because it is far too narrow term like previously mentioned EMR. THL representative had in the past tried to define term PIS with her colleagues. Their definition is that "PIS is information system that is meant for saving and handling patient information" [29].

The amount of different answers to this simple question – and the lack of (clear) answers – showed that the lack of definition is truly a problem. Organizations such as the Ministry of Social Affairs and Health (STM) should have a clear idea what a PIS is, but none of their representatives responded to survey. Even the answers from politicians repeatedly presenting ideas about PISs were lacking. This raises the question about their knowledge about PISs? It seems clear enough that many of these people know that the definition is lacking but only two of the whole set of participants showed interest for the existence of a proper definition. Does this mean that terminology is considered useless or is the question too hard to answer?

As shown before, it seems that no common terminology seems to be found within Finnish eHealth discussion. While the question of the definition of different eHealth terms – when arisen – should at least arise some interest, its importance to the people participating to the discussion seems to vary. This raises an alarming thought: if people are not interested in having a common terminology, are they having the discussion for other purposes than to develop the PIS in best way possible? In any case, this seems to be a matter to be fixed.

6   How Patient Information Systems Can Be Defined?

As mentioned before, instead of being considered as a stand-alone system PISs can be thought as a compilation of various systems and actors. Systems used in healthcare units vary according to their particular needs and thus is hard to define what typical PIS is and more, what subsystems are of PIS and what are not. Patient information is – or at least should be – the center of any PIS and it connects many systems together.

Treatment for health and wellbeing of the citizens is the process that is in common with all of these systems because for example treatment regulation dictionaries are also part of PISs. Thus it can be said that current PISs contain systems that support patients treatment process via information as well as many other subsystems directly or indirectly connected to the aforementioned process. These subsystems can include e.g. EMR, billing and ledger information, customer service www-portal, delivery room special services and service providence monitoring. [48, 49].

As mentioned in previous chapter: THLs definition of the PIS is "a system meant for saving and handling patient information." This seems to be a quite broad definition not really clarifying the term. As noted before, information systems can be people knowing and communicating verbally or via pieces of paper to large computerised systems. If we use this definition, all of the hospital staff that handle patient information in some way are part of PIS. What are the computerised parts of PIS?

Apotti program has so far been a somewhat public project. The planned infrastructure of the future system has been published. The system has been divided into two parts: core and integrated systems. The core systems include for example client and patient records, systems for controlling them and information about treatments and services. The systems are directly involved with patient care taking process. Also, the patient data is used for billing information, but this is not a crucial part of the process. [49]

Integrated systems are systems of specialized medical healthcare units and other systems which are involved with patient data but not in same amount as previously mentioned systems. For example laboratory systems are integrated systems.

Other PISs are like puzzles that have been put together accounting to healthcare units' needs. Which puzzle pieces the units have selected remains largely a mystery. PISs are collections of subsystems that use patient data in particular unit of healthcare. (e.g. [47].)

One approach could be the approach of functionalities and their levels of importance. While client and patient records, medication control and log data are obviously core functions in any PIS solutions, it can be argued that billing is not. This obviously leads to certain problems not the least being the subjective requirements from the system from different interest groups. E.g. a hospital could not fund its functions long, if it could not do billing. Therefore more than mere functionalities must be the key for the definition.

Another method for defining is an approach from the content. The most important information within the PIS is the patient information. The main goal of storing patient information is to give access to patient information. With this approach though PISs and EMRs, EHRs and EPRs can easily be equated with each other.

Third method for defining could be the definition through the structure, i.e. through the analysis of sublevels of the system. This seems to be the main definition method used to define Apotti system. Through this method patient information system could consist from various different systems with some overlapping functionalities. The sublevels could be patient information systems themselves, but they also could be mere EMRs, databases, registries or actors. In Apottis case the PIS can be defined to contain the core functions (see [49]). This, although clarifying definition, seems to be a case-specific method which always requires another method to support the definition.

Fourth method – and the most used method – is through examples and negations. With this method examples of PISs and non-PISs are delivered for the explanation and definition of a PIS. Although being the clearest of the methods available yet, this method suffers from the similar problems than the aforementioned Theory of Forms.

Therefore it seems that there is no easy way out of this yet important dilemma and it seems that a good and exact definition requires more analysis. While the approximate idea could be delivered from the aforementioned directions a usable – or even a more defined – idea still requires more analysis and discussion. Our future research will concentrate on the combination of the methodologies in defining the terminology more accurately within both national and international contexts.

7   Conclusions

As shown above, it seems that little common language exists in Finnish healthcare information system development discourse. Due to the lack of proper and meaningful discussion the problems not only appear as a linguistic one but yet a problem in the whole acquirement process of procurement, development, implementation and upkeep.

Due to the difficulties in defining eHealth [13], EHR [14] or the defining of PIS, it can be presumed that this problem is not unique to Finnish discussion but also exists in other countries. The global terms as well as the localised terms should be made if not unambiguous at least understandable.

To have a discussion with one another we require a common set of terms under-stood by everyone. To develop complex multidisciplinary information systems we need a possibility for discussion. To enhance our level of healthcare we require com-plex multidisciplinary information systems. Thus, the further development of termi-nology in the subject is not only recommended but required.

Therefore our future research on the topic will focus on more defined glossary concerning patient information systems and other healthcare information systems so that public discussion about the subject will have a possibility to flourish.

References

1. Coiera, E.: Guide to health informatics, 2nd edn. Oxford University Press Inc., New York (2003)
2. THL (National Institute of Health and Wellfare): KanTa-palvelut: Kansallinen potilastiedon arkisto Alustava käyttöönottoaikataulusuunnitelma v.2.2 (November 11, 2013) (Kanta services: National archive of patient information Preliminary implementation plan v.2.2.) (2013), http://www.kanta.fi/documents/12105/3494314/Potilastiedon+arkisto_suunnitelma+k%C3%A4ytt%C3%B6%C3%B6nottoaikatauluista_v+2+2.pdf/c490ae41-1c4e-4fc1-bc9d-4b841c3e753f (accessed January 6, 2014)
3. CGI: Historia: CGI:n tarina Suomessa (History: CGI's story in Finland) (2014), http://www.cgi.fi/historia-suomessa (accessed January 6, 2014)
4. Tieto: Historia (History) (2014), http://www.tieto.fi/tiedosta/historia (accessed January 6, 2014)
5. City of Helsinki: APOTTI-hanke usein kysytyt kysymykset(APOTTI Program FAQ) (2013), http://www.hel.fi/hki/apotti/fi/Apotti-hanke/FAQ (accessed: December 23, 2013)
6. Helsingin Sanomat / Tuomas Peltomäki: Uutisanalyysi: Apotti-hanke saa maksaa tietotekniikan vanhoista synneistä (News analysis: Apotti programwillpay for the oldsins of computing) (September 12, 2012), http://www.hs.fi/kotimaa/a1347361544072 (accessed January 3, 2014)
7. Helsingin Sanomat / Esa Juntunen: Apotti-järjestelmä tulee kaikkien kukkarolle (Apotti systemwillbeexpensive for everyone) (August 26, 2013), http://www.hs.fi/kaupunki/a1377399301286 (accessed January 3, 2014)
8. Kasvi, J.J.J.: Blog entry: Apotinsynti (The sin of Apotti) (January 26, 2013), http://jyrkikasvi.puheenvuoro.uusisuomi.fi/131025-apotin-synti (accessed January 3, 2014)

9. Tietokone / Seppo Lindstedt: Apotti-hankevaatiitehohoitoa (Apotti Program needs intensive care), http://www.tietokone.fi/artikkeli/uutiset/apotti_hanke_vaatii_tehohoitoa (accessed January 3, 2014) (March 14, 2013)

10. YLE (Finnish National Broadcasting Company) AnnamariIranto: Apotti-järjestelmäkehittyyvuorovaikutuksessa (Apotti system is being developed in interaction), http://yle.fi/uutiset/apotti-jarjestelma_kehittyy_vuorovaikutuksessa/6633702 (accessed January 3, 2014) (May 8, 2013)

11. IT-Viikko / Perttu Pitkänen: Viron potilasjärjestelmän kehittäjä pilkkoisi HUS:in Apotin osiin (The Estonian patient information system developer would modularise Apotti) (May 30, 2013), http://www.itviikko.fi/uutiset/2013/05/30/viron-potilasjarjestelman-kehittaja-pilkkoisi-husin-apotin-osiin/20137634/7 (accessed January 3, 2014)

12. City of Helsinki: Apotti-järjestelmän kustannushyötylaskelma (Cost-benefit calculation of Apotti-system) (2013), http://www.hel.fi/static/taske/apotti/asiakas-ja-potilastietojarjestelman-kustannushyotylaskelma-2013.pdf (accessed: January 3, 2014)

13. Oh, H., Rizo, C., Enkin, M., Jadad, A.: What Is eHealth (3): A Systematic Review of Published Definitions. Journal of Medical Internet Research (February 2005), http://www.ncbi.nlm.nih.gov/pmc/articles/PMC1550636/ (accessed: December 20, 2013)

14. Häyrinen, K., Saranto, K., Nykänen, P.: Definition, structure, content, use and impacts of electronic health records: A review of the research literature. International Journal of Medical Informatics 77(5), 291–304 (2008)

15. Plato (380 BC), The Republic. Multiple translations

16. Nurminen, M.I.: Kolme näkökulmaa tietotekniikkaan (Three perspectives on information technology). WSOY (1986)

17. Helsingin Sanomat / Karoliina Liimatainen: It-järjestelmän tilaaminen on taitolaji (Ordering information technology systems is skill based), http://www.hs.fi/talous/a1378456580086 (accessed January 6, 2014) (September 7, 2013)

18. Helsingin Sanomat: Professori: Perusterveyden-huollon romahtamisen syynä keikkalääkärit ja tietojärjestelmät (Professor: Reasons for collapse of primary healthcare are freelance doctors and information systems) (September 19, 2013), http://www.hs.fi/kotimaa/a1379554098791 (accessed January 5, 2014)

19. YLE (Finnish National Broadcasting Company) / Merja Niilola: Terveydenhuollon it-hankinnoissa lähes kaikki mennyt pieleen (In healthcare IT procurement almost everything gone wrong) (May 21, 2012), http://yle.fi/uutiset/terveydenhuollon_it-hankinnoissa_lahes_kaikki_on_mennyt_pieleen/6103664 (accessed November 5, 2014)

20. YLE (Finnish National Broadcasting Company) IT-asiantuntija: Husin uusi potilastietojärjestelmä menossa pahasti pieleen (IT specialist: Hus' new patient information system going terribly wrong) (May 7, 2013), http://yle.fi/uutiset/it-asiantuntija_husin_uusi_potilastietojarjestelma_menossa_pahasti_pieleen/6630873 (accessed January 5, 2014)

21. Kivekäs, O.: Blog entry 8.6.2012: Epicfail, eli sairaaloiden IT eilen, tänään ja huomenna (Epic fail i.e. hospitals' IT yesterday, today and tomorrow) (2012), http://otsokivekas.fi/2012/06/epic-fail-eli-sairaaloiden-it-eilen-tanaan-ja-huomenna/ (accessed January 5, 2014)

22. Östman, K.: Blog entry: Potilastietojärjestelmät ja niiden hinta – tolkkua tuhlaukseen (Patient information systems and their costs – making sense in wasting money), http://kimmoostman.blogit.hameensanomat.fi/2012/10/07/potila stietojarjestelmat-ja-niiden-hinta-tolkkua-tuhlaukseen/ (accessed January 5, 2014) (October 10, 2012)

23. Garets, D., Davies, M.: Electronic Patient Records EMRs and EHRs Concepts as different as apples and oranges at least deserve separate names. Healthcare Informatics (October 2005)

24. Hoidokki: Asiasanasto (Medical Subject Headings), Finnish Foundation of Nursing Education (2005-2014) (2014), http://www.hoidokki.fi/index.php?MITform=sanat_aihe&t= 5&aiheno=9 (accessed January 4, 2014)

25. City of Helsinki: What is the Apotti Program about? (2013), http://www.hel.fi/hki/apotti/fi/Apotti-hanke/English (accessed: January 3, 2014)

26. Valta, M.: Sähköisen potilastietojärjestelmän sosiotekninen käyttöönotto: seitsemän vuoden seurantatutkimus odotuksista omaksumiseen (The sociotechnical implementation of an electronic patient record. A seven-year follow-up study from expectations to adoption) Faculty of Social Sciences and Business Studies. Doctoral Thesis. Publications of the University of Eastern Finland. Dissertations in Social Sciences and Business Studies, no 62 (2013), http://urn.fi/URN:ISBN:978-952-61-1217-6 (accessed: December 20, 2013)

27. Winbland, I., Hyppönen, H., Väskä, J., Reponen, J., Viitanen, J., Elovainio, M., Lääveri, T.: Potilastietojärjestelmät tuotemerkeittäin arvioitu: Kaikissa kehitettävää (Patient Information Systems evaluated by brand: All of them require improvement) Suomen Lääkärilehti (The Finnish Medical Journal) 50-52/2010 vsk 65 (2010)

28. Arvola, T., Pommelin, P., Inkinen, R., Väyrynen, S., Tammela, O.: Potilastietojärjestelmien turvallisuusriskit hallintaan (To control the securityrisks in patientinformationsystems) Suomen Lääkärilehti (Finnish Medical Journal) 12/2012 vsk 67 (2012)

29. Vuokko, R., Mäkelä, M., Komulainen, J., Meriläinen, O.: Terveydenhuollon toimintaprosessit: Terveydenhuollon yleiset prosessit ja niiden tarkennukset (The healthcare processes: general healthcare processes and their specifications) Raportti 53/2011, ISSN 1798-0089; ISBN 978-952-245-535-2 (pdf). Terveydenjahyvinvoinninlaitos (THL) (Finnish National Institute of health and wellfare), Helsinki (2011), http://www.thl.fi/thl-client/pdfs/f2fd2a43-4e91- 42e7-b7fe-5607f86e4d79 (accessed: December 20, 2013)

30. Koskinen, J., Heimo, O.I., Kimppa, K.K.: A viewpoint for more ethical approach in healthcare information system development and procurement: the four principles. In: The 4th International Conference on Well-being in the Information Society – Exploring the Abyss of Inequalities, Turku, Finland, August 22-24 (2012)

31. Heimo, O.I., Kimppa, K.K., Nurminen, M.I.: Ethics and the Inseparability Postulate – How to make better critical governmental information systems. In: ETHICOMP 2014 - – Liberty and Security in an Age of ICTs, Paris, France, June 25-27 (in print, 2014)

32. Heimo, O.I., Koskinen, J.S.S., Kimppa, K.K.: Responsibility in Acquiring Critical Governmental Information Systems: Whose Fault is Failure? In: ETHICOMP 2013 – The possibilities of ethical ICT, June 12-14. University of Southern Denmark, Kolding (2013)

33. Avison, D., Torkzadeh, G.: Information Systems Project Management. Saga Publications, California (2008)

34. Fleischman, W.M.: Electronic Voting Systems and The Therac-25: What Have We Learned? In: ETHICOMP 2010 - The "Backwards, Forwards and Sideways" Changes of ICT, April 14-16. Universitat Rovirai Virgili, Tarragona (2010)
35. Mercuri, R.: Electronic Vote Tabulation: Checks and Balances. PhD thesis, University of Pennsylvania (2001), http://www.cis.upenn.edu/grad/documents/mercuri-r.pdf (accessed January 4, 2014)
36. Heimo, O.I., Fairweather, N., Ben, K., Kai, K.: The Finnish eVoting Experiment: What Went Wrong? In: ETHICOMP 2010 - The "Backwards, Forwards and Sideways" Changes of ICT, April 14-16. Universitat Rovirai Virgili, Tarragona (2010)
37. Robison, W.L.: Voting and Mix-And-Match Software. In: ETHICOMP 2010 - The "Backwards, Forwards and Sideways" Changes of ICT, April 14-16. Universitat Rovirai Virgili, Tarragona (2010)
38. Larsen, E., Ellingsen, G.: Facing the Lernaean Hydra: The Nature of Large-Scale Integration Projects in Healthcare. In: Kautz, K., Nielsen, P.A. (eds.) SCIS 2010. LNBIP, vol. 60, pp. 93–110. Springer, Heidelberg (2010)
39. Wijvertrouwenstemcomputersniet:Rop Gonggrijp, Willem-Jan Hengeveld - Studying the Nedap/Groenendaal ES3B voting computer, a computer security perspective. In: Proceedings of the USENIX Workshop on Accurate Electronic Voting Technology (2007), http://wijvertrouwenstemcomputersniet.nl/images/c/ce/ES3B_EVT07.pdf (accessed February 7, 2011) (see also http://wijvertrouwenstemcomputersniet.nl/English
40. Verzola, R.: The Cost of Automating Elections (2008), http://ssrn.com/abstract=1150267 (accessed January 4, 2014)
41. Heimo, O.I., Hakkala, A., Kimppa, K.K.: How to abuse biometric passport systems. Journal of Information, Communication and Ethics in Society 10(2), 68–81 (2012)
42. Aristotle, Nicomachean Ethics. Multiple translations
43. Danzon, P., Furukawa, M.: e-Health: Effects of the Internet on Competition and Productivity in Health Care. In: Internet, B.T.F. (ed.) The Economic Payoff from the Internet Revolution'. Brookings Institution Press, Washington DC (2001)
44. Mäkelä, K.: Terveydenhuollon tietotekniikka, terveyden ja hyvinvoinnin sovellukset (Health care information technology, health and welfare applications) Talentum Media Oy, Helsinki (2006)
45. Koskimies: Sairaalatietojärjestelmien historiaa (History of hospital information systems). In: Saranto, K., Korpela, M. (eds.) Tietotekniikka ja tiedonhallinta sosiaali- ja terveydenhuollossa, pp. 63–85. WSOY, Porvoo (1999)
46. Korpela, M., Saranto, K.: Peruskäsitteet,osa-alueet ja toimijat (Basic concepts, sectors and actors). In: Saranto, K., Korpela, M. (eds.) Tietotekniikka ja tiedonhallinta sosiaali- ja terveydenhuollossa (Information Technology and Information Management in Social and Health Care), pp. 18–44. WSOY, Porvoo (1999)
47. Pirttivaara, M.: Terveydenhuollon tietojärjestelmäinvestoinnit ja niiden arviointi – fokuksessa potilastietojärjestelmät (Healthcare information system investments and their evaluation – the focus on patient information systems). In: SITRAn selvityksiä 22, SITRA (2010)
48. Tolppanen, E.-M.: Elektroninen potilaskertomus (Electronic patient record). In: Saranto, K., Korpela, M. (eds.) Tietotekniikka ja tiedonhallinta sosiaali- ja terveydenhuollossa (Information Technology and Information Management in Social and Health Care), pp. 241–253. WSOY, Porvoo (1999)
49. City of Helsinki: APOTTI-hanke. Hankesuunnitelma (APOTTI Program. Programplan) ohjausryhmän hyväksymä versio (version approved by the steering group) (May 22, 2013), http://www.hel.fi/static/taske/apotti/Apotti-hankesuunnitelma-versio-4.pdf (accessed: December 21, 2013)

Author Index

Printed in the United States
By Bookmasters